A Sierra Club Naturalist's Guide to

THE
SIERRA NEVADA

By Stephen Whitney

SIERRA CLUB BOOKS   *San Francisco*

The Sierra Club, founded in 1892 by John Muir, has devoted itself to the study and protection of the earth's scenic and ecological resources—mountains, wetlands, woodlands, wild shores and rivers, deserts and plains. The publishing program of the Sierra Club offers books to the public as a nonprofit educational service in the hope that they may enlarge the public's understanding of the Club's basic concerns. The point of view expressed in each book, however, does not necessarily represent that of the Club. The Sierra Club has some fifty chapters coast to coast, in Canada, Hawaii, and Alaska. For information about how you may participate in its programs to preserve wilderness and the quality of life, please address inquiries to *Sierra Club, 530 Bush Street, San Francisco, California 94108*.

Copyright © 1979 by Stephen Whitney.

Library of Congress Cataloging in Publication Data

Whitney, Stephen, 1942–
    A Sierra Club naturalist's guide to the Sierra Nevada.

    Bibliography: p.
    Includes index.
    1. Natural history—Sierra Nevada Mountains.
2. Sierra Nevada Mountains.   I. Sierra Club.
II. Title.
QH104.5.S54W45   500.9′794′4   79-766
ISBN 0–87156–215–4
ISBN 0–87156–216–2 pbk.

Series design by Klaus Gemming, New Haven, Connecticut
All drawings and maps by Stephen Whitney
Printed in the United States of America

10 9 8 7 6 5 4 3 2 1

To Vandana and Aaron

TABLE OF CONTENTS

Contents   xi

ACKNOWLEDGMENTS

A BOOK OF THIS SORT is necesarily the work of numerous people, many of whom were not even aware that they had been enlisted in its preparation. I refer in particular to the many geologists, meteorologists, botanists, zoologists, and ecologists whose firsthand research in the Sierra accounts for the bulk of information contained in this guide. My contribution has largely been that of compiler, interpreter and illustrator. My sole purpose has been to make this information, much of it contained only in academic journals, available to the general reader. To all these unnamed professional naturalists this grateful amateur wishes to acknowledge his debt.

Special thanks are extended to the following people for their contribution to this manuscript:

Dr. Jack Major of the University of California at Davis for reviewing the entire manuscript and suggesting numerous improvements in the text.

Dr. Robert Curry of the University of Montana, for reviewing the chapter on geology and making available information that I had not encountered elsewhere in my research.

Dr. Robert Orr of the California Academy of Sciences for reviewing the sections on Sierra animals and clarifying many points that had formerly been obscure, and Dr. A. Starker Leopold of the University of California at Berkeley for reviewing the material on animals in its early form.

Dr. David Parsons, Research Biologist at Sequoia/Kings Canyon National Parks, for making available to me information that at the time had not appeared in publication.

Dr. Eugene Coan of the Sierra Club's conservation staff for his careful reading of the manuscript and numerous helpful suggestions for its improvement.

The author, of course, must bear final responsibility for this guide, and any mistakes or oversights should be laid at my door.

I would also like to thank Jon Beckmann, director of Sierra Club Books for supporting this project during the three years of its preparation and for his continued confidence in its author.

Special thanks go to Diana Landau, project editor at

Sierra Club Books, whose keen perceptions about the purposes of this guide have immeasurably improved it and whose cajolings, pleadings, and whip crackings at appropriate moments kept me at the typewriter when all other instincts urged me to retreat.

Finally, I would like to thank my wife Vandana for her constant support over the past three years, often in the face of great difficulties arising from my sometimes single-minded attention to this project. Without her good humor and encouragement, I should have been tempted to abandon the effort long ago.

Stephen Whitney
Belfair, Washington

Acknowledgments

Introduction

This guide provides in a single volume extensive information about the geology, climate, and ecology of the Sierra
Nevada, as well as detailed accounts of more than 200
species of plants and animals. It is intended as a field guide
for hikers and campers or as a general reference for use
either at home or in the mountains.

Chapter I describes the main physical features of the
Sierra and summarizes the history of human activities in the
range. A set of three maps depicts the region covered by
this guide. The maps show the locations of major roads,
towns, rivers, lakes, and peaks, as well as the boundaries of
existing national parks, forests, and wilderness areas. Most
place names used in the guide are shown on these maps.

Chapter II recounts the geological history of the Sierra
from the formation of its oldest rocks to their current destruction by the processes of weathering and erosion. Numerous diagrams illustrate many of the basic geological
processes that formed the Sierra and that continue to shape
the range today. Line drawings depicting most of the major
types of landforms occurring in the Sierra are intended to
serve as aids to identification in the field.

Chapter III describes and explains the weather and climate of the Sierra. Topics include mountain climates in
general and that of the Sierra in particular, seasonal
weather patterns, and basic meterological processes. The
chapter also includes a section on snow and the Sierra
snowpack.

Even people who seldom pay much attention to climate
or geology are likely to find themselves doing so in the
Sierra, where the effects of both are readily apparent and
often dramatic. Aside from their intrinsic interest, climate
and geology are essential to an understanding of the communities of plants and animals found in the Sierra, for together the processes at work in heaven and earth create the
physical environment on which life depends.

Chapter IV discusses how plants and animals in the
Sierra have responded to the various environments encountered in different parts of the range. It also explores the
ways in which organisms interact with one another and af-

fect the habitats of their neighbors. Central to the discussion is the concept of plant communities—predictable associations of plants occurring in response to local variations in climate, soil, available moisture, and other environmental factors. Plant communities also largely determine the types of food and shelter available to animals, and therefore the kinds of animals found in a given area.

The system used in this guide to classify plant communities corresponds closely to those used by other ecologists, and Table 5 in Chapter IV compares this system with four others from prominent sources. Chapter IV also contains a simple key intended to aid the novice naturalist in identifying plant communities in the field. (See page 138).

The four remaining chapters of the guide examine in detail the major plant communities found in the Sierra and the wildlife characteristic of each. Each of the four chapters is devoted to a particular region in which certain communities regularly occur together to create distinctive vegetation patterns, or mosaics. Each region can be distinguished readily from the others not only by its characteristic landscape, but also by its geographic location in the range. Readers who may be unfamiliar with the Sierra can thus quickly determine which regional chapter applies to the area in which they are interested. The location and characteristic vegetation of each major region is as follows:

The *Sierra foothills* (Chapter V) lie below the main coniferous forest on the west slope of the range. Their characteristic vegetation is a mosaic of woodland and chaparral, with grassland forming an important element at lower elevations.

The *coniferous forest belt* (Chapter VI) lies above the foothill woodland and chaparral on the west slope of the Sierra and above the pinyon–juniper woodland and sagebrush scrub on the east. Its upper margin is timberline, or tree limit. It is by far the largest and most diverse of the regions, comprising five major plant communities and extending over several thousands of feet of elevation, so this chapter is significantly longer than those devoted to the other three regions. The forest belt is the region in which most visitors to the Sierra spend the greater part of their time.

The *alpine region* (Chapter VII) extends from tree limit to the tops of the highest peaks. Trees are absent and shrubs are few. Vegetation consists primarily of low perennial herbs sparsely scattered over a landscape dominated by bare rock.

The *lower eastern slope* of the Sierra (Chapter VIII), extending from the coniferous forest to the base of the range, is covered largely by sagebrush scrub, with stands of pinyon–juniper woodland scattered along the upper margins. These communities are characteristic of the Great Basin, which stretches eastward for more than five hundred miles.

Each of these regional chapters is divided into two major sections, the first devoted to plant communities, the second to the wildlife found in each community. The emphasis throughout is on the ways in which both plants and animals have adapted to conditions within their respective habitats.

Plants and Animals

Each of the regional chapters contains checklists of plants and animals, both grouped according to the plant communities in which they occur. These lists do not include alien species that have become naturalized in the Sierra, even though some are locally common or even abundant. Most alien plants and animals are found below the forest belt because their upslope occurrence has been limited by snow, cold temperatures, short growing seasons, competing organisms, or some combination thereof. The alien plants found in the Sierra are too numerous to list here. The number of alien animals, however, is much smaller. The more common of these species are:

Bullfrog, *Rana catesbiana;* ponds and slow, warm streams in the lower foothills and Central Valley.
Starling, *Sturnus vulgaris;* foothill woodland, lower forest; along eastern base of range.
House Sparrow, *Passer domesticus;* near human dwellings.
Opossum, *Didelphis marsupialis;* western foothills.
Domestic Rats, genus *Rattus;* human dwellings.
House Mouse, *Mus musculus;* human dwellings.
Beaver, *Castor canadensis;* a few mountain streams, both slopes.

Lists also exclude nonvascular plants, invertebrate animals, or strictly aquatic plants and animals; this largely because of space limitations. Nevertheless, the importance of invertebrate animals and nonvascular plants to the life of various communities is stressed throughout the text. Aquatic communities are important to the terrestrial food chain in that they serve as spawning grounds for innumerable kinds of insects and other invertebrates, important food sources for numerous other species of animals.

The checklists of plants and animals included in this book serve as community rosters and narrow down the field of species that one can reasonably expect to encounter in a particular community. They may therefore facilitate species identification and at the very least give an idea of the range and variety of life to be found in each plant community. Plants and animals described or illustrated elsewhere in the text are so noted.

Separate lists of wildflowers, shrubs, trees, amphibians, reptiles, birds, and mammals are included for each community. In addition, important grasses and sedges are listed for the valley grassland and montane meadow communities —where these species are dominant—and common ferns are listed for the coniferous forest communities. Species occurring in more than one community are listed under each.

The following criteria were used in preparing the plant checklists:

TREES Trees are perennial woody plants having a single trunk. Most trees exceed 20 feet (6 meters) in height. Small trees may be shrubby. Near timberline, subalpine conifers often exhibit multiple trunks and shrubby or prostrate growth habits in response to severe environmental conditions.

The tree lists include all native species found in each community with the exception of a few extremely rare and local forms. Also excluded are normally shrubby plants. Lists are not provided for communities in which trees are at most an occasional and minor element.

Learning to identify trees is essential if one is to recognize most forest communities. This guide provides as aids to identification black-and-white line drawings of the leaves and fruit of most Sierra trees as well as detailed descriptions of each illustrated species.

SHRUBS Shrubs are woody perennial plants having multiple shoots branching from a base. They range in height from a few inches to 20 feet or more. Some shrubs are occasionally treelike. The lists of shrubs do not include trees that are sometimes shrubby, small perennial herbs with woody bases but soft stems, or extremely rare and local species. The lists do include woody vines. Shrub lists are not provided for communities in which they are at most an occasional and minor element. Dominant shrubs are described and illustrated for the chaparral, montane chaparral, and sagebrush scrub communities. Illustrations and descriptions are also provided for a few of the more common and conspicuous shrubs found in other communities.

WILDFLOWERS As used in this guide the term *wildflowers* refers to herbaceous plants having conspicuous flower parts. Grasses, sedges, and rushes are therefore excluded from this category. Herbaceous plants, or *herbs*, are annual or perennial flowering plants with little or no woody tissue. More than 2000 herbaceous plants occur in the Sierra; this guide of necessity lists only some of the more common types. More than 75 species are illustrated by black-and-white line drawings accompanied by brief descriptions of some of their more obvious features. Thirty-two additional species are shown in two sections of color plates.

Sedges and grasses are not illustrated because in most cases their identification is difficult at best and often requires botanical keys and close examination. The ability to distinguish particular species of grass or sedge is not essential to recognition of the communities in which they occur. A simple means of distinguishing grasses from sedges, however, is described in the introduction to montane meadows.

ANIMALS The animals of each plant community are listed under the headings of amphibians, reptiles, birds, and mammals. These lists include species regularly frequenting the community, even if that species is rather uncommon. Casual visitors and seasonal migrants only passing through the Sierra are not included. Selected animals are described in greater detail at the end of each regional chapter; the number of common animal species found in the Sierra precludes detailed descriptions of them all. The animals selected for extended discussion are merely a representative sample and were chosen for one or more of the following reasons:

1. They are especially common and conspicuous. Examples: Steller's jay and the yellow-bellied marmot.

2. They are especially characteristic of a particular community, regardless of how common or conspicuous they may be. Examples: the wrentit and the gray-crowned rosy finch.

3. They are common, though perhaps not conspicuous. Examples: the dusky-footed woodrat and grasshopper mice.

4. They exhibit anatomical or behavioral adaptations of particular interest. Examples: the dipper and the western spadefoot toad.

Even using the above criteria, numerous species had to be excluded for reasons of space. Nevertheless, those selected include a sampling of the birds and most of the mammals, reptiles, and amphibians that one is likely to encounter in the course of a walk in the Sierra. Some of these animals are also illustrated, but in many cases identification may be possible without resorting to visual aids. One can narrow down the possibilities by noting the general type of animal in question—small rodent, large predatory mammal, squirrel, and the like—and the plant community or region in which the observation occurred.

With the exception of certain species of birds, animals are by and large inconspicuous elements in a community. Many are active only at night; others are hard to observe even in broad daylight. Often, tracks or other signs are the only indications of their presence, and for this reason the tracks of most large mammals and a few of the smaller mammals are illustrated. Other signs are noted in the detailed descriptions of selected animals.

Although animals are listed and discussed in this guide according to the plant communities in which they are most commonly found, a word of caution is in order here. Animals by definition are mobile, and many Sierra animals may range or seasonally migrate over several elevational and vegetation zones, taking advantage of varying resource opportunities. Therefore, attempting to assign fauna to a specific community is to some extent arbitrary, depending on the creature's degree of mobility and ability to utilize a variety of habitats. It is, however, the most convenient means of portraying a total picture of life in a community, and animal ranges constitute a significant part of all discussion and description of animals in this guide.

Nomenclature

All species mentioned in this guide are identified by both their common and scientific names. The format used is as follows: canyon live oak, *Quercus chrysolepis*. A species may be known by several common names, but no other organism will bear the same scientific name. The canyon live oak, for example, is also known as the canyon oak, golden oak, gold cup oak, and maul oak, all of which can lead to a great deal of confusion. There is, however, only one *Quercus chrysolepis*. The common names employed in this book were chosen either because they are the most widely used or where this criterion doesn't apply, because they are especially descriptive.

Scientific names are based on Latin. The first name—in the above case, *Quercus*—indicates the genus; the second name—*chrysolepis*—the particular species. This system is used internationally, and though biologists sometimes do not agree on what name should be assigned a particular species, they never assign the same name to more than one species.

A full explanation of the criteria by which species are recognized and classified lies beyond the scope of this book, but they include such factors as mutual fertility, geographic range, anatomical features, and physiological similarities. Members of the same genus (plural *genera*) exhibit numerous traits in common, but in most cases are not mutually fertile. Lesser degrees of relationship are expressed in a series of larger hierarchies that include families, orders, classes, phyla, and kingdoms, among others.

Some species are further broken down into a number of geographic races designated as subspecies or varieties. In some cases these races may be readily distinguished by an interested observer with little training or special equipment. In others the differences are far more subtle and are unlikely to be evident to most observers in the field. Subspecies and varieties are indicated in this book only in a very few cases where their use has become conventional to

Introduction   7

identify the particular form of a species occurring in the Sierra. Examples include lodgepole pine, *Pinus contorta*, var. *murrayana*, and Anderson's alpine aster, *Aster alpigenus*, var. *andersonii*. Most amateur naturalists, however, need not be concerned with these distinctions.

Metric Equivalents

Metric equivalents are provided for all measurements used in this book. They are indicated in parentheses following the English units. The following conversions are applicable to the measurements in this book.

1 mile = 1.67 kilometers (km)
1 kilometer = 0.6 miles
1 foot = 0.3 meters (m)
1 meter = 3.28 feet
1 inch = 2.5 centimeters (cm)
1 centimeter = 0.4 inches
    4 inches = 10 centimeters or 1 decimeter (dm)

To convert degrees Fahrenheit (F) to degrees Celsius (C) or vice versa use the following equations:

$F = 9/5\ C + 32$
$C = 5/9\ (F - 32)$

Metric and English rulers are printed on the last page of this guide to facilitate the identification of wildflowers.

Additional Features

In addition to the features discussed above, this guide also includes the following elements designed to facilitate its use at home or in the field.

1. The table of contents lists all major subject heads found in each chapter. Often, one can find desired information simply by scanning these heads rather than resorting to the index.

2. The index lists all important terms, place names, and names of plants and animals mentioned in the text, checklists, or captions of this book. All species are indexed by both their common name and scientific name.

3. The text contains numerous cross-references to relevant information occurring elsewhere in the book.

4. A list of addresses of national parks and forests in the
Sierra Nevada follows Chapter VIII. Sources of additional
maps are also indicated.

5. A list of selected references directs readers to other
sources of information.

CHAPTER I

The Range of Light:
A Geographical Orientation

In APRIL 1776, Father Pedro Font, a Franciscan mission-ary attached to the Anza expedition, which had been sent north by the Spanish viceroy in Mexico to establish a colony in *alta* ("upper") California, stood on a hill near San Fran-cisco Bay and beheld to the east "an immense treeless plain" and, many miles beyond, "*una gran sierra nevada*"—a great snow-covered mountain range. Four years earlier two Franciscan fathers attached to the Gaspar de Portola expedition, which discovered San Francisco Bay, had been the first Europeans to see this great *sierra nevada,* but Font was the first to show its location on a map and give it the name that has endured to this day.

Almost a century later, in April 1868, a young man re-cently arrived in California by way of sailing ship around Cape Horn stood at Pacheco Pass, in the Coast Ranges south of San Francisco, and beheld to the east the great valley Font had seen and the snowy crest of the Sierra Nevada stretching north and south to the limits of vision. Barely thirty years old, John Muir had left San Francisco on foot just a few days before, bound for Yosemite Valley. Un-beknownst to him at the time, he would spend most of the next six years living in the valley, and most of his remaining 46 years exploring, interpreting, defending, and singing praise to the Sierra Nevada. Years later he would vividly recall his first glimpse of the range:

> When I first enjoyed this superb view, one glowing April day, from the summit of the Pacheco Pass, the Central Valley, but little trampled or plowed as yet, was one furred, rich sheet of golden compositae, and the luminous wall of the mountains shone in all its glory. Then it seemed to me the Sierra should be called not the Nevada, or Snowy Range, but the Range of Light. After ten years spent in the heart of it, rejoicing and wondering, bathing in its glorious floods of light, seeing the sunbursts of morning among the icy peaks, the noonday radiance on the trees and rocks and snow, the flush of alpenglow, and a thousand dashing waterfalls with their marvelous abundance of irised spray, it still seems to me above all others the Range of Light, the most divinely beautiful of all the mountain-chains I have ever seen.

Muir was a man of his time, and this extravagant praise, with its emphasis on the sublime, reflects the nineteenth-century Romantic in him. Yet Muir's language is no more extravagant than the Sierra itself, the beauty of which, while embracing the small, the intimate, and the serene, is more typically monumental—often downright awesome.

Size and Extent of the Sierra

The Sierra Nevada lies almost entirely in California, extending into neighboring Nevada only along the eastern shore of Lake Tahoe. More than 400 miles long (650 kilometers) and from 60 to 80 miles wide (100 to 130 kilometers), the Sierra forms a massive barrier separating central and northern California from more arid lands to the east. According to Francois Matthes, one of the pioneers of Sierra geology, the range covers an area greater than that of the French, Swiss, and Italian Alps combined.

The Sierra is the longest continuous mountain range in the coterminous United States. Its closest competitor in this regard, the Cascade Range of the Pacific Northwest, although about 700 miles long (1130 kilometers), has been cut through by the Columbia, Klamath, and Pit rivers. The resulting segments are by themselves far shorter than the Sierra. The Rocky Mountains and Appalachians, though more extensive than the Sierra, are actually vast mountain systems composed of numerous individual ranges, none of which even closely approach it in length. The magnificent Tetons, for example, are but 30 miles long (48 kilometers) and 10 to 15 miles wide (16 to 24 kilometers). The Front Range of Colorado, which rises above the city of Denver, is only 170 miles long (270 kilometers).

The Sierra's northernmost point is located just a few miles south of Mt. Lassen, the southernmost peak of the Cascade Range. Here, near Lake Almanor, the Sierra block disappears beneath a sheet of younger Cascade volcanic rocks. No obvious change in topography or vegetation marks the boundary, so without carefully examining the rocks themselves, it is difficult to know where one range ends and the other begins. Volcanic rocks are also found in the Sierra, but most of the range is composed of granite.

From Lake Almanor the Sierra extends in a southeast-erly direction for about 350 miles (560 kilometers) to the Mt. Whitney region, where it swings due south for another

Extent of the Sierra

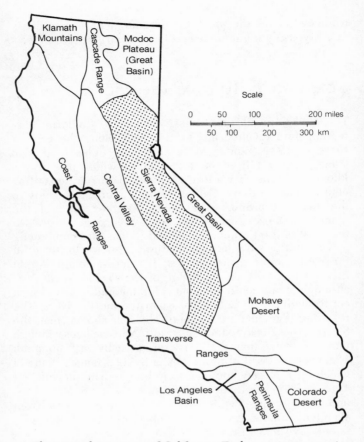

1. The natural provinces of California. Each constitutes a major geographic region characterized by its own distinctive blend of geology, climate, flora, and fauna. The Sierra Nevada province is roughly 400 mi (640 km) long and 40 to 80 mi (65 to 130 km) wide.

80 miles (130 kilometers) to Tehachapi Pass, the southern terminus of the range. South of this pass, the Tehachapi Mountains, a tiny, structurally distinct range, continue the trend of the Sierra for a few more miles to merge at last with the Transverse Ranges of Southern California.

THE RANGE OF LIGHT

The Central Valley

The Sierra Nevada is bordered on the west by California's vast Central Valley, a flat, low-lying plain almost entirely surrounded by mountains. Roughly 400 miles long (650 kilometers) and from 25 to 65 miles wide (40 to 105 kilometers), the valley parallels the general north–south trend of the Sierra on the east and the California Coast Ranges on the west. The northern half of the Central Valley is known to Californians as the Sacramento Valley, after the major river that drains it. Likewise, the southern half is called the San Joaquin Valley, after its most important stream.

Once covered by marshes and grasslands that supported one of the most impressive concentrations of wildlife in North America, the valley is now almost entirely given over to agriculture. The tule elk, pronghorn, wolf, and grizzly that once roamed the valley are gone; the great marshes along its west side have been mostly drained and filled; the carpet of wildflowers that once awed John Muir has been replaced by the orderly geometry of thriving farms. The valley is underlain by some 50,000 feet (15,250 meters) of sediments, most of which were washed down from the Sierra. The deep, fertile, alluvial soils derived from these sediments have made the Central Valley one of the nation's most productive agricultural regions. Because California summers are extremely dry, farmers must rely on irrigation. Water for Central Valley agriculture is derived largely from winter snowfall on the west slope of the Sierra.

The Great Basin

The abrupt east slope of the Sierra rises above a series of high desert basins which constitute the westernmost portion of the Great Basin Province. Stretching eastward to the Rockies, the Great Basin takes in most of Nevada and parts of eastern Oregon and California, southern Idaho, western Utah, and the southwest corner of Wyoming. The region exhibits pronounced "washboard" topography created by an alternation of high mountain ranges and intervening valleys. The mountains range in elevation from 9000 to over 14,000 feet (2750 to 4250 meters), and most of the valleys

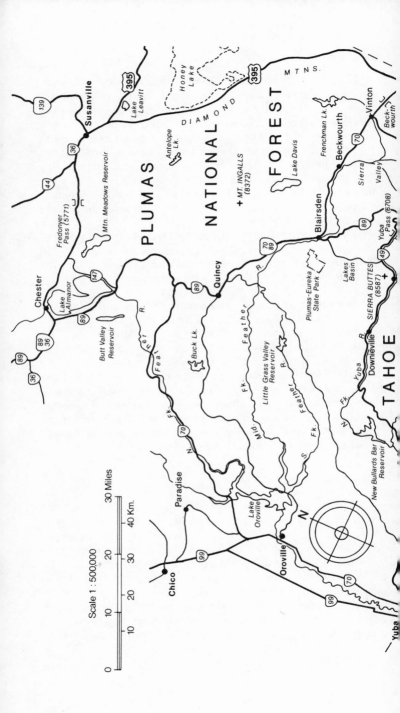

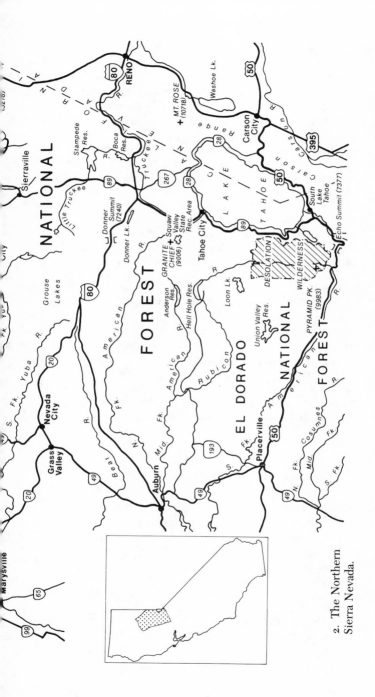

2. The Northern Sierra Nevada.

are more than 3000 feet high (900 meters). Like the Sierra, these desert ranges are uplifted fault blocks, and the valleys separating them, like those along the eastern base of the Sierra, are sunken blocks. Structurally, the Sierra could be considered the westernmost of the basin ranges except that its much larger size warrants its status as a separate geographic unit.

The Owens Valley is the largest and southernmost of the downfaulted basins along the eastern base of the Sierra. About 80 miles long (130 kilometers) and 10 miles wide (16 kilometers), it slopes gently downward toward the south, with elevations ranging from just over 4000 feet (1200 meters) near the town of Bishop to 3500 feet (1050 meters) south of Owens Lake. The Owens Valley forms a deep trough separating the Sierra on the west from the White Mountain and Inyo ranges on the east.

The White Mountain Range, which extends northward beyond the valley itself, culminates in 14,246–foot (4342 meters) White Mountain Peak, which rivals in elevation the highest summits of the Sierra. Southward from the White Mountain Range the Inyo Range reaches its greatest height at 11,127–foot (3392 meters) Waucoba Mountain. The White Mountains are known for their fine stands of bristle-cone pine, some of which exceed 4000 years in age, making them the oldest trees in the world. Both ranges are drier than the Sierra, which intercepts the moist Pacific air masses that might otherwise reach them.

Across the Sierra

The Sierra Nevada is essentially an enormous piece of the earth's crust that rose thousands of feet along a series of faults, or fractures, on its eastern side, tilting westward in the process to form an asymetrical mountain range with a broad, gently sloping western flank and narrow, precipitous eastern escarpment. Ranges formed in this way are known as tilted fault-blocks and include, in addition to the Sierra, the Basin ranges of northern Nevada.

Although the Sierra is structurally of a piece, it exhibits wide variations in topography and vegetation that are readily apparent to even the casual observer. In order to survey this variety, the following discussion traces an imaginary journey across the southern Sierra from the Central Valley to the Owens Valley, and from there northward to Lake Tahoe and beyond.

The Sierra Foothills

The west slope of the Sierra is a broad, gently sloping ramp 30 to 50 miles wide (50 to 80 kilometers). It rises eastward from the floor of the Central Valley at rates ranging from less than 2 degrees in the north to 6 degrees in the south. The emergence of the Sierra block from beneath the sediments of the Central Valley is marked by a narrow belt of undulating foothills and broad valleys covered by a patchwork of grassland, oak woodland, and chaparral. The foothills constitute that portion of the west slope from the valley floor to elevations of about 2000 feet (600 meters) in the north and 5000 feet (1500 meters) in the south. Although they are not geologically distinct from the Sierra as a whole, the foothills form a well-defined vegetational unit. Indeed, with respect to topography, climate, life forms, and overall aspect, the Sierra foothills more closely resemble the hot, dry California Coast Ranges than they do the upper portion of the Sierra itself.

The Conifer Forest

Above 2000 feet elevation in the north and 5000 feet in the south, the west slope of the Sierra is largely covered by a coniferous forest dominated by various species of pines and firs. Amidst the forest are large expanses of sparsely vegetated rock outcrops and meadows ranging in size from small plots of turf to great open subalpine fields up to several miles in length. As elevation increases the forest grows more open, and the portion of the landscape given over to rock outcrops and meadows increases.

During California's rainless summers, the Sierra forest serves as an oasis for vacationers seeking relief from the seasonal heat and drought of the surrounding lowlands. When inland hills and valleys are brown and sere for lack of

3. Nevada Falls, Yosemite National Park. Here, the Merced River plunges nearly 600 ft (180 m) over the face of a giant step carved in granite by an advancing glacier (see Figure 35).

rain, the Sierra forest, watered by the previous winter's snow, remains green and cool. Long after foothill grasses have withered, wildflowers bloom profusely in mountain meadows. When most lowland watercourses have become dry washes, Sierra streams continue to flow. Seeps, thundershowers, late-melting snow, and even a few small

THE RANGE OF LIGHT

glaciers provide enough water to keep the larger mountain streams running throughout the summer.

Yosemite Valley and Kings Canyon

The west slope of the Sierra, despite its relatively gradual incline, is extremely rugged, characterized throughout the length of the range by southwest-trending ridges separating deep river gorges. When the Sierra Nevada block began to be uplifted and tilted west— beginning sometime between 10 and 20 million years ago—the formerly meandering streams draining the region began to flow faster and cut deeper channels, eventually forming V-shaped canyons. Later, beginning perhaps three million years ago, the upper reaches of these canyons were invaded by glaciers, which quarried enormous amounts of rock from their sides, thereby transforming them into U-shaped valleys with steep, nearly vertical walls and broad, gently sloping floors.

The most famous of these glacier-carved canyons is Yosemite Valley, where steep granite cliffs rise more than 3000 feet (900 meters) above the meandering Merced River. A few miles north of Yosemite Valley, the walls of Muir Gorge rise a full mile above the Tuolumne River, forming a narrow canyon comparable in depth to the Grand Canyon. South of Yosemite National Park, the canyons are deeper yet, culminating in the awesome gorge of the south fork of the Kings River, which measures more than 8000 feet (2450 meters) from canyon floor to the tops of the adjacent ridges, making it the deepest river canyon in North America. Canyons between 6000 and 7000 feet deep (1850 and 2150 meters) are common in the southern Sierra.

The High Sierra

A spectacular landscape of jagged peaks, thousands of lakes and meadows, ice-scoured gorges, and high, rocky, windswept basins sprawls across the crest of the Sierra from Sonora Pass south to the Mt. Whitney region and the peaks above Mineral King. About 150 miles long (240 kilometers) and from 10 to 20 miles wide (16 to 32 kilometers), this

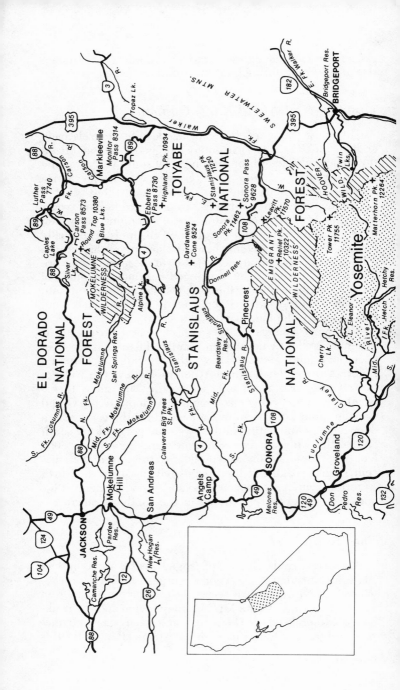

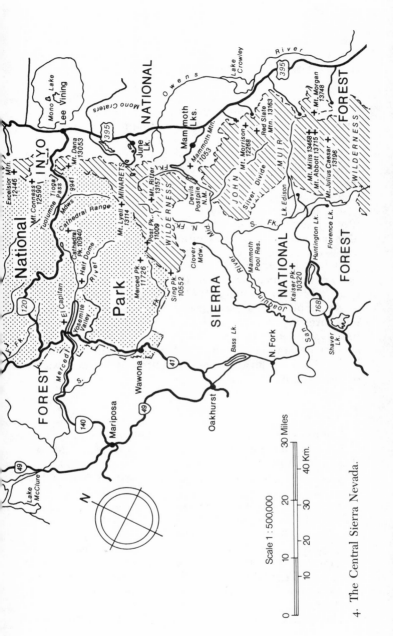

4. The Central Sierra Nevada.

"alpine" region contains some of the grandest scenery in the West and constitutes one of the largest roadless areas in the 48 states. Known as the High Sierra, this region lies mostly above 9000 feet elevation (2700 meters) and roughly coincides with the extent of the great ice caps that blanketed the upper slopes of the range during the Pleistocene Epoch, which lasted from three million to about ten thousand years ago.

Evidences of glaciation abound in the Sierra—in vast expanses of polished rock buffed to a high sheen by the heavy hand of moving ice; in U-shaped canyons with their sheer, elegantly sculpted cliffs towering over broad valley floors; in massive pyramidal peaks and giant glacial stairways; in high, curving ridges of debris that parallel ancient glacier courses; in the miscellany of boulders that, pushed and scattered by the glaciers, litter slopes, valleys, and river bottoms; and in the thousands of sparkling lakes and "sky parlor" meadows that fill the great amphitheaters quarried from mountainsides by moving ice.

North of Sonora Pass glacially scoured terrain occurs only intermittently along the crest, most conspicuously in the Desolation Wilderness southwest of Lake Tahoe. Still smaller pockets occur north of Lake Tahoe in the Grouse Lakes Basin and near the Sierra Buttes, at the headwaters of the Yuba River.

The Sierra Crest

For most of its length the Sierra culminates in a single main divide separating the watersheds of the east and west slopes. Summit elevations along the main crest tend to increase steadily from north to south. North of Lake Tahoe few peaks exceed 8000 feet (2450 meters), but on both sides of the lake they approach or exceed 10,000 feet (3050 meters). Eighty miles south, in Yosemite National Park, summit elevations along the main crest range from 11,000 to 13,000 feet (3350 to 3950 meters). From Duck Pass, just south of Yosemite, to Trail Pass, in the southern Sierra—a distance of 90 miles (145 kilometers)—the main crest does not drop below 11,000 feet. Peaks along this stretch commonly exceed 12,000 feet, and 13,000-foot summits are numerous.

The climax of the range is attained in two widely separated groups of 14,000-foot peaks (4250 meters). The north-ernmost group, known as the Palisade Crest, is situated due west of the town of Big Pine. It comprises six peaks over 14,000 feet, the highest being North Palisade, at 14,242 feet (4341 meters). Forty miles south along the main crest, the Mt. Whitney group, sometimes called the Muir Crest, includes six more 14,000-foot summits. South of the Muir Crest elevations decrease steadily until, at the southern end of the range, the highest ridges seldom exceed 7000 feet (2150 meters). Altogether, more than 500 peaks rise above 12,000 feet, over 160 exceed 13,000 feet, and 12 are higher than 14,000 feet.

The Sierra does not culminate in a single ridge, but rather in a complex of lofty crests, some paralleling the main divide, others branching away from it. Most of these secondary crests have names of their own—the Ritter Range, Crystal Range, Cathedral Range, Silver Divide, Le Conte Divide, Kaiser Ridge, Glacier Divide, Kaweah Peaks, Great Western Divide, and many others—but they are not separate mountain ranges, for all are perched atop the same uplifted block. They often approach and some-times exceed the main crest in both elevation and scenic beauty, and if situated elsewhere would be considered major mountain ranges in their own right. In Sequoia Na-tional Park, for example, the Great Western Divide—comparable in size to the Teton Range—has many peaks exceeding 12,000 feet (3650 meters) and some exceeding 13,000 feet (3950 meters). Paralleling the main crest for some 30 miles (50 kilometers), the Great Western Divide rises more than 5000 feet (1500 meters) above the interven-ing Kern River and some 7000 feet (2150 meters) above the middle fork of the Kaweah River on the west.

In the Mammoth Lakes region, a popular resort area on the east slope of the Sierra near Yosemite National Park, the main crest is an unimpressive volcanic ridge seldom reaching even 10,000 feet (3050 meters) in elevation and displaying few of the glacial features that lend grandeur to the High Sierra. As if in compensation for this lapse, how-ever, a secondary crest—the jagged Ritter Range—rises only six miles (ten kilometers) to the west, towering nearly 2000 feet (600 meters) above the main divide and more than 4000 feet (1200 meters) above the middle fork of the San

5. The Ritter Range, southeast of Yosemite National Park.

Joaquin River, which separates the two ridges. Generally considered one of the most spectacular massifs in the Sierra, the Ritter Range exhibits most of the features— lakes, meadows, sawtooth ridges, even small glaciers—for which the High Sierra is noted.

The Eastern Escarpment

Viewed from the Central Valley the Sierra Nevada is inconspicuous, appearing as a low range of foothills on the eastern horizon. From this vantage the high peaks, which lie 30 to 50 miles (50 to 80 kilometers) east of the valley, are seldom visible. On the east side of the range, however, the Sierra presents an imposing mountain wall rising steeply from adjacent lowlands. The eastern escarpment is most impressive in the southern Sierra, especially along the west side of Owens Valley, where a monolithic ridge extends unbroken for more than 70 miles (110 kilometers), its numerous peaks rising from 9000 to 10,800 feet (2750 to 3300 meters) above the valley floor, which ranges from 3500 to 4000 feet in elevation (1070 to 1220 meters). By comparison, the Teton Range of Wyoming rises only about 6000 feet (1800 meters) above Jackson Hole, and the Front Range of Colorado, only about 9000 (2750 meters) above the High Plains. North of Owens Valley the height of the main crest gradually decreases, while the valleys at its base tend to increase in elevation. As a result, the difference in elevation between the two steadily diminishes from about 9900 feet (3020 meters) near the town of Bishop to 6700 feet (2040 meters) at Mono Lake, 4300 feet (1310 meters) at Sonora Pass junction, and 3700 feet (1130 meters) in the Tahoe Basin.

Conifer forest mantles the upper slopes of the eastern escarpment and extends to lower elevations along stream-courses. This forest contains fewer species of trees than that of the west slope, but otherwise resembles it closely. Above the forest lies the same complex of lakes, meadows, and bare rock characteristic of the High Sierra, and below it pinyon–juniper woodland and sagebrush scrub extend downslope to the desert valleys at the base of the range.

East-slope canyons are shorter and steeper than those on the west side of the Sierra. Their streams drain far smaller areas and carry off less meltwater, owing to diminished precipitation east of the crest. Many of the canyons were once filled with glacial ice, particularly in their upper reaches, but none approach the gorges of the west slope in depth or monumental beauty. There are no Yosemites on the east side of the Sierra.

Spur Ranges

The single, unbroken escarpment characteristic of the southern Sierra gives way near the town of Bishop, at the northern end of the Owens Valley, to a more complex structure consisting of staggered spur ranges branching north and east from the main crest. The southernmost of these spurs extends eastward from the main crest just north of Mammoth Lakes, dividing Long Valley from Mono Basin to the north. The east-side highway, U.S. 395, crosses this upland at Deadman Summit. Extending eastward for 20 miles (32 kilometers) to Glass Mountain, this broad ridge also includes the picturesque Mono Craters, volcanic domes east of the highway just south of Mono Lake.

The Bodie Hills, another spur range, tumble down from the Sierra crest just north of the town of Lee Vining and skirt the north end of Mono Basin, dividing it from the higher, less arid Bridgeport Valley, the lush pastures of which are subirrigated by the East Walker River. Highway 395 crosses the Bodie Hills at Conway Summit, where the view southward of Mono Basin and the Sierra crest beyond is magnificent.

The Bridgeport Valley is bounded on the south by the Bodie Hills and the main crest of the Sierra, which here swings westward in an impressive series of rugged pinna-

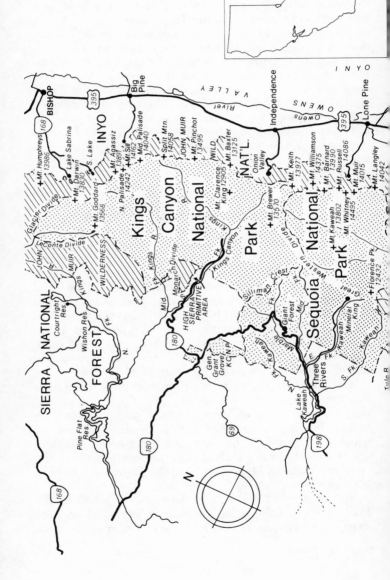

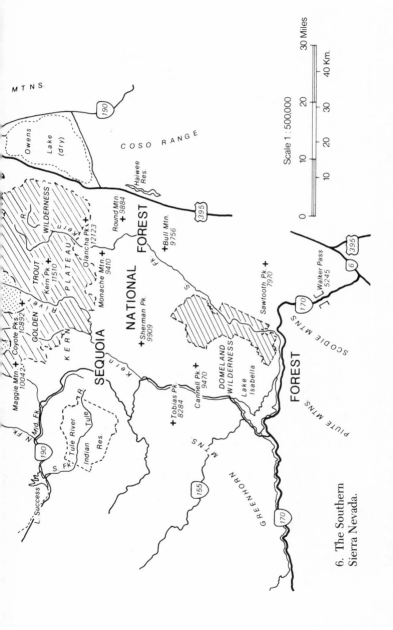

6. The Southern Sierra Nevada.

cles appropriately named Sawtooth Ridge. The west side of the valley is bordered by the Sweetwater Mountains, another spur range, which extend from the Sierra crest northward for some 50 miles (80 kilometers). Patterson Peak, the highest summit in the Sweetwater Mountains, attains an elevation of 11,673 feet (3558 meters), making it higher than any of the nearby Sierra peaks. Highway 395 crosses the Sweetwater Mountains at Devils Gate Summit.

A few miles northwest of Sonora Pass junction the Pine Nut Range leaves the Sierra crest to parallel the course of the Sweetwater Mountains into Nevada. The highest peak in the Pine Nut Range, which divides the watersheds of the Walker and Carson rivers, is Mt. Siegel, a 9450-foot (2880-meter) peak situated several miles east of Carson City, the state capital of Nevada. Highway 395 crosses the range north of Topaz Lake, just across the Nevada line. South of the lake, in California, Highway 89 branches west, crossing the Pine Nut Range at Monitor Pass enroute to the small mountain town of Markleeville, the seat of remote and sparsely populated Alpine County.

Lake Tahoe

The Carson Range branches north from the Sierra crest between Carson Pass and Echo Summit. Lake Tahoe fills the basin lying between the Carson Range on the east and the Sierra crest on the west. It formed when the original drainage of the Truckee River, the lake's only outlet, was blocked, first by volcanic debris and later by glacial moraines.

Twenty-two miles (35 kilometers) long, 12 miles (19 kilometers) wide, and 1600 feet (490 meters) deep, Lake Tahoe is the largest mountain lake in North America, and despite the extensive commercial development along its shoreline it is still among the most beautiful. Many people, including this author, feel it is a shame that the lake and its surrounding mountains, which together form one of the crown jewels of the Sierra, were not turned into a national park long ago. Certainly no area now included in the park system is any more deserving of preservation. Yet back in the 1920s, when only a small portion of the lakeshore was developed, an investigator assigned by the federal government to determine the area's suitability for national park status advised against this course on the grounds that too much development had already occurred around the lake.

The Northern Sierra

North of Lake Tahoe, the Sierra diminishes in stature and rather than culminating in a single crest, consists of a series of undistinguished parallel ridges, one of which happens to be the main crest of the range. The highest peaks in this region barely top 8000 feet elevation (2450 meters), and while beautiful in its own right, the landscape rarely exhibits the rugged grandeur characteristic of the southern Sierra. Most of the region north of Lake Tahoe is drained by the westbound Feather River system, the middle fork of which cuts through the low ridge that is the northernmost extension of the main crest. Although Sierra Valley, a northern extension of the Tahoe Basin that was cut off by the volcanic flows that also impounded the lake, is situated east of the main crest, its waters are carried west. The drainage divide in this, the northernmost part of the Sierra is formed by two spur ranges, the Bald Mountain Range and the Diamond Mountains, which continue the northward trend of the Carson Range.

Sierra Waters

West-Slope Streams

Eleven major river systems carry the runoff of the west slope into the Central Valley. The Feather, Yuba, and American rivers drain the Sierra from Lake Tahoe north, emptying into the Sacramento River, which begins in the Klamath Mountains and flows south down the Sacramento Valley (the northern half of the Central Valley). The Mokelumne, Stanislaus, Tuolumne, and Merced rivers all empty into the San Joaquin River, which begins high in the central Sierra and flows north up the San Joaquin Valley (the southern half of the Central Valley). The Sacramento and San Joaquin rivers converge in the west-central part of the Central Valley to form a complex delta system comprising marshes, diked farmlands, dozens of islands, and hundreds of miles of meandering sloughs. From there the combined waters flow through the Carquinez Strait, the valley's only outlet, into San Francisco Bay.

The southern end of the Sierra is drained on the west by three major streams—the Kings, Kaweah, and Kern rivers—all of which terminate in the southern San Joaquin Valley. Mountains west and south of the valley have for millions of years prevented these streams from reaching the ocean. Prior to the advent of extensive agriculture in the valley, the waters of the Kings and Kaweah rivers flowed into the vast Tule Basin, which was filled by a large, shallow lake bordered by marshes. Diversion of most of this water for irrigation began early in this century, and Tule Lake now appears only briefly and occasionally during seasons of excessive runoff. Similarly, the Kern River once emptied into a shallow lake at the extreme southern end of the valley, but this lake too has now vanished in the service of agriculture.

East-Slope Streams

The east slope of the Sierra is drained by four major streams and hundreds of smaller creeks, none of which empty into the ocean. Like other streams in the Great Basin, those flowing eastward from the Sierra empty finally into desert lakes and playas.

North of Lake Tahoe numerous small streams drain the eastern slope of the Diamond Mountains, flowing but a brief way to their destination in nearby Honey Lake. This vast, shallow body of water, like other desert lakes along the east side of the Sierra and elsewhere in the Great Basin, is a remnant of the much larger lakes that occupied the region during the Pleistocene Epoch, when runoff was much greater than today.

Lake Tahoe itself and the high country to the west are drained by the Truckee River, which flows north and then east from the lake, tumbling down a steep canyon to the city of Reno. From there it flows northward into the desert, emptying finally into Pyramid Lake in northwestern Nevada.

THE RANGE OF LIGHT

Immediately south of Lake Tahoe the 35-mile (56-kilometer) section of the crest bounded by Carson Pass on the north and Sonora Pass on the south is drained by the east and west forks of the Carson River, which flow northeastward into Nevada, where they dissipate finally in a vast marshy sump known as the Carson Sink, now the Newman Reservoir.

The east and west forks of the Walker River drain the east slope from Sonora Pass to the Sawtooth Ridge. They are separated by the Sweetwater Mountains, joining north of it and emptying finally into Walker Lake, in the Nevada desert north of the town of Hawthorne.

From the Bodie Hills south to Deadman's Pass, the east slope of the Sierra is drained by several small streams, all of which empty—or did so at one time—into Mono Lake, the large, extremely saline lake east of Tioga Pass. Today much of this streamflow is being diverted south for use by the city of Los Angeles. As a result, the water level is now falling at an alarming rate, and the lake could deteriorate into a vast salty wasteland by the end of the century.

South of the Mono Basin the east slope of the Sierra is drained by small streams flowing swiftly downslope to join the Owens River, or rather, what remains of it. The Owens River rises as a series of streams in the high country near Mammoth Lakes. Until the early decades of this century, when the river's water was diverted southward in an aqueduct for use by, again, the city of Los Angeles, the Owens River flowed south for 120 miles (190 kilometers) to Owens Lake, near the town of Lone Pine. Owens Lake, like Honey and Mono lakes, was a remnant of larger Ice Age lakes, but today it has been reduced to a dry alkaline basin shimmering white in the desert sun. The Owens Valley, in the words of Mary Austin, has been a "land of little rain" for thousands of years, but prior to the 1930s, when water diversion began in earnest in the region, agriculture flourished along the river. Today most of the old farms are abandoned, the river flows in concrete channels, and desert scrub has invaded streamside flats where lush meadows once prospered.

The Thin Edge of Drought

With somewhat less drastic consequences the story of the Owens River has been repeated for virtually every major stream on the west slope of the Sierra. A vast system of dams, aqueducts, and irrigation canals has been built at a cost of billions of dollars to distribute the waters of the Sierra to drier parts of the state. Semiarid Southern California takes the lion's share to quench the thirst of its huge population, but in some degree most of California depends on runoff from the Sierra snowpack to provide water for agriculture, industry, hydroelectric power, and home use. When occasional dry winters reduce the Sierra snowpack, tremors of discontent shake the entire state. The two-year drought of 1975 to 1977, when Sierra snowfall was about one-third of normal, forced numerous communities, including most of the populous San Francisco Bay Area, to institute strict water rationing. Many farmers and ranchers suffered heavy financial losses, and some went out of business altogether. It is generally agreed that a third year of drought would have brought economic disaster to the state, not only through additional agricultural losses, but also through the forced closing of industries heavily dependent on ample water. California's population, particularly that of the Los Angeles area, has far outstripped the capacity of local water supplies to support it. Depending almost entirely on runoff from the Sierra, residents of the Golden State will continue to live on the thin edge of drought.

Visitors

For centuries before Father Pedro Font saw *una gran sierra nevada* in 1776, numerous Indian settlements were scattered through the western foothills and along the eastern base of the range. Small trading parties often crossed the mountains to barter with tribes living on the opposite side. The peoples inhabiting the west slope based their diet on acorns, which they traded for pinyon nuts, the staple food of Indians living on the east side of the Sierra. During the summer entire settlements often moved upslope, where food plants, game, and water were more plentiful. But like today's vacationers, they also took to the slopes to escape the blistering heat of California's interior valleys. The Tahoe Basin and Yosemite Valley were favorite summer retreats for certain tribes.

Following Pedro Font's sighting, the Sierra was largely ignored by the Spaniards and Mexicans who settled in California's coastal hills and valleys. At least, there is no record of any *Californios* having ventured farther upslope than the western foothills. The first non-Indian known to have crossed the Sierra was Jedediah Smith, who led two companions westward over the range in October 1827, probably crossing somewhere near Ebbetts Pass. Four years later a large party led by Joseph Walker crossed the range through what is now Yosemite National Park. The following year, after wandering throughout much of the length of California, Walker led his party back over the Sierra from the west. In the winter of 1844 Captain John C. Fremont and his scout, Kit Carson, headed a small party that successfully crossed the range in the vicinity of Carson Pass. Indians in the region knew better than to venture into the high country during the winter, and when informed of Fremont's intention to do so, one man could only mutter in dismay, "Rock upon rock, snow upon snow." During the late 1840s several parties of immigrants crossed the Sierra to settle in California, among them the ill-fated Donner Party, many of whom perished in the deep snows east of Donner Summit during the winter of 1846–1847.

The attention of the nation—and indeed, much of the world—turned to the Sierra following the discovery of gold near the foothill settlement of Coloma in 1848. Over the next decade thousands of fortune-seekers swarmed over the Sierra foothills chasing the elusive "big strike" in the streams and gravels of the Mother Lode. Such foothill towns as Sonora, Angels Camp, Placerville (formerly "Hangtown"), Jackson, Mokelumne Hill, and Nevada City sprang up overnight as rough-and-tumble mining camps. Today, many of the old buildings and mining equipment dating from the Gold Rush can be seen in these and other foothill communities. Angels Camp provided the setting for Mark Twain's famous tale "The Jumping Frog of Calaveras County." Many of Bret Harte's stories, including "Tennes-

Visitors   35

see Pardner" and "The Outcasts of Poker Flat," are also set in the Sierra foothills.

Yosemite Valley was discovered in 1851 and in 1864 was given to the state of California by the federal government for designation as a state park, thereby becoming the first large wilderness park established in the United States. Giant sequoias were discovered in 1852, but their preservation would not come until the following century, and before it did, many of the finest specimens would be cut down for timber or the amusement of the curious.

The first methodical exploration of the Sierra came in 1863–1864, when the California State Geological Survey, led by Josiah Whitney, surveyed much of the central and southern portions of the range. John Muir first visited the Sierra in 1869, and in a series of national magazine articles broadcast its glories and the need to preserve them to all who would hearken to his word. His efforts in this behalf led in 1892 to the founding of the Sierra Club.

Table 1: Parks and Wilderness Areas of the Sierra Nevada

Unit	Acres
Yosemite National Park	761,320
Devils Postpile National Monument	798
Kings Canyon National Park	460,331
Sequoia National Park	385,863
Desolation Wilderness	63,500
Mokelumne Wilderness	50,400
Emigrant Wilderness	97,000
Hoover Wilderness	42,800
Minarets Wilderness	109,500
Kaiser Wilderness	22,500
John Muir Wilderness	504,263
Golden Trout Wilderness	306,000
Domeland Wilderness	62,561
Plumas-Eureka State Park	4,632
Malakoff Diggins State Park	2,590
Indian Grinding Rock State Park	44
Calaveras Big Trees State Park	5,437
Donner Memorial State Park	353
Sugar Pine Point State Park	1,975
D. L. Bliss State Park	1,237
Emerald Bay State Park	595
Grover Hot Springs State Park	519
Columbia State Historical Park	241

THE RANGE OF LIGHT

As a consequence of the work of Muir and his followers, much of the Sierra Nevada has been set aside in national parks and wilderness areas which together account for more than 3.5 million acres. Many people still seek gold in Sierra streams, but millions more flock to the range each year to fish its waters, ski its slopes, climb its peaks and cliffs, ramble through its high country, or just enjoy its magnificent scenery, clear waters, and sweet air. Indeed, the Sierra has become so popular that today it stands in danger of being loved "not wisely, but too well." Campgrounds in popular areas such as Yosemite Valley and Lake Tahoe are crowded throughout the summer, and on many weekends even remote wilderness trails are aswarm with hikers. Many backcountry campsites have deteriorated from overuse and carelessness, and in too many areas meadows have been damaged by trampling feet and lakes have been polluted by waste and garbage. Loving the Sierra "wisely" requires knowing it well, and to that purpose this book is dedicated.

CHAPTER II

Fields of Granite,
Rivers of Ice:
A Geological Survey

THE WORLD'S great mountain ranges, rather than being scattered randomly over the globe, occur in distinct belts, or *cordillera*. One of these belts extends along the western margins of North and South America, from Alaska to Tierra del Fuego. It includes the Alaska Range, Rocky Mountains, Cascade Range, Sierra Nevada, Sierra Madres of Mexico, and the Andes, to name only a few. Another, even larger cordillera extends across southern Europe and Asia, from Gibraltar to China, and includes the Pyrenees, Alps, Carpathians, Caucasus, Hindu Kush, Karakoram, Himalaya, and Tien Shan, among other ranges. Less massive mountain belts extend down the east side of Africa and border the western Pacific.

Altogether, the mountains of the world account for only about a quarter of its exposed land surface. Obviously, tremendous earth-moving, or *tectonic*, forces are at work in the cordillera that are, for a time at least, less active elsewhere. That these forces are still active today is evidenced by the concentration of volcanic and seismic (earthquake) activity along the cordillera.

Compared to the age of the earth, which is now estimated at 4.5 to 5 billion years, the events that produced these mountain belts occurred fairly recently. The oldest rocks in the Sierra Nevada, for example, date back 475 million years, a span of time nearly incomprehensible in human terms, yet representing but one-tenth of the time that has passed since the earth was formed. If the earth's age were compared to the passage of a single day, the history of the Sierra rocks would not begin until around 9:30 P.M. Actual uplift of the Sierra commenced only 2.5 to 3 million years ago—a couple of minutes before midnight—making it just about the youngest nonvolcanic mountain range in the world.

Plate Tectonics

Ideas about the forces responsible for movements in the earth's crust (Figure 7), including the creation of mountain ranges, have changed dramatically in the last decade in response to geologic, geophysical, and oceanographic evi-

Table 2: Geologic Time

Era	Period	Epoch	Years before present	Geologic events in the Sierra Nevada
CENOZOIC	Quarternary	Holocene (Recent)	10,000	Sierra enters a warming period following the retreat of the last major glaciers 10,000 years ago. Minor glacial advances occur 2000 and 700 years ago. Uplift continues to present. Intermittent volcanic activity.
		Pleistocene		Climate becomes cooler and wetter. Oldest Sierra glaciation dates back about 2.7 million years. From then until 10,000 years ago, the range is repeatedly overwhelmed by glaciers, with maximum advance occurring 20,000 years ago. Warm, interglacial periods separate glacial advances. Uplift begins in southern Sierra about two to three million years ago and continues throughout Pleistocene.
	Tertiary	Pliocene	±2.5 million	By the opening of the Tertiary the Sierra region is a gentle, rising plain with a few modest hills and ridges in the east, which must have resembled the Adirondacks today. The climate is warm and moist. Volcanic activity begins again about 30 million years ago. The northern Sierra is buried beneath ash and volcanic mud. Uplift of the northern Sierra begins about 10 million years ago. Tahoe region reaches present height by opening of Pleistocene.
		Miocene	9 million	
		Oligocene	25 million	
		Eocene	40 million	
		Paleocene	60 million	
MESOZOIC	Cretaceous		70 million	Sea-floor sediments are folded, tilted, and stuffed into the subduction zone between the Pacific and North American plates. Rocks on the diving Pacific plate melt to form magma, some of which is expelled from both offshore and inshore volcanoes, the rest cooling in place to form the Sierra batholith. Gold and other minerals are formed. Sea-floor volcanic and sedimentary rocks are transformed by heat and pressure into metamorphic rocks. Crust is uplifted to form a folded mountain range that was the forerunner of the Sierra. Beginning about 130 million years ago this pre-Sierran range begins to be leveled by subsidence and erosion.
	Jurassic		135 million	
	Triassic		180 million	
			225 million	

Era	Period	Epoch	Years before present	Geologic events in the Sierra Nevada
PALEOZOIC	Permian		270 million	For more than 200 million years, the Sierra region lies beneath the sea, receiving sediments from the North American continent, which is drifting westward. Toward the end of this period, the sea-floor sediments begin to be folded as the Pacific plate collides with the North American plate. Oldest rocks in the Sierra deposited on the sea floor 475 million years ago.
	Pennsylvanian Mississippian (Carboniferous)		350 million	
	Devonian		400 million	
	Silurian		440 million	
	Ordovician		500 million	
	Cambrian		575 million	
Pre-Cam-brian			4.5 billion	Age of Earth

dence that the crust, rather than being immobile, is composed of numerous plates that glide over the more plastic rocks of the mantle. This theory of *plate tectonics* was advanced in 1967 as an explanation for *continental drift*.

It is now generally agreed that during most of the Paleozoic era (600 to 225 million years ago) the earth's continents were united in a single supercontinent, or perhaps two continents situated side by side. For reasons yet undetermined this great land mass began to break up about 230 million years ago and the continents were carried away on moving plates. A rift developed between the Americas on one side and Europe and Africa on the other. The former began to move west and the latter east from their shared boundary, widening the rift, which was invaded by the sea to become the Atlantic Ocean. Today the rift is marked by the Mid-Atlantic Ridge, an undersea volcanic chain that runs down the center of the Atlantic, its course mimicking the west coasts of Europe and Africa.

Some plates are covered with thin (about five miles/eight kilometers), dense oceanic rocks, some with lighter but thicker (up to 25 miles/40 kilometers) continental rocks, and a few with both. Precisely why plates move is uncertain, though one plausible explanation attributes the phenomenon to convection currents in the mantle, the solid, 1800-mile (2900-kilometer) thick shell of iron and magnesium rocks immediately beneath the crust. It is thought that

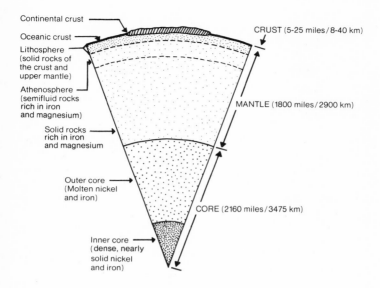

Continental crust

Oceanic crust

Lithosphere
(solid rocks of
the crust and
upper mantle)

Athenosphere
(semifluid rocks
rich in iron
and magnesium)

Solid rocks
rich in iron
and magnesium

Outer core
(Molten nickel
and iron)

Inner core
(dense, nearly
solid nickel
and iron)

CRUST (5-25 miles / 8-40 km)

MANTLE (1800 miles / 2900 km)

CORE (2160 miles / 3475 km)

7. Cross section of the earth's interior. The earth is made up of a series of concentric shells surrounding a core of nickel and iron. The outermost shell, or *crust*, ranges from 5 mi (8 km) thick beneath the ocean floors to as much as 25 mi (40 km) thick beneath the continents. It consists of several segments, or *plates*, which move about on the surface of a shell of denser rock called the *mantle*. Consisting of rocks rich in iron and magnesium, the 1800-mile-thick (2900 km) mantle in turn surrounds the earth's core.

these currents may push the lighter crustal rocks about in much the same way as pot herbs are swirled about on the surface of hot soup.

Plates move away from midocean rises—such as the Mid-Atlantic Ridge—where upwelling lava, rising through zones of crustal weakness, is added to the trailing edges of outward-bound rocks. The lava that spews forth from these rises flows down both slopes, cooling to form the dense black rocks of the sea floor. As additional lava is generated, older flows are pushed away from the rises toward the continents, a process known as *sea floor spreading*. Measurements of the ages of various flows confirm that the oldest rocks on the ocean floor occur near the continental margins, the youngest immediately next to the mid-ocean rises.

As plates move over the globe they slide past and collide with other plates, and as one might expect, the great earthquake belts of the world coincide with these boundaries. Plates passing each other form zones of lateral shear called *transverse faults*. California's San Andreas Fault is the most famous example. It forms the boundary between the Pacific and North American plates, which are sliding by each other at this time, though they have collided in the past. The lands west of the fault are moving northward at a rate of about two inches (five centimeters) a year, not smoothly, but in jerks and starts, one of which leveled San Francisco in 1906, when the Pacific plate in the space of a few seconds shot northward as much as 21 feet (6.4 meters).

Where the leading edges of oceanic plates encounter the margins of continental plates head on, the denser oceanic crust dives beneath the lighter continental crust, forming troughlike areas of subsidence called *subduction zones*, which correspond to the deep oceanic trenches found along many continental margins throughout the world. The Pacific plate, for example, is now plunging into the Aleutian Trench, which parallels the island chain of the same name. The great Anchorage earthquake of 1964, which elevated 70,000 square miles (182,000 square kilometers) of land, occurred in response to tensions deep in the earth's crust that built up as the plunging Pacific plate jostled against the overriding continental rocks.

Most of the world's greatest earthquakes originate deep in subduction zones and apparently occur in response to the massive crumpling, folding, and breaking of the earth's crust that accompanies plate collision. Rocks on the ocean floor, along with those on the continental margin, are squeezed in a huge vice as one plate slides beneath the other. Some are scraped off on the leading edge of the continental plate; others are borne downward in the earth, where they melt to form *magma*, or molten rock.

The magma rises buoyantly into the denser, heavier rocks above it, causing some of them to melt as well. A fraction of this molten rock makes its way to the surface, where it erupts from volcanoes. The remainder is trapped deep in the earth by the rocks above and cools in place to form granitic rocks such as those exposed in the Sierra.

The world's cordillera mark the boundaries along which current or geologically recent plate collision has occurred. The Himalaya, for example, seem to consist of gigantic folds in the earth's crust produced while the plate bearing the Indian subcontinent smashes headlong into the Eurasian plate. Most other mountain chains seem to have formed along the boundaries between continental and oceanic plates, where uplift through buckling is supplemented by vertical movement of crustal blocks in response to enormous pressure from below.

The Foundations of the Range

Plate Tectonics and the Sierra Nevada

During most of the Paleozoic era, the region now occupied by the Sierra Nevada lay beneath the sea receiving sediments from the North American continent to the east. Tens of thousands of feet of sand, silt, mud, and the skeletal remains of marine organisms, along with miscellaneous volcanic materials erupted from submarine or island volcanoes, were deposited layer upon layer on a subsiding continental shelf, the submerged western margin of North America. These layers were compacted and cemented together over the eons to form sedimentary rocks such as sandstone, mudstone, siltstone, shale, and limestone. In this way the continent gradually extended itself westward at the expense of the ocean floor.

Toward the end of the Paleozoic era the long ages of deposition began to draw to a close as the North American plate, perhaps 230 million years ago, began to break loose from Europe and Africa along the Mid-Atlantic Ridge and move westward, encountering the eastbound Pacific plate, which was forced to dive beneath it. Magma distilled from the upper side of the diving plate rose into the overlying rocks, where it eventually cooled and solidified to form the granites exposed in the Sierra today. Part of the magma, however, worked its way to the surface, forming island volcanoes that spewed ash and other materials over the sea floor, covering the older, Paleozoic sediments. These Mesozoic volcanic sediments were mixed with lesser

The Foundations of the Range   45

amounts of continental deposits being washed into the sea at this time.

During the next 60 million years or so, the Pacific plate continued to dive smoothly beneath the North American plate. Volcanic sediments were piled deeply onto the sagging sea floor, and granitic magmas rose into place beneath the surface rocks. Then, about 150 million years ago, the North American plate, for reasons undetermined, began to move faster, which caused it to collide violently with the Pacific plate. The Paleozoic and Mesozoic sea-floor sediments, along with slices of oceanic crust, were squeezed in the subduction-zone vice, brutally folded, and piled up as westward-tilting slabs separated by faults. The result was a pre-Sierran mountain range as much as 15,000 feet (4600 meters) high rising between the present Sierra crest and the White and Inyo mountains to the east.

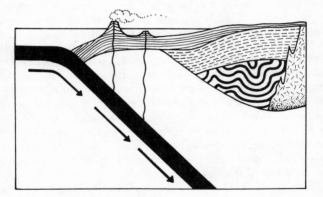

8. Evolution of the Sierra Nevada

A. During most of the Paleozoic era (600 to 225 million years before the present), the region now occupied by the Sierra lay beneath a shallow sea receiving sediments eroded from the continent to the east. At the beginning of the Mesozoic era, about 225 million years ago, the North American plate began to drift westward, overriding the thinner, eastward-bound Pacific plate, which was forced to dive beneath it. Rocks on the upper surface of the diving plate melted to form magma. Part of the magma rose to the surface, spewing forth from offshore volcanoes. The rest cooled beneath the earth's surface to form the granite exposed today in the White Mountains to the east of the Sierra.

FIELDS OF GRANITE, RIVERS OF ICE

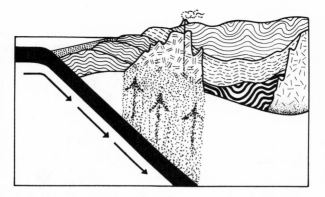

B. About 150 million years ago the North American plate began to push westward at a faster rate, which caused it to collide violently with the diving Pacific plate. Slices of ocean floor were scraped off onto the leading edge of the continent, and along with the continental rocks were brutally folded and thrust upward to form a mountain range that may have been as much as 15,000 ft (4600 m) high. The enormous heat and pressure accompanying the birth of this mountain range altered the composition and structure of the rocks to form the metamorphic rocks found in the Sierra today. Magma generated on the surface of the diving plate erupted from onshore volcanoes or cooled within the earth to form the granitic core of the Sierra Nevada.

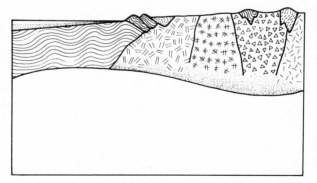

C. Between 210 and 80 million years ago, more than 100 pulses of granitic magma rose off the diving Pacific plate. Then, activity in the Sierra region subsided as the advancing North American continent pushed the plate boundary westward. Beginning about

130 million years ago, the pre-Sierran mountains entered an erosional phase, and over the next 55 to 80 million years were reduced to a gently rolling upland rising toward the east. The once-buried granitic rocks now lay at the surface, interrupted only occasionally by remnant "islands" of older metamorphic rocks. The sediments eroded from the range were deposited into the long trough now occupied by California's Central Valley.

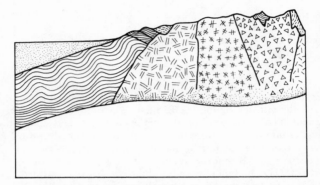

D. Beginning about 10 million years ago the region began to be uplifted again, this time to form the modern Sierra Nevada. In the north, the range rose along faults on its eastern side, tilting westward in the process. In the south it bulged upward between parallel fault systems bounding both its eastern and western flanks.

Metamorphic Rocks

As the sedimentary and volcanic rocks were squeezed and piled up on the leading edge of the advancing continent, they melted in part and later cooled and solidified under conditions of enormous pressure. Old minerals were largely replaced by new ones which pressure caused to be aligned in thin sheets. This process, known as *metamorphosis*, produced entirely new kinds of rocks from the old. Paleozoic shale, mudstone, siltstone, and sandstone were metamorphosed into slate, phyllite, chert, and hornfels. Limestone was transformed to marble, as at Convict Creek in the eastern Sierra and near San Andreas in the western foothills. The younger volcanic rocks of the Mesozoic era were metamorphosed into schist and graywacke.

Several types of metamorphic rocks exhibit prominent bands, built up from numerous layers of flattened minerals. The word *schist*, like *schism* and *schizophrenia*, comes from a Greek root meaning 'to split' and refers to the laminated structure of such rocks. The metamorphic rocks in the Sierra show signs of having been repeatedly folded, though in many the banded structure is still evident. Near Convict Lake, for example, the mountains underwent intense folding and their variously hued mineral bands now resemble huge chocolate sundaes or slices of marble cake.

Sierra Bedrock

As the North American plate continued to push westward, the pre-Sierran mountain range was stretched to breaking. Faults formed along what is today the Owens Valley, and the mountains began to sink. At the same time, they were being eroded at a rate of about one-half foot (fifteen centimeters) per thousand years, and over the next 55 to 80 million years, at least seven miles (eleven kilometers) of rock was removed from the range, partly by volcanic eruptions, partly by the weathering and stream transportation of older metamorphic rocks. These and later sediments were deposited on the continental margin, which subsided beneath their weight to form the long, sediment-filled trough known as the Central Valley. Since these pre-Sierran mountains were at most perhaps 15,000 feet high— and they may have been even lower—uplift must have continued throughout this period in order to account for so much erosion. By the beginning of the Tertiary period, some 65 million years ago, the Sierra region had been reduced to a gentle, rolling upland.

The removal of the Paleozoic *metasedimentary* rocks and Mesozoic *metavolcanic* rocks revealed the now-solidified granitic rocks that had formed beneath them. These granites today constitute more than 60 percent of the exposed rock south of Sonora Pass and occur as scattered outcrops to the north. Metamorphic rocks now exist in the Sierra only as isolated *roof pendants* perched on top of underlying gran-

9. The Mt. Emerson roof pendant, east of Bishop, California, as seen from the trail leading to Blue Lake.

ite or as *septa*, slices of rock sandwiched between adjacent granite blocks. Together, the metamorphic rocks and underlying granites make up what geologists call the *basement complex* or *subjacent series*—bedrock, in other words. Beginning about 30 million years ago renewed volcanic activity in the Sierra buried these older rocks in places beneath layers of younger rocks, which constitute the *superjacent series*. These younger volcanics cover large areas north of Yosemite but occur sparingly southward.

The largest exposure of metamorphic rocks in the Sierra, consisting of adjacent tilted slabs of Paleozoic and Mesozoic age, extends through the Sierra foothills northward from the San Joaquin River to Oroville, and eastward to Lake Almanor, at the northern end of the range. Interbedded with these slabs are slices of serpentine, a metamorphic rock derived from peridotite, a dark, iron- and magnesium-rich rock similar in composition to that making up the earth's mantle. Whether the serpentine was intruded into the adjacent rocks in the manner of granite or originated as upwelling magma along the East Pacific Rise is not certain.

Roof pendants of both Paleozoic and Mesozoic age are scattered as well through the eastern part of the Sierra, forming such prominent peaks as the Sierra Buttes, Mt. Tallac, Mt. Dana, and many others. The spectacular Ritter Range east of Yosemite is but the exposed tip of a roof pen-

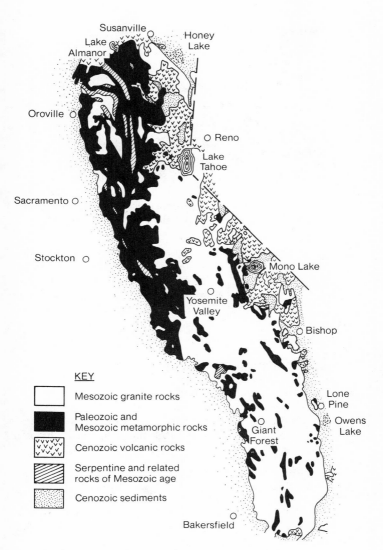

KEY

☐	Mesozoic granite rocks
■	Paleozoic and Mesozoic metamorphic rocks
⌄⌄⌄	Cenozoic volcanic rocks
⫽	Serpentine and related rocks of Mesozoic age
∴	Cenozoic sediments

10. Rocks of the Sierra Nevada.

The Foundations of the Range

11. Tombstone slates are scattered among the grass and oaks of the western foothills of the central and northern Sierra.

dant consisting of 30,000 feet (9000 meters) of metavolcanic rocks of Mesozoic age. A few miles south the rocks composing the peaks near Convict Lake are part of a section of metasediments estimated to be 50,000 feet (15,000 meters) thick and up to 475 million years old. Among these are the oldest rocks known in the Sierra.

Sierran metavolcanic and metasedimentary rocks can generally be distinguished by color. Metasedimentary rocks, such as those making up Mt. Morrison, near Convict Lake, Mt. Emerson, west of Bishop, or Mt. Dana, at the east end of Tuolumne Meadows, are generally deep reddish or chocolate brown. Metavolcanic rocks, however, range from dark gray to nearly black, and their color is reflected in such place names as Black Kaweah, Black Divide, and Blackcap Mountain.

Granitic Rocks

The Sierra granites are part of a vast field of rock known as the Sierra *batholith* (Greek *bathys*, 'deep,' and *lithos*, 'rock'), so called because it solidified deep in the earth. The Sierra batholith also underlies the White and Inyo mountains to the east, the ranges of northwestern Nevada, and the Klamath Mountains of northeastern California. It consists of numerous distinct blocks known as *plutons* (after Pluto, Roman god of the underworld), which originated as separate pulses of magma distilled off the diving Pacific plate.

Between 210 and 80 million years ago more than 100 plutons intruded into the overlying metamorphic rocks. Plutonic rocks are therefore called *intrusive* to distinguish them from volcanic, or *extrusive*, rocks, which are also derived from magma. Together, plutonic and volcanic rocks are classified as *igneous* (from the same root as the word *ignite*) in reference to their common molten source.

Types of Granite

The magma from which plutonic rocks are formed can be visualized as a thick, extremely hot mineral soup. Over millions of years, as this viscous broth slowly cools, crystals begin to form, each of the different minerals found in the broth solidifying at a different temperature. Darker minerals, such as pyroxene, amphibole, biotite, and olivine, which are rich in iron and magnesium, have the highest melting points and thus are the first to crystallize and settle out of solution. With continued cooling of the magma, one mineral after another solidifies, the last to do so being plagioclase feldspars and, finally, quartz. This process is called *magmatic differentiation* (See Figure 12).

The type and texture of granitic rocks depend on such factors as rate of cooling, the degree to which the mineral soup was agitated, and—most important—the minerals present to begin with. Fine-textured granites suggest rapid cooling that did not allow time for large crystals to form. Porphyritic granites, in which large, conspicuous crystals are imbedded in a finer-grained matrix, suggest a shift in the rate of cooling or perhaps agitation of the magma. An even distribution of various minerals also suggests that the soup was homogenous—as if stirred—during crystal formation.

The color of Sierra granites ranges from off-white to nearly black. The darker types consist primarily of darker minerals, with or without a sprinkling of orthoclase feldspar, a light-colored mineral with a high melting point.

The Foundations of the Range

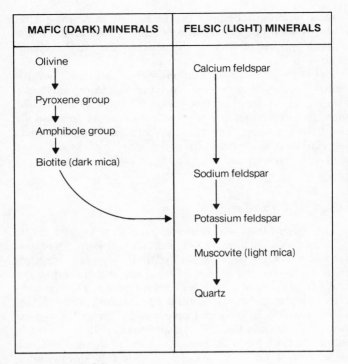

MAFIC (DARK) MINERALS	FELSIC (LIGHT) MINERALS
Olivine	Calcium feldspar
↓	↓
Pyroxene group	
↓	
Amphibole group	
↓	↓
Biotite (dark mica)	Sodium feldspar
	↓
	Potassium feldspar
	↓
	Muscovite (light mica)
	↓
	Quartz

12. Magmatic differentiation.

Whitish or pale-gray granites contain mostly plagioclase feldspars with varying amounts of quartz. Medium-gray types contain roughly equal amounts of light and dark minerals. The salt-and-pepper appearance of many lighter-colored granites is created by specks of darker minerals — mostly biotite (black mica)—imbedded in the lighter quartz and feldspars.

We commonly use the word *granite* to describe the familiar light-gray rock with the salt-and-pepper appearance that is used for headstones, monuments, government buildings, and other structures of comparable solemnity. What we casually lump together as granite, however, comprises several types of plutonic rocks known to geologists by a variety of names. They have divided granitic rocks into numerous types based on mineral composition and restrict

Table 3: Igneous Rocks

The rock types listed are broad categories that include numerous variations known to geologists by other names, e.g., "granite" includes granodiorite, and quartz monzonite, among others.

MINERALS	Volcanic rocks (magma cools at the surface of the earth after eruption as lava or volcanic fragments; rocks fine-grained)	Plutonic rocks (magma cools deep in the earth's crust; rocks coarse-grained; minerals visible to the naked eye)
Mostly light minerals; few or no dark minerals	Rhyolite (rocks buff, tan, yellowish or pinkish; rhyolite tuffs found in Sierra foothills, on tableland north of Bishop, and along crest of northern Sierra)	Granite (rocks white, pale gray, buff, or pinkish; often have salt-and-pepper appearance; the most common type of rock in the Sierra)
Mostly light minerals, but a large proportion of dark minerals	Andesite (rocks medium to dark gray, weathering to deep reddish brown; common north of Yosemite; also on east side of range south of Mono Lake)	Diorite (rocks medium to dark gray; scattered throughout Sierra)
Mostly dark minerals; few or no light minerals	Basalt (rocks dark gray to black; found in foothills near Oroville, on table mountain near Friant, and on east slope from Mammoth Lakes south to Independence)	Gabbro (rocks dark gray to black; scattered throughout Sierra)
All dark minerals	No extrusive rocks equivalent to peridotite	Peridotite (rocks blackish, though weather to pinkish; not found in Sierra, but common in Klamath Mountains)

The Foundations of the Range

their use of the word *granite* to designate a particularly light-colored type, which just so happens to be rather scarce in the Sierra.

Although fine distinctions of this type are essential to professional geologists, they are less useful to amateur naturalists and seldom obvious even at that. Moreover, the word *granite* has a long history of popular use predating the more restricted definition assigned to it by geologists. Therefore, following the lead of other popular works, this guide uses the singular *granite* to describe such light-colored plutonic rocks as granodiorite and quartz monzonite, the most common types found in the Sierra. Medium-colored granitic rocks are similarly grouped under the heading diorite and the darkest types under the heading gabbro. The plural *granites* refers to both light- and dark-colored plutonic rocks. The basic mineral composition of each type is shown in Table 3.

Gold and Minerals

As the plutons cooled, superheated quartz solutions distilled from the magma steamed upward into the numerous faults that folding and tilting had created in the overlying metamorphic rocks. Cooling as they rose, these solutions solidified, sealing the faults with great meandering sheets, or *veins*, of quartz, which often contained concentrations of iron, asbestos, chromite, copper, nephrite jade, silver, and gold. As the Forty-niners would discover, however, some quartz veins contained significant amounts of gold, while others were barren. Old timers claimed to be able to distinguish "live" quartz, which tends to be milky, from the worthless kind, which is clear. Many veins of milky quartz, however, were found to contain no gold whatsoever. Networks of gold-bearing quartz are called *lodes*, and the metamorphic belt of the northern Sierra foothills, which had produced more than $750 million worth of gold by 1865, is today still known as the Mother Lode.

During the mid-Tertiary period, when erosion stripped most of the metamorphic cover from the range, quartz and gold as well as other minerals contained in these veins were deposited in Sierra streams. Being heavier than most other rocks, those bearing gold were transported shorter distances, sinking to the bottoms of gravel beds as other debris was carried farther downstream. During the California Gold Rush successful miners soon learned that gold tended to accumulate behind obstacles in the streambed, or on the wide sides of bends, where currents are slower. Gold freed from bedrock by erosion and carried downstream, *placer gold*, was what James Marshall found in the tailrace of Sutter's mill, in the foothill settlement of Coloma, on January 24, 1848, touching off the gold rush of '49.

From about 60 million to 9 million years ago successive showers of volcanic ash buried some of the gold-bearing gravels in foothill streams. Subsequent lava flows raced down many stream channels, adding a new layer and diverting the water to new courses. The diverted streams cut their new channels more deeply in response to the uplift of the range, which began around this time, with the result that the old Tertiary streambeds, with their buried gold, became elevated benches perched well above the new river channels. During the gold rush enterprising miners backed by ample capital began to go after this buried gold by using giant hydraulic monitors, or water cannons, to wash away the overlying gravel. The monitors were supplied with water from nearby streams or distant lakes, which they delivered with enormous force. Entire hillsides and ridges were washed away. The debris was channeled through sluice boxes, where the much heavier gold settled out, leaving the residue to be washed downslope by nearby streams, many of which are today still lined with boulder tailings from the hydraulic operations.

Because of the increased sediment loads, streams entering the Central Valley overflowed their banks, flooding valuable farmland. In response, the angry farmers took their complaint to court, with the result that in 1884 the California Supreme Court prohibited the dumping of mine tailings into streams, virtually ending hydraulic mining in California.

The destructive power of the great hydraulic cannons is vividly apparent at Malakoff Diggins State Park, near the Mother Lode town of North Bloomfield, in the Sierra foothills east of Nevada City. The park's colorful, intensely eroded cliff, which is now slowly being reclaimed by vege-

13. Malakoff Diggins, an old hydraulic mine in the northern Sierra foothills, is now preserved as a state park. Huge water cannons were used to blast gold-bearing gravels from the hillsides.

tation, was produced by hydraulic monitors, one of which, the "Hendy Giant," is on display nearby. From 1866 to 1884, Malakoff Diggins produced about $3.5 million worth of gold and about 50 million tons of tailings, which were diverted down the Yuba River. The monitors at Malakoff Diggins created a hole roughly 7000 feet (2150 meters) long, a half-mile (800 meters) wide, and 600 feet (180 meters) deep. The pond at the base of the cliff was once a reservoir built to supply the monitors with water pumped from the Bowman Lake area 15 miles (24 kilometers) east. Altogether, more than 1.5 billion tons of debris were washed from the Sierra foothills during the era of hydraulic mining.

Granitic Landforms

Granites are extremely hard. Owing to their fused crystalline structure, they resist crumbling and chemical weathering and may be shaped only through the application of enormous force. In the Sierra moving glaciers once provided such force, but in places even they were unable to alter the rocks significantly. For example, Muir Gorge, in northern Yosemite, largely retained its preglacial V-shaped profile despite being filled with 4000 feet (1200 meters) of ice. The great expanses of bare rock characteristic of the High Sierra reflect the slowness with which granite weathers to soil. Pleistocene glaciers stripped away the soil cover from much of the upper slopes of the range, and today, 10,000 years after the retreat of the last great glaciers, plants have been able to reclaim only a small fraction of the rocky high country.

Joints

Visitors to the High Sierra will notice that vegetation is frequently able to invade rocky areas by means of crevices, where enough soil and moisture can collect to support not only herbs, but even shrubs and trees. Often lines of trees mark the courses of extensive crevices in the granitic bedrock. On many rocky slopes vegetation even forms checkerboard patterns where two sets of crevices are oriented at right angles to each other. These crevices develop along *joints,* lines of structural weakness in the granite that range in length from a few feet to several miles and extend to unknown depths in the rock. The distance between two parallel joints may be anywhere from less than an inch to hundreds, or even thousands of feet. There are two major sets of joints in the Sierra, one paralleling the southeast–northwest trend of the range, the other running perpendicular to the first.

A recent hypothesis suggests that joints are stress fractures created by the slow northward creep of the Sierra block. According to this hypothesis, as the Pacific plate moves northward along the San Andreas Fault (see page 44) it tends to drag the adjacent slice of continental crust along with it. This block in turn nudges its neighbor—the Sierra block—northward. Joints would form in response to the immense strain generated as the Sierra, bound by a stationary block on the east, is dragged along by its western neighbor.

Weathering

Weathering is the process by which rock is eventually reduced to soil by the chemical and mechanical action of

14. Frost-riven rock near Silver Pass in the central Sierra. Note the jigsaw-puzzle effect created as the rock fragments were pushed apart.

moisture and air temperature. In Sierra granites this process begins along joints, which must first be widened into crevices before further weathering can occur.

CHEMICAL WEATHERING   Initially, minute amounts of moisture invade joints and chemically alter the feldspars and micas present in the granite. As a result, these minerals expand and slowly wedge the rock apart.

FROST RIVING   Once a crevice has formed, further wedging occurs as a result of the repeated freezing and thawing of moisture seeping into the crack. When water freezes, its expansion exerts an outward pressure as high as 1000 pounds per square inch. Moisture entering a crevice during the day freezes on cold enough nights and thus

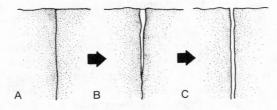

15. Frost riving. When air temperatures are cold enough—such as at night and during much of the winter—water seeping into granite crevices (A) freezes and expands, slightly wedging the rock faces apart (B). This allows even more moisture to enter and freeze, thus pushing the rocks even farther apart. Eventually they are severed completely (C).

FIELDS OF GRANITE, RIVERS OF ICE

widens the fissure. In this way large pieces of rock eventually break away along joints.

SAWTOOTH RIDGES The serrated mountain crests found in the eastern Sierra are produced by frost riving on sheer mountain walls where vertical joints are closely spaced. Excellent examples in the Sierra include the Whitney pinnacles west of Lone Pine, the Cathedral Range near Tuolumne Meadows, and the Sawtooth Ridge south of Bridgeport. Metamorphic rocks may also be jointed, however, and the Minarets of the Ritter Range, one of the most spectacular arrays of pinnacles in the Sierra, were formed from such rocks.

Sawtooth ridges are characteristic of the eastern Sierra, where granites tend to be coarse-grained and joints closely spaced. Rounded, more massive landforms dominate the western part of the range, where granites are finer grained and joints farther apart. A trip from Yosemite Valley, where massive cliffs and domes are the dominant features, northeast to the spires and knife-edged ridges of the Cathedral Range beautifully reveals this contrast in terrain.

TALUS AND SCREE Rocks removed from a cliff or mountain wall by frost riving accumulate at its base to form spreading aprons of debris known as *talus*, if coarse, or

16. Frost riving in rocks with close vertical joints has produced the numerous serrated ridges so characteristic of the High Sierra. Rock fragments plucked from the mountainsides collect at their bases to form rubble slopes known as *talus*.

scree, if fine. Rocks in a talus slope may range in size from particles smaller than gravel to large blocks several feet in diameter. They are for the most part arrayed from the top of the slope to the bottom in order of ascending size for the simple reason that larger rocks dropped from above tend to roll farther downhill. Slope angle cannot exceed 40 degrees—the *angle of repose*—but most talus slopes are not so steep.

SOIL FORMATION   Frost riving on gentler slopes may produce rubbly surfaces consisting of great masses of small to medium-sized rocks. Where such metamorphic rocks as slate or schist occur, large areas may be covered with accumulations of thin slabs, which reflect the laminated structure of these rocks. Through continued frost riving, rocks are reduced eventually to *gruss,* the fine-grained rubble that chemical weathering converts to soil. Since soil formation requires the presence of moisture, it proceeds most rapidly where the gruss is buried—by avalanche-borne rubble or rockslides, for example. Sufficient soil may accumulate in crevices or among rubble for plants to become established. In turn, they hasten soil formation by trapping moisture and soil transported from other areas, contributing organic matter, and further wedging the crevice open with their roots (see Crevice Invasion, Chapter VI).

In the western Sierra, primarily at low altitudes, some granites that have remained largely unweathered where exposed have decomposed under a deep soil mantle on flat areas where soil could accumulate. The dry exposed granite resists chemical weathering, while the buried granite, which is subjected to moisture, decays. The result is a stepped topography of flats bordered by escarpments.

Exfoliation and Domes

Enormous granite domes occur on the west slope of the Sierra from the Tahoe region south, particularly in the watersheds of the Tuolumne, Merced, and San Joaquin rivers. Although some show signs of having been wholly or partly overridden by glaciers, they were not produced by glacial sculpting. Nor do they seem to be products of chemical weathering. They may well represent the response of

17. Liberty Cap, a granite dome overlooking the Little Yosemite Valley, was overwhelmed by glacial ice during the Pleistocene. Nearby Half Dome, however, was not.

certain types of Sierra granite to the release of pressure attending the removal of the miles of metamorphic cover that once buried them—in other words, a magnificent "sigh" of relief.

Domes develop only in massive—that is, widely jointed—granites. They are produced by the leafing away, or *exfoliation,* of rounded shells of rock. When the burden

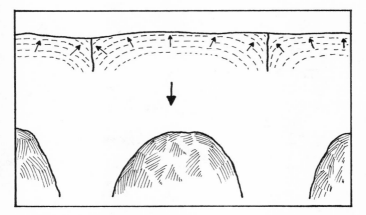

18. Dome formation. The release of pressure occasioned by the removal of overlying rock may have caused rounded sheets of granite to pop away from the rock beneath. The sheets would be rounded because the pressure-release reaction would be directed toward free rock surfaces, i.e., joint faces on the sides and the exposed rock surface above.

Granitic Landforms 63

of overlying rock is removed to expose the granite beneath, these shells pop loose as pressure is released. They are curved because separation tends to follow the "free" rock faces—that is, the exposed surface above and the joint surfaces on the sides—where pressure is less (see Figure 18). Continued *pressure-release exfoliation* produces first an undulating topography and ultimately the great domes we see in the Sierra today.

Exfoliation may also occur without attendant dome formation, which would be determined in large part by the location of vertical joints. Great slabs of exfoliated granite can be seen throughout the central and southern Sierra, such as along the Tioga Pass Highway near Tenaya Lake, where great overlapping sheets of rock terminate at the very shoulders of the road. In this region glacial ice was once extremely thick, and its retreat may have stimulated a pressure-release reaction in the underlying rocks. This is pure speculation, however, and has been disproven in areas outside the Sierra. Until the phenomenon is studied in the Sierra itself, it remains a possibility that should not be dismissed out of hand.

19. Exfoliating granite, showing a curved shell already in the process of separating from the rock beneath it.

Volcanic Activity

Prelude

The mountain range that preceded the Sierra began to be eroded away in the late Cretaceous period and by the mid-Tertiary had been reduced to a rather low complex of ridges comparable in elevation and topography to the present-day Adirondacks. Streams draining these mountains flowed westward down a gently sloping plain to the shallow sea that then filled the Central Valley. Its waters lapped at the base of what are today the western foothills, but which then was a low, swampy coastline of lagoons and bayous. Not far inland, ridges of erosion-resistant greenstone, a metamorphic rock derived from volcanic sediments, paralleled the northerly trend of the coast. Streams draining the uplands to the east crossed these ridges through steep rocky gorges.

The climate during this period was warm and humid, with abundant summer rainfall that supported dense semitropical vegetation. All in all, the region must have somewhat resembled today's Gulf Coast in climate and vegetation as well as topography. Highly acidic, nutrient-poor lateritic soils, which are characteristic of warm, humid climates, formed in the region and today outcrop in the Ione area (see page 245), where they are distinguished by several rare, endemic plants. The higher ridges in the east, which contained only a few peaks approaching 5000 feet (1500 meters) elevation (one of them being Mt. Dana), cast little rain shadow over the lands farther eastward, and fossil evidence suggests that these hinterlands were then covered by a deciduous–hardwood/evergreen–dicotyledon forest, with conifers at highest altitudes.

During the early Tertiary period the Sierra region experienced little in the way of dramatic geological activity. The action now lay farther west, where islands rising in the sea marked the collision zone of the advancing continent and the Pacific plate. Situated about 50 miles (80 kilometers) offshore, these islands were the infant California Coast Ranges, which were being buckled upward along the plate boundary as the pre-Sierran mountains had before them.

Then, about 30 million years ago, the long, relatively quiet period ended rather abruptly as a succession of violent volcanic explosions shook the northern Sierra. Originating from vents near the present crest of the range, these explosions buried most of the region north of Yosemite beneath deep layers of volcanic "ash"—actually tiny particles of rock—which subsequently cooled to produce beds of *tuff*—a light-colored volcanic rock derived from rhyolite lava—that today exceed 400 feet (120 meters) in the foothills and 1000 feet (300 meters) in the eastern part of the range. Thus began the second major episode of volcanic activity in the Sierra region, the first having occurred during the formation of the pre-Sierran range.

Volcanic Rocks

Before recounting the events that followed these volcanic explosions, a brief review of volcanism and volcanic rocks is worthwhile. Volcanic rocks originate in the same molten soup that produces plutonic rocks (see page 52), but instead of cooling deep in the earth the magma wells upward through fissures to the surface, where it spews forth from vents in the form of lava and volcanic fragments of various sizes. Although volcanic and plutonic rocks are comparable in terms of mineral composition (see Table 3), they differ greatly in texture and appearance. Whereas plutonic rocks are composed of crystals visible to the naked eye, volcanic rocks typically consist of particles too small to detect without the aid of powerful magnification. Upon being suddenly exposed to the drastically lower pressures at the earth's surface, upwelling magmas cool too rapidly for large crystals to form.

Like their plutonic equivalents volcanic rocks also show wide variation in color, texture, and mineral composition, and they too can be separated into three large categories—basalt, rhyolite, and andesite.

BASALT Basalt is derived from lavas with an abundance of iron- and magnesium-rich minerals but lacking in quartz. It is therefore the volcanic equivalent of gabbro and other dark plutonic rocks. Basaltic lavas tend to be highly fluid, erupting with ease and flowing rapidly over the surrounding terrain to form broad volcanic tablelands such as

Oroville Table Mountain in the northern Sierra. Highly dissected by streams, this formation appears as a complex of mesas and canyons in the foothills east of Oroville and Chico. It was formed perhaps 30 million years ago, about the same time as the explosions of rhyolite. Basaltic lavas build up layer upon layer to form broad, gently sloping *shield volcanoes*, those of the Hawaiian Islands being typical. Although no shield volcanoes now exist in the Sierra, they can be found in Mt. Lassen National Park, just north of the range.

RHYOLITE This light-colored volcanic rock is similar in composition to granite. Rhyolitic lavas, owing to their comparatively low melting points, are stiff and pasty, close to being solid even when red hot. Rather than flowing freely, like basaltic lavas, they are pushed upward slowly, like toothpaste, often plugging the lava conduit to form steep-sided, domelike peaks. The formation of such *plug-dome volcanoes* is typically accompanied by violent explosions as hot gases and lava trapped by the plug periodically burst free. The volcano is like a giant pressure cooker in which the pressure eventually becomes so great that the mountain literally "blows its stack." Holes may be ripped in its side by escaping gases, and the plug itself, along with pasty lava below, violently propelled upward like a champagne cork. Mammoth Mountain is a good example, having finally blown a giant crater out of its east wall 40,000 to 30,000 years ago.

Lava fragments ranging in size from tiny particles of *ash* and *lapilli* to *blocks* and *bombs* several feet in diameter

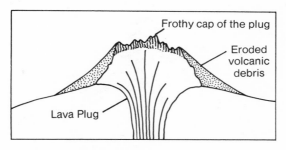

20. Cross section of a plug-dome volcano.

Volcanic Activity

are hurled violently from the volcano. The larger framents generally fall within a short radius of the vent, but clouds of volcanic ash may be borne by the wind for hundreds or thousands of miles. Some fragments are solid when they are ejected. Others solidify as they are cooled by the outside air. The fragments are usually porous because of trapped gases released during cooling. *Pumice*, for example, is so full of holes that it floats on water.

A *nuée ardente*, or 'fiery cloud,' composed of volcanic ash charged with superheated steam may rush downslope from a plug-dome volcano or other source vent for many miles, incinerating everything in its path and burying the old land surface beneath hundreds of feet of ash. In 1902 a fiery cloud rolled down the slopes of Mt. Pele, on the Caribbean island of Martinique, killing 30,000 people in the town of St. Pierre. In 1915 Mt. Lassen, a plug-dome volcano just north of the Sierra, erupted violently, first with a great mudflow, then with a *nuée ardente* that swept down its northeast slope. If the volcanic ash is still hot when it settles, the particles fuse together as they cool to form the light-colored, fine-grained rock called *tuff*. Volcanic tuffs occur in the northern Sierra and along the east side of the range intermittently between Mono Lake and Independence. Buildings fashioned out of tuff are common in the Sierra foothills, for the rock is soft enough to be cut and dressed easily by stone masons and fine-grained enough to require little mortar. A tuff quarry is located near the town of Mokelumne Hill, among other places in the region.

ANDESITE This medium-gray rock, which often weathers to a rusty brown, contains large amounts of both

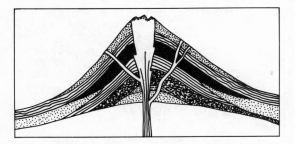

21. Cross section of a composite volcano, or strato volcano.

light and dark minerals and is therefore the volcanic equivalent of diorite. Andesitic lavas are only slightly less stiff than those of rhyolite and tend to flow only very short distances. Following such a flow, the vent is usually plugged with lava for a time, which leads to explosions. Volcanic fragments ejected from the vent cover the preceding flow and are covered in turn by a subsequent flow. Then the vent is plugged again, followed by further explosions, further flows, and so on. Alternate layers of lava and volcanic fragments gradually form steep-sided, symmetrical *strato volcanoes*, or *composite volcanoes*, such as Mt. Rainier and Mt. Shasta in the Cascade Range and Mammoth Mountain in the central Sierra.

Tertiary Andesite Eruptions

The rhyolite explosions that began in the mid-Tertiary began to subside about 20 million years ago, only to be succeeded by eruptions of andesite from vents along the crest of the northern Sierra, which at this time was beginning to rise and tilt westward. Mt. Rose, Squaw Peak, Mt. Ellis, Sonora Peak, Relief Peak, and Dardanelles Cone were among the sources of these andesite flows, which over a period of almost 20 million years covered the region north of Yosemite with 2000 cubic miles of volcanic rock. Although subsequent erosion has stripped most of this rock from the range, significant outcrops occur along the crest from Sonora Pass north to Alpine County and from Lake Tahoe northward. Dardanelles Cone, which dominates the northern skyline a few miles west of Sonora Pass, is a plug of andesite lava surrounded by skirts of more easily eroded volcanic fragments. Other volcanic plugs, or *necks*, are found throughout the northern crestal region, often resembling castles, battlements, or gravestones erected by giants. The rocks have weathered to a rich, reddish brown owing to the oxidation of iron present in the lava. Castle Peak and Mt. Lincoln near Donner Summit and the Carson Spur near Kirkwood all exhibit fine andesite flows.

Some of the andesite flows mixed with water from lakes, streams, and melting snow to produce *lahars*, great rivers of steaming mud. As it flowed downslope, the mud gradually cooled, solidfying first on the surface, while the hotter material inside continued to move. The rock already formed was broken by the movement, giving volcanic mudflows a chaotic structure comprising large fragments, assorted mineral crystals imbedded in the rock, smaller particles, and miscellaneous debris swept up in the muddy river. Rock formed in this way is called *breccia*, (Italian 'broken'), and the process is referred to as *autobrecciation*.

TABLE MOUNTAINS Mudflows invaded the foothills via streamcourses, filling up canyons to great depth and diverting water to new channels. Subsequent erosion removed less resistant rocks from both sides of the flows to produce elevated mesas, or table mountains, the winding courses of which preserve in stone the ancient Tertiary channels of Sierra streams. Stanislaus Table Mountain, which is conspicuous along Highway 120 from Oakdale to Sonora, is the finest example in the Sierra of such a perched mudflow. Although discontinuous, it extends for more than 40 miles (65 kilometers), marking the prevolcanic course of the Stanislaus River, which was diverted north by the lava. In places the flow is 2000 feet (600 meters) wide and up to 300 feet (90 meters) thick. Several comparable but less impressive volcanic table mountains are scattered throughout the foothills of the central and northern Sierra. In the southern Sierra a few basalt flows occurred at widely scattered locations during this same period. San Joaquin Table Mountain, near the town of Friant, was produced when basaltic mud filled the channel of the San Joaquin River. Oroville Table Mountain in the northern Sierra is also made of basalt, but is a remnant of a vast sheet of lava rather than a volcanic mudflow.

Cenezoic Volcanism

About three million years ago the center of volcanic activity in the Sierra shifted from the region north of Yosemite to the central part of the range, along the east side south of Mono Lake. This shift occurred as volcanoes formed along the fault system that developed in conjunction with the subsidence of the Owens Valley block. Eruptions occurred near Mammoth Lakes and were climaxed some 700,000 years ago by an enormous explosion originating

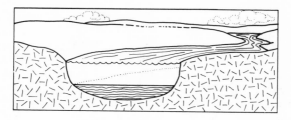

22. Formation of Volcanic Table Mountains

A. Prevolcanic landscape. Prior to the volcanic activity of the mid to late Tertiary period, large, lazy streams meandered through the gently rolling terrain now occupied by the Sierra. Layers of gravel eroded from the upper slopes of the ancestral Sierra lined the streambeds.

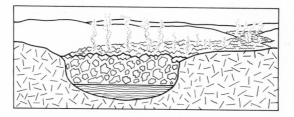

B. Volcanic landscape. Beginning about 20 million years ago, stratovolcanoes near the present-day Sierra crest began to erupt. The lava mixed with water to form a thick volcanic mud, which filled streamcourses and diverted their water to new channels.

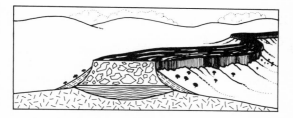

C. Postvolcanic landscape. The volcanic mud soon hardened into rock. Subsequent erosion removed the softer rocks around it, producing a sinuous table mountain tracing in stone the ancient course of a Sierra river.

Volcanic Activity

from Glass Mountain, a plug volcano situated a few miles east of the Sierra.

THE VOLCANIC TABLELAND A *nuée ardente* swept 30 miles (50 kilometers) southward from Glass Mountain into Long Valley, incinerating everything in its path and burying a 350-square-mile (900-square-kilometer) area beneath 500 feet (150 meters) of volcanic ash. Temperatures within the incandescent cloud are estimated to have exceeded 1000° F (560° C). The ash cooled to form the broad, gently sloping Volcanic Tableland, which is abruptly buried beneath younger rocks just north of Bishop. Travelers on Highway 395, which crosses this steep southern escarpment at Sherwin Grade, can readily identify in the road cuts the pale pink and yellow rhyolite tuff formed from the ash. Cross-sections of this "Bishop tuff" can be examined at leisure in Owens River Gorge and in Red Canyon, where Indian petroglyphs adorn the soft rock. Both places are accessible by side roads heading north from Bishop.

Between 690,000 and 680,000 years ago rhyolite ash began erupting from vents located in and around Long Valley. Mammoth Mountain was as yet unborn when these early explosions of rhyolite occurred, but the magma source that generated them would later give birth to the peak itself. The tuff produced by these explosions, which were much smaller than the Glass Mountain eruption, can be seen in nearby Red Meadows.

DEVILS POSTPILE About 600,000 years ago basaltic lava erupted from vents in the same area and flowed into the canyon of what is now the middle fork of the San Joaquin River. At that time the water flowing down the canyon emptied eastward into the Owens River, but the lava blocked its course, diverting the stream westward into the drainage of the San Joaquin.

Filling the canyon to a depth of 600 to 700 feet (180 to 210 meters), the lava cooled rapidly and apparently all at once, shrinking and cracking in the process to form a tight cluster of vertical columns having four, five, six, or seven sides. Similar columnar basalts include the Giants Causeway in Ireland, the Palisades of the Hudson River, and Devils Tower in Wyoming. Smaller formations of this type occur near Sonora Pass, Lake Tahoe, the Kern River canyon, and elsewhere in the Sierra. About half the columns

72   FIELDS OF GRANITE, RIVERS OF ICE

23. Devils Postpile is one of the finest examples of columnar basalt in the world. It is located in the gorge of the middle fork of the San Joaquin River, just west of the east-side resort town of Mammoth Lakes.

in the Postpile—a higher portion than in the above formations—are hexagonal, a degree of regularity suggesting that conditions at the time of cooling were remarkably uniform throughout the flow.

Subsequently, glaciers moved down the canyon to the middle fork, overriding the Postpile and destroying much of it in the process. The columns that remain today are but a remnant of the original flow, as are similar, though smaller formations scattered on both sides of the canyon. The glaciers also polished the top of the Postpile so that it resembles a new tile floor. Over the years frost action has pried columns loose from the formation, and broken sections lie at the base like the rubble of an ancient temple.

MAMMOTH MOUNTAIN Immediately east of Devils Postpile rises the appropriately named Mammoth Mountain, a massive composite volcano formed of alternating layers of glassy quartz latite, a rhyolitic rock, and volcanic debris produced by periodic explosions that blew holes in the side of the peak and showered much of the surrounding country with pumice. The mountain began to rise about 200,000 years ago atop earlier basaltic, andesitic, and rhyolitic debris, reaching its present 11,053 feet (3369 meters)—or higher—about 180,000 years ago.

MONO CRATERS Mammoth Mountain is the oldest and southernmost peak in a volcanic chain of sorts that extends northeast for about a dozen miles including the picturesque series of plug domes known as the Mono Craters and culminating in Black Point, a basaltic crater erupted into Mono Lake. Rising abruptly from the southern shore of Mono Lake, the Mono Craters stand some 2000 feet (600 meters) above the sagebrush-covered Pumice Valley to the west. These so-called craters actually consist of plugs of dark volcanic glass, or obsidian, which have been pushed upward like toothpaste into the centers of cones made up of rhyolite tuff. In places the plugs have pushed through the walls of the cone to flow short distances downslope. The Mono Craters are much younger than Mammoth Mountain, having formed through a series of explosive eruptions that occurred from 60,000 to only 1600 years ago. The Inyo Craters immediately to the south are volcanic explosion pits that formed about 1000 years ago.

RED MOUNTAIN   Basaltic flows and cinder cones less than 90,000 years old occur along the base of the eastern escarpment between Big Pine and Independence. Travelers along Highway 395 can pull off along the side of the road and closely examine the black, highly porous basaltic rocks that cover the valley floor. As in other volcanic rocks the holes and pockets in this basalt were produced by escaping gases that bubbled through the partially cooled rocks like steam escaping from simmering oatmeal. The most prominent volcanic landform in this region is Red Mountain, a rust-colored, beautifully symmetrical cinder cone that rises more than 1000 feet (300 meters) above the plain. It seems rather less grand than it might otherwise, however, for the nearby Sierra crest rises abruptly from the valley floor for nearly 9000 feet (2700 meters), culminating in Split Mountain, which is more than 14,000 feet (4250 meters) high.

Despite current inactivity the Sierra is still in the midst of a volcanic era, as evidenced by eruptions from the Inyo Craters within the past 200 years, the numerous hot springs found throughout the range, and wisps of steam that escape from the sides of Mammoth Mountain. In fact, volcanic activity in the past probably occurred no more frequently than today. Reservoirs of hot magma still lie buried beneath the peaks, and this suggests that additional plutons may also be forming. Indeed, it is virtually certain that pluton formation is occurring today in places—Long Valley, for instance—along the eastern rampart of the range.

The Rise of the Sierra Nevada

At the onset of volcanic activity in the northern Sierra about 30 million years ago, the region was still a low plain rising gently toward the east and culminating in a crest of low hills. The uplift that would produce the range we know today began about 10 million years ago at about the same time that andesite eruptions commenced in the northern Sierra. The precise times and amounts of uplift and tilting, as well as the degree of deformation that resulted, are still subjects of vigorous debate. Since there is neither space nor need in a guide such as this to explore the methodologies and points of controversy in depth, the following account is intentionally a general summary of the mountain-building events that produced the highest range in the contiguous United States.

Uplift occurred along a series of *en echelon* faults, (staggered, parallel faults) running along the eastern base of the Sierra. Movement along these faults is mostly vertical, with some lateral slippage as well. They separate blocks of crust that have been broken apart by pressures deep in the earth. Some of the blocks, such as the Sierra itself, have risen; others have sunk. For most of its length, the total displacement along the Sierra's eastern escarpment was produced not only by the rise of the Sierra block, but also by the subsidence of adjacent blocks to the east. The magnitude of this displacement is often obscured by thousands of feet of sediments lying on top of the sunken valley blocks. In the southern Sierra, for example, the total displacement between the Sierra crest and the Owens Valley block is about 19,000 feet (5800 meters), but only the upper 9000 to 11,000 feet (2750 to 3350 meters) are apparent.

The northern Sierra had risen to its present height by about two million years ago. Displacement in the Tahoe region is estimated to have been about 5000 feet (1500 meters). Older faults on the western margin of the northern Sierra did not participate in this uplift, which occurred entirely along the eastern side, so the Sierra block, rather than rising straight up, tilted downward toward the west. The western edge of this block is buried deep beneath the sediments of the Central Valley, where it is in contact with Coast Range rocks along a fault.

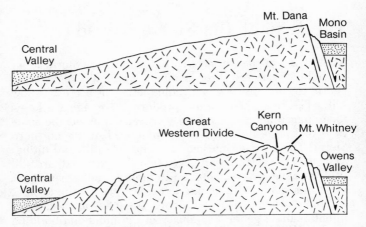

24. Uplift of the northern Sierra (A) and southern Sierra (B).

The story in the southern Sierra is less well known and more complicated. Here, a vast section of the earth's crust, which included not only the region now occupied by the Sierra but also that embracing the Owens Valley, Inyo Mountains, and basins and ranges farther east, began to bulge upward. As the crust was stretched, parallel sets of north–south faults developed in response to the pressure, dividing the region into a series of long blocks. The Owens Valley block sank between the Sierra and Inyo blocks. At the same time, faults also developed along the west side of the Sierra, so that the block was not simply tilted, as in the north, but rose upward as well between two parallel fault systems. The Greenhorn Mountains, a spur range along the west slope south of Sequoia National Park, were produced by this faulting.

The more complicated structure of the southern half of the Sierra is also reflected in the strange course of the Kern River, which alone among west-slope streams flows not west, but due south for about 70 miles (115 kilometers) before swinging westward to empty into the southern end of the San Joaquin Valley. Kern Canyon developed along a fault that has been inactive for the past three million years at least. More than 6000 feet (1800 meters) deep, Kern Canyon separates the Sierra crest on the east from the Great Western Divide on the west. The river rises in glacier basins high on the slopes of the Kings–Kern Divide near Mt. Whitney, and during Pleistocene times the upper reaches of Kern Canyon were invaded by valley glaciers.

Upland Surfaces

Gently sloping benches on either side of Kern Canyon—the Chagoopa Plateau on the west and the Boreal Plateau on the east—have been identified as the remnants of ancient land surfaces that were elevated during episodes of faulting. So too have the gently sloping summit platforms of Cirque Peak and Mt. Whitney, both located in the same region. Each of these four surfaces lies at a different elevation and together they are supposed to reflect stages in the uplift of the southern Sierra. According to this view the Mt. Whitney surface, which is the highest of the four, represents the oldest terrain, that which existed prior to the commencement of uplift in the region. After movement along the Sierra Nevada fault had elevated this surface, stream action presumably leveled the terrain below it, producing the Cirque Peak surface. A second episode of uplift then elevated this surface as well and produced that of the Boreal Plateau. A third episode produced the Chagoopa surface, and so on. These upland surfaces are not continuous over the landscape, and those who believe them to be remnants of older terrain attribute the discontinuity to subsequent erosion wasting away the areas in between. Some geologists, however, doubt that the surfaces represent stages of uplift, arguing that they were produced naturally by normal processes of erosion working in granite. They attribute the discontinuity not to erosion having destroyed much of the intervening terrain, but to the independent erosional histories of the surfaces themselves (see page 62).

Tabular Peaks

Numerous Sierra peaks rise gradually on one side to fairly level, tablelike summit platforms and plunge steeply on the other. Mt. Whitney, the highest summit in the range, is a particularly striking example of such a *tabular peak*. Viewed from the east, it crowns a precipitous moun-

25. The gently sloping summit of Mt. Whitney, in Sequoia National Park. Such "tabular peaks" may be ancient lowland surfaces that were later uplifted to their present lofty heights.

tain wall that seems virtually unscalable, and from this direction anyone unfamiliar with the peak would have no way of knowing that its summit is a gentle platform sloping gradually westward. In a land of glacier-carved gorges and pinnacles these tabular summits are islands of gentle terrain preserved during the Pleistocene, when ice caps covered much of the crestal region, by high southwesterly winds that kept them swept free of snow. The northern and eastern sides of such peaks, however, are typically steep and deeply eroded by frost action, avalanches, and glacial plucking. Such processes were presumably more vigorous on the leeward slopes owing to increased snow depths and reduced rates of melting, which thereby allowed glaciers to form.

Recent Uplift

Although the region occupied by the southern Sierra may have first began to bulge upward some 10 million years ago, most of the uplift along faults has occurred within the last 700,000 years. Measurements taken along the crest suggest that the Sierra is continuing to rise in places by as much as 15 inches (38 centimeters) a century. An even higher rate is implied by the great earthquake that rocked the Owens Valley in 1872. Within a few minutes the eastern front rose 13 feet (4 meters) and moved 20 feet (6 meters) laterally in places. Assuming that such a quake might occur every 500 years, the rate of uplift would be 26 feet (8 meters) per thousand years, for an average of about 31 inches (79 centimeters) per century. Since the rate of erosion is about 1½ feet (46 centimeters) per thousand years, rates of uplift are more than sufficient to have produced the amount of displacement observed in the range today. Consequently, there is good reason to believe that one day the Sierra may be significantly higher than it is now.

The 1872 earthquake, which killed 30 people in the town of Lone Pine, occurred along the Owens Valley fault system, which extends from the Garlock Fault in the south to just below the town of Bishop, a distance of more than 100 miles (160 kilometers) . The impressive eastern escarpment of the Sierra along the west side of Owens Valley is not itself the face of the fault scarp, having been produced by subsequent erosion of that scarp. The actual fault line runs a few miles to the east, and consists of a succession of offset scarps from 5 to 20 feet (1½ to 6 meters) high. North and south of the town of Lone Pine a prominent fault scarp, which appears as a small cliff dropping toward the east, parallels Highway 395 for seven miles.

The Alabama Hills, west of Lone Pine, are composed of granite of comparable age to that of the Sierra itself. They sit between two faults, occupying a slice of crust that has subsided less than the neighboring Owens Valley block on the east. Therefore, the Alabama Hills were not buried by sediments, and weathering along closely spaced joints produced the rounded, pillowy forms they show today.

A vast apron of alluvial wastes forms a ramp extending from the Sierra escarpment to the floor of Owens Valley. It is composed of overlapping alluvial fans that developed at the mouths of the many canyons dissecting the eastern face of the range. Such fans are typical of steep mountain fronts and are best represented in arid regions, where flash-flood deposition is most common. Broad alluvial ramps formed from overlapping fans are known as *bajadas*. They form along the bases of ranges where abundant precipitation at higher elevations, combined with steep escarpments, produces periods of heavy streamflow and the resulting transportation of large amounts of sediment. Sierra streams flowing out onto the ramp diminish in volume as part of their water percolates downward through the sediments and emerges in cold-water springs along the eastern front.

The monolithic appearance of the eastern escarpment

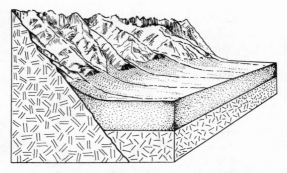

26. East slope of the Sierra Nevada west of Owens Valley. The mountain wall is a deeply eroded fault scarp. The valley floor is underlain by thousands of feet of sediment eroded from the mountains and carried downslope by swift streams. The broad, gently sloping ramp forming a transition between the valley floor and the mountain wall—a *bajada*—developed as alluvial fans at the mouths of canyons eventually coalesced.

south of Bishop gives way northward to more complicated structures as a single fault zone is replaced by sets of widely spaced parallel faults. Spur ranges branching northward from the main crest—such as the Sweetwater, Pine Nut, and Carson ranges between Yosemite and Lake Tahoe— reflect uplift along these faults.

Formation of Lake Tahoe

The Tahoe Basin, like the Owens Valley, has sunk between two uplifted fault blocks, the Sierra on the west and the Carson Range on the east. The Carson Range's spectacular eastern escarpment drops 8000 feet (2450 meters) to the floor of Carson Valley, which is the downward end of a tilted fault block that culminates eastward in the Pine Nut Range. Both the Carson and Pine Nut ranges merge with the main crest of the Sierra south of Lake Tahoe.

The lake was created when andesite flows from vents along its current north shore blocked the ancestral drainage of the Truckee River. Eventually the river was able to cut through these flows, causing the lake to drop drastically, but subsequent depositions of glacial debris dammed the

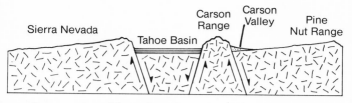

Carson
Range

Carson
Valley

Sierra Nevada

Pine
Nut Range

Tahoe Basin

27. Cross section of the Lake Tahoe region, showing the relative movement of the various crustal blocks. The Tahoe Basin sank between the Sierra and Carson blocks. The Pine Nut Range, like the Sierra itself, is a tilted fault block.

basin once again. Though the Truckee has succeeded in breaching these as well, its current outflow is matched by the waters flowing into the lake from the surrounding mountains. Lake levels have fluctuated greatly in the past, rising during wet glacial periods and dropping during drier interglacials. The present lake level is 700 to 800 feet (215 to 245 meters) below former maximums, which are indicated by old shoreline benches preserved on adjacent slopes. Each year Lake Tahoe receives some 50,000 tons of sediments, at which rate it will fill one foot (25 centimeters) in 3200 years. The Tahoe Basin is structurally continuous with the Sierra Valley to the north, but the two are now separated by volcanic flows. The Diamond Mountains on the east side of the Sierra Valley are a granitic block that rose along the Honey Lake Fault on its east side.

Glaciers and Glacial Landforms

The Pleistocene epoch, or Ice Age, which began about 2.5 million years ago, was marked by four to ten periods during which large ice sheets covered much of northern Europe, part of Asia, the southern tip of South America, Antarctica, and the northern third of North America. Separating these glacial advances were progressively shorter periods when the climate was as warm or warmer than today, causing the ice sheets to retreat. Most meterologists believe that the last 10,000 years constitute yet one more interglacial period, after which ice will once again return. This proba-

Table 4: Glacial Episodes in the Sierra Nevada

Epoch	Glacial episode*	Years before present
Holocene (Recent)	Matthes	700 to present
	Recess Peak	2000–3000
Pleistocene (Ice Age)	Hilgard	11,000
	Tioga	20,000
	Tahoe	60,000
	Mono Basin	87,000
	Donner Lake	250,000
	Casa Diablo	400,000
	Sherwin	750,000
	McGee	1.5 million
Pliocene	Deadman Pass	2.75 million

*The glacial episodes are named for specific deposits of glacial debris, or till; one should not infer that glacial ice during these episodes was limited to the geographic regions named. The dates are based on tentative reasoning and are debatable. Casa Diablo, for example, is thought by some to be less than 200,000 years old and may correspond to the Mono Basin episode.

bility was first demonstrated by geologist Francois Matthes in his pioneering work on Sierra glaciation.

During periods of glacial advance a number of mountain ranges, including the Andes, Alps, Rockies, and Sierra Nevada, were also covered by smaller ice caps. The Sierra was repeatedly overwhelmed by glacial ice between three million and ten thousand years ago, a fact first recognized and promulgated by John Muir (see Table 4). Sierra geologists Francois Matthes and Eliot Blackwelder later identified, respectively, three and four periods of major glacial advance in the Sierra during the Pleistocene. As many as ten separate advances have been identified more recently on the basis of glacial debris, or *till*, scattered throughout the Sierra. In addition, four minor advances have been recognized for the period since the close of the Pleistocene. The 60 to 70 small glaciers, or *glacierets*, remaining in the central Sierra were formed during the most recent of these advances, which began about 700 years ago.

The largest glacier now found in the Sierra, the Palisade Glacier, is about a half-mile (800 meters) long and a mile and a half (2400 meters) wide. It occupies a northeasterly basin about 12,000 feet (3650 meters) in elevation on the

28. The Kuna Glacier lies in a northeasterly cirque on Kuna Peak, near the eastern border of Yosemite National Park. A series of recessional moraines is visible at its foot.

steep flanks of the Palisade Crest. Several other glaciers occur nearby and a few much smaller patches of permanent ice are scattered along the main crest for another 10 miles (16 kilometers) south. The northernmost Sierra glaciers occur near 11,000 feet (3350 meters) elevation on the northeast side of Sawtooth Ridge, which is plainly visible along the south side of Bridgeport Valley some 80 miles (130 kilometers) north of the Palisade Crest.

The Sierra Ice Cap

Maximum glacial advance in the Sierra occurred between 60,000 and 20,000 years ago, when an ice cap some 275 miles (445 kilometers) long and from 20 to 40 miles (32 to 64 kilometers) wide stretched across the range from Mt. Whitney to Sierra Buttes. At its northern and southern ends, the ice cap was discontinuous, and numerous peaks rose above its surface throughout. These islands, or *nunataks*, to use the Eskimo word, were untouched by glaciation largely because high winds prevented snow from accumulating on them. Numerous valley glaciers branched off the ice cap and moved down canyons on both slopes of the range. The longest and deepest rivers of ice flowed down the broad, snowy west slope of the Sierra, plucking rocks from canyon walls to form the spectacular U-shaped glacial canyons of which Yosemite Valley is the most famous and spectacular example. The longest west-slope glacier flowed down the canyon of the Tuolumne River, a few miles north of Yosemite Valley, for a distance of 60 miles (100 kilometers), filling Muir Gorge, the deepest part of the canyon, with 4000 feet (1200 meters) of ice. Most Sierra glaciers were much shorter, however, only a few exceeding 15 miles (24 kilometers) in length. Those on the east slope, owing to decreased precipitation and the steepness of the escarpment, were shorter yet.

Glacier Formation

Two conditions are essential for glaciers to form: abundant snowfall and summertime temperatures low enough for snow to remain on the ground year around. Neither condition by itself is sufficient. The Sierra, for example, today receives enough snow to promote glacier formation, but very little remains on the ground past mid-July. The Brooks Range of Alaska, on the other hand, experiences cool enough summers for glaciers to form but receives insufficient snow during the winter, and thus has only a few small glaciers despite its extreme northern location.

The lower boundary of perennial ice and snow is called the *firn limit*, firn being the coarse-grained old snow from which glaciers are made. During the Pleistocene the firn limit in the Sierra ranged from below 8000 feet (2450 meters) in the Tahoe region to below 11,000 feet (3350 meters) near Mt. Whitney. Today, what would be the firn limit in the southern Sierra is probably well over 15,000 feet, higher than any peak in the range, with the result that none are covered with perennial snow. The few glaciers remaining in the Sierra persist in cool, snowy northern and eastern exposures, where the firn limit is lowered by topographic factors. Even such small remnant ice fields as these are absent from the peaks south of Kings Canyon.

Glacial ice, which is 90 percent as dense as an equal volume of water, begins, of course, as snowflakes, which are only 1 to 10 percent as dense. The process by which these airy crystals are compacted and reshaped to form glacial ice capable of quarrying canyons out of obdurate granite is known as *destructive metamorphosis* and is described in Chapter III.

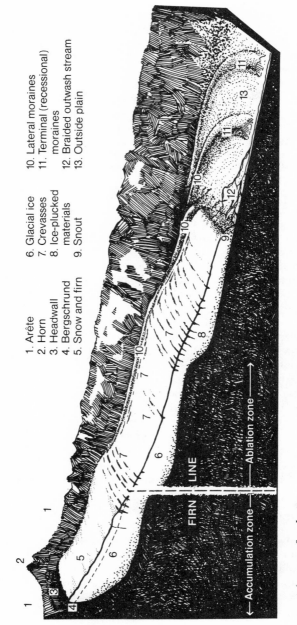

1. Arête
2. Horn
3. Headwall
4. Bergschrund
5. Snow and firn
6. Glacial ice
7. Crevasses
8. Ice-plucked materials
9. Snout
10. Lateral moraines
11. Terminal (recessional) moraines
12. Braided outwash stream
13. Outside plain

FIRN LINE

←——— Accumulation zone ———→←——— Ablation zone ———→

29. Anatomy of a glacier

Structure of a Glacier

When ice accumulates to depths of 100 feet (30 meters) or more, the weight of the mass may initiate downslope movement, and mountain glaciers, which flow down canyons already carved by streams, are essentially rivers of ice. Glacial movement usually amounts to a few inches or feet a year, though much faster speeds have been recorded. A glacier continues to advance so long as ice accumulation at its *head*, or upslope end, exceeds ablation, or melting, at its *snout*, or downslope terminus. The zone of accumulation lies above the firn limit, the zone of ablation below.

The lower depths of a glacier usually consist of fused, solid, unfractured ice, but the surface layers crack readily in response to the bending and stretching that occurs as a glacier moves over obstacles, negotiates bends in a canyon, and scrapes against rock walls on either side. Cracks, or *crevasses*, also form where a glacier's faster-flowing middle portion pulls away from its slower margins. A crevasse may range in size from a narrow separation of the surface ice to a giant chasm dozens of feet wide and as much as 200 to 250 feet (60 to 75 meters) deep. The upper end of a glacier is separated from its adjacent rock face, or headwall, by a large crevasse known as a *bergschrund*, which forms as the downward flowing ice pulls away from the rock.

Overhanging snow cornices and bridges often obscure the presence of a crevasse, and if they are unable to support a person's weight can pose a severe hazard to mountaineers attempting a glacier crossing. Anyone venturing onto the surface of a glacier, even the small ones found in the Sierra, should be trained in snow and ice techniques and should be roped to his companions. Even experienced climbers occasionally find themselves dangling by a rope in the glimmering blue depths of a crevasse.

Glacial Erosion

Glaciers are powerful agents of erosion, quarrying and transporting huge amounts of rock debris from the sides and bottom of their canyons. The process by which glaciers quarry into bedrock is known as *ice plucking*. Under great pressure, such as that provided by the weight of glacial ice, water can melt at temperatures below freezing. This occurs within and at the margins of glacial ice. The subfreezing meltwater flows to regions of lower pressure, which include cracks and crevices in the adjacent rock, where it refreezes. In the process the water expands and forces the crevice apart just as it does in frost riving (see page 60). After this has occurred repeatedly, a rock fragment is broken loose and borne away by the moving glacier. The resulting debris ranges in size from huge boulders to *rock flour*, fine-grained particles created by rocks grinding against one another in the course of glacial movement.

Below the firn limit, in the ablation zone, where the glacial *surface* begins to retreat through melting, the debris is exposed and transported on the surface. Some of the debris is pushed to the sides of the glacier, where it is deposited in ridges known as *lateral moraines*. When two valley glaciers come together a *medial moraine* is formed along their mutual boundary. If a glacier remains stationary for a prolonged period, debris deposited by melting at the snout accumulates to form a crescent-shaped *terminal moraine*. A retreating glacier may leave a series of *recessional moraines* in its wake, each one a terminal moraine formed during a pause in its upslope retreat.

Moraines may be hundreds of feet tall and several miles long. They consist of glacial *till*, random assortments of various-sized rocks rounded and smoothed by glacial abrasion. Although moraines occur on both slopes of the Sierra, they are more conspicuous on the east, particularly between Lee Vining and Bishop, where glaciers moved out of the mountain canyons onto the open plain. These excursions are commemorated by sinuous, rounded moraines extending from the mountain front out onto the gentle, sagebrush-covered flats. On the west side of the Sierra, moraines tend to be obscured by abundant vegetation and degradation through weathering, both occasioned by heavy precipitation. Visitors to Yosemite Valley will find well-preserved terminal moraines in Bridalveil Meadow and just below El Portal. The two moraines were formed during separate glacial advances.

As a glacier retreats, rock debris within the ice is released through melting at the snout, so that areas once glaciated are commonly covered with randomly scattered rocks of

30. An *erratic*, or perched boulder, carried downslope by a glacier, then stranded when the ice retreated. Such erratics are often composed of a different rock type from that on which they have come to rest.

31. Glacial polish creates a shiny finish on vast expanses of rock in the High Sierra. Here, portions of the glacial polish have eroded away.

various sizes and types, including a number of huge boulders. Stranded rocks, or *glacial erratics*, are abundant throughout the High Sierra and most conspicuous where they are of a different type from the rock on which they were deposited. In such cases it may be possible to determine where they originated upslope and thereby calculate the distance traveled.

Moving glaciers strip soil away from bedrock, which is polished to a high sheen as small rock particles are dragged over it like scouring powder. *Glacial polish* is still very much in evidence throughout the High Sierra, despite the passage of 10,000 years since ice last covered the region. In the thin dry air of the high country, sunlight reflected off polished granite can be blinding and often necessitates the use of sunglasses if one is to avoid perpetual squinting, as well as possible eye damage. In many areas, weathering has removed the glacial polish; it is best preserved in widely jointed granite, such as that of the Yosemite region.

Glaciated rock surfaces may also bear grooves, "chatter" marks, and potholes. Grooves mark the paths of small rocks dragged over the surface by the ice. Chatter marks are similarly formed, except that the transported rock fragments were used to chip crescent-shaped gouges in the bedrock. Chatter marks point in the direction of glacial movement. Potholes occur where eddies of water in a glacier employ trapped rock particles to drill into the bedrock below.

Glacial Sculpture

Glaciers are responsible for some of the most glorious mountain scenery in the world, including that of the Alps, the fjords of Norway and New Zealand, the northern Rockies, North Cascades, and Sierra Nevada. Glacial quarrying produces broad, steep-walled valleys, such as the Yosemite; great rockbound amphitheaters; knife-edged ridges; pyramidal peaks; vast polished basins; and hanging canyons graced by waterfalls and cascades. The landforms produced by glacial quarrying reflect patterns of weakness and strength in the structure of the underlying bedrock. Enormous amounts of rock may be ɩ asted away in closely jointed granite, for example, while massive granite is vulnerable only along its widely distributed joints. The difference is reflected in the contrast between the monolithic landforms produced in the massive granites of the west slope of the Sierra and the more irregular, heavily dissected forms characteristic of the closely jointed rocks of the crest and east slope of the range. Although glaciers are able to quarry most deeply in softer or more easily fragmented rocks, obdurate types, such as the massive granites of the Yosemite region, retain the shapes imposed on them for longer periods.

32. A glacial horn, or pyramidal peak, rises above the headwaters of Bishop Creek on the east slope of the Sierra near Bishop.

Mountain glaciers form at high elevations in the gentler terrain at the heads of stream canyons, where air temperatures are cool enough and precipitation abundant enough for snow to accumulate to great depths and persist throughout the year. As a glacier begins to move it plucks rocks from surrounding slopes and scoops out the bottom of its accumulation basin to form a broad, dished amphitheater, or *cirque,* bound on three sides by steep cliffs. The headwall of a cirque may be hundreds, or even thousands, of feet tall, depending on local jointing and the depth of the glacier. Pyramidal peaks, or *horns,* mark where glaciers have scooped out several sides of a mountain. Knife-edged ridges, or *arêtes,* occur where two cirques form back to back on either side of a ridge or where two parallel glaciers erode the ridge between them. Low, rounded notches, or passes, along a ridge mark where glaciers overrode the rock.

Glacial Valleys

Glaciers radically alter the shape of the stream canyons they occupy. Viewed end-on, a stream canyon typically exhibits a V-shaped profile produced by the downward cutting of the stream followed by the wasting away of materials on either side. Glacial quarrying in the canyon sides produces steep, even vertical, rock walls, widening the canyon floor in the process. The result can be a classic U-shaped valley such as the Yosemite, which was invaded by several glaciers, the largest more than 6000 feet (1800 meters) deep

33. The glacially carved valley of the north fork of Mono Creek. The peaks in the distance are part of the Silver Divide, a high granitic ridge branching west from the main crest. The dark summit just visible in the distance is Red Slate Mountain, a peak on the main crest composed of metamorphic rock.

and 37 miles (60 kilometers) long. Many other Sierra canyons were less radically excavated into a modified V-shape, either because the rock was more resistant, quarrying was less intensive, or there was less subsequent filling with downwashed sediments than occurred, for example, in Yosemite Valley (Figure 34).

As glaciers excavate a river canyon the channels of tributary streams flowing in from each side are steepened as rocks are quarried from the canyon walls. In cases of radical excavation, such as occurred in Yosemite and Hetch Hetchy valleys, both in Yosemite National Park, the tributary channels may be abruptly truncated, leaving them perched high above the valley floor. Streams debouch from these *hanging valleys* as free-falling cataracts such as Yosemite and Bridalveil falls.

Yosemite Falls plunges over the north wall of the valley in two great leaps separated by a short stretch of cascades. The upper fall descends 1430 feet (436 meters); the lower, 320 feet (98 meters). Including the cascades, the total drop of Yosemite Falls is 2565 feet (782 meters), making it one of the highest waterfalls in the world. Across the valley Bridalveil Fall plunges 620 feet (189 meters). Its name aptly describes the gossamer curtain of spray formed by the wind during the summer, when runoff is low. Other notable free-falling cataracts in the Yosemite region include Ribbon Fall, 1612 feet (491 meters); Illilouette Fall, 370 feet (113

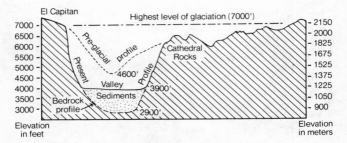

34. Cross section of Yosemite Valley. Prior to glaciation, it had the V-profile typical of stream-carved canyons. Glacial quarrying and later filling by sediments have produced its present U-shaped profile. The depth of glacial quarrying is now obscured by some 1000 ft (300 m) of sediments which today underlie the valley floor.

meters); Vernal Fall, 317 feet (97 meters); and Nevada Fall, 594 feet (181 meters)—all in Yosemite Valley; Tueeulala Fall, about 1000 feet (300 meters); Wapama Fall, 1200 feet (365 meters)—both of which plunge into Hetch Hetchy Valley's Hennessey Reservoir; and Rainbow Fall, 150 feet (45 meters)—just south of Devils Postpile. Rainbow Fall flows over a brink of columnar basalt.

Glacial Staircases

Nevada and Vernal falls occur where the Merced River plunges over steps on a giant rock staircase leading from Little Yosemite Valley to Yosemite Valley. Such staircases are produced because as a glacier flows down a canyon it is able to quarry the floor more deeply in some places than in others. *Glacial staircases* occur throughout the High Sierra, and hikers who have climbed up the region's glacially carved canyons will clearly recall the alternation of fairly gentle stretches—the treads—and precipitous rocky head-walls—the risers.

John Muir suggested that staircase formation was linked to joint spacing—that glaciers ride up and over zones of widely jointed rock and quarry downward in zones of closely jointed rock. Thus the risers would correspond to the former, the treads to the latter. Muir may have been correct, though his theory has not yet been verified.

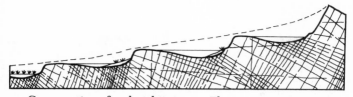

35. Cross section of a glacial staircase. The top step is a cirque containing a frigid, rockbound tarn. Below it another lake occupies the second step. Some sedimentation has occurred at the mouth of the stream connecting the two lakes. On the third step sedimentation has progressed even further, and the lake is well on its way to becoming a meadow, such as the one on the lowest step. According to John Muir and, later, Francois Matthes, glacial staircases reflect alternating areas of closely jointed, easily quarried rock and widely jointed, more resistant rock. A second hypothesis suggests that staircases may occur in response to pressure waves within the glacier rather than the joint structure of the underlying rock.

A more recent explanation links step formation to waves of pressure in a moving glacier. According to this hypothesis glaciers do not flow at constant pressure, but in a series of pressure waves. Such waves may produce the conspicuous ripples on the surfaces of some large glaciers. Where pressure is greatest increased melting of glacial ice and resultant ice plucking would produce the steps of a staircase. The risers would correspond to zones of lesser pressure. This explanation, like Muir's, has not yet been verified, but European scientists are now boring into a glacier with the purpose of measuring internal pressure variations.

Glacial Lakes

Lakes form on the treads of a glacial staircase when streamflow is impounded in the dished-out areas behind the risers. Sediments transported by the stream will eventually fill the lake, and even before this occurs may obscure the backward slope of the underlying bedrock. A series of step lakes on a glacial staircase linked together by their connecting stream are known as *chain lakes* or *paternoster lakes*. (The latter name is derived from the practice in Catholic alpine countries of locating shrines corresponding to stations of the cross at each lake.) Step lakes occur on most glacial staircases in the Sierra, though one or more of the lower steps may have already been filled in with downwashed sediments, which typically support meadow.

Cirques constitute the top steps of glacial staircases, and like those below, they commonly hold a glacial lake, or *tarn*, formed by snowmelt impounded behind either a rock ridge or moraine. Most cirque lakes in the Sierra are of the former variety. The water levels in cirque and step lakes remain more or less constant from year to year because their outlet streams carry away only excess water. In a dry year the streams simply stop flowing.

Lakes also form behind moraines deposited on lower glacial steps. While less common than lakes dammed by rock sills, moraine lakes include some of the largest in the Sierra. Cascade Lake and Fallen Leaf Lake, on the southwest shore of Lake Tahoe, are both dammed by moraines. Picturesque Emerald Bay is a former moraine lake that was flooded by the rising waters of Lake Tahoe. Gold Lake, Truckee Lake, Echo Lake, Convict Lake, and Moraine Lake all lie behind recessional moraines. Twin moraine lakes, which commonly occur along the east side of the northern Sierra, develop behind two recessional moraines.

Altogether, more than 2000 glacial lakes occur in the High Sierra, ranging in size from tiny ponds to deep bodies of water several hundred acres in size. They are one of the most distinctive features of the High Sierra, lending it enormous charm and exquisite scenic beauty. Lake Tulainyo, which lies in a cirque just below Mt. Russell, in the Whitney region, is, at 12,865 feet (3921 meters) elevation, said to be the highest lake in the contiguous United States. The lowest cirque lakes in the Sierra occur in the far northern end of the range at elevations above 7000 feet (2150 meters). In some areas of the central Sierra, where glaciation was most extensive, a dozen or more lakes may occur in a single square mile, jewels set in fields of granite by vanished rivers of ice.

36. Columbine and Cyclamen lakes occupy the top two steps of a glacial staircase on Sequoia National Park's Great Western Divide. The outlet stream draining the lower lake empties into yet a third tarn, which is not shown. Together, these three lakes constitute one of the finest examples of chain, or *paternoster*, lakes found in the Sierra.

Glaciers and Glacial Landforms

CHAPTER III

Winter Storms and Summer Drought: Weather and Climate in the Sierra

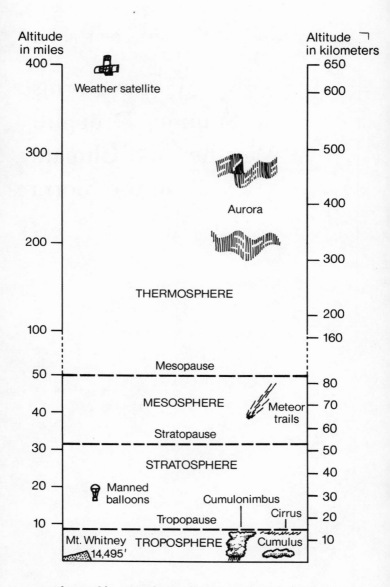

37. The earth's atmosphere, showing various phenomena occurring in each layer. Meteorological phenomena are confined to the troposphere.

WEATHER AND CLIMATE

CLIMATE comprises the overall conditions of air temperature, precipitation, water availability, humidity, wind, and
other factors characteristic of a particular region over an extended period of time. It encompasses not only average
conditions, but extremes as well. Weather is the day-to-day
fluctuations in climate caused by physical changes occurring from place to place in the air mantle covering the
earth.

Mountain ranges, by virtue of their great height and
abrupt topography, are cooler, wetter, and windier than
the lowlands around them. This is true whether we are
speaking of the Sierra Nevada, the Andes, or the Karakoram.
Air becomes thinner and cooler with increasing altitude. It
flows erratically through diverse mountain topography and
is accelerated in its passage over crests and through narrow
canyons and passes. Mountain ranges not only intercept
winds aloft that go unnoticed at lower elevations, they generate breezes of their own. They are cloudier and receive
more precipitation than lowland areas because moist air
masses forced upward over their slopes are cooled to the
point where water vapor condenses into raindrops or
freezes to form snowflakes. Mountains act as barriers to the
passage of air and thus profoundly affect the climates of regions around them, including those of other mountain
ranges. By subjecting air masses to such sudden and radical
fluctuations in speed, direction, temperature, and density,
mountain ranges create their own weather, which can
change, as any mountaineer knows, with alarming rapidity.

The Elevation Factor

Anyone who has ever ascended a mountain range knows
that the higher one travels the cooler the air becomes.
Even when temperatures in the lowlands soar into the 80s
and 90s, visitors to the high country may require a sweater
or windbreaker for comfort. Air also becomes thinner as
elevation increases. Above 8000 feet (2450 meters) most
people experience some shortness of breath, which persists
until their bodies adapt to the lower levels of oxygen in the
air. Mountain air also tends to be drier than that of sur-

rounding valleys because air moving upslope often cools to the point where its moisture condenses to form clouds, leaving the air itself drier. These characteristics of mountain air—coolness, thinness, dryness—are all functions of increasing elevation.

Mountain Air

DENSITY Air is densest at sea level because it is compressed by all the air above it. With increasing elevation, the amount of air overhead decreases, allowing the air beneath to expand. The gas molecules contained in a cubic yard of air at sea level would fill about 1⅓ cubic yards at an elevation of 10,000 feet (3050 meters). Thus, at 10,000 feet one must, in effect, gulp in a third more air to obtain the same amount of oxygen as at sea level. Shortness of breath may persist for a day or two until the body becomes acclimated to the thinner air. As additional oxygen-carrying red blood corpuscles are manufactured and as circulation increases, the shortness of breath and occasional feeling of light-headedness gradually disappears. The higher one ventures, of course, or the greater the level of exertion, the longer it will take the body to adapt.

People who overexert themselves before their bodies have had a chance to become adapted to reduced oxygen levels may become ill from oxygen deprivation. The first symptoms of what is known as *mountain,* or *altitude, sickness* are persistent headache and fatigue. Treatment consists of returning to lower elevation immediately (8000 feet/ 2450 meters or below is usually sufficient). After recovering, which may take a day or two, the victim may return to higher elevations, but should proceed slowly and rest often. Failure to treat the symptoms of mountain sickness immediately can result in serious complications, such as pulmonary edema, leading to death.

TEMPERATURE As air rises, its heat is converted to the kinetic energy of expansion, producing an average drop in temperature of 3.5° F for each 1000-foot gain in elevation (0.6° C per 100 meters). Thus, when air temperatures in the Owens Valley (about 4000 feet/1200 meters elevation) hover in the mid-80s, those atop the Sierra crest (about 13,500 feet/4100 meters) may register only in the 50s.

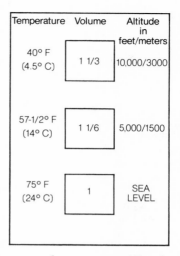

Temperature	Volume	Altitude in feet/meters
40° F (4.5° C)	1 1/3	10,000/3000
57-1/2° F (14° C)	1 1/6	5,000/1500
75° F (24° C)	1	SEA LEVEL

38. As air rises, its volume increases and temperature falls. If a volume of air at 75° F (24° C) near sea level rises to 10,000 ft (3050 m), it will expand by one-third and cool down to about 40° F (4° C).

Conversely, sinking air gains heat at roughly the same rate.

The loss or gain of heat as a function of altitude is known as the *lapse rate,* and it varies according to such factors as air speed, temperature differences between lower and higher altitudes, vegetation cover, amount of insolation (*in-*coming *sol*ar radi*ation*), slope aspect, and most important, the amount of moisture contained in the air. Since water vapor warms and cools more slowly than do other gases in the air, rising moist air masses lose heat at a lower rate than do drier air masses. During the summer, when air passing over the Sierra is quite dry, we would expect the average lapse rate to be higher than during the winter, when moister air often moves upslope. Temperatures for particular stations, however, are also affected by local conditions, so variations from the expected pattern are common. In addition, temperature records for high elevations are scanty and do not permit accurate generalizations about actual lapse rates for the range as a whole (see Figure 39).

TEMPERATURE CHANGES AT HIGH ALTITUDE   Thin, dry mountain air gains and loses heat readily, so that after sunset, for example, temperatures drop sharply as heat acquired during the day is rapidly reradiated into space. Cloudy nights tend to be warmer than clear ones because the cloud cover serves as a blanket of insulation. Air temperatures are lowest between three and six in the morning but rise rapidly with the appearance of the sun.

Should the sky become overcast during the day, as happens on many summer afternoons in the Sierra, temperatures will again drop sharply. Even in the shade of a single passing cloud or a grove of trees, the air will be significantly cooler than in nearby sunny areas. The higher one goes, the more striking the contrast will be. The thin, dust-free air of the high country also admits considerable ultraviolet radiation, that part of the spectrum responsible for sunburns. Visitors to the High Sierra will remember numerous occasions when they alternately shivered in the shade of a rock or tree and roasted in the intense, burning high-country sun.

Mountain Winds

Mountain ranges are windier than nearby lowlands partly because they intercept upper-level winds that pass unnoticed below and partly because their great height produces temperature differences that generate upslope and downslope flows of air.

Winds and breezes passing over a rugged mountain range such as the Sierra follow tortuous courses over and around ridges, up and down canyons, through gaps in the crest. Eddies set up by the irregular terrain blow here and there in vigorous gusts that rattle trees and shrubs one minute only to abruptly die down the next. In the protection of a large boulder or grove of trees there may be scarcely any wind at all, while just a few yards away, in a more exposed area, it howls furiously.

VALLEY AND MOUNTAIN BREEZES   On a warm summer morning the air next to the ground surface is heated and rises. Cooler air nearby moves in to replace it and rises in turn. This movement is felt during the day as an upslope breeze. It typically begins about three hours after sunrise, reaches a peak during the hottest part of the day, and tapers off toward dusk. Since the air movement is directly related

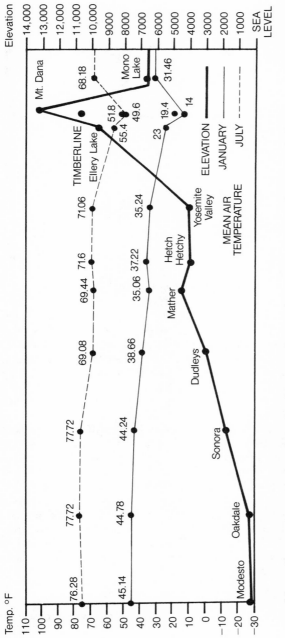

Temp. °F

Elevation

ELEVATION
JANUARY
JULY

MEAN AIR
TEMPERATURE

Modesto Oakdale Sonora Dudleys Mather Hetch Hetchy Yosemite Valley Ellery Lake Mono Lake Mt. Dana TIMBERLINE

76.28 77.72 77.72 69.08 69.44 71.6 71.06 55.4 51.8 68.18
45.14 44.78 44.24 38.66 35.06 37.22 35.24 49.6 31.46
23 19.4 14

39. Mean air temperatures across the central Sierra. This graph is meant to give only a general idea of the effect of elevation on air temperatures. The figures apply only to the various stations shown and should not be considered necessarily typical for the Sierra as a whole, nor even for other stations in the Yosemite region.

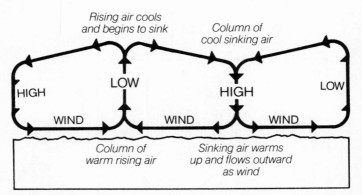

Rising air cools
and begins to sink

Column of
cool sinking air

HIGH

LOW

HIGH

LOW

WIND

WIND

WIND

Column of
warm rising air

Sinking air warms
up and flows outward
as wind

40. Convection cells, showing the circulation of air resulting from uneven heating of the earth's surface. Winds blow from high-pressure centers of cool sinking air toward low-pressure centers of warm rising air.

to surface heating, the breeze is faster on warm, sunny slopes than on cool, shady ones. This daily movement of air upslope is known as a *valley breeze* because winds are commonly named for their direction of origin.

As the valley breeze subsides in the late afternoon, lake surfaces rippled all day become glassy. The period of calm usually lasts until around midnight, when colder air aloft begins to sink toward the earth's surface, initiating a downslope drainage of air known as a *mountain breeze*. By morning, valley bottoms and basins may be filled with a layer of cold, heavy air, while surrounding ridgetops are comparatively warmer.

The difference may be large enough to affect the kinds of plants able to grow in each place. Yosemite Valley, for example, is only about 4000 feet (1200 meters) elevation, yet supports plants, lodgepole pine for one, that are more commonly found at higher locations. Overnight campers in the Sierra will find that campsites situated on the sides of a ridge are often warmer than those in the bottoms of canyons and lake basins, thanks to the mountain breeze. By midmorning the cold air that flowed downslope the night before is warmed up and begins to rise, beginning the daily cycle once again.

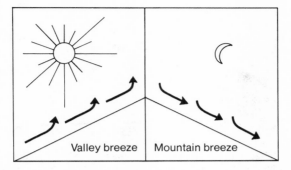

Valley breeze   Mountain breeze

41. Valley and mountain breezes. During the day, sun-warmed air moves upslope, creating the valley breeze. At night, cool air flows downslope, creating the mountain breeze.

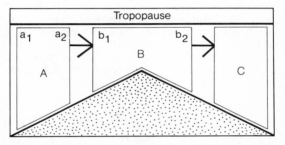

42. Wind speeds increase over mountain crests and through canyons and passes because air—like any fluid—accelerates when forced through a narrow passage. As a volume of air moves upslope (A), it is increasingly squeezed between the mountains and the tropopause, the inversion layer acting as a lid on the lower atmosphere. Since the volume of the air remains the same as it squeezes over the mountain crest, it becomes elongated (B). And since volume B must cover the distance from b_1 to b_2 in the same interval as volume A moves from a_1 to a_2, the speed of volume B must be greater. Air forced to squeeze through a canyon or mountain pass is accelerated in much the same way.

The Orographic Effect

By forcing air upward, mountain ranges increase precipitation on their slopes and even produce it where none existed at lower elevations. Known as the *orographic effect*,

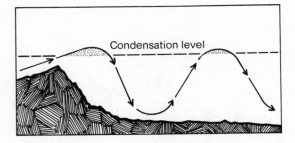

43. During the winter, air passing over the Sierra oscillates between layers of colder air above and warmer air near the surface. As the air moves downwind from the Sierra, each oscillation, like the successive bounces of a ball, is smaller than the preceding one as the energy that generated the wave gradually dissipates. These oscillations, or *mountain waves,* are made visible in the form of lens-shaped clouds that seem to hang motionless over the Sierra crest and valleys to the east. The flat bottoms of wave clouds mark the elevation above which the water vapor in the rising air condenses. Their rounded tops inscribe the upper curves of the waves. Wave clouds seem motionless because while the air moves through them, their upper and lower boundaries remain much the same.

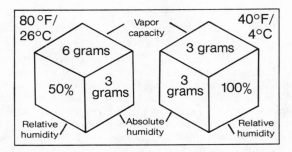

44. The amount of water vapor present in a given volume of air—usually expressed as so many grams of vapor per cubic meter of air—is its *absolute humidity.* This same amount, expressed as a percentage of the air's vapor capacity, is its *relative humidity.* For example, if a cubic meter of air can hold 6 g of water vapor, but actually contains only 3 g, its absolute humidity is 3 g/m^3 and its relative humidity is 50%. However, if this same volume were cooled by 20° (11° C), its vapor capacity would be cut in half. Consequently, while its absolute humidity would remain the

WEATHER AND CLIMATE

same, its relative humidity would increase to 100%. At this point the air would be saturated. Any further cooling would reduce vapor capacity below the amount of moisture present, causing the excess to condense into tiny visible droplets, forming fog, clouds, steam, frost, and dew.

45. Orographic precipitation. As a moist air mass (A) moves up the west slope of the Sierra (B), its vapor capacity is lowered and increased rainfall results. As the air mass continues to move upslope, precipitation changes from rain to snow as the air temperature drops to freezing (C). Snowfall accounts for roughly one-half the precipitation at 6000 ft (1800 m) and increases upslope toward the crest (D). As the air sinks down the east slope of the Sierra it becomes warmer, increasing its vapor capacity so that precipitation rapidly decreases, then stops altogether (E).

this phenomenon occurs because air's capacity for holding water vapor varies with changes in temperature. When air is heated, its vapor capacity increases, approximately doubling with each increase of 20° F (11° C). Conversely, when air is cooled, as in its passage up a mountain slope, its vapor capacity decreases at the same rate.

If the vapor capacity of air is reduced to the point where condensation occurs, clouds form. Mountain crests often are capped with clouds even when lowland skies are clear. During summer afternoons, for example, Sierra skies are often littered with puffy, white cumulus clouds with rounded tops and flat bottoms. These clouds "pop" suddenly into being as rising air reaches a level where it has been cooled to the point of saturation. Their flat bottoms mark this level.

If the air mass is already close to saturation, as are those

The Elevation Factor 107

associated with winter storm systems moving in from the Pacific, the cooling produced by ascending a mountain slope will cause significant precipitation. And if temperatures aloft are below freezing, the water vapor in the air, rather than condensing to form raindrops, will freeze directly to form snow, a process known as *sublimation*.

In the Donner Pass region precipitation increases on the west slope of the Sierra at the rate of just over 7 inches per each 1000-foot gain in elevation (61 millimeters per 100 meters). On the abrupt eastern slope the rate is roughly 17 inches per 1000 feet (140 millimeters per 100 meters). North of Donner Pass the rate on the west slope increases to about 13½ inches (100 millimeters per 100 meters). Rates in the foothills west of Yosemite are surprisingly high (200 millimeters per 100 meters), indeed much higher than those recorded near the crest of the range, but this apparent anomaly probably reflects inaccuracies in measuring snowfall.

Geographic Factors Affecting Mountain Climates

Mountain climates differ according to the geographical positions of various ranges with respect to such factors as latitude, maritime and continental air masses, and other mountain ranges. The Sierra Nevada, for example, enjoys a milder climate than the Cascades, which are situated farther north, or than the Rockies, which are cut off during the winter from the moderating influence of marine air.

Latitude

As one moves northward, air temperatures tend to drop at the rate of about 1° F per each 70 miles (1° C per 200 kilometers). As a result, the Washington Cascades are significantly cooler year around than the Sierra. The effect of latitude on temperature is particularly evident in the northward drop in climatic timberline, the level above which temperatures are too cold during the summer to support tree growth. In the Yosemite region timberline occurs at about 10,500 feet (3200 meters); on Mt. Rainier, between 6500 and 7000 feet (2000 to 2150 meters). The drop in air temperatures northward is also evidenced by a steady increase in the number and size of glaciers found on the higher peaks. Although the Sierra receives heavy winter snowfall, summer air temperatures are too high for snow to persist through the season, a condition essential to the formation of glacial ice.

Moreover, owing to their more northerly location, the Washington Cascades not only receive more total precipitation than the Sierra, but it is more evenly distributed throughout the year. And because of warmer air temperatures in the Sierra, snowfall begins later in the autumn and ceases earlier in the spring than in the Cascades.

Marine Air

The deep snows and generally mild temperatures characteristic of Sierra winters are both occasioned by the range's proximity to the Pacific Ocean. Prevailing westerly winds during this season bring comparatively warm and extremely moist marine air masses to the western slope of the range, which is situated roughly 80 to 100 miles (130 to 160 kilometers) from the coast. At the same time, mountain ranges immediately east of the Sierra protect it somewhat from the frigid continental air masses that bring fierce blizzards and prolonged periods of subzero temperatures to the Rockies. Nevertheless, the continental influence is appreciable, if somewhat tempered, on the east side of the Sierra, where winter temperatures tend to range lower than those recorded for stations of comparable latitude and altitude on the west slope.

Seasonal Storm Patterns

The climate of the Sierra Nevada is characterized by warm, dry summers and snowy winters that are surprisingly mild for a range of such great elevation. More than 95 percent of the range's total annual precipitation falls between October

and May. This wet-winter/dry-summer climate is characteristic of California as a whole and is classified by
climatologists as Mediterranean because it resembles that
of the lands of southern Europe.

Storms usually begin to move into California in late October and increase in frequency through January, the wettest month. Precipitation throughout the state drops off
sharply in April during most years and more or less ceases
by the end of May. In some years one or more tropical
summer storms may blow northward into California, bringing scattered thunder showers, or sometimes only widespread cloudiness, to the central part of the state. Such
storms may bring heavier than normal precipitation to the
upper slopes of the Sierra, but over the long run they do
little to alleviate California's perennial summer drought.

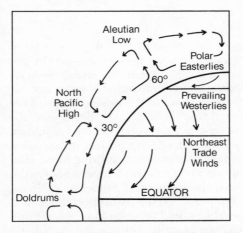

46. Convection cells over the North Pacific. Air heated at the
equator rises and flows northward, sinking somewhere between
Hawaii and California to form the North Pacific High. Winds
emanating from the high blow in a clockwise direction, producing
the prevailing northwesterlies of the Pacific Coast and the northeast tradewinds of Hawaii. In the vicinity of 60 degrees north
latitude air flowing north from the Pacific High encounters the
cool polar easterlies along a boundary known as the Polar Front.
Along this front the warmer, wetter southern air is forced upward
to produce the Aleutian Low, spawning ground for most of the
cyclonic storms that strike California during the winter.

WEATHER AND CLIMATE

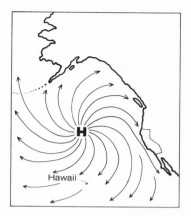

47. Summer winds in the northern Pacific emanate from the North Pacific High and circulate in a clockwise direction, deflecting possible storm systems northward from California.

Pacific Air Masses

The cycle of winter precipitation and summer drought is directly related to shifting patterns of air circulation over the northern Pacific Ocean.

THE NORTH PACIFIC HIGH   Near the equator sun-warmed air rises and flows north aloft, becoming cooler and denser as it goes, until somewhere midway between Hawaii and California it sinks to earth, forming a center of cold, heavy air known as the North Pacific High. Winds radiate in all directions from this high-pressure center, and because of the earth's rotation veer to the right and flow in a clockwise direction around the high, forming what is called an *anticyclone*. Winds north of the high curve eastward to become the prevailing northwesterlies of the Pacific Coast. Those to the south curve westward to become the cooling trade winds that moderate Hawaii's tropical climate.

THE POLAR FRONT   Between 40 and 60 degrees north latitude, the northwesterlies encounter the polar easterlies sweeping down from the Polar High, a column of cold, sinking air that hovers over the top of the globe. This boundary, known as the *polar front*, is not smooth, but consists of great waves where salients of air from each side make in-

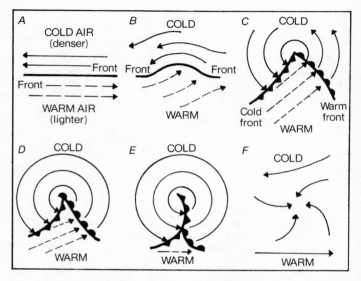

48. Formation of cyclonic storms. The Polar Front is not regular (A), but consists of great waves where salients of air from each side invade the territory of the other (B). Within these waves, wedges of warm and cold air tend to deflect each other in a counter-clockwise direction to form cyclones (C) consisting of a warm-front and a cold front. Together, the two fronts constitute a low-pressure center characterized by abundant precipitation as the moist southern air is forced upwards and cooled. The two fronts chase each other around the center (D) until one finally over-takes the other (E), producing what meterologists call an *occluded front*. Eventually, after a trip of perhaps thousands of miles, the energy of the cyclonic cell dissipates (F).

roads into the territory of the other. Within these waves, or loops, wedges of colliding air tend to deflect each other in directions opposite to their original flow, producing cells of counterclockwise motion known as *cyclones*. At the same time, the colder, polar air slides beneath the warmer, lighter, Pacific air, pushing it upward, so that these cyclonic cells are characterized by low-pressure centers of rising air. Abundant precipitation is associated with these lows because the warm marine air is extremely moist after its long journey over the ocean and, as it rises and cools, releases this moisture as rain and snow.

THE PACIFIC STORM TRACK   Cyclonic storms move eastward along the polar front, sweeping over the west coast of North America and from there into the interior of the continent. Since the winds associated with these storms move in a counterclockwise direction, they strike the coast from the southwest, and a shift in wind to this direction usually signals an approaching front. As the storm system passes to the east, the winds shift to the northeast, and after it leaves an area entirely, back to the northwest as the Pacific High reasserts its influence.

Whether storms enter California depends on the position of the polar front, which in turn is directly tied to that of the North Pacific High. The high is normally situated farther north during the summer than in the winter. The reasons for this seasonal shift are extremely complex and as yet imperfectly understood, but they result in part from the

49. Types of frontal systems.

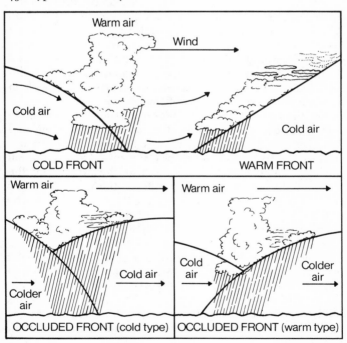

COLD FRONT   WARM FRONT

OCCLUDED FRONT (cold type)   OCCLUDED FRONT (warm type)

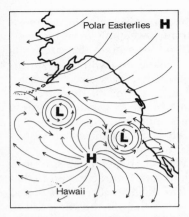

50. As winter approaches, the North Pacific High moves south-ward, permitting storm systems along the Polar Front to move into California.

interplay among such factors as (1) the seasonal tilting of the earth's axis toward and away from the sun in response to orbital position, (2) ocean temperature gradients between the equator and the pole, (3) ocean circulation patterns, and (4) the relative shifts in the polar jet stream, the broad "river" of air that circles the polar region at great altitude. Detailed discussion of these factors, worthy of a book in itself, lies outside the scope of this guide.

For the purpose of the present discussion it is enough to know that during the spring the North Pacific High and polar front shift northward, causing the prevailing summer storm track to lie well north of California. During the fall the high and polar front usually shift southward, moving the cyclonic storms to a more southerly track and bringing rain and snow to California. If the high remains in the north during the winter—as it did during the winters of 1975–1976 and 1976–1977—the state may experience se-vere drought.

Even during normal winters the position of the polar front is constantly changing. Most winter storms entering California originate in the Gulf of Alaska, but some are gen-erated farther south in the Pacific. These southern storms tend to be warmer and wetter than those formed to the north, and they deliver greater amounts of precipitation.

The heaviest snowfalls of the season in the Sierra are usually associated with these southern, or "Hawaiian," storms.

Sierra Winters

The combination of great snowfall and relatively mild temperatures characteristic of Sierra winters is well illustrated by conditions at Huntington Lake, located on the west slope of the central Sierra at 6950 feet elevation (2120 meters). During January, usually the coldest and snowiest month in the Sierra, the mean temperature at Huntington Lake is just over 30° F (-1° C), and snowfall for the month averages 53 inches (135 centimeters).

The average daytime high at Huntington Lake in January is about 41° F (5° C), the average nighttime low, about 19° F (-7° C). On the hottest day of the month temperatures typically range into the mid-60s, dropping on the coldest day only to the high teens. Anyone familiar with winter conditions in North Dakota, Vermont, or the northern Rockies will appreciate how congenial Sierra Januaries are by comparison. Huntington Lake, by the way, receives about 260 inches (660 centimeters) of snow a year—nearly 22 feet (6.7 meters). (For winter temperatures at other Sierra stations, see Figure 39.)

Precipitation

THE SNOWY RANGE   In Spanish, *sierra nevada* means "snowy mountain range," an appropriate name because the Sierra is one of the snowiest places in North America. Only the coastal ranges of the Pacific Northwest, from Oregon to Alaska, regularly receive greater snowfall than the Sierra. Above 6000 feet (1850 meters), a seasonal snowfall of 30 feet (9 meters) or more is common. Tamarack, which is located between Lake Tahoe and Yosemite National park at an elevation of about 8000 feet (2450 meters), receives an average of 38 feet (11.6 meters) of snow each year. In mid-March the snowpack at Tamarack is typically 17 feet deep (5.2 meters). In the winter of 1906–1907 Tamarack received 73.5 feet of snow (22.4 meters), a record for the Sierra and for many years the greatest known snowfall in the world. (Snow records were begun in the Sierra in 1870, long before they were kept in other western ranges. Nowadays, stations in the northern Cascade Range regularly record greater snowfall than the Sierra.)

GEOGRAPHIC DISTRIBUTION The west slope of the Sierra receives between 20 and 80 inches (50 and 200 centimeters) of precipitation a year, depending on elevation and latitude. Precipitation generally increases northward through the range, with maximum recorded amounts falling in the region between Sonora and Yuba passes. Below about 2000 feet (600 meters) in the central Sierra almost all precipitation falls as rain. Above 6000 feet (1800 meters) all but a tiny fraction of precipitation occurs as snow. Snow covers the ground more or less continuously throughout the winter and spring. The lower limit of the snowpack—the "snow line"—usually occurs somewhere around 4000 feet (1200 meters), but varies greatly from year to year, as well as during the course of a single winter.

Maximum recorded precipitation occurs between 5000 and 6000 feet (1500 and 1800 meters) on the west slope, about half of it falling as snow. Above this elevation precipitation seems to decline, but this apparent anomaly may again reflect inadequate snow-survey techniques rather than actual conditions. Information on snowfall is surprisingly scant for much of the High Sierra, and the apparent drop-off in precipitation above 6000 feet may well turn out to be illusory once adequate data is available.

Moist Pacific air masses forced upward over the Sierra during the winter are cooled to such an extent that they precipitate most of their moisture content as snow on the west slope. Consequently, the east slope of the range receives comparatively little precipitation—only 10 to 30 inches a year (25 to 75 centimeters). Indeed, the aridity of the Great Basin, which extends from the base of the Sierra eastward to the Rockies, can be attributed largely to this "rain shadow" cast by the Sierra.

Not only do air masses passing over the Sierra bring comparatively little moisture to the east slope of the range, they also rob the region of what precious little moisture it may already have. Once past the crest these air masses begin to sink somewhat, growing warmer in the process. As a result their vapor capacity increases and they are able to absorb greater amounts of moisture, not only from the atmosphere—causing clouds to dissipate—but from the surfaces of soil and vegetation as well.

A notable exception to the decline in precipitation experienced on the east slope occurs in the Mammoth Lakes region in the central part of the range. Here storms move through a significant gap in the crest, bringing an annual snowfall that may approach 500 inches (1270 cm). The conifer forest here extends well downslope to cover lands that anywhere else along the east side would be dominated by desert vegetation.

The Sierra Snowpack

The first snows of autumn are usually light, and because the ground is still warm, melt within a few days—or hours. By mid-November the ground is normally cool enough for snow to persist. The snowpack increases during the winter months and reaches maximum depth in mid-March, at which time storms usually begin to taper off and the rate of melting surpasses that of accumulation.

SNOW CRYSTALS Though most people think of snowflakes as flat, hexagonal stars—which, indeed, they often are—many other shapes also occur: plates, columns, needles, and irregular crystals (see Figure 51). Snow forms when precipitation occurs at or below freezing. The shape and size of the crystals depends on combined conditions of air temperature and humidity, both at the time of formation and en route to earth.

Snow crystals may be altered significantly by the air through which they fall. If it is above freezing, for example, they will melt en route and arrive as rain, or perhaps sleet. If the air is cold and moist, they may acquire a coating of ice called *rime*, forming round pellets known as *soft hail* or *graupel*. Snowflakes are about one-tenth as dense as liquid water. Very cold, comparatively dry air such as found over the interior of the continent is most conducive to snowflake formation, and so the Rockies, in the minds of skiers, are "blessed" with especially light, dry—that is, completely frozen—snow. Heavier forms, such as graupel, develop

SYMBOL	EXAMPLE	TYPE OF SOLID PRECIPITATION
		1. Plates
		2. Stars
		3. Columns
		4. Needles
		5. Spatial dendrites
		6. Capped columns
		7. Irregular particles
		8. Graupel, or soft hail
		9. Ice pellets, or sleet
		10. Hail

51. International snow classification.

when the air is moist and at or just below freezing, conditions that more commonly occur in maritime ranges such as the Sierra and Cascades than in the colder, drier interior. Air temperatures during the winter are often low enough in the Sierra, however, for splendid snowflakes to form.

Snowpack Structure

The snowpack is built up layer by layer, each differing in density and texture according to weather conditions at the time it was deposited, the air temperatures thereafter, and the amount of snow subsequently piled on top of it. A layer

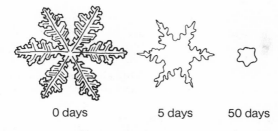

0 days   5 days   50 days

52. Destructive metamorphosis of a snow crystal, showing its
deterioration over a period of 50 days. The process consists
basically of the migration of minute amounts of water vapor from
the extremities of the crystal towards the center, where it
refreezes.

of *new snow* consists of loosely packed crystals. Shortly after
falling to earth the crystals begin to lose their elegant
geometric shapes as vaporization commences at their tips.
Minute amounts of water vapor migrate from the extremities of the crystals toward the more massive centers,
where it refreezes to form more rounded particles. These
are able to settle more closely together and form a denser,
more compact mass. After weeks or months of progressive
deterioration, coarse, granular *old snow* is produced. (*Powder snow*, beloved of skiers, is a transitional stage between
new and old snow.) Additional layers of snow compress
those beneath them, and after years of accumulation and
compaction, the snow crystals are converted to glacial ice.
In the Sierra this process, known as *destructive metamor-
phism*, does not currently progress to the final stage, for
under the climatic conditions now prevailing snow does not
remain on the slopes throughout the year.

Heat Exchange at the Snow Surface

The snowpack continues to build so long as the rate of
accumulation exceeds that of melting. (Evaporation occurs
only to a limited extent in the Sierra and is usually balanced
by condensation.) The temperature of the snow surface
fluctuates, but never exceeds the freezing point of water. If
additional heat is applied, the surface retreats, through
melting, but its temperature always remains at or below
freezing. The snowpack gains heat primarily from solar

radiation and the air moving over its surface. Rainfall also supplies heat, but is much less important in this regard.

EDDY CONDUCTION If the air is cooler than the snow surface, the latter will become cooler, that is, it will lose heat to the air. Conversely, if the air is warmer, it loses heat to the snow, the temperature of which may be raised enough for melting to occur. (Melting would not occur if the temperature of the snow were raised only, say, to 30° F.) When the air over the snow surface is calm, the amount of heat exchanged between the two is quite small. When the air begins to move, the amount of heat exchanged increases directly with wind speed, a phenomenon known as *eddy conduction*. A warm, dry wind is the most efficient medium for melting snow, but over the long run, in the Sierra at least, is less important in this regard than solar radiation. Scattered trees warmed by the sun are also efficient melters of snow because they re-radiate their absorbed heat.

SOLAR RADIATION The sun supplies heat to the snow surface in two forms: visible sunlight and infrared radiation. Snow absorbs virtually all of the infrared radiation it receives, but may lose it just as readily. On clear days the snow surface loses more than it receives. On overcast days it loses infrared radiation to the clouds if they are cooler, as they usually are in midwinter, and gains it from them if they are warmer, as they increasingly tend to be as summer approaches. The snow surface behaves quite differently to visible radiation than it does to infrared. Newly fallen snow reflects up to 90 percent of the sunlight striking it, but as destructive metamorphosis and other factors increase the irregularity of the snow surface, the amount of light reflected may drop to 60 percent or below.

During the winter the snow surface is seldom exposed to the elements for long because it is quickly covered by new snowfall. Consequently, reflectivity tends to remain high and melting proceeds slowly if at all. Moreover, because of the sun's low position in the winter sky, the amount of heat received by the snowpack in the form of sunlight may actually be less than that lost through the radiation of infrared waves into space; in other words, the snow surface may become cooler even while the sun shines.

From late winter on, however, a number of events that

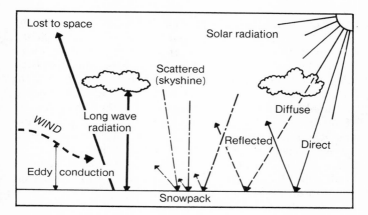

53. Heat exchange at the snow surface.

contribute to the melting of the snowpack begin to come together.

SPRING THAW   After mid-March, as storms taper off in the Sierra, the snow surface is exposed to the elements for increasingly longer periods. Throughout the spring and early summer, melting proceeds rapidly as the snow surface becomes more and more irregular and littered with dirt, leaves, and other debris, all of which reduce its reflectivity at precisely the time when the intensity and duration of sunlight are increasing from day to day. As air temperatures rise, greater amounts of snow also melt as a result of eddy conduction. In addition, spring storms tend to be warmer than those arriving earlier in the year, so rainfall becomes more common as summer approaches. Rain furthers melting not only by warming the snow surface, but by increasing its irregularity. Clouds accompanying such storms also tend to be warmer than the snow surface, which therefore gains additional heat in the form of infrared radiation. As melting continues through the spring, water accumulating on the snow surface heats the layer just beneath or trickles downslope, creating ridges, gullies, and other irregularities.

Spring thaw proceeds from lower to higher elevations, working its way upslope from mid-March to mid-July, when the last snow usually disappears from the higher peaks and basins. At any given elevation, open areas and warm, south-facing slopes are the first to be free of snow; dense forests and cool, shady northern exposures, the last. From one to four inches (2.5 to 10 centimeters) of snow melt each day, supplying from one-half to two inches of water (1.25 to 5 centimeters). Every little ditch and gully becomes a channel for runoff. Even gopher holes may spout water. Flooding downslope may occur if the melting proceeds too rapidly, but not so often as formerly because most of the major rivers are now interrupted by one or more reservoirs. May and June are the best months for viewing the famous waterfalls of Yosemite Valley, which then are swollen with meltwater.

The rate of melting varies from year to year, of course, depending on the depth of the snowpack, the frequency of spring storms, and the warmth of the season. After the winter of 1978, for example, a year of heavy snowfall in the Sierra, good-size drifts remained in the high country throughout the summer. At the other extreme, in the spring of 1976, following the second driest winter on record for California, Humphreys Basin, at about 11,000 feet (3350 meters) in the central Sierra, was largely free of snow by mid-May.

Snow Features and Phenomena

ROTTEN SNOW During the spring, meltwater coursing through the snowpack may carve out substantial cavities that are not apparent at the surface. The snow above these cavities eventually collapses, often prematurely under the weight of unwary skiers or early-summer hikers.

The term "rotten snow" also applies to recrystallized particles known as *depth hoar*. In the cold days of early winter the surface of a shallow snow layer may well be much colder than that of the ground, which usually stays at the freezing point. The sharp difference in temperature from relatively warm ground to cold snow surface over a short distance causes *constructive metamorphosis* of the snow crystals. Water distills upward to form large, cup-shaped hexagonal crystals, which are structurally unstable and tend to collapse rather easily. It is by no means certain that depth hoar occurs in the Sierra. The snowpack at Donner Summit, for example, is isothermal, that is, its temperature is constant from the ground to the surface and the sharp temperature gradient essential to the formation of depth hoar is lacking.

CORN SNOW Partial melting during the day followed by refreezing at night produces large, rounded grains called *corn snow*. It is most common during the spring, when daytime temperatures are fairly warm while nighttime temperatures continue to fall below freezing.

SNOW CRUSTS When melting of the snow surface during the day completely melts the upper layer of crystals, the resulting sheet of water may freeze at night to form a *meltwater crust*. Winds also produce snow crusts through blowing and breaking up surface crystals, which then resettle more compactly than before.

RIME AND HOARFROST Rime is a deposit of frozen water droplets that may encrust the surfaces of objects exposed to the wind. Hoarfrost is produced by the sublimation of water vapor in the air onto various surfaces. It is distinguished from rime by its pronounced crystalline structure.

SUNCUPS Scalloped snow surfaces—called *suncups*— are produced by uneven heating and melting. Suncups usually form on warm, clear days as dry air moves over a snowfield where surface irregularities have already developed to some degree. The raised areas diminish as a result of evaporation caused by the wind, while the hollows, protected from the wind, are melted by solar radiation. Since several times more heat is required to evaporate than melt a given amount of snow, the high points on the snow surface diminish less rapidly than the hollows. As a result, surface irregularities are steadily accentuated until distinct scallops form. They may approach three feet in depth, presenting a tedious obstacle to travel.

CORNICES Overhanging lips of snow often develop on the brinks of leeward cliffs and mountain walls as a result of drifting caused by the wind. These *cornices* build up layer by layer, extending outward gradually and curving downward in response to gravity. Cornices may be hard and stable or soft and prone to breaking away from the mountain. Unstable cornices pose a severe hazard for mountaineers, since the danger may not be readily apparent. Some cor-

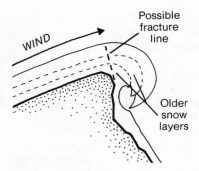

54. Snow cornice.

nices can bear considerable weight and will persist throughout the winter, but anyone untrained in snow mountaineering should stay well back on what is known to be solid ground. Falling cornices often generate avalanches.

PINK, OR WATERMELON, SNOW During the late spring and early summer, portions of snowbanks may be stained a bright watermelon pink. The color is derived from algae living in the snow. These minute plant organisms are actually green, but they secrete a pink, gelatinous coating around themselves, perhaps as protection against the extremely intense solar radiation of their chosen environment. Pink snow is uncommon in the winter, for some melting must occur in order to provide the algae with water. One should not eat pink snow, since it is a pronounced laxative.

AVALANCHES Avalanche danger is high in the Sierra, where deep snows, steep slopes, and frequent warm days during the spring and early summer combine to create instability in the snow pack. Avalanches consist of either large slabs or loose snow. Slab avalanches occur when upper layers of snow break away *en masse* from a layer of rotten snow beneath them. Loose-snow avalanches usually occur on very steep slopes where the weight of accumulated snow finally succumbs to gravity. Or they may occur when over-developed cornices break away. Avalanches may also be classed as airborne—as when a cornice falls—or surficial. Although avalanches are commonplace, there is little data on what types are most common in the Sierra.

Sierra Summers

Although snow still lies thick on the ground in mid-April, many Sierra animals emerge from winter burrows at this time. Mule deer begin to move upslope from their winter quarters in the lowlands, following the retreating snow line in their quest for nutritious young plant shoots. The black oaks in Yosemite Valley and elsewhere on the lower west slope begin to leaf out in May. Wildflowers form great swatches of color in the foothill grasslands, and near the crest of the range mountain alders bloom and fat buds on willows and aspens threaten to burst.

The ice on subalpine lakes normally begins to break up around the middle of May, melting first along the shoreline to form huge flat icebergs in the middle of the lakes. At night downslope winds push the floating ice toward one end of a lake. During the day upslope winds blow it toward the opposite end. The ice will have melted entirely by mid-

	Cooling		Warming
mid-60s	↑	ICE	↑
40-foot thermocline	40°F (4.5°C)	32° (0°C)	40°F (4.5°C)
45°F (7°C)	↓	↓ 40°F (4.5°C)	↓
AUGUST	OCTOBER	JANUARY	JUNE

55. Thermal circulation of lake water. High Sierra lakes exhibit seasonal temperature stratification. During the summer a comparatively warm, light layer of water sits on top of a cooler, heavier layer that begins abruptly at a depth of about 40 ft (10 m). As air temperatures drop in the fall, the surface waters cool more rapidly until for a time the entire lake is about 40° F (4.5° C), the point at which water is heaviest. Continued cooling of the surface water results in ice formation. At this time the water is coolest and lightest just beneath the ice, warmest and heaviest at the bottom. After the ice melts in late spring the surface waters warm up, and wind-driven waves encourage circulation until for a time the entire lake is about 40° F once again.

Sierra Summers

June, though clear, thin layers will continue to form each morning into early summer on the still, shallow waters along the shore.

Summer Weather

Summer in the Sierra begins in earnest in July, the hottest month of the year. Snow has melted from all but the highest peaks and basins. The lakes are free of ice. And backpackers almost equal the hordes of mosquitos. A typical July day in the Sierra begins with clear skies. The air is still nippy right after sunrise, but quickly warms up. Around midmorning valley breezes begin to blow upslope toward the crest, and puffy, isolated cumulus clouds lazily float eastward. The surfaces of glacial lakes ripple in response to the wind. On many days, if air movement aloft is slight, the cumulus clouds formed by the upslope movement of valley winds will begin to gather together by mid-afternoon, casting broad shadows over meadows and lake basins. The air cools rapidly as the clouds pass overhead, warming immediately with the return of the sun.

Sierra summers tend to be warmer and drier than those of the Cascades or northern Rockies, but somewhat cooler and moister than those of comparable mountain ranges to the east and in Southern California. Less than 5 percent of the range's total annual precipitation falls during the summer months; consequently, the amount of solar radiation falling on the range is comparatively high, since cloud cover is sparse.

The mean maximum temperature for July in Yosemite Valley (elevation 3966 feet/1209 meters) is about 90° F (32° C), falling to the low 50s at night. Temperatures on the warmest day of the month typically exceed 100° F (38° C, and on the coldest night drop only into the high 30s. Even near 10,000 feet elevation (3000 meters) summertime temperatures in the Sierra are warm enough to be comfortable. For example, the mean maximum temperature for July at Ellery Lake (elevation 9489 feet/2892 meters), about 20 miles northeast of Yosemite Valley is nearly 68° F (20° C); the mean minimum, about 42° F (5.6° C). Temperatures on the warmest day of the month at Ellery Lake normally range into the low 80s. On the coldest night of the month, however, they may drop to the mid-20s.

Thunderstorms

Summer thunderstorms are fairly common in the Sierra during July and August, but only when the air rising up-slope contains sufficient moisture and when the vertical movement of air aloft exceeds the wind speed. Under such conditions, puffy cumulus clouds may collect along the crest of the range, piling up to form towering cumulonimbus clouds, or thunderheads. The top of a thunderhead commonly reaches 25,000 to 30,000 feet (7600 to 9150 meters), flattening out against the troposphere (see Figure 37) to produce the anvil shape typical of such clouds.

The rising warm air in a thunderhead replaces cooler air aloft, which begins to sink. This sinking air blows out of the bottom of the cloud, forming the cool, gusty wind that often precedes a thunderstorm. The entire process of thunderhead formation is often extremely rapid, taking only 15 to 20 minutes for scattered cumulus clouds to mass together and pile upward. In the Sierra this usually takes place between two and three o'clock in the afternoon, sometimes later.

LIGHTNING   For reasons still not understood, a thunderhead acts like an electric generator, with positively charged particles in its upper portion and negatively charged ones in the lower. Electrical current flowing between these poles is called *sheet lightning* because it is experienced as a flash rather than a stroke. *Fork lightning*, which actually consists of several strokes spaced about 1/1000 of a second apart, is a giant, visible, electric current passing from the lower, negatively charged portion of the cloud to the positively charged earth below. Lightning tends to take the shortest route between two poles, so mountaintops and trees are frequent targets. Anyone caught in a thunderstorm in the High Sierra should avoid high, exposed ridges and tall trees. The magnitude of the danger can be appreciated by realizing that lightning generates more than 100 million volts.

Along the course of a lightning stroke, whether within

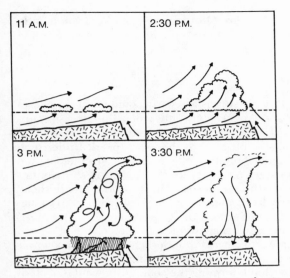

| 11 A.M. | 2:30 P.M. |
| 3 P.M. | 3:30 P.M. |

56. Formation of a summer thunderstorm in the Sierra. The times indicated are merely approximate and are intended only to convey a typical interval for the events shown. For a description of these events, see the text.

the cloud or from cloud to ground, the air is for a micro-second heated to 15,000° C, causing it to expand and contract violently, which produces the tremendous explosions of thunder. The rumbling or rolling effect occurs because sound waves emanating from various points along the lightning track reach our ears at slightly different times. One can calculate how far away a lightning strike has occurred by estimating the number of seconds that elapse between the flash and the following thunder. Since sound travels about 1100 feet per second through air (335 meters per second), a 10-second lapse between flash and thunder would mean that the lightning struck about 11,000 feet (1100 × 10), or two miles away (3.2 kilometers). If the lightning is more than 18 miles away (29 kilometers), the thunder will not be heard, owing to the dissipation of the sound waves over such a distance.

HAIL AND RAIN   About the time lightning and thunder begin, water vapor in the rising air is cooled to form large drops, and rain or hail starts to fall. Hail forms when temperatures in the upper part of the cloud are cold enough to freeze the drops and when updrafts are strong enough to swirl falling hail back upward repeatedly. On each ascent the hail grows larger by the addition of another layer of ice. Hailstones fall out of the cloud when they become so large and heavy that the updrafts can no longer support them.

Precipitation generally lasts between 15 and 30 minutes, after which the thunderhead begins to dissipate as the frictional drag caused by the precipitation sets up a strong downdraft. At this stage lightning activity reaches a climax, and the top of the cloud may reach 40,000 feet altitude (12,200 meters) or more, often flattening out against the tropopause. When the downdraft finally prevails over the movement of air upward, precipitation stops because air is no longer being cooled. In turn, the end of precipitation diminishes the downdraft, and the thunderhead begins to dissipate into scattered cloudlets floating downwind. The entire storm may take less than an hour and will almost certainly be followed by bright skies and calm, cool evenings.

Thunderstorms often occur only locally, and people sitting on one ridge can watch the lightning dance on another a couple of miles away. At other times, a storm may cover a vast area and carry on violently for the entire afternoon. This is typically the case when tropical storms move north from Mexico during the summer. Although they may bring little precipitation to the lowlands, their movement up the west slope of the Sierra often generates rains that may last several days. Such storms freshen the landscape and reinvigorate small streams, at least for a time, but because of their infrequency they do little to relieve the drought characteristic of Sierra summers. Even the precipitation delivered by normal afternoon thundershowers does little in this regard.

Waiting for Winter

Many veteran Sierra wanderers consider autumn the most beautiful season in which to visit the range. After Labor Day the number of visitors drops off markedly, and though nights grow increasingly cool as the season progresses, daytime temperatures may continue to be warm well into October or later. Thunderstorms become less common as summer turns into fall, and September and October typically bring a long succession of clear, brilliant days in which every object in the landscape, from the highest peaks to the smallest stones, is thrown into dramatic relief by the low autumnal sun. The predominant green of the forest and gray of the granite is accented by patches of bronze and gold from the turning leaves of aspen, cottonwood, maple, and willow. The pace of life slows down as many animals, having completed their preparations for the coming winter, seek out warmer quarters in logs, rockpiles, burrows, or holes in trees. Deer slowly make their way downslope to winter quarters. Bighorn sheep leave the high country for the sagebrush steppe of the eastern slope. Migratory birds head south or downslope to the valleys and foothills on both sides of the range. The days are quiet as life everywhere retreats and waits.

CHAPTER IV

The Mountain Environment: An Ecological Overview

ALL FORMS OF LIFE rely ultimately on the ability of green plants to convert the radiant energy of sunlight into the chemical energy of carbohydrates. Plants—the *producers*—use these carbohydrates, along with other substances, to manufacture proteins, which thus become available to *herbivores,* or *primary consumers.* The herbivores, in turn, supply protein to the *carnivores,* or *secondary consumers.* Green plants, herbivores, and carnivores each constitute what ecologists call a *trophic* ("nutrition") *level,* and these levels together compose a *food chain.*

Eating is the means by which energy is transferred from one level to the next, but as in other forms of energy exchange, a certain amount is lost in the process as waste heat. It has been estimated that herbivores and carnivores alike are able to utilize on the average only about 10 percent of the energy stored in the food they eat. In other words, of 100 calories of plant production, an herbivore obtains only 10 calories on the average, and a carnivore only one. Thus a large number of plants are necessary to support a single mule deer, and a great many deer to maintain a single lion. This relationship is usually expressed as a pyramid of decreasing numbers.

Decomposer organisms such as fungi and bacteria complete the cycle. The remains of plants and animals alike provide food for decomposer organisms, which in the process of digestion synthesize compounds essential to plant nutrition. Through performing the absolutely essential ecological function of recycling the nutrients bound up in organic materials, decomposers, in a very real sense, make continuing life possible on earth. They convert not only litter but sewage into useable forms.

Nature thus seems to be organized into dynamic systems—*ecosystems*—designed to obtain energy, give it form, and pass it on. The prefix *eco-* is derived from a Greek root, *oikos,* meaning "household." Ecosystems are nature's households, and the branch of biology devoted to their study is *ecology.* Ecosystems consist of organisms and their physical environment, which includes conditions of climate, moisture availability, and soil. Although no single strand connects all elements in an ecosystem, all are ultimately linked in a vast web of mutual accommodation. The enormous variety and complexity apparent in nature seems

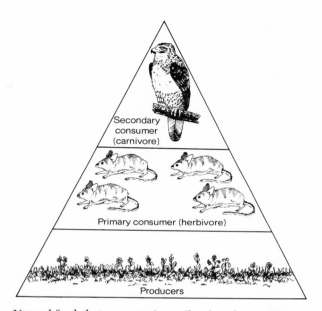

57. Natural food chains consist basically of producers (plants), which obtain energy from the sun; primary consumers (herbivores), which obtain it by eating the plants; and secondary consumers (carnivores), which obtain it by eating the herbivores and/or one another. Since energy is lost in the transfer from one trophic ("eating") level to the next, the number of consumers that can be supported at each successive level diminishes. Thus, it takes a large number of plants to support only a few deer mice, and several mice to feed a single hawk (the numbers shown here should not be taken literally). As evidenced by the diagram, this relationship is commonly depicted as a pyramid of decreasing numbers. Not shown are the fungi and bacteria that feed off the remains of plants and animals alike, returning nutrients to the soil and thus helping plants begin the cycle anew.

to be essential to the stability of ecosystems, for the greater the number of strands in a web, the less critical is the loss or malfunction of any single one.

The specific environment in which an organism lives is its habitat, which is defined by climatic, edaphic, physiographic, and biotic factors. *Climatic* factors include air temperature, precipitation, humidity, wind, and the like.

Edaphic factors refer to soil conditions, including texture, moisture, chemical composition, and the bedrock from which soils are derived. *Physiographic* factors include geographic location, altitude, and local topography, all of which profoundly affect climate. Since each living component in an ecosystem affects and is affected by others, the habitat for any single plant or animal also includes other organisms living with it—the *biotic* factor.

Basic Plant Processes

Green plants, through the process of *photosynthesis*, provide the primary means by which the energy of the sun is made available to all other forms of life. In this process sunlight is absorbed by chlorophyll, the green pigment present in the leaves of plants, and the energy thus obtained is used to synthesize carbohydrates—which fuel growth and reproduction—from carbon dioxide and water. The process in which plant cells burn the carbohydrates thus produced is called *respiration*, which is analogous to respiration in animals. Oxygen is an important by-product of photosynthesis.

Plants require moisture, which they derive primarily from the soil, not only for photosynthesis but also to maintain *turgor*, the quality of firmness characteristic of cells. Water is also the medium through which plants obtain nutrients from the soil and circulate them to stems and leaves. Plants having specialized tissues to circulate water are known as *vascular plants*, as opposed to others, such as algae and fungi, in which each cell absorbs moisture directly from the outside environment. Water obtained from the soil by the roots of vascular plants passes upward through the stems to the leaves, where it is released to the atmosphere through minute cellular openings known as *stomata*. This process is called *transpiration*.

Through transpiration, plants rid themselves of waste products and make way for the circulation of additional nutrient-rich water. The evaporation of moisture from leaf surfaces also serves to cool plant tissues. Stomatal transpiration accounts for almost all of the water loss experienced by plants. In addition, a tiny fraction is also transpired directly through the *cuticle*, or skin, of plants.

When the amount of water lost through transpiration exceeds the amount absorbed by the roots, plants are subject to moisture stress. If the water deficit drops below a certain point, which varies from one species to another, a plant loses turgor—it wilts. Wilting involves a collapse of structure within the cells, and though all plants can withstand a certain amount of wilting and still survive, prolonged moisture stress may cause the cells to lose their resilience permanently so that even if additional water is forthcoming they will not be able to recover their turgidity.

Plant Communities

One need not be trained in ecology to understand that the vegetation patterns evident in natural landscapes—the arrangements of forest, meadow, marsh, woodland, grassland, desert scrub, and the like—are not accidental, but reflect (1) the availability of particular kinds of plants in a given region, and (2) geographic variations in climate, soil, and other environmental factors as they have evolved over prolonged periods of time ranging from a few decades to millions of years. Wherever certain habitats occur, certain plants are consistently found growing together, their association reflecting mutual accommodations to competing needs in the light of available resources. Thus, we can recognize different habitats by the kinds of plants growing there. Associations of this kind are called *plant communities*, and the natural vegetation of any given region typically consists of several plant communities arranged according to local patterns of soil and climate. Such arrangements are known as *vegetation mosaics*, a term that draws an analogy between natural patterns and those apparent in the contrasting shapes and colors of mosaic tiles.

No landscape is entirely uniform, not even the sagebrush flats of the Great Basin or the rolling grasslands of the High Plains. Studies of the former, for example, have revealed several distinct communities that to most observers would

Plant Communities

pass unnoticed. Variation in vegetation is most pronounced in rugged terrain because of the profound impact topography has on local climates. Several vegetation mosaics are apparent in the Sierra and are described more fully in later sections of this guide. For purposes of illustrating the concept, however, the pattern of grassland, woodland, and brush found in the Sierra foothills is an excellent example.

Sierra Plant Communities

The concept of plant communities is enormously useful for purposes of discussion and demonstrably corresponds to vegetational units readily observed in nature. But like all human categories, the plant community is ultimately an intellectual construct that at best only approximates reality. Nature is seldom as neatly divided as the idea of a plant community may suggest, and there is always some difficulty in knowing precisely where to draw the boundaries.

For example, within a single Sierran meadow some areas may remain wet throughout the entire growing season, others will have ample moisture only for a few weeks following snowmelt, and still others will fall somewhere between these two extremes. Each site will have some plants it shares with the other two and some that they lack. If one were to record the kinds and abundance of species on each type of site, one would discover both differences and similarities among them with regard to floristic composition, which raises a difficult question. Should wet, moist, and dry meadows be considered separate plant communities based on their demonstrable differences? Or should they merely be considered local variations within a single larger community?

If a plant community is too broadly defined, important differences among its components may be obscured. For example, if the entire Sierra coniferous forest were considered to be a single community—which no one assumes, by the way—the profound ecological and floristic differences between, say, the mixed coniferous forest and subalpine forest would have to be ignored.

If a plant community is too narrowly defined, important and useful similarities among closely related formations

Table 5: Plant Communities of the Sierra Nevada

This Book	Munz[1]	Niehaus[2]	Ornduff[3]	Storer & Usinger[4]
Valley Grassland	Valley Grassland	Foothill Grassland	Valley Grassland	Dry Grassland
Chaparral	Chaparral	Chaparral	Chaparral	Foothill Chaparral
Foothill Woodland	Foothill Woodland	Foothill Woodland	Valley and Foothill Woodland	Pine–Oak Woodland
Riparian Woodland			Riparian Woodland	Streamside Woodland
Mixed Coniferous Forest	Yellow Pine Forest	Mixed Coniferous Forest	Montane Forest	Mountain Conifer Forest
Red Fir Forest	Red Fir Forest	Subalpine Forest		
Lodgepole Pine Forest	Lodgepole Pine Forest			
Subalpine Forest	Subalpine Forest		Subalpine Forest	Subalpine Forest
Montane Chaparral			Montane Chaparral	Mountain Chaparral
Montane Meadow		Mountain Meadow	Montane Meadow	Meadow
Rock Outcrops				Rocky Areas
Alpine Meadow and Rock Communities	Alpine Fell Fields	Alpine	Alpine Fell Field	Rocky Areas and Alpine Meadow
Pinyon–Juniper Woodland	Pinyon–Juniper Woodland	Pinyon–Juniper Woodland	Pinyon–Juniper Woodland	Juniper Woodland
Sagebrush Scrub	Sagebrush Scrub	Sagebrush Scrub	Sagebrush Scrub	Sagebrush

[1] Philip A. Munz and David D. Keck, *A California Flora and Supplement* (Berkeley: University of California Press, 1968).
[2] Theodore Niehaus, *Sierra Wildflowers* (Berkeley: University of California Press, 1974).
[3] Robert Ornduff, *Introduction to California Plant Life* (Berkeley: University of California Press, 1974).
[4] Tracy I. Storer and Robert L. Usinger, *Sierra Nevada Natural History* (Berkeley: University of California Press, 1964).

may be overlooked. It is not surprising that ecologists have not adopted a uniform system of classifying plant communities. Those who prefer to emphasize broad similarities among several units of vegetation tend to recognize larger, more varied plant communities than those who place greater stock in differences.

Several systems have been applied to the vegetation of the Sierra, each with its particular biases but all of them workable. In some instances the systems differ only in the names used. In others the variations reflect substantive differences of opinion regarding the relative importance of criteria used to distinguish one community from another. For most readers it is enough merely to know how one system roughly translates into another so that no confusion will arise from comparing several sources. Table 5 compares four prominent systems with the one used in this guide. The latter was selected because it includes all the communities found in other sources.

A Key to Sierra Plant Communities

The following key is provided to assist readers in the field identification of Sierra plant communities, This key is applicable only in a general way, and ambiguities may arise in places where climax vegetation has been disturbed by natural or human causes or in places where community boundaries overlap. Moreover, the criteria used here for identification are not the only, or even necessarily the most important, ones by which Sierra plant communities are distinguished. They are, however, those easiest for an untrained observer to use in the field.

To identify a community, begin at 1a and if it applies proceed to the chapter and section indicated. If it does not, continue on to 1b and then to the number indicated. Proceed in this fashion through the key until you have identified the community in question.

    1a. Vegetation at or above timberline; trees dwarfed or absent. See **Alpine Communities**, Chapter VII.

      1b. Vegetation below timberline. *Go to 2*.

      2a. Dominant plants are grasslike. *Go to 3*.

      2b. Dominant plants are shrubs or trees. *Go to 4*.

3a. Community below the coniferous forest belt, west slope. See **Valley Grassland**, Chapter V.

3b. Community within the coniferous forest belt, mostly above 6000 feet (1800 meters), both slopes. See **Montane Meadow**, Chapter VI.

4a. Dominant plants are shrubs. *Go to 5*.

4b. Dominant plants are trees. *Go to 7*.

5a. Community below coniferous forest belt. *Go to 6*.

5b. Community, within coniferous forest belt, mostly above 6000 feet. See **Montane Chaparral**, Chapter VI.

6a. West slope. See **Chaparral**, Chapter V.

6b. East slope. See **Sagebrush Scrub**, Chapter VIII.

7a. Dominant trees are broad-leaved, either evergreen or deciduous. *Go to 8*.

7b. Dominant trees are conifers. *Go to 9*.

8a. Streamside woodland below main forest, west slope. See **Riparian Woodland**, Chapter V.

8b. Broadleaf woodland away from streams, below main forest, west slope. See **Foothill Woodland**, Chapter V.

9a. Coniferous woodland below main forest, east slope; pines are large rounded shrubs or small trees; stands consist primarily of open groves scattered amongst sagebrush. See **Pinyon–Juniper Woodland**, Chapter VIII.

9b. Coniferous forest, both slopes. Identification of the four major types of coniferous-forest community found in the Sierra depends largely on recognition of the dominant trees in each. To identify these trees refer to the figures listed below, which depict the cones and needles of each species and include a description of other identifying characteristics. *Go to 10*.

10a. Dominant trees are ponderosa pine (Fig. 130), Jeffrey pine (Fig. 142), white fir (Fig. 136), or a combination thereof. Sugar pine (Fig. 137), incense cedar (Fig. 135), black oak (Fig. 131), or giant sequoia (Fig. 141) may be locally abundant. See **Mixed-coniferous Forest**, Chapter VI.

10b. Dominant tree is lodgepole pine (Fig. 152). See **Lodgepole Pine Forest**, Chapter VI.

10c. Dominant tree is red fir (Fig. 144). See **Red Fir Forest**, Chapter VI.

10d. Dominant trees are whitebark pine (Fig. 155), mountain hemlock (Fig. 157), or foxtail pine (Fig. 156). See **Subalpine Forest**, Chapter VI.

Ecological Tolerance

Plant communities reflect variations in habitat as they affect the distribution of species making up the local flora. Each species has its own particular set of environmental requirements, its unique ranges of tolerance for sunlight, heat, water, nutrients, and numerous other commodities supplied by its habitat. Some plants tolerate a wide range of conditions and therefore are able to occupy a variety of habitats. Others are able to survive only within certain narrow limits. All plants, however, are able to grow only where the environment supplies neither too much nor too little of all the elements essential to their survival.

The distribution of a particular kind of organism is controlled by the environmental factor for which it has the narrowest range of tolerance. Lodgepole pine, for example, a common subalpine conifer in the Sierra, requires full sunlight at all stages of growth but is able to tolerate a wide range of soil moisture. Sunlight is therefore the more critical factor limiting its distribution. Different species of plants occuring together do not necessarily have identical tolerance ranges, merely overlapping requirements that are satisfied by the habitats they share, and one species' tolerance for a given factor is modified by the presence of other plants that are better competitors for that factor. Lodgepole pine does not normally grow on the best-watered soils in the Sierra, but red fir does, and the lodgepole is found on the driest and wettest sites, from which red fir is absent. The two species grow together, however, on sites where their preferred habitats overlap.

Dominance

Plants compete for light, heat, moisture, and nutrients, and since these are never sufficiently plentiful to allow for the maximum development of all the plants in a community, some are severely handicapped by the comparatively

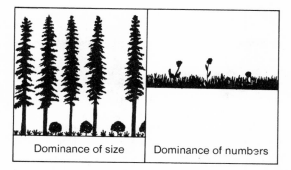

| Dominance of size | Dominance of numbers |

58. Trees dominate woodland and forest communities because their size affects the amount of sun, wind, precipitation, soil moisture, and nutrients received by other plants around them. Grasses and sedges dominate meadows by virtue of sheer numbers.

greater efficiency with which others are able to exploit their shared habitat. The resulting process of selection determines the particular mix of species occurring in each community, as well as the location of the community with respect to others.

Competition is most rigorous where one or more of the environmental commodities essential to plant growth is in short supply. On arid soils such as occur above timberline and on the east slope of the Sierra, for example, the spacing of plants reflects adjustments among them with respect to available moisture. Seedlings attempting to establish themselves on bare soil among older plants will probably die, victims to the more extensive root systems of their neighbors. The greater the deficiency of any single environmental commodity in a given habitat, the fewer the species able to grow there. Above timberline, heat, soil, and moisture are all in short supply, so fewer species of both plants and animals inhabit the alpine zone than any other in the Sierra.

Some plants exert a greater influence on the character of a community than others, and their removal would be tantamount to destroying the community entirely. Such plants are the *dominant* species of that community. For example, if fire removes all the red firs from a stand of red fir forest, the community ceases to exist and is replaced by another one. But if the common wildflower mountain pennyroyal were to disappear from the red fir forest, the overall character and operation of the community would remain the same.

In communities such as forest or woodlands, which are characterized by plants of varying height, the tallest are usually the dominants because they profoundly affect the amount of moisture, heat, and light available to the plants beneath them. (For examples of how forest trees affect the environment of associated plants, see Forest Influences, page 172.) Trees, therefore, are commonly dominants wherever they occur. In grasslands, chaparral, meadows, and other communities in which most plants are more or less the same height—including forests comprising several species of comparable size—community dominants are usually the species represented by the largest number of individuals. Their abundance is a measure of their success in utilizing the habitat and is responsible for the distinctive appearance of the community.

By virtue of their success, community dominants limit the sites available to other plants and alter the environment in ways that affect the kinds and distribution of plants associated with them. The sedges and grasses that dominate Sierra meadows, for example, reproduce vegetatively by means of aggressive underground shoots called *rhizomes*. A rhizome extending from one plant develops buds along its length from which others of its kind—*clones,* or genetic replicas of the first—sprout and push upward through the soil surface. Meadow soils support elaborate networks of rhizomes—as do home lawns—which tightly bind individual soil particles, thereby reducing the air spaces between them. Consequently, meadow soils tend to drain slowly and because of their high moisture content are cooler than others. They are also oxygen poor because most of the spaces between the soil particles are filled with water instead. Moreover, the dense sods formed by meadow plants prevent young shoots from penetrating the soil surface and thereby may even inhibit the growth of species otherwise able to tolerate meadow soils. In short, numerous species of plants are unable to colonize meadow sites largely because of the ways in which the dominant sedges and grasses modify the habitat to suit their own needs.

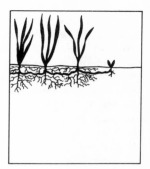

59. Most species of grass and sedge found in Sierra meadows reproduce by means of rhizomes, underground shoots that sprout new plants. This method is much more rapid and dependable than reliance on seeds, an important advantage in the High Sierra's short growing season.

Ecotones

Adjacent communities usually share several species in common, species whose tolerance ranges allow them to exist with varying degrees of success in both. The community dominants will be different, however, and a species dominant in one may be a subordinate in the other. Ponderosa pine, for example, is a codominant with white fir in the mixed coniferous forest, but also occurs locally in the foothill woodland and chaparral. Shorthair sedge, the dominant species in the dry-meadow community of the High Sierra, commonly forms a sparse ground cover beneath lodgepole pines and occurs as a subordinate member of wetter meadow types dominated by other sedges. Sagebrush dominates vast tracts throughout the Great Basin but also occurs as an understory shrub in the pinyon–juniper woodland and in several east-slope forest communities.

Community boundaries, though sometimes rather abrupt, more often reflect gradual environmental changes in the landscape. Consequently, a certain degree of blending usually characterizes community boundaries, with representatives from each side occupying a zone of overlap, or *ecotone*. Where forest meets meadow, for example, meadow sedges, grasses, and wildflowers commonly intermingle with scattered young trees, shrubs, and wildflowers from the forest. Animals characteristic of each community are also likely to meet along the ecotone. The resulting mixture of organisms may actually be richer in species than either community by itself, for dominants exert considerably less influence in ecotones, where conditions, though tolerable, are seldom optimal for their development. The species found in ecotones are usually among those from both communities that have the widest ranges of ecologic tolerance.

Ecotones vary in width according to environmental gradients, the rates at which various factors change over a given distance. For example, the savanna of the Sierra foothills, an ecotone between valley grassland and foothill woodland, may be several miles wide, defining a belt in which conditions are not optimal for either community. The boundary between a subalpine meadow and adjacent rock outcrop, in contrast, is usually abrupt, showing little or no overlap in plant species, though animals may range freely between the two. The forest–meadow ecotone may vary in width from a few feet to several yards.

Ecotones may or may not be stable. They represent long-term dynamic balance between adjacent communities or a temporary stage in the invasion of one by the other. Such invasion can occur only when the habitat has in some fashion been altered by outside events. These may be natural, such as landslide, fire, volcanic eruption, and climatic changes, or of human origin, such as logging, road building, trampling of vegetation, introduction of alien plants or animals, and—once again—fire.

Community Succession

The process by which communities replace one another on a given site is called *succession*. The invasion by plants of areas that formerly supported no vegetation whatsoever is

60. *(facing page)* Examples of ecotones in the Sierra Nevada: (A) the grassland–woodland ecotone (savanna) of the western foothills; (B) the forest–meadow ecotone; (C) two riparian ecotones; (D) the meadow–rock outcrop ecotone; and (E) the timberline ecotone.

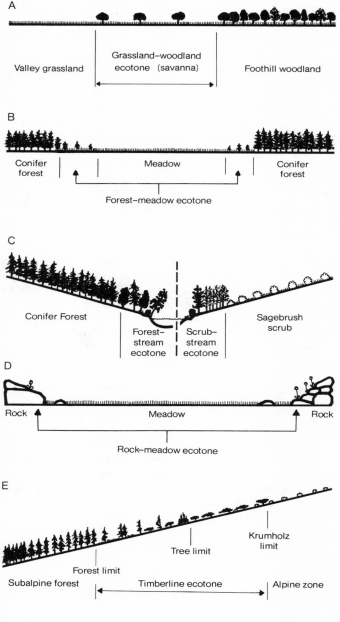

A

Valley grassland   Grassland–woodland ecotone (savanna)   Foothill woodland

B

Conifer forest   Meadow   Conifer forest

Forest–meadow ecotone

C

Conifer Forest   Forest–stream ecotone   Scrub–stream ecotone   Sagebrush scrub

D

Rock   Meadow   Rock

Rock–meadow ecotone

E

Subalpine forest   Forest limit   Tree limit   Krumholz limit   Timberline ecotone   Alpine zone

Plant Communities

called *primary succession.* Examples from the Sierra include the occupation of bare outcrops of rock and the invasion of wet soils around the borders of lakes (see, respectively, Crevice Invasion and Meadow Formation, Chapter VI.) The replacement of one community by another in response to a natural or human disturbance is known as *secondary succession.*

When plants first begin to establish themselves on bare ground, the success of each species is largely controlled by physical factors such as available sunlight, moisture, and soil. As vegetation becomes denser some plants grow taller than others or are able to occupy more space, and the habitat of each plant is increasingly altered by the activities of its neighbors. Dominants gradually emerge as some plants are forced out of the mix or are severely restricted in the sites available to them by the activities of others.

SERES Succession typically involves several stages or *seres* (coined from the word "series") that over a period of time replace one another on a given site. For example, after a fire, burned areas for a time support numerous herbs that in unburned forest stands are absent, or restricted to sunny openings. By removing the dominant trees, fire opens up the forest and allows these sun-loving understory plants to proliferate. The pioneer herbs are soon shaded out by rapidly growing shrubs that reproduce through seeds or sprouts following the fire. For a time shrubs dominate the site, but eventually are replaced in turn by the maturing offspring of dominant forest trees. Each stage—herb, shrub, tree—is a sere in post-fire forest succession.

CLIMAX COMMUNITIES The process of succession ends when the plants occupying a particular site reach a state of equilibrium between their competing needs and the resources available. From then on equilibrium is maintained by community dominants, which, in the ways described earlier, perpetuate the environmental factors conducive to their indefinite occupation of a site. Communities that achieve such stability, so that barring outside changes they will occupy a given habitat indefinitely, are called *climax communities.*

No concept in plant ecology has occasioned more vigorous and long-standing debate than that of the climax community. Virtually all ecologists accept some form of the concept in principle, but disagreements as to its precise definition and application in field work continue to be common. Rather than attempting to summarize the host of complex issues dividing ecologists on this question, this guide will merely indicate the current consensus of opinion regarding the plant communities of the Sierra shown in Table 5. Most authorities agree that foothill woodland, mixed-coniferous forest, red fir forest, subalpine forest, alpine communities, pinyon–juniper woodland, and sagebrush scrub are climax formations. Rock communities may be safely considered seres in the course of primary succession leading from bare rock to climax forest. Montane chaparral is also best considered a transitional community, though it may occupy talus slopes for extremely long periods. The status of valley grassland, chaparral, lodgepole pine forest, and montane meadow remains uncertain.

It should be remembered that a given kind of plant may be a climax species under one set of habitat conditions, but seral under another.

Vegetation Zones

Ascending either slope of the Sierra, one passes through a succession of plant communities, each occupying a particular elevation range. The distribution of Sierra plant communities according to elevation is shown in Figure 61. In the 1890s the eminent American botanist C. Hart Merriam, observing comparable zonation on the slopes of the San Francisco Mountains of northern Arizona, attributed this phenomenon to the effect of altitude on air temperature. Merriam observed that the drop in temperature and change in vegetation encountered in ascending a mountain slope are comparable to those encountered on a journey northward (or southward in the southern hemisphere) toward the pole. He expressed this correlation by means of a system of *"life zones,"* most of which he named for representative geographic regions. Thus, in ascending the Sierra, one travels through a series of temperature–vegetation zones comparable to those encountered on a journey from northern Arizona to the Arctic.

The impact of Merriam's work on the emerging science

of plant ecology was profound, for he gave it a method of classifying vegetation according to environmental principles. The usefulness of the life-zone system was limited, however, because it relied exclusively on air temperature, ignoring equally important factors such as precipitation and soil, as well as locally critical influences such as wind and snow. Furthermore, the vegetational units embraced in Merriam's zones, while superficially similar in most cases, often differed dramatically with regard to ecological and floristic details. For example, life zones could not account for the significant differences in alpine vegetation among the Sierra, Rockies, Cascades, and other ranges, nor between Arctic tundra and alpine vegetation as a whole, all of which were subsumed in a single category, the "arctic–alpine zone."

Nevertheless, some system of zones is useful, if only as a convenient way of referring to particular elevational ranges. The system shown in Figure 61 is more or less comparable to Merriam's but employs names specifically appropriate to the Sierra. It does not imply any particular correlations between the vegetation of the Sierra and that of other mountain ranges or latitudinal belts. Other systems for the Sierra have been devised, but these do not differ substantively from the one used here. Zones, which reflect climatic belts, should not be confused with plant communities, which describe vegetation types composed of particular plant species. A single zone commonly contains several plant communities.

Air Temperature and Vegetation

Major vegetative processes such as photosynthesis, respiration, growth, reproduction, and transpiration are in various degrees sensitive to changes in air temperature. For example, photosynthesis occurs only within a certain range of temperatures, which varies from one species of plant to the next. As elevation increases, plants must be able to carry out photosynthesis at progressively lower temperatures. The upper elevational limit for many plants therefore occurs where air temperatures drop so low that the rate of

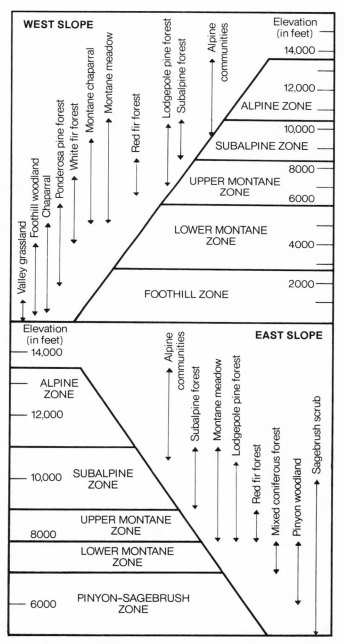

61. Life zones and plant communities of the Sierra Nevada.

photosynthesis is roughly equal to that of respiration. When this happens there is no surplus of carbohydrates to invest in the production of new shoots or in reproduction, both of which are sacrificed to the needs of minimal plant maintenance. Above timberline, for example, air temperatures are too low for trees to carry out photosynthesis at a rate fast enough to support even minimal growth. The dwarf trees characteristic of timberline reflect in part the paucity of carbohydrates available for growth at that elevation and air temperature.

Each species of plant has its own upper elevational limit analogous to timberline, though in any given place the plant may be prevented from attaining this limit by other factors. Plants native to high elevations share an ability to carry out photosynthesis efficiently even at air temperatures approaching the freezing point.

An imbalance between the rates of photosynthesis and respiration can also be crucial in determining the lower elevational limits of plants. As temperatures increase above a certain optimum, which varies from species to species, photosynthesis may decline while respiration continues to rise. Once again, carbohydrates would be burned faster than they could be synthesized.

Frost Damage

Frost damage, a function of air temperature, is a critical factor limiting the upward distribution of mountain plants. When nighttime temperatures fall below freezing, the formation of ice crystals within and around plant cells may cause tissue damage severe enough to kill a plant. The degree of damage depends on several factors, including minimum temperatures, the rate of drop, and how long the subfreezing cold persists. Below roughly 5000 feet (1500 meters) in the northern Sierra and 7000 feet (2150 meters) in the south, temperatures seldom drop below freezing during the summer. As elevation increases, however, nighttime freezes become increasingly common, last longer, and are characterized by lower minimum temperatures. In the subalpine and alpine zones, frosts may occur any night of the year. Because air gains and loses heat more rapidly as it becomes thinner, the disparity between day and night temperatures also tends to increase with elevation, an important factor because the faster temperatures drop, the less time plants have to become adjusted to the change and the greater the likelihood of damage. For example, during the winter thin-barked trees and shrubs sometimes crack because of the sudden formation of ice crystals in the bark and outer woody layers. The crystals force the plant tissues apart in much the same fashion as frost riving in rocks, often with such force that a loud report is produced. Such frost cracks may not themselves be fatal to the plant, but through allowing easy entry to insects or fungi may thereby contribute to the plant's ultimate demise.

The Growing Season

As used in agriculture and horticulture, the term "growing season" has traditionally designated the period between the last killing frost of spring and the first of autumn. This definition is useless, however, in high mountain ranges, where frosts may occur any month of the year. The ability to continue growth despite occasional frosts is a prerequisite for plants inhabiting cold areas.

Nor is the frost-to-frost definition of the growing season particularly applicable to the Sierra foothills, which are subject to summer drought, a more severe restriction on plant growth in this region than frost. The growing season for most foothill plants coincides with the rainy months from autumn through spring. By mid-summer all but the most drought-resistant foothill plants, or those growing near perennial sources of moisture—riverbanks, for example—become dormant and remain so until the arrival of rain in the fall. Trees and shrubs may simply shut down operations for the duration of the dry season; most herbs are annuals which scatter their seeds and die before the drought begins. Since most foothill plants are active during the winter, they are subject to periodic frosts, which they routinely survive.

Above the foothills, persistent winter snow cover shifts the growing season to the summer months. Although the disappearance of snow cover in the spring and its reappearance in the fall determines the outer possible limits of the growing season, the onset and end of growth for most plants is actually triggered by other factors. Each species has particular requirements with regard to such factors as air temperature, soil temperature, soil moisture, and the number of hours of sunlight each day, all of which must be met before dormancy is broken. Plants thereby reduce the possibility of commencing growth too soon—as during a dry winter, when snow might be absent in places but air temperatures and daylight hours insufficient for survival. During a normal winter, it is the rising air temperature, of course, that is primarily responsible for the melting of the snowpack, and this event in turn profoundly affects soil temperatures and moisture levels.

Since air temperatures drop as elevation increases, the growing season also becomes shorter, beginning progressively later and ending progressively earlier as one moves upslope. The length of the growing season for each vegetation zone in the Sierra (including the Central Valley as a point of comparison) is roughly as follows:

Central Valley	7–11 months
Foothill zone	6–10 months
Lower montane zone	4–7 months
Upper montane zone	3–4½ months
Subalpine zone	7–9 weeks
Alpine zone	6–8 weeks
Pinyon–Sagebrush zone	2–5 months

The relatively unimportant role of frost in determining these growing seasons is apparent when one considers that during the 3–4½ months available for plant growth in the upper montane zone, the frost-free period is only 40–70 days long. In the subalpine and alpine zones, there are no frost-free periods.

Although the first permanent snows of autumn mark the latest dates at which plant growth is possible in the upper zones, most species have begun to shut down for the winter by the time the storms arrive. Once again, as with the breaking of dormancy in the spring or early summer, air temperature, soil moisture, and the number of daylight hours are as important as snow in determining its resumption in the late summer or early autumn.

Since the onset of plant growth occurs at progressively later dates as elevation increases, so too does the period of flowering. The best time to see foothill wildflowers is from March through June, with a maximum display occurring in April and May. Forest wildflowers are most abundant in June and July; subalpine and alpine wildflowers, in July and August.

Snow and the Growing Season

The upward distribution of some plants is limited by their inability to withstand prolonged snow cover and by the resulting brief growing season. There is a strong correlation between snow depth and the kinds of plants able to grow on a particular site. The deeper the snowpack, the longer it takes to melt and the less time that remains for plants to complete their cycles of growth and reproduction. Many plants in the foothill and lower montane zones can withstand occasional snows that are not too deep and do not remain on the ground for more than a day or two, but not the deep, persistent snows found at higher elevations. Ponderosa pine, for example, is seldom found where snow is deep. Although the mature pines can tolerate such conditions, the seedlings cannot.

The briefest growing seasons in the Sierra occur on sites beneath or downslope from lingering snow patches, where soils may not be exposed till late July or early August and may remain cold and soggy for the remainder of the summer. Distinctive plant communities, dominated by sedges and a few other rapidly growing species that require constantly moist soils, develop on these snowbeds. Trees are usually absent from such sites partly because cold, wet soils inhibit germination and growth in the brief time available. The progressively shorter growing season as snow depth increases is an important factor limiting the distribution of many plants.

Moisture and Vegetation

Moisture stress in plants occurs when moisture is evaporated from the surfaces of leaves and stems faster than it can be replaced from the soil. The evaporative power of the air largely depends on relative humidity, though wind also increases evaporation. Saturated air absorbs no moisture, but as relative humidity drops, the air is able to suck up increasing amounts from the surfaces of plants, animals, and soil, causing many mammals to perspire and plants to move additional water upward into their leaves to replace that lost. Thus, transpiration rates increase with evaporation rates. The entire process by which water is thus lost from plant surfaces is called *evapotranspiration*. If available soil moisture is inadequate to keep up with loss through evapotranspiration, moisture stress will result.

Since warm air can hold more water vapor than cool air, the relative humidity of the air during the summer in regions such as California, where this season is both hot and dry, is generally very low, ranging down to 20 percent or less in the hills and valleys of the interior. Even at higher elevations in the Sierra, relative humidity during the summer is rather low. This is partly offset by the lower vapor capacity of the cooler mountain air, but even so, plants growing on dry sites at any elevation in the Sierra must possess ways of reducing water loss through evapotranspiration.

Xerophytes, Hydrophytes, and Mesophytes

Plants adapted to arid soils are called *xerophytes* (Greek *xéros*, dry, and *phyton*, plant). Dry, or *xeric*, sites in the Sierra include alpine gravel patches, rock outcrops, and most soils occupied by grassland, chaparral, foothill woodland, and sagebrush. Xerophytes are plants that are able to endure drought because they have evolved ways of reducing their use and loss of water during the driest seasons of the year. Xerophytes are numerous in the foothill, alpine, and pinyon–sagebrush zones.

Plants growing wholly or partly submerged or in perennially waterlogged soils are called *hydrophytes* (Greek *hudór*, water). In the Sierra, hydrophytic soils are limited to the bottoms and the shores of lakes, ponds, and streams, and hydrophytes account for a small percentage of the total flora. For this reason, they are not further discussed in this guide. The common cattail, which lines ponds at lower elevations, is one of the more familiar hydrophytes.

Most soils in the Sierra fall somewhere between the above extremes, containing a moderate amount of moisture and requiring no particular adaptations either to seasonal drought or flooding. Plants preferring such soils are called *mesophytes* (Greek *mesos*, medium). Most *mesic* sites in the Sierra are occupied either by coniferous forest or montane meadow. Crevices that hold soil and moisture may provide mesic habitats in otherwise xeric rock outcrops.

Since xeric habitats tend to be hot and sunny, adaptations to drought, heat, and intense sunlight are difficult to separate and often occur together in the same plant. Similarly, mesophytic adaptations are often responses as well to conditions of cool temperatures and low light. Taken as groups, xerophytes and mesophytes differ in numerous ways, both in structure and physiology.

ROOTS   Xerophytic plants tend to be smaller and therefore require less water. Their root systems, however, are often much more extensive than those of mesophytic plants of the same size. Xerophytes tend to have long taproots that allow them to utilize deep sources of moisture, and the entire root system is typically much heavier and more extensive than the leaves and stems.

LEAF SIZE   The leaves of xerophytes tend to be smaller than those of mesophytes, thereby reducing the area exposed to sun, wind, and dry air, all of which tend to increase evapotranspiration. Some xerophytes, notably manzanitas, hold their leaves in a vertical position to further reduce exposure to the elements.

Xerophytic leaves are typically thicker than those of mesophytes, so the ratio of exposed surface to volume is smaller.

SCLEROPHYLLS   Xerophytes tend to have smaller and fewer stomata per unit of leaf area. In addition, their leaves have thicker cuticle and are often covered with a layer of varnishlike lipids (fats) that further serves to inhibit water loss. Plants with leaves of this type are called *sclerophylls*, (Greek *skléros*, hard) or "hard-leaved" plants. They include conifers, as well as the broadleaf trees and shrubs of the foothill woodland and chaparral, which are classified as "broadleaf sclerophyll communities." The thick varnished cuticle of sclerophylls not only reduces water loss, but insulates leaves from both overheating and freezing. It is thus an extremely important adaptation for mountain conifers, which during the winter are exposed not only to freezing temperatures, but to high winds that otherwise might induce moisture stress (see "Snow, Wind, and Vegetation").

PUBESCENCE Hairiness, or *pubescence*, is more widespread among xerophytes than mesophytes. Coats of fine, pale hairs covering leaves and stems reduce evaporation by (1) reflecting sunlight and thereby cooling the plant surfaces and (2) reducing air movement. Like the thickened cuticle of sclerophylls, hair coats also insulate plants from freezing temperatures and as a result are commonly found not only on desert species, but also on those inhabiting the alpine zone. The pale green or gray color and silvery sheen characteristic of many xerophytes are produced by these surface hairs.

MOISTURE AVAILABILITY Xerophytes tend to bear flowers and fruit early in the season, while moisture is still plentiful. Mesophytes, which are assured of moisture throughout the growing season, are apt to be more leisurely in this regard.

LONGEVITY Xerophytes tend to live longer than mesophytes. This is necessary because given the more hostile conditions of xeric habitats, rates of success for flowering, fruiting, germination, and seedling establishment are correspondingly lower.

Factors Affecting Soil Moisture

PRECIPITATION For the most part soil moisture varies directly with precipitation, which tends to increase with elevation. Precipitation is seldom critical with regard to the upward distribution of plant species and communities, but it is often the principal factor affecting their lower elevational limits. On the floor of the Central Valley, for example, annual rainfall is so sparse that irrigation is necessary for agriculture, and native trees are for the most part confined to streamsides. Prior to the beginning of irrigated farming, the valley was largely grassland. Though cultivated fields now dominate the valley landscape, grassland remains the typical plant cover of drier sites in the adjacent foothills. With a further slight increase in elevation, pre-

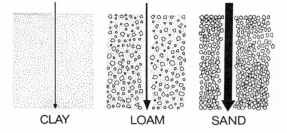

CLAY   LOAM   SAND

62. The rate at which soils drain is related directly to the size of the particles composing them. Clay soils drain very slowly and often tend to be waterlogged for long periods. Sandy soils dry out rapidly. Most plants prefer loams, where a blend of both clay and sand result in moderate drainage.

cipitation increases enough to support trees and shrubs over widespread areas, and thus foothill woodland and chaparral replace grassland as the dominant communities in the upper foothill zone. Still further upslope, coniferous forest replaces woodland and brush, primarily in response to increasing precipitation. A similar sequence—from sagebrush to pinyon–juniper woodlands to coniferous forest—reflects increasing precipitation as one ascends the east slope of the Sierra.

PARTICLE SIZE   The moisture capacity of soil is largely determined by the size of the particles making it up. Soil scientists have divided soil particles into six size classes: coarse gravel, fine gravel, coarse sand, fine sand, silt, and clay. Coarse gravel includes particles larger than five millimeters (about 1/5 inch) in diameter. Individual clay particles, which are smaller than 0.002 millimeters (about 1/12,500 inch) in diameter, cannot be distinguished with the naked eye. Most soils are composed of soil particles of various sizes. *Loams* are soils in which clay, silt, and sand are all well represented.

The smaller the particles in the soil, the more tightly they tend to be packed. Rainfall or snowmelt penetrate coarse soils more readily than they do fine ones because in the former there are larger air spaces between the particles composing them. Runoff—moisture in excess of the soil's infiltration capacity—is therefore greater on slopes with fine soils, since less moisture is able to penetrate the soil surface. The same quality that allows coarse soils to absorb

Moisture and Vegetation

water more easily, however, also assures they will lose it more rapidly. Soil moisture exists primarily as a film or coating around larger particles. Excess moisture drains downward through the spaces between particles. The larger these spaces are, the faster the water drains.

Coarse sandy or gravelly soils, which are common in the High Sierra, absorb large amounts of moisture from melting snow but lose it quickly. Plants occupying such soils are able to commence growth soon after snowmelt, but must complete their annual cycles within the space of a few weeks. They generally have long taproots, which allow them to draw upon moisture that has percolated to lower levels.

Fine soils absorb water less readily, but also drain less rapidly. Extreme saturation occurs when the spaces separating soil particles are so small that drainage is inhibited by the surface tension of the water itself. Waterlogged soils may contain little or no oxygen because air spaces have been largely or entirely filled with water. Plants require soil oxygen for respiration and germination, and oxygen deficiency is the most critical factor limiting the occupation of waterlogged soils. Since water warms up more slowly than air, wet soils remain cool longer than dry ones, and this too inhibits the growth of many species of plants.

TOPOGRAPHY   Except for the bottoms and shores of lakes, streams, and ponds, the wettest soils in the Sierra are found beneath moist meadows. Since these generally occupy topographic depressions, runoff is minimal, sometimes virtually nil. Moist meadow soils are waterlogged at least during the first few weeks following snowmelt, and standing water may remain on the lowest sites for most or all of the summer.

The steeper the slope, the greater and more rapid the runoff. Hilltops and ridgecrests are often significantly drier than the lower slopes, and this difference is always reflected in the vegetation, which may differ in type, density, or relative abundance of the species making it up.

PLANT COVER   Vegetation itself also affects soil moisture in a variety of ways. Dead plant materials decomposed by soil organisms increase the moisture capacity of coarse soils and improve the aeration and drainage of fine ones. The litter and duff (partly decomposed litter) that accumu-

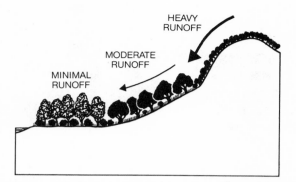

HEAVY
RUNOFF

MODERATE
RUNOFF

MINIMAL
RUNOFF

63. Moisture runoff increases directly with the steepness of the terrain. This affects the kinds of plants able to grow on various slopes. As shown here, for example, deep-rooted chaparral plants occupy the steepest foothill slopes, where runoff is greatest. Shallow-rooted riparian species cover moist streamside flats, and the more drought-resistant plants of the oak woodland dominate intermediate slopes.

late on the soil surface reduce moisture loss through evaporation. Plants further reduce evaporation by shading and thus cooling the air above the soil and by increasing humidity through transpiration. On steep slopes roots anchor soil in place, helping to prevent runoff and erosion. Plants also reduce erosion by sheltering soil from the direct impact of raindrops. Moreover, the denser the vegetation on a slope, the slower the water is able to flow downhill and the greater the amount absorbed by the soil as a result.

Frozen-Ground Phenomena

Frozen-ground phenomena result from the churning of soil and buried rocks by the expansion and contraction accompanying the freezing and thawing of moisture in the soil. The process is analogous to frost action in rocks and occurs most widely in regions where a thin layer of saturated ground sits on top of permanently frozen soil, or *permafrost*. The climate of the Sierra is too warm for permafrost to form, the absence of which, combined with dry summers and rapidly draining gravel soils, tends to limit frozen-ground phenomena to wet meadows, damp lakeshores, and slopes below late-melting snowbanks.

64. Needle ice forms in wet soils exposed to freezing air temperatures. Crystals begin to form near the soil surface, which freezes first (A). They grow as freezing extends downward and as moisture is drawn up by capillary action (B). The expanding ice crystals heave up soil particles at the surface, imparting a granular texture to the soil (C).

NEEDLE ICE   The most common and widespread type of frozen-ground phenomenon in the Sierra, occurring for a short time after snowmelt, when bare soils are still water-logged, is *needle ice*. As air temperatures slowly drop below freezing at night, ice crystals form near the soil surface and extend downward as water below is drawn upward by ice formation above. Needle ice can form at any elevation where bare, saturated soils are exposed to freezing temperatures, but it is most characteristic of the subalpine and alpine zones, where such conditions occur throughout the summer. Campers in the high country who arise shortly after dawn, when the air is often still quite chilly, will often find needle ice in bare, gravelly soils near lakes and streams. The soils typically have a granular, sugary texture that results from having been churned and heaved upward by expanding ice crystals, many of which protrude slightly above the ground. As the day warms up, the needle ice will melt. Vigorous needle-ice activity often prevents plant establishment because the expanding ice crystals may heave up seedlings or sever their roots.

PATTERNED GROUND   The churning of the soil that accompanies ice formation heaves buried rocks upward to the surface, where they roll into slight depressions to form geometric figures known as *patterned ground*. Polygons, circles, and ovals occur in gentle terrain where soil is saturated and frost-heaving intense. *Rock streams* form along depressions running downslope. *Rock stripes* lie across gentle slopes, and *rock garlands* occur on steeper slopes, where gravity, solifluction, or both have caused a rock stripe to sag in the middle. Frost-heaved rocks may also be scattered randomly over the ground.

PEAT HUMMOCKS   Bare, level ground adjacent to lakes or streams, where the water table remains high throughout the summer, are often decorated with small, turf-covered mounds known as *peat hummocks*. The formation of peat hummocks has not been definitively described for the Sierra; the following account, however, has been proposed for hummock formation in the Rockies and may well apply in the Sierra as well. Freezing and thawing churns the saturated soils, thrusting buried rocks to the surface to form rock polygons, several of which may intersect to create a pattern resembling a parquet floor. At first, these rock nets are entirely submerged. Frost-churning prevents plants from occupying the centers of the polygons, but sedges are able to invade the raised perimeters. Through contributing organic matter to the soil, the sedges initiate peat formation. Slowly, small mounds of peat begin to rise above the surface of the water, assisted by continued frost heaving from below. At this point, the hummocks are invaded by mosses, willows, and a few grasses and forbs (herbs other than grasses) tolerant of extremely moist soils. Eventually, hummocks may be several inches high and several feet long, standing well above the water. When this occurs, meadow plants intolerant of saturated soils are able to invade the drier hummock crowns. In the Rockies dessication and abrasion of the crown by blowing dust and snow leads to hummock degradation, but this does not seem to occur in the Sierra, where peat formation and upward thrusting apparently keep pace with erosion.

Solifluction

Here and there in the High Sierra, tiny ponds lie amid the lush turfs that grow on moist slopes downhill from lingering snowbanks. These ponds are impounded behind small

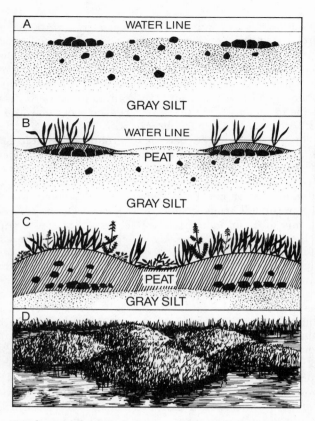

65. Peat hummocks, which form in submerged cold soils near timberline, may form in the following manner. During the winter freezing churns the soil, heaving buried rocks to the surface, where they roll to the perimeter of the raised mounds to form rock polygons (A). Continued churning prevents plants from invading the centers of the polygons, but moisture-loving sedges may become established among the submerged rocks of the perimeter (B). The sedges contribute organic matter, initiating the formation of peat hummocks, which eventually protrude above the water surface. As the mounds increase in height they become somewhat less soggy so that wet-meadow plants such as elephants head and alpine willow can become established (C). Mature peat hummocks appear as groups of low, grassy mounds in moist meadows.

THE MOUNTAIN ENVIRONMENT

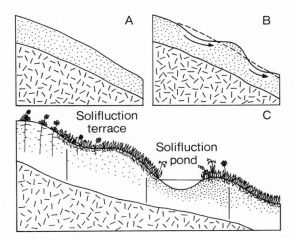

66. Solifluction occurs in bare, waterlogged soils on fairly steep slopes (A). In the Sierra such conditions are largely restricted to areas just below lingering snowpatches at high elevation. The soil begins to creep downslope in response to gravity because the particles are lubricated by abundant moisture and no longer adhere to one another. Small terraces form where the soil piles up (B). Eventually, moisture-loving sedges and grasses may invade the slope, inhibiting further creep (C). Tiny ponds impounded behind solifluction terraces are common features of moist alpine meadows in the Sierra.

ridges of soil known as *solifluction terraces*. Solifluction is the downward creep of soil saturated with water, usually from snowmelt. The moisture lubricates the soil particles so that they no longer adhere to one another, but begin to "flow" downslope. The terraces form where the soil comes to rest, piling up slightly in the process. Solifluction usually occurs in bare soils, which are not anchored in place by plant roots. Vegetation may subsequently invade and stabilize the slope, making further slumping unlikely.

Microclimates

Local variations in climate occur in response to topography and patterns of vegetation. A forest opening, for example, is sunnier and windier than the forest understory. The lee-ward side of a mountain, or even a single boulder, receives less wind and more snow than the windward side. Such variations profoundly influence the types of plants growing in various areas within a region and are herein referred to as *microclimates*. Some sources prefer to limit this term to apply only to the warmer, less windy climate occurring within a few feet of the earth's surface, using the term *mesoclimate* to refer to broader differences resulting from local topography and vegetation, but the difference between the two is, in any case, a matter of degree. There is no general agreement among authorities on where micro-climate ends and mesoclimate begins. Regardless of which term one prefers, local variations in climate, in conjunction with those in soil, water availability, and other factors, are responsible for the patchwork of habitats producing vegeta-tion mosaics, as well as less pronounced variations within single plant communities.

Slope Aspect

Variations in local topography affect the amounts of wind, sunlight, and snow received by various sites within a given area, and these factors in turn influence local air tem-peratures and the length of the growing season. The role of topography in producing local wind phenomena, including mountain and valley breezes and the acceleration of winds through canyons and passes, as well as over mountain crests, is discussed in Chapter III (see page 102 and Figure 42). The following discussion will focus on *slope aspect*—the direction faced by a slope—as it affects insola-tion, wind, and snow depths.

INSOLATION   In the northern hemisphere slopes fac-ing south receive more hours of sunlight during the year and more intense radiation than those facing north. As a result they tend to be warmer than northern exposures, and since soil moisture evaporates more rapidly as air tempera-tures increase, drier as well. The disparity is greatest dur-ing the winter, when steep north-facing slopes may receive no sunlight whatsoever. As the sun moves higher in the sky with the approach of summer, northern exposures receive

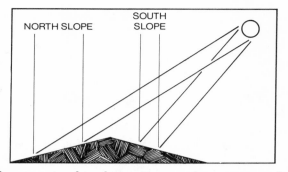

67. Slope aspect and insolation. Since northern exposures face away from the sun in the northern hemisphere, they receive its rays more obliquely. Therefore, a given amount of solar radiation is spread over a larger area than on comparable south-facing slopes. Because of this "dilution" of sunlight, north-facing slopes tend to be cooler and moister (owing to slower rates of evaporation), a difference that is reflected dramatically in the types of vegetation characteristic of each slope.

increasing amounts of sunlight—though always less than south-facing slopes, regardless of the season. Contrasts in sunlight and air temperature, along with resulting varia-tions in such factors as moisture availability and length of growing season, produce detectable differences, even in relatively gentle terrain, in the vegetation found on south- and north-facing slopes. In the lower foothills of the west slope of the Sierra, for example, grassland may cover both slopes, but the mix of species on each may be somewhat different. Along the eastern base of the range, sagebrush plants may grow farther apart on southern exposures than they do on northern ones. The kind and frequency of as-sociated species may also vary from one slope to the other.

As slopes become steeper the effects of slope aspect be-come even more pronounced, and the resulting differences in vegetation are accordingly more dramatic. In the upper foothills, for example, a canyon wall facing south is com-monly covered by chaparral, while the facing slope—at the same elevation—supports oak woodland. On the east side of the Sierra, sagebrush may cover a southern exposure while pinyon–juniper woodland or coniferous forest occur on the opposite slope.

Slope aspect, then, produces differences in air temperature and related factors similar to those encountered with a change in elevation, and as a result, individual plants and entire plant communities tend to range farther upslope on southern exposures and farther downslope on northern exposures. In other words, they exhibit relative constancy with regard to site preference. In the central Sierra, for example, foothill chaparral may extend up to 5000 feet (1500 meters) elevation on south-facing slopes, but only to 3000 feet (900 meters) or so on north-facing ones. Plant communities thus tend to "interfinger" with those immediately above and below them, with the result that the boundaries of vegetation zones are seldom tidy and almost never consistently tied to a particular elevational limit. The upper and lower limits given for Sierra vegetation zones in Figure 61 are therefore generalizations, with which local topography frequently plays havoc.

East- and west-facing slopes exhibit less pronounced microclimatic differences since both receive comparable amounts of sunlight during the day. Nevertheless, western exposures tend to be somewhat warmer. Maximum solar radiation occurs about midday, when the sun is highest in the sky, but the hottest part of the day comes two to four hours later, the lag being the amount of time required for the air to heat up. At this point steeper eastern exposures may lie in shadow and remain cooler than comparable west-facing slopes. Near timberline, where the climate is cool to begin with, any loss of sunlight, however brief, can be critical in determining whether a plant is able to survive on a given site. Moreover, because of the thinness of the air, the drop in temperature produced by shading is much more pronounced than at lower elevations. On the other hand, moisture loss through evaporation will be lower on eastern exposures and may allow the growth of plants that could not tolerate the warmer, drier conditions on west-facing slopes. Mountain hemlock, for example, prefers cool, relatively moist sites near timberline. Its distribution in the northern Sierra is not nearly so affected by slope aspect as in the south, where the tree becomes increasingly confined to cooler, moister northeastern exposures.

WIND AND SNOW   North-facing slopes are the first on which snow sticks in the autumn and the last from which it

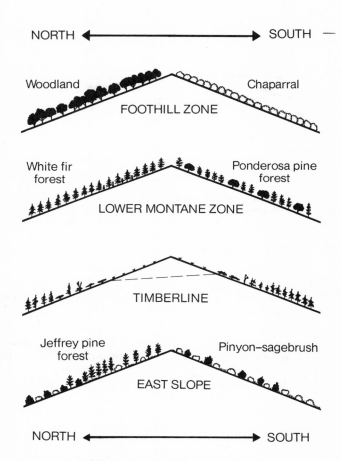

NORTH ◄─────────► SOUTH —

Woodland FOOTHILL ZONE Chaparral

White fir forest LOWER MONTANE ZONE Ponderosa pine forest

TIMBERLINE

Jeffrey pine forest EAST SLOPE Pinyon–sagebrush

NORTH ◄─────────► SOUTH

68. Vegetational differences between comparable north- and south-facing slopes in the Sierra Nevada.

disappears the following summer, partly because they receive less sunlight, and are therefore cooler, and partly because they receive more snow. Local differences in snow depths primarily reflect the interplay of wind and topography. After snow has settled and compacted, it is only superficially affected by the wind, but while falling, or shortly thereafter, it is extremely susceptible to being

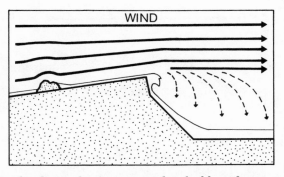

69. Wind and snow depth. Snow tends to be blown from exposed windward slopes and deposited in deep drifts on protected leeward slopes and basins. In the Sierra the deepest snows are found on the northeastern sides of mountain crests because prevailing winter winds strike the range from the southwest.

blown about. Since winter storm winds in the Sierra generally blow from the southwest, slopes facing this direction tend to receive less snow than sheltered northern and eastern exposures. Snow is blown up and over windward slopes to be deposited on the leeward sides of ridges and peaks, where calmer air allows it to settle in deeper drifts. The steeper the slope, the greater the discrepancy in wind speeds, and therefore snow depths, between the windward and leeward sides is likely to be.

After the passing of a storm, or at other times when clouds are not obscuring the crest, one can often see this process at work as long streamers of snow—*snow banners*—are blown downwind from peaks and ridgetops. Banner Peak, a prominent summit in the Ritter Range, east of Yosemite National Park, was named for this phenomenon.

Wind Damage and Snow Cover

High winds can break limbs, strip away foliage, and subject plants to dessication and abrasion by blowing sand or snow. High winds near the Sierra crest chill plant surfaces sticking above the snow and rapidly carry away moisture. During the winter, if the snowpack is shallow and the soil is

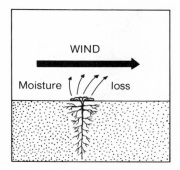

70. Few plants can survive High Sierra winters on windy slopes swept free of snow. Under such conditions high winds carry off moisture from the plants, which are unable to replace it because the soil moisture is frozen and therefore unavailable.

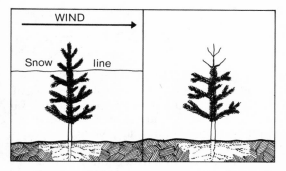

71. Abrasive wind-blown snow can strip the needles from the crowns of young trees that extend just above the surface of the pack. As shown by the tree on the right, the minimum snow depth in a particular place often can be gauged roughly by the point at which crown damage begins.

therefore frozen, plants thus exposed may succumb to moisture stress because they cannot replace the water lost at the plant surfaces. Plants growing on xeric sites are subject to similar stress during the latter part of the summer, when soil moisture has declined from early-season highs. Although some of the hardier alpine plants can withstand a certain amount of exposure to wind, many require the protection afforded by snow cover if they are to survive the

Microclimates 169

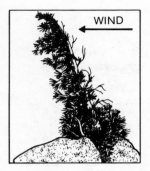

72. Flagging. High winds often strip needles and branches from the windward sides of timberline trees while leaving much of the foliage intact on the sheltered sides of the trunks.

winter. In exposed areas the height of plants may be largely determined by snow depth, since shoots projecting above the surface of the pack are quickly killed by dessication, abrasion, chilling, moisture stress, or a combination of all these.

Although snow is often taken as a symbol of winter's harshness, most plants that inhabit cold regions, especially above timberline, where winds are nearly constant, rely on snow to protect them from extremely low air temperatures and dessication. Since temperatures deep within the snowpack are at the freezing point in the Sierra, the snow serves to insulate plants from the frequently lower outside air temperatures.

Ridgetops and summits, where winds prevent snow from settling for long, are among the most inhospitable environments for plant life in the Sierra and often may support no vascular plants whatsoever. Plants whose seeds are carried upslope to such sites by wind or animals may manage to germinate and set out a tiny stem or two during their first summer but will not likely survive the following winter. The dwarfed, streamlined shapes typical of many subalpine and alpine plants are primarily adaptations to wind. Prostrate plants are not only less exposed to wind, but require less snow to cover them. The sprawling mats formed by many timberline trees create their own protective blankets by trapping snow blown across the ground.

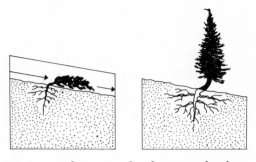

73. Young saplings on snowy slopes are often bent over by the slow downslope creep of the snowpack. Older trees may often show curvature of the trunk, or "snow knees," as a result of this wintertime deformation in their youth.

Snow Damage

Although snow is essential to the survival of many plants during the winter, it can injure plants in several ways. The weight of the snow can break branches and bend seedlings and saplings to the ground. As snow settles, it may tear out limbs. The tapered crowns exhibited by many conifers facilitate the shedding of snow and thus reduce the chances of damage. Subalpine conifers typically have flexible branches that resist breaking. Whitebark and limber pines, the latter named for this characteristic, are notable examples. Species lacking such resilience may be broken or permanently deformed by the deep snows of the subalpine zone. For example, many aspens in the Sierra are deformed in bizarre ways never seen in the Rockies. By bringing branches in contact with the ground, heavy snows also expose plants to soil fungi that ultimately may prove fatal. The lower branches of conifers, for example, may be killed by brown felt fungi if covered by snow for prolonged periods.

Mature conifers in the upper-elevation forest often exhibit *snow knees,* trunks bent at or just above the ground by the gradual downslope movement of snow. Smaller plants can even be uprooted by snow creep. On steeper slopes the downward movement of snow may take the awesome and destructive form of an avalanche, which can destroy all the vegetation in its path, including mature coni-

74. Avalanche tracks often appear as treeless corridors running downslope through the forest.

fers. Throughout the High Sierra, paths cleared through the forest mark zones of high avalanche danger. Trees and shrubs along these courses are scant or absent because they are repeatedly destroyed each winter. Skiers and other winter visitors to the Sierra should, for their own safety, learn to recognize this pattern in the landscape.

Forest Influences

Trees intercept sunlight and precipitation and reduce the impact of the wind, thus creating different conditions of soil and microclimate beneath them than occur in nearby open areas. To a lesser extent this is also true of shrubs and herbs, but since these effects are most dramatic beneath trees, they are commonly called *forest influences*.

In dense forests the ground beneath the trees may receive as little as one percent or less of the light striking the canopy, making the growth of photosynthetic plants nearly impossible on the forest floor. In the Sierra such is often the case in the red fir forest, where understory vegetation, except in openings, largely consists of *saprophytes*, plants that lack chlorophyll and therefore the ability to engage in photosynthesis. Saprophytes, such as the beautiful red snow plant, obtain energy instead from decaying organic matter in the soil or by parasitizing the roots of other plants.

Forest conifers receive ample amounts of light by virtue of their great height. The tapered crowns of many conifers not only allow them to shed snow, but permit light to

172   THE MOUNTAIN ENVIRONMENT

penetrate to lower layers of branches. This classic Christmas-tree shape, however, is seldom exhibited by conifers characteristic of open habitats. The trunks of some species of conifers, giant sequoia for example, may be bare of branches for several tens of feet above the ground. Since the lowest branches receive scarcely any light anyway, some trees simply quit supplying them with water and nutrients, thereby allowing them to wither away. Again, this habit of self-pruning, an adaptation to low light, seldom occurs in conifers adapted to open areas.

Trees are most vulnerable to shading when they are seedlings or saplings. Species able to tolerate shade for long periods are usually represented by more offspring in the understory than those which are not. Some trees, such as ponderosa pine and lodgepole pine, require full sunlight at all stages of growth. Others, such as white fir, red fir, and incense cedar are able to withstand long periods of shading in the juvenile stages, during which time they grow very

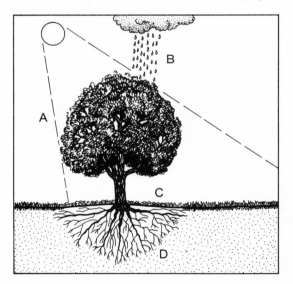

75. Mature trees affect the environment of plants around them in many ways, including casting shade (A), intercepting precipitation (B), contributing leaf litter to the soil (C), and monopolizing available soil moisture and nutrients (D).

76. Saplings of shade-tolerant trees, such as the young white fir shown here, grow very slowly beneath the dense forest canopy, but when the death of a mature tree opens up the forest, their growth rapidly accelerates in response to increased sunlight.

slowly. Eventually, lightning, disease, fire, logging, or some other agent kills one or more of the mature trees, producing an opening in the forest. When this occurs, young firs and cedars emerge from their shade-induced lethargy and begin to rapidly add new growth, often gaining several feet of height within only a few years.

Sun-loving trees are seldom able to compete with shade-tolerant species in habitats capable of supporting dense forest, so they often exhibit adaptations to extreme environments where competition for sunlight will be reduced. For example, lodgepole, whitebark, foxtail, and limber pines are able to grow in thin, dry, rocky soils at high elevations, habitats where most forest trees cannot survive. Lodgepole pine, willows, quaking aspen, and other species avoid competition for light by inhabiting soils too moist for dominant forest conifers. Ponderosa pine is adapted to periodic fires, which create conditions favorable to sun-loving plants.

When a green plant is not actively engaged in photosynthesis, as at night, for example, its weight drops as a result of respiration. In order for growth to occur, photosynthesis must exceed respiration. The amount of light necessary for this to occur is lower for plants able to grow in the shade than it is for those that prefer full sun because the former usually respire more slowly. The leaves of shade plants are also designed to catch as much sunlight as possible. They are commonly larger than the leaves of sun plants and have more chloroplasts, the cell structures that contain chlorophyll, which is essential for photosynthesis.

Low light is by no means the sole factor limiting plant growth in dense forests. It is typically accompanied by the following environmental conditions, and shade tolerance is the relative measure of a plant's ability to thrive in such circumstances.

TEMPERATURE   Since a portion of sunlight is experienced directly as heat, air temperatures during the day are lower in the forest than in sunny openings. At night, however, the forest remains warmer, since the dense canopy of vegetation inhibits the loss of heat to the atmosphere. Nevertheless, since the effect of plant cover on air temperatures is more pronounced during the day, average air temperatures within the forest are lower overall than in open areas. As a result, soil temperatures also tend to be lower.

PRECIPITATION   Snow depths are generally greater in open areas than within the forest because a good deal of snow is intercepted by the canopy and may be blown into openings or evaporate before it reaches the ground. Even so, open areas, thanks to greater exposure to sun and wind, are free of snow earlier in the spring and thereby enjoy longer growing seasons.

HUMIDITY   The relative humidity of the air beneath the forest canopy is often higher than that over open areas because trees transpire enormous amounts of moisture by virtue of their sheer size. As a result, shade plants are less likely to be subjected to moisture stress than sun plants occupying soils of comparable wetness.

WIND   Forest trees reduce wind velocities by 20 to 60 percent. The higher the wind speed, the greater the reduction. Within the forest, winds average one to two miles per hour, to some degree sparing shade plants from the effects of chill, dessication, and destructive breakage produced by the wind in open areas.

SOIL MOISTURE   Forest soils lose moisture to the atmosphere slowly, thanks to the greater humidity produced by cooler air temperatures and reduced wind speeds. Nevertheless, forest soils are often drier than those in open areas because the forest trees take up enormous amounts of

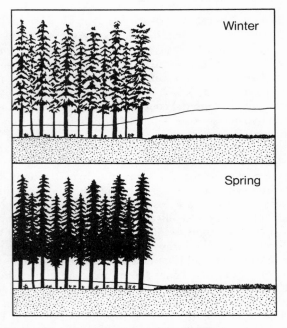

77. During the winter the snowpack is often deeper in open areas than on the forest floor because deep drifts may form in the lee of trees. In the spring, however, snow persists longer in shady forests than in sunny meadows.

water, thereby creating drought conditions for understory plants. The ability of seedlings to survive dry forest soils is an important factor in determining which species of plants are able to grow there.

SOIL NUTRIENTS   Lower air temperatures in the forest may result in slower rates of decomposition of forest litter, thus producing a nutrient deficiency at times great enough to inhibit establishment of understory plants.

Since available light also affects these and other environmental factors, it is difficult to separate adaptations to light alone from those directed to the entire complex of conditions associated with varying amounts of sun and shade. For example, many adaptations to intense sunlight seem to be concerned more with reducing heat and consequent moisture loss than with cutting down on light per se.

Fire and Vegetation

Each summer dozens of wildfires break out in California, burning hundreds of thousands of acres of forest, brush, and grassland, costing millions of dollars in property damage, lost resources, and human labor, and causing widespread public consternation. Conditions during the summer in most of California, including much of the Sierra below timberline, are ideal for fires: high air temperatures, low relative humidity, frequent winds, and little rain. During this season much of the state is one large tinderbox waiting for ignition. Although human carelessness causes most fires that occur in the state today, fires ignited by lightning are a natural part of the California and Sierra environments. Unlike most parts of the country, California experiences few summer thunderstorms, except at high elevations, yet they do occur from time to time when tropical storms from Mexico manage to push their way northward into the state. During the exceptionally dry summer of 1977, one such storm set off more than a hundred fires from one end of the state to the other.

Although such storms do not occur every summer, most California plant communities are to some degree adapted to fire. Some of them depend on periodic burning to maintain their vigor or dominance on a site, and many Sierra plant species need fire in order to complete their life cycles or to eliminate competitors that otherwise would crowd them out. Certain chaparral plants, such as chamise, even contain flammable substances in their sap. Better adapted to fire than some competitors, such plants may have developed greater flammability to ensure their competitive advantage. Such adaptations do not develop overnight, but indicate a long and intimate relationship between fire and many Sierra plant communities.

Prior to the early 1900s, when public agencies began the program of fire suppression that has continued in most areas to this day, any given patch of forest or brushland on the west slope of the Sierra could be expected to burn every three to fifteen years, the average interval being eight or nine years. Occasional lightning strikes at lower elevations were supplemented by fires intentionally set by local Indian tribes to open up the forest and thereby create more favorable conditions for wildlife and understory plants, both of which were sources of food.

Most of these blazes were comparatively cool groundfires that consumed underbrush but left mature trees largely unscathed. Destructive crown fires, which turn trees into giant torches and commonly devastate thousands of acres, were less common than today because the short periods between burns did not allow huge amounts of fuel to accumulate on the forest floor. Today, after some 70 years of suppressing fires, most areas are so cluttered with dead wood, downed timber, deep litter, and dense understory vegetation that when a fire does occur—as it inevitably will—the resulting conflagration is far worse than if small, periodic groundfires had been allowed to burn.

Today both the U.S. Forest Service and National Park Service have designated certain "let burn" areas in the Sierra in an attempt to reduce the number of destructive burns and restore fire to its former role in forest ecology. These areas are generally situated well away from populated areas and are characterized by fuel conditions unlikely to produce destructive crown fires. In addition, prescribed burns have been carried out in a number of areas, not only to reduce accumulated fuel and thereby reduce future fire hazard, but also to learn more about how various plant communities respond to burning. Although much remains to be learned in this regard, the following ecological functions of fire are fairly well understood.

Succession

Through opening up forest or brush stands, periodic fires favor sun-loving plants over those favoring shade. In the mixed-coniferous forest, for example, fire suppression has favored shade-tolerant seedlings and saplings of white fir and incense cedar over sun-loving ponderosa pines, black

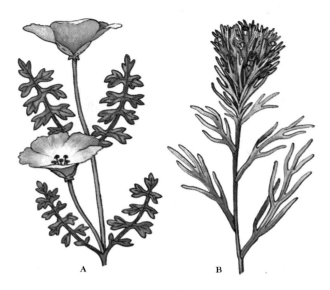

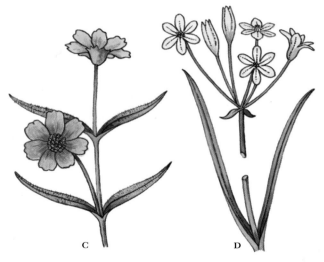

A. Baby Blue-Eyes, *Nemophila menziesii* (page 215)
B. Purple Owl's Clover, *Orthocarpus purpurascens* (page 215)
C. Goldfields, *Lasthenia chrysotoma* (page 215)
D. Prettyface, *Triteleia scabra* (page 215)

PLATE 1

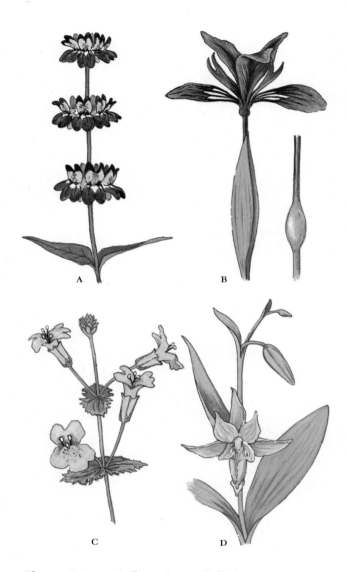

A. Chinese Houses, *Collinsia heterophylla* (page 227)
B. Bowl-Tubed Iris, *Iris macrosiphon* (page 228)
C. Common Monkeyflower, *Mimulus guttatus* (page 234)
D. Stream Orchid, *Epipactis gigantea* (page 234)

PLATE 2

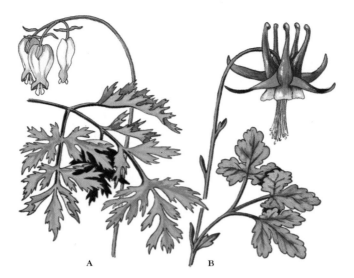

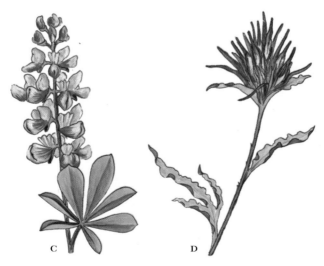

A. Bleeding Heart, *Dicentra formosa* (page 361)
B. Crimson Columbine, *Aquilegia formosa* (page 361)
C. Broadleaf Lupine, *Lupinus latifolius* (page 362)
D. Indian Paintbrush, *Castilleja applegatei* (page 362)

PLATE 3

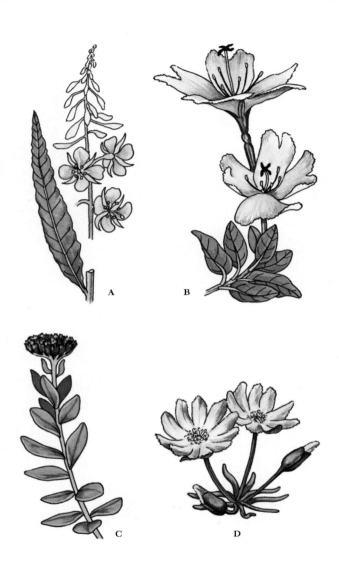

A. Fireweed, *Epilobium angustifolium* (page 362)
B. Rock Fringe, *Epilobium obcordatum* (page 362)
C. Rosy Stonecrop, *Sedum rosea* (page 362)
D. Bitterroot, *Lewisia rediviva* (page 362)

PLATE 4

oaks, and understory shrubs. As a result, the latter are gradually being eliminated from the forest mix, for when the mature plants die there will be fewer offspring to replace them. In the red fir forest sunny openings conducive to lodgepole pines are slowly eliminated as a result of fire suppression. The forest becomes denser and more uniform as the dominant red firs invade the openings and shade out the pines and other plants. Fire suppression may also allow trees to invade and eventually take over meadows, while periodic burning would keep them at bay. In the chaparral fire not only rejuvenates old, unproductive stands, but opens them up to grasses and wildflowers, as well as to other shrubs, that are rare or absent prior to burning.

Since fires burn irregularly, occurring on different lands at different times and, even in a single burn, varying in intensity from one site to the next, they tend to produce a mosaic of forest stands characterized by differences in age, density, and constituent species. In other words, fires create greater diversity in habitats, thereby encouraging a greater variety of plants and animals in a given area. California Indians understood this relationship and routinely carried out their own programs of prescribed burns. The conflagrations that might occur today, however, can destroy vegetation over tens of thousands of acres, producing not diversity, but a different and less desirable sort of uniformity than existed prior to the blaze.

Soil Conditions

Deep forest litter inhibits the germination of many plants, including ponderosa pine and giant sequoia, as well as numerous shrubs and herbs. Litter provides little in the way of nutrients and during the summer is generally drier than the soil below. The very presence of litter, of course, implies a canopy overhead, which shades out many plants. Because of the cooler temperatures in the forest, litter decomposition proceeds slowly, and mature trees remove nutrients from the soil faster than they can be replaced. As a result, forest soils are usually deficient in nutrients essential to seedling survival. Periodic fires reduce or remove forest litter, thereby exposing the soft, friable mineral soils favored by most plant seedlings. In the years following a fire, litter decomposition accelerates because more light is able to reach the forest floor. Moreover, burned litter retains moisture better than unburned. Nitrogen, potassium, calcium, phosphorus, and magnesium tied up in both the litter and living plants are returned to the soil when these are burned. Although extremely hot fires may vaporize nutrients and thereby reduce soil fertility, cool fires tend to improve overall soil chemistry. Even hot fires may prove useful in some cases, however, through killing destructive soil organisms.

Hot fires may produce severe erosion by removing all vegetation, burning even the partially decomposed duff layer beneath the litter, and baking the exposed mineral soil to bricklike hardness. Cool fires, however, generally improve soil permeability and leave enough materials and vegetation to prevent disastrous runoff and consequent erosion and flooding.

Insects and Disease

Through removing dead and diseased trees, fires may keep forest pests under control, thereby improving the overall vigor of the community. There is reason to believe that outbreaks of spruce budworm and bark beetles may have been less frequent and severe under natural fire cycles. Dwarf mistletoe, as well as other parasites on forest trees, may have been held in check by periodic burns.

Symbiosis and Parasitism

Although there has been a good deal of debate among biologists regarding the concept of *symbiosis*, most use it to designate a mutually beneficial relationship between dissimilar organisms living in close association. For example, bees and butterflies obtain food from flowers in the form of nectar. In the process they transfer pollen from one flower to another, thereby assisting plant reproduction. Many plants are entirely dependent on pollination by insects and have devised various strategies for attracting them or otherwise furthering the process.

Parasitism, like symbiosis, involves the intimate association of dissimilar organisms, except in this case the activities of one are detrimental to the other. Examples include fungal invasion of plants and animals, mistletoe on
trees, fleas on cats and dogs, streptococci in humans, and
wasps that lay their eggs in the larvae of other insects.

Commensalism refers to a third category of interaction,
in which one partner in the relationship derives benefit
from the other without inflicting harm in return. For example, in the Sierra foothills and lower montane zone, mice
and other small animals often take up residence in the
large, elaborate nests constructed by dusky-footed wood
rats, but the latter are not adversely affected by their unin-
vited tenants. Another, more widespread example is the
creation of plant galls—swollen growths appearing on
leaves and stems—caused by several species of small
wasps. The insects lay their eggs inside the plant tissue, and
the hosts produce the galls as a way of sealing off the invaded areas. In most cases the host plants are not seriously
damaged by the arrangement.

Symbiosis

Examples of symbiosis in nature are legion, so common,
in fact, that cooperation seems at least as important as competition, or "survival of the fittest," in the web of life. The
symbiotic relationship between flowers and certain insects
has already been mentioned. Lichen, to cite a second example, is a compound organism formed from the symbiotic
union of algae and fungi. (For a full discussion of lichens,
see Chapter VI). The western juniper also presents a fascin-
ating instance of symbiosis. During the winter its seeds provide welcome food to several species of Sierra birds and
mammals. A few of the seeds are not fully digested, however, and are passed in the feces. As it happens, only those
juniper seeds that have passed through the digestive tracts
of birds and animals will germinate. These consumers also
transport the seeds to new areas, where competition from
already established trees may be reduced.

Two additional examples of symbiosis deserve extended
discussion because they play such crucial roles in the overall health and maintenance of plant communities. The re-

Symbiosis and Parasitism

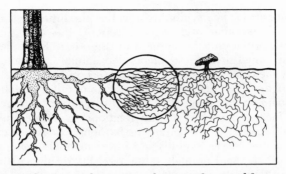

78. Mycorrhiza, a symbiotic union between fungi and forest trees.

mainder of this discussion, then, will focus on mycorrhizal fungi and symbiotic bacteria.

MYCORRHIZAL FUNGI   The nutrition of many types of vascular plants is tied intimately to that of soil fungi. This relationship has long been recognized in the case of conifers, but research has shown it to be even more widespread than was formerly thought. Mushrooms are the fruiting bodies of soil fungi, which largely consist of elaborate networks (*mycelia*) of branching filaments (*hyphae*). Enzymes produced by the hyphae penetrate dead plant and animal tissues in the soil, decomposing them into simpler substances that are absorbed by the fungi. In the process basic minerals bound up in these organic materials are released to the soil and thereby become available to plants. In soils deficient in nutrients, fungal hyphae may surround or invade the roots of certain plants, forming a symbiotic structure called a *mycorrhiza*, which allows each partner to obtain nutrients more efficiently than either could by itself. Although the relationship is initially parasitic—the fungus living off the vascular plant but giving little in return—it soon becomes fully reciprocal.

Plants growing in nutritionally deficient soils may have stunted root systems unable to absorb sufficient water and nutrients. When invaded by fungal hyphae, however, the roots begin to branch and spread, increasing the amount of surface in contact with the soil and thus improving their absorptive power. At the same time, the hyphae proliferate as well, further extending the effective range of the partnership. The fungus provides the plant with water and nutrients in excess of its needs. The plant in turn uses these materials to synthesize carbohydrates essential to the fungus.

For reasons outlined on page 176, forest soils are commonly deficient in such nutrients as nitrogen, phosphorus, potassium, and calcium. Consequently, conifers and many other plants form mycorrhiza and without them could not compete for water and nutrients. Some mycorrhizal fungi are host specific, occurring under only one species of tree. This is the case, for example, with *Suillus tomentosus*, which is found growing only in close association with lodgepole pine. Most mycorrhizal fungi, however, form unions with several species, though they may prefer particular types, such as conifers or hardwoods. Mushroom genera such as *Boletus*, *Amanita*, *Suillus*, *Leccinum*, *Cortinarius*, and *Rhizopogon* have elaborated numerous species closely associated with various conifers and hardwoods. *Leccinum scabrum*, for example, occurs under quaking aspen; the poisonous *Boletus satanus*, under foothill oaks.

SYMBIOTIC BACTERIA: NITROGEN FIXATION Farmers have long known that one way to increase soil fertility is to plant a crop of beans. In nitrogen-deficient soils, most members of the bean, or legume, family develop root nodules inhabited by *Rhizobium* bacteria, which have the useful and uncommon ability to convert atmospheric nitrogen into amino acids, which can be used by plants. This process is called *nitrogen fixation*. In return for this service the host plants furnish the bacteria with nutrients and water.

Rhizobium bacteria exist freely in most soils, but do not form root nodules if the organic nitrogen supply is ample. In their free state these rod-shaped microorganisms are unable to fix nitrogen. Neither can the host plants by themselves. When nitrogen levels are too low, however, the bacteria invade the roots of legumes via root hairs. Since legumes constitute the second largest family of flowering plants and are found in most terrestrial communities, they perform an important service in maintaining soil fertility. Legumes in the Sierra include clovers, lupines, vetches, lotuses, locoweeds, red bud, and chaparral pea. Nitrogen levels increase in soils inhabited by legumes, benefitting all the plants associated with them. Precisely how plants obtain and make use of the amino acids produced by *Rhizobium* bacteria is not known.

Symbiotic nitrogen fixation has also been observed in plants of the genus *Ceanothus*, which in the Sierra includes such common shrubs as buck brush, squaw carpet, deer brush, snow bush, and tobacco bush. In the case of *Ceanothus*, however, the bacterial partners are *Actinomyces*, rather than *Rhizobium*. *Actinomyces* bacteria also form nodules on the roots of alders, wax myrtle, buffalo berry, bitterbrush, and others.

Parasitism

Parasitism has been called a form of predation in which smaller organisms feed on larger ones. Parasites that prey on humans, or on plants and animals that humans value, are understandably regarded as evil, organisms to be eradicated if possible. From an ecological point of view, however, parasites are neither good nor bad, but merely organisms that like all others, conscious or not, seek to survive and to perpetuate their kind.

Some parasites, moreover, actually perform "beneficial" services, not only for humans, but also for other members of the ecosystems in which they occur. Numerous species of tiny wasps lay their eggs inside the larvae of various kinds of destructive caterpillars, whose numbers otherwise would swell to such size as to pose a serious threat to the trees or other plants on which they feed. In the upper montane zone of the Sierra, for example, the lodgepole needle-miner, a parasitic caterpillar, sometimes defoliates large stands of lodgepole pine, but most of the time its population is kept under control by parasitic wasps, as well as numerous hungry birds. But even the lodgepole needle-miner performs a useful service insofar as humans are concerned, for by destroying stands of lodgepole, it may well be an important agent preventing these trees from invading adjacent meadows.

Parasites are not outlaws within their native ecosystems; they evolved conjointly with the species on which they feed and on those that in turn feed on them. All populations adjust themselves not only to the resources available, but also to losses suffered as a result of predation and parasitism. Under normal conditions parasites are kept under control by organisms that prey on them or by the natural resistance of their hosts. Parasites—or any organisms—alien to an ecosystem can, however, raise havoc if, as is often the case, the ecosystem has evolved no effective mechanisms of control. Imported fungal diseases of forest trees, for example, have caused widespread damage among certain species, and in one case, the American chestnut, have virtually eliminated a species once common in the eastern hardwood forest.

FUNGI AS PARASITES Fungi constitute a large and varied division of simple-structured plants that, like bacteria, lack chlorophyll and therefore cannot manufacture their own food from the raw ingredients of sunlight, carbon dioxide, and water. Instead, they obtain nutrients by "feeding" on the tissues of plants and animals, both living and dead.

Familiar types of fungi include yeasts, bread molds, mildews, rusts, blights, truffles, and mushrooms. Parasitic fungi, those that feed on living tissue, are responsible for numerous diseases in both plants and animals, diseases such as athlete's foot, ringworm, powdery mildew, chestnut blight, white pine blister rust, and heartwood rot.

Numerous parasitic fungi are responsible for destructive forest diseases, the control of which has occasioned extensive research. The non-native white pine blister rust is perhaps the most destructive of these parasites, having damaged or killed thousands of "white pines" in the western United States. (White pines constitute an informal grouping of closely related species within the genus *Pinus* and in the Sierra include sugar pine, western white pine, foxtail pine, limber pine, and whitebark pine, all of which grow their needles in bundles of five.)

Spores produced by the blister-rust fungus in the spring invade the leaves of gooseberries and currants (genus *Ribes*) in the summer, germinating, spreading, and by autumn producing a second generation of spores. Winds blow these new spores to adjacent white pines, where they settle on the needles and subsequently invade the trees' inner bark.

Symbiosis and Parasitism 185

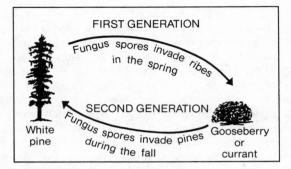

Fungus spores invade ribes in the spring

SECOND GENERATION

White pine

Fungus spores invade pines during the fall

Gooseberry or currant

79. Life cycle of white pine blister rust.

Within a couple of years after infection has occurred, the bark becomes discolored and swollen, and after another year or two, whitish spore sacs erupt through the diseased bark. These release millions of minute orange spores, which are carried by the wind to nearby currants and gooseberries to begin the cycle again. This pattern of alternate hosts is essential to the life cycle of the fungus, and though the currants and gooseberries are not adversely affected by the parasite, the host pines are eventually killed when their trunks are girdled by the spreading infection.

Other fungi that parasitize living forest trees in the Sierra include red belt fomes, white pouch fungus, sulfur bracket fungus, rainbow shelf fungus, and incense cedar dry rot. Some feed on heartwood, others on living sapwood. Some fungi contribute as well to the decomposition of fallen logs, thereby improving the soil through the addition of humus. Fungal spores commonly enter host trees via wounds in the bark inflicted by insects, mammals, or birds, and by mechanical damage resulting from wind, lightning, frost, snow, and the like. The action of fungal enzymes produces the dry, crumbly punkwood characteristic of infected trees and fallen logs.

Wildlife in the
Mountain Environment

Communities include animals as well as plants, though animals are much less numerous and conspicuous. While some animals are narrowly restricted to a single plant community or vegetation type, most range through several in the course of a year, a day, or an hour. And animals that are restricted to a particular plant association may be neither its most conspicuous nor its most numerous form. Because of their mobility and often secretive habits, animals are more difficult to study than plants, and their impacts on a community are less easily detected. Attempts to describe *biotic communities*—predictable associations of both plants and animals—has met with some success, and indeed some associations, such as that of the grazing herds on the African savanna, are well known. Nevertheless, the concept of biotic communities remains less fully elaborated than that of plant communities.

Yet one need only recall, for example, the importance of insects to pollination or of earthworms to soil development to realize that animals play crucial roles in the lives of plants and plant communities. The effects of parasitic insects have already been discussed, as has the role of birds in ensuring the distribution and germination of the seeds of the western juniper. Birds and mammals are both instrumental in distributing the seeds of many plants. To encourage this process, plants have evolved seeds that are appetizing to various animals or that possess hooks, barbs, or other devices that enable them to cling to fur and feathers.

Grazing animals, in preferring some types of plants over others, may for a time improve the competitive position of less appetizing forms. Browsing animals prune shrubs and trees much as a gardener would, thereby promoting shoot proliferation, which in turn provides yet more food. If herbivorous animals reproduce beyond the capacity of their food supply, favored food plants may be eliminated, at least temporarily, from certain areas.

These are but a few of the many ways in which animals affect plants, and in so doing, animals, in turn, alter their own environment, which is largely determined by the types and abundance of plants found in a given area.

Wildlife Habitats

Plant habitats are largely defined by physical factors in the environment—air temperature, precipitation, soil, humidity, and so on. Animal habitats, while including these elements, are instead tied directly to the types of food and shelter provided by different kinds of vegetation. Within a single plant community there may be several animal habitats, as, for example, in the mixed-coniferous forest, where the canopy, understory shrubs, streamsides, rocky openings, grassy areas, and others offer particular opportunities for food and shelter to animals equipped to take advantage of them. At the same time, different communities may offer comparable habitats that some animals are able to utilize more or less equally. Mountain chickadees, for example, feed largely on insects that inhabit the outer branches of conifers. Since most any conifer will do in this regard, mountain chickadees range throughout all the forest communities in the Sierra.

The amount and distribution of food, water, and shelter in a given area largely governs how many animals will live there. The types of food and shelter provided by various habitats limit the kinds of animals that can make use of them. Some animals are able to satisfy most or all of their requirements in a single habitat. The dipper, for example, spends almost all of its life along Sierra streams. The pocket gopher seldom if ever leaves its meadow home, and the pika rarely ventures far from the High Sierra rockslides it inhabits. Many animals, however, use different habitats for different purposes. The yellow-bellied marmot, for example, seeks shelter in the same rockslides as the pika, but relies largely on nearby meadows for food. Sage grouse, which occur on sageflats east of the Sierra, require dense brush for food, nesting, and cover from predators, but open areas for carrying out their elaborate mating dance. Migratory animals such as mule deer commonly utilize a variety of habitats in the course of a year, as do large predators such as the mountain lion and fisher, which must travel great distances to secure enough food.

Ecotones and Waterholes

The variety and number of animals are usually greatest where two or more habitats converge, a phenomenon known as the *edge effect*. Along the boundary between meadow and forest, for example, conditions are suitable for organisms typical of both habitats, so this "edge," or ecotone, is usually richer in wildlife than either meadow or forest alone. Birdwatchers know this fact well and often station themselves near such habitat boundaries, a practice that anyone wishing to observe wildlife would do well to imitate. Other examples from the Sierra include areas where woodland, chaparral, and grassland converge; almost any streamside or lake border; where meadows and rock outcrops meet, especially if a few trees are present as well; and where open sagebrush gives way to pinyon woodland or coniferous forest. Naturally, these are but a few of the numerous ecotones occurring in the Sierra, any of which will usually prove to be fruitful places for observing wildlife.

In hot, arid regions such as the Sierra foothills and pinyon–sagebrush zone, reliable sources of water also attract a greater number of animals than occur generally. Although several animals are able to obtain sufficient water from their food or have developed various other ways of conserving moisture, studies have shown that the number and variety of species declines with increasing distance away from a water source. These oases also attract wide-ranging animals that spend most of their time elsewhere. This is true even in the forest, though there, because of the greater abundance of water overall, the concentration at any single water source may be less dramatic than in drier areas.

Animal Mobility

If the genius of green plants is their ability to manufacture food from scratch, that of animals surely consists of being able to move about in order to take advantage of shifting resource opportunities. A plant must be adapted to conditions as they exist throughout the year on its particular patch of ground, but an animal can range freely through a variety of habitats, using them wherever possible, enduring them for a time if necessary. Animals are therefore less vulnerable than plants to rapid environmental changes, to which they may respond by moving to different quarters. The price of mobility, however, is the enormous amount of energy animals must expend in the process: to pay this price animals must consume correspondingly large amounts of food, an activity that becomes increasingly critical as the size of an animal decreases.

The smaller an animal, the greater its surface area compared to its volume, and hence the more rapidly it loses body heat. This is critical for warm-blooded animals, which maintain body heat through their own metabolic activity. Larger mammals and birds can go without food for relatively long periods because their rates of heat loss are comparatively slow. Small animals, however, must spend most of their time securing and consuming food simply to keep pace with heat loss. Shrews, which are common in the Sierra, are the smallest of all mammals and therefore extraordinarily voracious. Were they any smaller, they would not be able to eat enough food to sustain themselves. With the shrew, the advantage of mobility seems to have reached the point of diminishing returns: it moves to eat and eats to move—period.

Food Quality

Carnivores and seed eaters rely on foods that are reliable sources of high protein, so their only problem is finding enough. Herbivores that feed primarily on plant shoots, rather than seeds, however, must be extremely selective in regard to which plants they eat and when they eat them. Not all plants are equally nutritious, and inferior types will be eaten only after more nourishing species are unavailable. The lack of preferred food plants may result from such factors as the onset of winter snow, depletion through overgrazing, or seasonal shifts in protein content.

Even the most nutritious species of plants vary greatly in protein content through the year. Plant shoots are most nutritious during the period of early growth and flowering, when proteins are being actively manufactured. They become less so during seed production, when proteins are being transferred from the shoots to the seeds. Plants are least nutritious after seed production and during dormancy, at which times the old shoots are composed mostly of cellulose.

Animals contend with shifting protein levels in plant shoots by switching to a new food source as necessary or by migrating to areas where more nutritious forage is available. Sierra chipmunks, for example, prefer new shoots in the spring and early summer, but switch increasingly to seeds as the season progresses. They also supplement their late summer diet with berries and mushrooms. Similarly, the black bear subsists largely on bulbs and young plant shoots during the spring and early summer, shifting in late summer and fall to such foods as nuts, berries, grubs, and acorns, which promote fat production in preparation for a long winter sleep.

Mule deer spend the winter and spring in the Sierra foothills and sagebrush flats along the eastern base of the range, where new shoots may appear all winter. As summer approaches, plants in these lowland areas commence seed production and a decline of protein in their shoots results. So most of the deer begin to move upslope, following the spring, as it were, to feed on plants recently emerged from winter dormancy and beginning to set forth new shoots. Since the onset of new plant growth occurs progressively later as elevation increases, upslope migration ensures the mule deer a steady succession of nutritious food throughout most of the summer.

Food and Population

Animal populations are in balance with their food supply when enough remains after feeding to ensure replacement of the amount eaten. Plants must be left with enough reserves to permit maintenance, growth, and reproduction. Populations of prey animals must be large enough to replace the individuals lost to carnivores and disease, but not so large as to diminish their own food supply. When an animal population grows too large, it may be reduced through the movement of some individuals to new areas or by death from starvation, disease, and predation. Weakened deer are easier targets for mountain lions. Meadow mice experience huge population explosions every few years and would quickly outstrip their food supply except that predators such as hawks, owls, coyotes, and foxes rapidly converge on overrun areas and help to reduce the population to its former sustainable level.

Home Range and Territory

The amount of land occupied over a period of time by an individual animal is a function of its mobility in relation to available food supplies. The area in which an animal normally roams in its search for food is called its *home range*. The home range of a gopher may consist of a few square yards of meadow; that of a pine marten, of several square miles of forest, meadow, and rock outcrops. Predators generally have larger home ranges than herbivores of comparable size because they must eat more food to obtain a comparable supply of protein. Large herbivores, however, often range over wide areas in order to take advantage of changing forage conditions during the year.

That part of an animal's home range defended against others of its kind, generally for mating purposes, constitutes its *territory*. In recent years, the territoriality of animals has received widespread attention in popular books and articles, but in fact relatively few animals exhibit territorial behavior. Deer, for example, have large home ranges, but do not actively defend particular territories. Gophers, on the other hand, stake out certain areas for their burrow systems and will drive off all other gophers who trespass, regardless of whether it is the mating season or not. Many species of birds, which along with fish are among the most territorial of creatures, vigorously defend breeding territories against all comers, but after the young are fledged show little concern for geographic boundaries. The western kingbird, a large flycatcher of the foothill zone, is one of the more pugnacious territorial species in this regard.

Home ranges and territories both ensure that the members of an animal population are sufficiently spread out to be able to obtain sufficient resources for survival with a minimum of conflict with others of their kind. Out of a given population of territorial animals, there are often a few members that are unable to establish and hold a territory for themselves. These tend to be the weaker, less assertive individuals in the population. Harried on all sides by stronger neighbors and forced to settle for inferior territories and thereafter scramble for food and water, such animals are prime candidates for both predators and disease. In this way, only the stronger individuals in a population are likely to survive and perpetuate the species.

A distinction should be made between the range of a species and the home ranges of individual animals. The range of a species encompasses the entire geographic area occupied by all representative individuals. Within this range there are typically several local populations, which may or may not be separated, each member of which has its own home range. The deer mouse, for example, ranges throughout the Sierra Nevada (as well as the rest of the western United States), but an individual mouse spends its entire life within a home range comprising less than five or six acres.

Elevational Ranges

Some animals, such as the mule deer, coyote, and red-tailed hawk, occur from lowland valleys to timberline, but most species are more restricted in their elevational distribution. Climatic conditions are largely responsible for this, either directly or indirectly.

The ranges of cold-blooded vertebrates are directly affected by climate. Although a few, such as the Yosemite toad and the Mt. Lyell salamander, can survive at high elevations, most amphibians and reptiles are intolerant of the severe cold that prevails near timberline for much of the year. Indirectly, elevational differences in climate account for the distribution of certain animals by determining the distribution of various specific vegetation types. For example, the brush rabbit of the lower western Sierra slope is restricted to foothill chaparral, while the varying hare or snowshoe rabbit is a resident of the high coniferous forests. Neither species would survive in the habitat occupied by the other, and the differences in these habitats are controlled essentially by climate.

Rarely, however, can the elevational ranges of animals be attributed to only one or two factors. More often, they are governed by the interplay of numerous factors, including the presence of other closely competing species in adjacent elevational zones. In many instances we simply do not know enough about the habits of an animal to ascertain why it occurs in one place but not another. Even in instances where much is known the answer is seldom clear-cut.

The gray squirrel illustrates several factors relevant to the elevational distribution of Sierra animals as a whole. This rather large arboreal squirrel is most characteristic of the oak woodlands of the Sierra foothills, but ranges upslope in the mixed pine–oak forest of the lower montane zone to about 6000 feet (1800 meters). It depends largely on oaks for both food and shelter, and its upper limit in the Sierra roughly corresponds to that of the black oak and canyon live oak. It is likely that the increasing scarcity of oaks about 6000 feet is responsible at least in part for the upper limit of the gray squirrel's range. Yet this cannot be the only factor, for in the lower montane zone the gray squirrel also nests in pines and eats large quantities of conifer seeds as well as acorns.

Deep, persistent winter snow cover above 6000 feet may inhibit the gray squirrel's feeding habits and thereby restrict its upslope occurrence. The squirrel buries surplus acorns and conifer seeds in underground caches for retrieval during the winter, when food is scarce. It later relocates some of these caches by smell. Above 6000 feet, the elevation at which deep, persistent snow becomes the rule during the winter, this technique is probably not workable. The caches would remain undiscovered, and starvation would shortly follow.

This problem does not exist for the chickaree, the counterpart of the gray squirrel in the upper montane forest. The chickaree stashes cones away for winter use, but rather than burying them, it stacks them in small piles next to rocks or logs near its home tree. It later recovers them by digging through the deep snow. It is likely that both its sense of smell and memory help the animal to locate these caches.

Another factor excluding the gray squirrel from the upper montane forests might be the presence of the pine marten, a swift, agile treetop predator that can overtake even the fastest squirrel. Even the resident chickaree, which is much faster than the gray squirrel, is no match for the marten, so gray squirrels in the upper montane zone would no doubt be easy prey.

The gray squirrel and the chickaree utilize comparable habitats in roughly the same way. In an ecological sense they can be considered analogous species, and were they to coexist throughout the same geographic range, competition between them would be considerable. As it is, each squirrel is better adapted to conditions within its particular geographic range—which in the Sierra is largely defined by elevation—and there enjoys a competitive advantage over the other. The very fact that the chickaree is present in the upper montane zone might well be sufficient to limit the upward distribution of the gray squirrel. Consequently, the range of the latter is also determined in part by all the factors governing the range of the former—and vice versa.

The case of the gray squirrel demonstrates how difficult it can be to pinpoint the reasons why an animal occurs in one place but not another. The presence of appropriate food and shelter is a necessary but not a sufficient condition; the habitat must also be free of close competitors for those resources.

Segregation by Elevation

The gray squirrel and chickaree constitute but one of many examples from the Sierra fauna of the *ecological segregation* of potential close competitors by elevation. Numerous examples could be cited, but a few will suffice.

Three species of jay occur in the Sierra, as well as the Clark's nutcracker, which is related to the jays and exhibits many of the same behavioral traits. Each of these four analogous birds occupies a different elevational belt. The scrub jay occurs in the foothill zone of the west slope. The pinyon jay frequents the pinyon–sagebrush zone of the east slope. Steller's jay is the common forest form on both sides of the range, but Clark's nutcracker replaces it in the open subalpine forest.

The dusky-footed wood rat of the foothills and lower montane zone is replaced in the upper forest by the bushy-tailed wood rat. The white-tailed jackrabbit of the upper montane and subalpine zones is the high-elevation counterpart of the common black-tailed jackrabbit of the lower eastern and western slopes.

In the central and northern Sierra the western toad ranges from the Central Valley to the lower margins of the upper montane zone, where it gives way to the very similar Yosemite toad, which occupies comparable habitats upslope to timberline. In the southern Sierra, however, where the Yosemite toad does not occur, the western toad is able to range upslope to nearly 10,000 feet (3050 meters). This example, more than any other from the Sierra, demonstrates that the presence of a competing species, in some cases at least, can be the critical factor governing the upper or lower range limits of another.

An extreme case of ecological segregation by elevation is provided by Sierra chipmunks, of which nine separate species have been identified. Different species occur at various elevations on both slopes, and in the few locales where the ranges of two or three overlap, they tend to prefer different foraging areas, such as trees, rocks, or understory brush and debris. Thus, ecological segregation both by elevation and foraging habits reduces competition among species of Sierra chipmunks.

Winter Survival

With the coming of winter, animals inhabiting the middle and upper slopes of the Sierra must contend with an acute food shortage. Cold weather is also a problem, but probably less of one than is commonly supposed. Most birds and mammals found in the Sierra, protected by coats of feathers or fur, are able to withstand prolonged cold so long as food and shelter are available. Many small mammals spend the winter beneath the snowpack in burrows warmed by their own body heat. Most active species are able to subsist on foods available in the winter—conifer seeds and needles, bark, buds, and the like—and therefore remain in the high country throughout the season, continuing about their business in all but the coldest, most inclement weather. All Sierra predators except the black bear (an occasional and half-hearted predator at best) remain active during the winter, though they often move downslope locally, where temperatures are warmer and food more plentiful. Squirrels, mice, and other rodents are important sources of food for predators during the winter. A few animals hibernate, but many more do not.

Migration

Most species of birds and a few mammals avoid winter food shortages by migrating downslope, or in the case of certain birds, out of the region entirely. Mule deer and bighorn sheep, which rely on green shoots for food, move downslope in the fall, the sheep to the sagebrush scrub on the east slope of the Sierra, mule deer to lower elevations on both slopes. Food is not the only consideration compelling sheep and deer to move downslope. Because of their small hooves, these animals are poorly equipped to travel through deep snow and thus are particularly vulnerable to predators under such conditions.

Of the thirty-odd species of birds regularly found in the subalpine and alpine zones during the summer, only about ten remain during the winter. Hammond's flycatcher, the calliope hummingbird, and the hermit thrush migrate to Mexico and Guatemala. The rest move downslope, some into the forest belt, some into the foothills, valleys, and basins on either side of the Sierra. A few species stray as far as the coast, especially during unusually severe winters. Clark's nutcracker, the white-crowned sparrow, and the gray-crowned rosy finch spend their winters in the pinyon–sagebrush belt on the lower east slope of the Sierra. Mountain bluebirds congregate in large flocks in the Central Valley and in lowlands east of the Sierra. Robins move westward into the foothills, and spotted sandpipers migrate to the sandy shores and mudflats of the Pacific Coast. The yellow-rumped warbler, the dark-eyed junco, Brewer's blackbird, the Lincoln sparrow, and other species all move downslope to some degree or another, ranging throughout central California and on the east side of the Sierra. Rosy finches, the most alpine of birds, occasionally may be found above timberline even during the winter.

Amid all this downslope flight, the blue grouse is a distinct anomaly. Spending its summers in the mixed-coniferous forest and red fir forests, it works its way upslope during the late summer and fall to spend winter in the upper montane zone, where it roosts in densely foliaged red firs. The needles of this tree constitute the blue grouse's sole food during the winter months.

Nonmigratory Birds

Several species of birds regularly remain in the high country during the winter, mostly in the red fir forest, where food and shelter are more available than in the sparser, colder subalpine forest. The number of birds found in the lower forest communities during the winter is even greater. Williamson's sapsucker, which feeds on the sap of lodgepole pines during the summer, relies during the winter, when the flow of sap is greatly reduced, on insects found in the bark of these trees. These same insects form the bulk of the diet of the black-backed three-toed wood-pecker all year long. Small, noisy bands of mountain chickadees, among the most common and conspicuous winter residents of the Sierra, feed during this season on dormant insects, larvae, pupae, and insect eggs gleaned from the outer foliage of conifers. The chickadee eats enormous amounts of the larvae of the lodgepole needleminer, which it obtains by snipping open the needles with its beak and deftly extracting the tiny caterpillar within. Red-breasted nuthatches, which occasionally join bands of chickadees, search for insects on the upper branches of conifers. Brown creepers continue their endless spiralling probe of tree trunks for insects, and dippers remain along their still-flowing streams. The pine grosbeak and red crossbill, both uncommon and erratically distributed red finches of the lodgepole pine forest, subsist on pine nuts during the winter. Juniper berries, which remain on the trees throughout this season, provide food for many species of birds.

Hibernation

Hibernating mammals, such as marmots, ground squirrels, chipmunks, and western jumping mice, store up fat

THE MOUNTAIN ENVIRONMENT

during summer for use during winter. In the fall they retreat to underground dens, where they spend from seven to
eight months in a torpid state. Their food requirements are
sharply reduced during this period because their
metabolism slows down radically. Breathing becomes very
shallow, body temperature drops to just a few degrees
above that of the sleeping quarters, and the heart rate slows
down to just a few beats per minute. In this state energy
expenditures are minimal, so the fat acquired during the
summer is ample to sustain life for the long hibernation
period. Most species do not eat from the time they enter
hibernation in the fall till they emerge in the late spring.
They may occasionally awaken briefly to urinate, at which
time metabolism temporarily returns to normal levels.

Although black bears den up during the winter, their
body temperature and respiration remain close to normal;
in other words, they do not physiologically hibernate, but
merely sleep the season away. As some people have discovered to their chagrin, these bears can easily be aroused and
display at such times the same surliness as roughly
awakened humans.

Winter-Active Mammals

Most Sierra mammals remain active during the winter,
having devised various strategies for securing food, finding
shelter, keeping warm, and traveling over and within the
snowpack. Winter, in fact, is one of the best seasons for
observing animal tracks, which are beautifully preserved in
the snow.

FOOD STORAGE Pikas, deer mice, pocket gophers,
and tree squirrels live during the winter on food stored the
preceding summer. Pikas spend the entire season within
talus slopes, eating vegetation gathered in late summer and
fall and stacked into piles for curing. Chickarees hole up in
tree cavities when the weather is bad, emerging on warmer
days to feed on buried caches of cones, which they dig
through the snow to retrieve, and dried mushrooms cached
in the crotches of trees. Deer mice store large amounts of
seeds, sprouting shoots, buds, nuts, berries, insects, and
tender bark. Relying on snow cover for protection against
cold and predators, they burrow close to the ground

80. Gopher cores in a meadow.

throughout the winter, only occasionally venturing out onto the snow surface.

Pocket gophers may store some food in their tunnels but subsist chiefly on roots, supplemented with plant stems and leaves obtained by burrowing through the snow at or above ground level. As summer approaches, gophers begin cleaning old tunnels and building new ones, pushing the excavated earth out into the snow burrows. After the snow melts, these cores of earth remain, winding like snakes through the meadows. They are sure signs that the animals were active in an area during the previous winter.

ACTIVE FORAGING Meadow mice also remain active during the winter, burrowing through the snow in search of young shoots and the bark of shrubs and trees. The mountain beaver, or aplodontia, feeds on bark and shoots of plants growing along streams and ponds. The porcupine spends the winter in conifers, feeding on bark. The winter diet of shrews consists of earthworms, small rodents, and the dormant larvae and pupae of insects. Given their voracious appetites, competition among shrews in the winter is probably fierce, and cannibalism is considered a distinct possibility by some authorities.

ANATOMICAL ADAPTATIONS White-tailed jackrabbits and snowshoe hares turn white during the winter, a form of protective coloration that, along with their speed and agility, offers some protection from predators. Weasels also develop white coats in winter, camouflaging them not only from cruising hawks and owls, but also from their own prey. A few mammals, including the white-tailed jackrabbit and the mountain coyote, grow thick fur on their feet, which not only provides insulation from cold, but improves the animal's maneuverability by turning its paws into snow-shoes of a sort.

Adaptations to Heat and Drought

Animals inhabiting the Sierra foothills and the lower, desert slopes along the east side of the range must contend with severe heat and drought during the summer. Furthermore, the nutritional value of many common food plants drops drastically following seed production in the spring, making food shortages a problem for some animals.

NOCTURNAL ACTIVITY   Most mammals beat the heat by sleeping during the day and emerging at dusk to spend the night foraging. Nocturnal activity also affords greater protection from predators. Among the diurnal animals — those abroad during the day—afternoon siestas are common. Snakes and lizards are particularly vulnerable to hot summer temperatures and commonly retire to underground burrows or shady areas beneath rocks and shrubs during the hottest part of the day. Some animals, such as the California ground squirrel and western spadefoot toad, spend much of the summer in a torpid state known as *estivation,* a hot-weather version of hibernation.

UPSLOPE MIGRATION   Many birds of the foothills and sagebrush scrub begin breeding in late winter and early spring, when food and water are plentiful, then move upslope in the summer into the forests and meadows, which by then are at the peak of activity. Larger predators such as coyotes and mountain lions also move upslope into the forest during the summer, as do deer herds that winter at lower elevations. By moving to higher rangeland, deer conserve the browse which must sustain them during the winter.

WATER CONSERVATION   Animals that remain at lower elevations during the summer must contend with drought as well as heat. Vernal pools and many smaller streams have dried up by early summer. A number of animals stay within easy reach of what reliable water sources remain, but those particularly adapted to desertlike conditions often are able to obtain sufficient water from their food—insects, seeds, leaves, and stems. This is true, for example, of kangaroo rats, pocket mice and antelope ground squirrels. Like most small mammals, they are unable to make long pilgrimages to water. Some desert rodents conserve what moisture they do obtain by virtually eliminating it from their wastes. The feces are typically hard and dry; the urine may consist of uric acid with most water removed. Nocturnal activity and midday inactivity, of course, are important stratagems for conserving body moisture, since loss of water is thereby reduced.

LIGHT COLORATION   Animals characteristic of hot, arid regions also tend to be lighter colored than their counterparts in cooler, moister areas. Light coloration reflects heat away from the body and thereby conserves moisture as well. Merriam's chipmunk, which lives in the Sierra foothills, is significantly lighter than its forest cousins, its body stripe scarcely being noticeable. Other foothill rodents, as well as those of the pinyon–sagebrush zone on the east slope also tend to come in shades of pale gray and tan.

Adaptations to Fire

Fire is an important if relatively infrequent environmental factor for most California animals, particularly for those occupying foothill communities, but also for residents of forest and sagebrush scrub. Despite posters depicting raccoons and deer evicted from their homes by flames, most wild animals survive fires. Larger animals and most birds are generally able to flee to safety, either leaving an area entirely or finding refuge on cooler, moister, north-facing slopes that commonly escape the flames. Smaller animals find sanctuary below ground or sometimes in deep rock crevices in outcrops surrounded by little flammable material. Other islands of safety may include trees with little or no understory or beneath logs or trunks protected by living bark and therefore less apt to burn. Young birds and mammals, of course, are more vulnerable than adults, but most creatures born early in the year can fend for themselves reasonably well by the time the fire season commences in late summer. Foothill animals commonly have their young in late winter and spring, when cool weather, ample moisture, and minimal amounts of dead plant materials make fire unlikely.

Most fire-caused deaths among wild animals result from *hyperthermia,* or excessive body temperature. As the air heats up, the evaporation of moisture from the body surface helps to keep an animal cool, but beyond a certain point, so much moisture has already been lost that the amount remaining is insufficient to produce further cooling. Most small animals, however, will survive a fire if they can find shelter in a well-ventilated burrow at least three inches, and preferably five or more inches, below the ground surface. In one controlled burn undertaken to determine animal responses to fire, the temperature of surface litter rose to 670° F (354° C) after 12 minutes of burning, cooling to 360° F (182° C) a half-hour later, and continuing to cool for three hours thereafter. Soil is an extremely efficient insulator, however, and only two inches below the ground surface, temperatures reached only 156° F (69° C) during the first hour. While this is still too hot for most animals to survive, temperatures only an inch or two deeper would have been well within the tolerance ranges of most species.

Fires can improve wildlife habitat in several ways. For example, mature chaparral shrubs offer poor browse for deer because few new shoots are produced and the older ones contain relatively little nourishment. Furthermore, much of this browse is inaccessible because old chaparral is tall and its thickets virtually impenetrable to animals as large as deer. Fire not only opens up such areas, but encourages the production of nutritious young shoots, as well as many herbaceous species that formerly were unable to grow beneath the dominant shrubs. Similarly, fires open up dense forests, admitting more sunlight and thus encouraging shrubs and herbs to proliferate. This improves the variety of available food plants in such areas and thereby permits a larger number of species to live there. (See Fire and Vegetation, page 177.) Fires also expose seeds that were once buried in deep litter, thus providing increased food for small birds and rodents. In general, fires encourage vegetation mosaics comprising tracts of land in various stages of community succession, thus increasing the number of different habitats available and the variety of wildlife as well.

Wildlife in the Mountain Environment 203

CHAPTER V

The Western Margin: Foothill Communities

THE FOOTHILLS of the Sierra Nevada form a belt 10 to 30 miles (16 to 48 kilometers) wide and from 500 to 5000 feet (150 to 1500 meters) elevation on the eastern border of the Central Valley. They begin where the tilted Sierra block emerges from the valley sediments, a transition marked by a gradual but conspicuous shift from flat to gently rising terrain. The Sierra foothills cannot be separated geologically or topographically from the range as a whole. They constitute a vegetation zone rather than one primarily distinguished by rock types or terrain. The foothill zone is defined by a distinctive vegetation mosaic comprising grassland, woodland, and chaparral, and its upper limit, by custom, coincides with the lower limit of the coniferous forest.

The foothills receive between 15 and 40 inches (40 and 100 centimeters) of rain a year, all but a small fraction falling from November through April. December, January, and February are the months of heaviest precipitation. Snow is exceptional and rarely amounts to more than an inch or two, falling only during the coldest storms and melting within a few hours or a couple of days at most. Average minimum temperatures during the winter range from 29 to 42° F (−2 to 6° C), so while frosts are not uncommon, hard freezes are rare. Daytime highs in January average in the mid-50s, reaching the 70s and even low 80s on the warmest days of the month. In some years rains may arrive as early as September or continue through June. For the most part, however, the period from mid-May to mid-October is characterized by virtually no rain whatsoever. Summers are very hot, with maximum temperatures usually ranging between 75 and 96° F (24 and 36° C); temperatures exceeding 100° F (38° C) are common. Relative humidity during the summer may drop to 20 percent or less.

Foothill plants, more than any others in the Sierra, must contend with pronounced drought during the warmest months of the year. Not only do they occupy the zone of highest summer temperatures and lowest annual precipitation, but unlike plants upslope they must endure the drought season without the benefit of runoff from the snowpack of the previous winter. Consequently, most foothill plants exhibit adaptive strategies designed to reduce water loss and prevent heat damage. Moreover, instead of commencing growth in the late spring or early

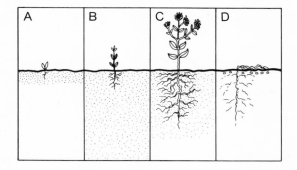

81. Life cycle of a foothill annual. The seed germinates and growth commences in the fall after the first rains (A). During the winter (B), growth proceeds slowly, for even though soil moisture is abundant, temperatures are too low for maximum activity. When air and soil temperatures rise in the spring (C), growth rapidly accelerates in order to take advantage of available soil moisture. Flowering and seed production are completed by the onset of summer drought (D), at which time the plant dies, leaving its seeds behind to sprout with the first rains of autumn.

summer, as plants growing at higher elevations do, foothill species tend to be most active during the winter and spring, when soil moisture is ample. Most species commence germination or growth in the late fall or early winter. The maximum amount of growth for most foothill plants occurs in March and April, when the air has warmed up, yet soil moisture is still ample. By the first of June most foothill plants have begun to shut down for the summer. Annuals have died, leaving numerous seeds behind to sprout the following rainy season. Perennials are becoming dormant, drastically slowing their rates of photosynthesis, respiration, and transpiration for the duration of the dry season.

FOOTHILL PLANT COMMUNITIES

FOOTHILL VEGETATION consists of four major plant communities: valley grassland, foothill woodland, chaparral, and riparian woodland. *Valley grassland* covers the gentle rolling terrain of the lower foothills and extends upslope as an understory beneath the foothill woodland. Patches of valley grassland also occur on dry, open flats in the ponderosa pine forest, just above the foothill zone.

The *foothill woodland* occurs on fairly deep, comparatively well-developed soils in the middle and upper foothills. It is dominated overall by blue oak and digger pine, locally by valley oak or interior live oak. Widely spaced trees scattered over an understory of grasses—a formation known as *savanna*—occurs on drier woodland sites throughout the foothills and may be considered an ecotone between woodland and grassland communities. On moister sites woodland stands are denser, but grasses remain a conspicuous part of the community on most sites. Understory shrubs may be sparse or absent in shadier or drier stands, more common in those where adequate sunlight and moisture exist.

Meandering corridors of willows, cottonwoods, sycamores, and other moisture-loving deciduous trees form a distinct *riparian woodland* along foothill streams, extending from the coniferous forest downslope and out onto the valley floor. Members of the riparian woodland community, unlike other foothill plants, are assured of moisture throughout the summer and lack the adaptations to heat and drought exhibited by grassland, woodland, and chaparral plants. Unlike their drought-resistant neighbors, riparian plants remain active during this season, entering dormancy in the fall, when plants in other foothill communities are just beginning to emerge from months of torpor.

On steep slopes or other areas underlain by thin, rocky, or otherwise inhospitable soils, foothill woodland is replaced by *chaparral,* a dense, fire-adapted shrub community dominated by chamise and several species of manzanita and ceanothus. Chaparral often forms extensive cover on steep, hot, south-facing slopes, but occurs on other aspects as well. Areas underlain by serpentine or other sterile rock types (see page 244) are often marked by abrupt changes from woodland to chaparral. Transitional stands composed of scattered woodland trees rising above a dense chaparral understory occur throughout the foothills. Often, however, chaparral boundaries are abrupt, especially those shared with grassland.

Valley Grassland

Grassland covers most of the lower foothills surrounding the Central Valley. Originally most of the valley floor was also given over to grassland, but with the introduction of irrigation the rich soils were rapidly converted to agricultural use. Soil moisture is the most important factor governing the distribution of the valley grassland community in that grasses dominate sites where moisture is insufficient to support shrubs or trees. In the Sierra this community is largely restricted to the lowest portion of the western foothills, where rainfall seldom exceeds 20 inches (50 centimeters) a year. Grassland species common to the community—though not the community itself—also range upslope, where they occur as elements in the understories of the foothill woodland and ponderosa pine forest. Grasses are present among chaparral shrubs only following fires. In mature chaparral stands the germination of grasses and forbs is inhibited by failure to compete successfully for light, moisture, and nutrients, as well as by the presence of plant toxins in the soil.

Like chaparral and foothill woodland, valley grassland is a widespread and characteristic element in the foothill landscape of central California, yet unlike these companion communities, it is now dominated by alien plant species, most of which are native to the Mediterranean region. Although evidence is scanty, it is generally agreed that the pristine California grassland was dominated by perennial bunchgrasses such as purple needlegrass, *Stipa pulchra*, and foothill bluegrass, *Poa scabrella*. Bunchgrasses grow in clumps from root systems that remain alive during the dry summer season, when the above-ground shoots die back. In the fall, with the arrival of rain or even before, new shoots

82   83

82. California Poppy, *Eschscholtzia californica*. Flowers brilliant yellow or orange, bowl-shaped; leaves lacy; stems branched, 6 to 24 in (1.5 to 6 dm). The California poppy is the state flower, commonly occurring below 5000 ft (1500 m) on the west slope in dry grasslands or disturbed areas. It is often seen along roads in the company of lupines. The California poppy blooms from April through August in the Sierra. It is unlawful to pick the flowers.

83. Williamson's Clarkia, *Clarkia williamsonii*. Flowers white to pale lavender with a purple spot on each petal; leaves linear; stem 4 to 40 inches (1 to 10 dm). Williamson's clarkia is one of several rather similar species found in the Sierra foothills. All go by the popular name, Farewell-to-Spring. Williamson's clarkia occurs in dry grassy areas upslope to 6000 ft (1800 m), blooming May–August.

develop from the living roots. Such plants, though well adapted to California's climate, have within the past century been replaced on most sites by such alien annuals as wild oats, *Avena fatua* and *A. barbata;* soft chess, *Bromus mollis;* red brome, *B. rubens;* and foxtail fescue, *Festuca megalura.* Today alien annual grasses account for up to 90 percent of the plants making up the California grasslands. Native perennial bunchgrasses are now plentiful only in scattered, ungrazed, unplowed stands.

Annuals sprout each year from seeds left behind the previous year. Growth is rapid because they do not need to develop permanent root or branch systems. Energy is concentrated into producing just enough stems and leaves to carry out photosynthesis and support flowers. Annuals are therefore in an excellent position to take advantage of optimal soil and temperature conditions during the spring, when soils are moist but not soggy and temperatures high enough for rapid growth. By early summer most annuals have died, leaving only their seeds behind, so they are not subjected to the rigors of the hot dry season.

Most of the alien grasses arrived in California along with Spanish and Mexican explorers and settlers. Some seeds were brought along purposely in feed for livestock or for planting in the cultivated fields that were part of every mission settlement. Others arrived unnoticed, attached to the coats of domestic animals, or to clothes, or hidden among gear and provisions. Some authorities have speculated that a few alien grasses may have arrived prior to the first Europeans, perhaps borne north to California from Mexico by migrating birds.

Whatever the form of transportation, by 1850 alien annual grasses were well on their way toward replacing native perennial bunchgrasses throughout the California prairie. Having evolved in a climate comparable to California's, the alien annuals were well adapted to their new home, and even better equipped than native bunchgrasses to endure the changes in environment that occurred in the latter half of the nineteenth century.

Prior to European settlement in California the valley grassland, then dominated by perennial bunchgrasses, was grazed primarily by large herds of tule elk and pronghorns. The native grasses, having evolved along with these ruminants, were more or less equal to the feeding pressures to which they were subjected. With the arrival of domestic livestock, sheep and cattle began to replace the native grazers. From 1850 to 1880 livestock grazing increased dramatically in the state, reaching a peak in the 1860s and 1870s. The grasslands were subjected to overgrazing, which the alien annuals were better equipped to endure, having coexisted for centuries with livestock. Moreover, their annual seeding habit not only guaranteed their reappearance the following year but allowed them to rapidly invade areas where bunchgrasses had been overgrazed. In similar fashion they were also able to reinvade abandoned fields that had been cleared for cultivation, growing so abundantly that perennial bunchgrasses were effectively excluded thereafter. On experimental plots in the Sierra foothills annual grasses have continued to exclude native perennials despite the absence of livestock grazing for periods up to 40 years. When grazing is halted wild oats and soft chess, rather than giving way to native bunchgrasses, actually increase in numbers and dominance.

The replacement of bunchgrasses by alien annuals was further encouraged by a decade of drought beginning in the 1850s. Not only were the annuals better able to take advantage of the sparse moisture available during these years, but since their seeds could remain viable through several seasons of drought, they were able to establish themselves quickly during intermittent rainy periods. Today there is no chance that the California grassland will ever be returned to its original condition, and some botanists have suggested that the new community be recognized as a "California annual type."

Although it is tempting to wax nostalgic about a vast, pristine bunchgrass prairie that no person now living has ever seen, this should not blind one to the beauty of the annual grassland as it exists today. Emerald green from fall through spring and tawny gold thereafter, the annual valley grassland is not only superlatively adapted to its environment, but a beautiful and now integral part of the California landscape.

The annual grasses and forbs constituting the valley grassland germinate in the fall, grow slowly during the cool winter months, and then rapidly increase growth during the warm moist months of March and April. Flowering reaches a climax in April and May, and by mid-June, as soon as seeds have been set, the plants die. Wildflowers are particularly profuse in the numerous small rainwater catch basins scattered throughout the foothills. During the rainy season, these basins fill with water to form *vernal pools*. After the water has deeply soaked the soil and then evaporated, wildflower growth is rapid and the resulting displays of color spectacular. Vernal pools provide a moister habitat—at least for a few weeks—than occurs in the foothills as a whole and thus support a number of moisture-loving herbaceous species that are unable to grow on drier sites. Among these species, white meadowform, *Limnanthes alba*, is especially conspicuous, forming massed displays from March through June.

84. Fremont's Tidytips, *Layia fremontii*. Flower yellow with white tips divided into three lobes; leaves compound, with numerous leaflets; stem 2 to 12 inches (5 to 30 cm). Fremont's tidytips are common in dry grasslands below 4000 feet on the west slope, where they bloom May–June. The related Sierra layia, *Layia pentachaeta*, has completely yellow flowers and hairy, rather than smooth, leaves.

85. Meadowfoam, *Limnanthes alba*. Flowers white, aging pink, bowl-shaped, with white hairs on sepals; leaves hairy, divided once or twice, 1 to 4 in (2.5 to 10 cm); stems 4 to 12 in (1 to 3 dm). Meadowfoam grows abundantly in moist grassland depressions, often in areas formerly occupied by vernal pools. Massed displays of flowers deck the foothill grasslands with white from April through early June.

The Sierra foothills are most beautiful in the spring, when the grasses are brilliant green and decorated with great swaths of native wildflowers. No matter how many times one has seen the dramatic change wrought in the grassland with the coming of rain, after the dessicated appearance of the summer hills the profusion of bloom and color during the winter and spring always seems miraculous.

Grassland Grasses

The following species are alien annual grasses, which now are dominant in all but a few small, widely scattered stands.

Wild Oats, genus *Avena.*
Soft Chess, *Bromus mollis.*
Red Brome, *Bromus rubens.*
Foxtail Fescue, *Festuca megalura.*

The following native perennials were dominant in the valley grassland prior to European settlement.

Purple Needlegrass, *Stipa pulchra.*
Foothill Bluegrass, *Poa scabrella.*

Grassland Wildflowers

The following are a representative sample of the more common species and genera.

Larkspurs, genus *Delphinium.*
Buttercups, genus *Ranunculus.*
Cutleaf Geranium, *Geranium dissectum.*
Meadowfoam, genus *Limnanthes,* Fig. 85.
Wind Poppy, *Stylomecon heterophylla.*
California Poppy, *Eschscholtzia californica,* Fig. 82.
Fringepod, *Thysanocarpus curvipes.*
American Winter Cress, *Barbarea orthoceras.*
Wild Buckwheats, genus *Eriogonum.*
Hooker's California Plantain, *Plantago hookeriana,* var. *californica.*
Canchalgua, *Centaurium venustum.*
Milkweeds, genus *Asclepias.*
Slender Phlox, *Phlox gracilis.*
Evening Snow, *Linanthus dichotomus.*
Gilias, genus *Gilia.*
Baby Blue-Eyes, *Nemophila menziesii,* Plate 1A (see description below).
Popcorn Flower, *Plagiobothrys nothofulvis.*
Fiddleneck, *Amsinckia intermedia.*
Purple Owl's Clover, *Orthocarpus purpurascens,* Plate 1B (see description below).
Paintbrush, genus *Castilleja.*
Pygmy Stonecrop, *Tillaea erecta.*
Lupines, genus *Lupinus.*
American Vetch, *Vicia americana.*
Lotuses, genus *Lotus.*
Williamson's Clarkia, *Clarkia williamsonii,* Fig. 83.
Long-Spurred Plectritis, *Plectritis ciliosa.*
Common Madia, *Madia elegans.*

Fremont's Tidytips, *Layia fremontii*, Fig. 84.
Goldfields, *Lasthenia chrysotoma*, Plate 1C (see description below).
Prettyface, *Triteleia scabra*, Plate 1D (see description below).

COLOR PLATES

Plate 1A. Baby Blue-eyes, *Nemophila menziesii*. Flowers bright to pale blue; leaves lobed; stems sprawling and succulent, 4 to 12 in (1 to 3 dm) long. Blooms March–May, often forming massed displays in moist grasslands and woodland openings. Ranges upslope to 5000 ft (1500 m). Several other *Nemophilas* also occur in the foothill grasslands.

Plate 1B. Purple Owl's Clover, *Orthocarpus purpurascens*. Flowers and bracts deep reddish purple in terminal spikes; leaves narrow, threadlike; stem erect, 4 to 16 in (1 to 4 dm). Blooms March–May, forming great masses of purple flowers. Ranges upslope to 4000 ft (1200 m). Other species of owl's clovers occur in the grasslands, as well as upslope to about 7000 ft (2150 m).

Plate 1C. Goldfields, *Lasthenia chrysotoma*. Flowers compound; ray flowers deep yellow at base, lighter at tips; leaves narrowly lance-shaped, opposite, slightly hairy; stem erect, many-branched, 1 to 4 in (2 to 10 cm). Forms vast yellow carpets in grassland March–May. Ranges upslope to 4000 ft (1200 m).

Plate 1D. Prettyface, *Triteleia scabra*. Flowers light yellow, borne in terminal umbels; petals bend at right angles and fuse to form tube below; leaves linear, growing from base; stem erect, free of leaves, 4 to 16 in (1 to 4 dm). Common in grasslands below 5000 ft (1500 m); blooms April–June. The form growing in the Sierra is subspecies *scabra*. Other forms occur elsewhere in the state.

Lists of trees and shrubs are not included for the grassland because neither is characteristic of the community.

Foothill Woodland

Although large areas in the Sierra foothills are given over to grassland and chaparral, the region's most characteristic and widespread vegetation is an open woodland dominated by the deciduous blue oak, *Quercus douglasii*, and the rangy, open-crowned digger pine, *Pinus sabiniana*. These trees are more or less constant associates throughout their

Foothill Woodland   215

86. Chaparral, with foothill woodland in background.

geographic ranges, forming a distinctive woodland on the foothills surrounding California's Central Valley. In the Sierra, foothill woodland occupies a variety of habitats between 300 and 5000 feet (90 and 1500 meters), depending on latitude and other factors. It forms a transition of sorts between the valley grassland of the lower foothills and the ponderosa pine forest above. Both the upper and lower boundaries of the community largely reflect increasing rainfall with elevation.

Woodland Phases and Types

Woodland stands vary in density, type and composition of understory vegetation, and dominant trees. The factors that cause this variation are latitude, elevation, slope aspect, and local conditions of soil, precipitation, moisture availability, and air temperature. Four distinct phases, based on the dominant trees, have been recognized in the Sierra Foothills: (1) the *valley oak phase*, which most commonly occurs on low, fairly moist sites adjacent to riparian woodlands; (2) the *blue oak phase*, which dominates the foothill woodlands of the Sierra, occupying slopes of moderate steepness and soil moisture; (3) the *live oak* phase, which replaces the blue oak phase farther upslope, just below the conifer forest; and (4) the *north slope phase*, a

87

88

87. White Globe Lily, *Calochortus albus.* Flowers white, sometimes tinged with pink, globular, pendulous; leaves grasslike;
stem ½ to 2½ ft (2 to 8 dm). The nodding white globe lily, or fairy
lantern, is fairly common in shady thickets below 5000 ft (1500 m)
on the west slope, blooming May–June. Several other species of
Calochortus—in colors of cream, yellow, rose, and white—occur
in various habitats throughout the Sierra.

88. California Indian Pink, *Silene californica.* Flowers, bright
red, starlike, 5 petals each with 4 deep lobes, 1 to 2 in (2.5 to 5
cm) in diameter; leaves narrowly elliptical, opposite; stem 6 to 18
in (15 to 45 cm). California indian pink is rather common in
semishady woods below 6000 ft (1800 m) on the west slope of the
Sierra. Several other members of the genus *Silene* (usually known
as campion or catch-fly) are found in various habitats throughout
the Sierra. Indian pink blooms March–August.

mixed woodland largely restricted to cooler, northern exposures from the Yosemite region north.

The foothill woodland may also be divided into three
types based on stand density and type of understory: (1) the
woodland type, in which trees—usually blue oak, interior
live oak, and digger pine—form a moderate to dense cover
over an understory of scattered shrubs and grasses; (2) the
woodland–grass type, or savanna, in which valley oak or,
more commonly, blue oak form an open woodland of widely
spaced trees over a grassland understory; and (3) the *woodland–chaparral type,* in which scattered blue oak, interior
live oak, and digger pine form an open woodland over an
understory dominated by chaparral shrubs.

VALLEY OAK PHASE   Approaching the Sierra Nevada from the west, the first native trees to appear away from streamcourses or other sources of reliable moisture are likely to be widely spaced oaks scattered over gentle grass-covered hills and valleys. This open parkland, or savanna, is an ecotone between the valley grassland and denser stands of foothill woodland upslope. As a general rule, however, savanna occupies the driest woodland sites, regardless of elevation.

Parklands dominated by the stately valley oak, *Quercus lobata*, once covered large areas in the Central Valley, generally occupying higher ground adjacent to major streams. Today only a few such stands remain, most having been replaced by cultivation. Notable stands still occur on the deeper, moister soils of valley bottoms in the lower Sierra foothills, as well as in portions of the adjacent Central Valley from Oroville south to Tulare County. Stands along major Sierra highways occur near Auburn and Grass Valley, northeast of Sacramento; along Highway 88 west of Jackson, in Amador County; along the Yosemite highway east of China Camp, in Tuolumne County; southeast of Mariposa, in Mariposa County; and east of Visalia, in Tulare County. Valley oaks also occur sparingly in denser woodland stands farther upslope.

BLUE OAK PHASE   On thinner, drier soils characteristic of steeper slopes, valley oaks are replaced by blue oaks, which form a similar, though less impressive, savanna formation. Both trees belong to the deciduous "white oak" group, but blue oak is generally a shorter, more spindly

89. Cross section of blue oak savanna, showing the wide spacing of the trees and the uniform grassland understory.

90. Blue Oak, *Quercus douglasii*. *Height:* 20 to 60 ft (5 to 15 m). *Bark:* gray, checked with small scales. *Leaves:* deciduous, leathery, blue-green above, paler below; 1½ to 4 in (4 to 10 cm) long, ¾ to 2 in (2 to 5 cm) wide; margins shallowly lobed or smooth. *Fruit:* acorns, ¾ to 1½ in (2 to 4 cm) long, ½ to ¾ in (1 to 2 cm) wide; oval with small, shallow cup. *Range:* abundant in foothill woodland below 4000 ft (1200 m); commonly associated with digger pine.

tree. Its trunk and branches are less massive and its crown much less broad than that of its lowland cousin. Blue oak is the most drought-resistant foothill tree and often is found alone on hot, arid hillsides, where it persists through the long rainless summers with the help of extremely deep roots. Although deciduous, and therefore inactive during the winter, blue oaks have small leathery leaves like those of the evergreen sclerophylls.

Savanna gives way on somewhat moister sites to denser, more extensive woodlands in which blue oak is joined by the pale green digger pine. Such stands are typically quite open, the branches of one tree often not touching those of its neighbors. The understory consists largely of annual grasses and forbs typical of the valley grassland, along with such shrubs as common buckbrush, *Ceanothus cuneatus*; whiteleaf manzanita, *Arctostaphylos viscida*; Mariposa manzanita, *A. mariposa;* coffeeberries, genus *Rhamnus;* and poison oak, *Toxicodendron diversiloba*. While seldom so numerous as blue oak, digger pine is a constant and especially conspicuous member of the foothill woodland, easily recognized even at a distance by its lacy, gray-green foliage, which resembles that of no other foothill tree. Unlike its stately, spirelike relatives in the coniferous forest, the digger pine is a rangy, open-crowned tree that often

Foothill Woodland   219

91. Poison Oak, *Toxicodendron diversiloba*. *Height:* 2 to 8 feet; may occur as an erect or spreading shrub or climbing vine; deciduous; leaves alternate, compound, usually in sets of three; leaflets 1 to 4 inches (2.5 to 10 cm) long, usually lobed or toothed, sometimes entire; foliage turns red to purple in fall; may be tinged with red in spring; flowers small, drooping, greenish white, appear with leaves. A common deciduous shrub or vine in woodlands below 5000 ft (1500 m) on the west slope. Poison oak is easily recognized by its sets of three leaflets. In spring and summer, the foliage is bright green, sometimes reddish on plants growing in sunny places. The shrub is most conspicuous in the fall, when it is the only foothill plant with bright red leaves. Most people develop a blistery, oozing rash within a day or two after coming in contact with poison oak, so it should be admired from a distance. Especially severe reactions may result from inhaling the smoke of the burning plants. People who come into contact with poison oak should wash the exposed skin with Fels Naphtha soap as soon as possible, as this sometimes will prevent the rash from developing. In addition, the clothes worn at the time of exposure should be taken off and washed. Commercial ointments are available to relieve itching and inflammation. In severe cases, victims should consult a physician immediately. Contrary to popular belief, poison oak remains toxic during the winter, after its leaves have fallen. People who are immune to poison oak at one time may suddenly lose their immunity upon their next exposure.

lacks the single, straight trunk and radial branches of its clan. The tall tapered shape of forest pines is largely an adaptive strategy for obtaining maximum light in crowded conditions. Since digger pines seldom form even moderately dense stands, they have little need to grow either tall or straight, though trees exceeding 50 feet (15 meters) are not uncommon.

FOOTHILL PLANT COMMUNITIES

92. Digger Pine, *Pinus sabiniana*. *Height:* 50 to 70 ft (15 to 21 m). *Bark:* dark brown, often with a purple cast; broad ridges and large scales. *Leaves:* needles, gray-green, 7 to 13 in (18 to 33 cm) long, 3 per bundle. *Fruit:* cones, light brown, 6 to 10 in (15 to 25 cm) long, globular. *Range:* foothill woodland, chaparral, below 4500 ft (1400 m), west slope.

Digger pines are admirably suited to the foothill environment and may be seen growing in a wide variety of situations. Isolated pines leaning precariously outward from steep chaparral slopes are common sights in foothill canyons. Digger pines also grow on rocky outcrops and thin, poor soils unsuitable to other foothill trees. Like the knobcone pine, they are able to tolerate serpentine soils. At the same time, they often grow in moderately dense woodland stands scattered over rolling, grassy hillsides. Deep probing roots enable the pine to persist on dry, rocky sites. Its sparse, pale foliage reduces to a minimum the amount of dessicating solar heat intercepted during the summer months.

LIVE OAK PHASE   Interior live oak, *Quercus wislizenii*, is a common associate of blue oak and digger pine in nearly all situations. At lower elevations scattered interior live oaks may occur in the blue oak savanna, but they are more characteristic of rocky outcrops, where moisture is often available to deeply probing roots. The roots of both interior live oak and blue oak may penetrate the fractured metamorphic bedrock of the central and northern foothills to depths of 40 feet (12 meters) or more. A shrubby form of live oak also occurs in the chaparral. Live oaks tend to be-

93. Interior Live Oak, *Quercus wislizenii. Height:* 25 to 75 ft (8 to 24 m). *Bark:* smooth, gray, becoming ridged in older trees. *Leaves:* evergreen, dark green above, yellow-green below; 1 to 3 in (2.5 to 7.5 cm) long, ¾ to 1¾ in (2 to 4.5 cm) wide; shape variable, from oblong to lanceolate; tip rounded or pointed; margins toothed or smooth. *Fruit:* acorns, 1 to 1½ in (2 to 3 cm) long, oblong and pointed, with turban-shaped cups. *Range:* common, locally dominant in foothill woodland; also in chaparral and ponderosa pine forest; west slope below 5000 ft (1500 m).

come more common as elevation increases, especially on cooler northern exposures. Just below the ponderosa pine forest it often is much more abundant than blue oak, forming a woodland from which the latter is commonly absent. Numerous chaparral plants occur in such stands, but the oaks tend to be trees rather than shrubs. Black oak, *Quercus kelloggii,* an important associate in the ponderosa pine forest, here occurs with canyon oak, *Quercus chrysolepis,* which ranges through both communities in canyon bottoms and rock crevices, where moisture is close to the surface. Digger pine also occurs in these stands, but blue oak is often absent. A stand of digger pine found in Hetch Hetchy Valley, separated by many miles of forest from the nearest stands like it in the foothills, is thought to be a relict from a time when the foothill woodland may have extended farther upslope than it does today.

NORTH SLOPE PHASE   California buckeye, *Aesculus californica,* another common associate in the foothill woodland, grows as a large shrub or small tree on a variety of sites. In the central and northern Sierra it forms a dense, somewhat shrubby, but distinctive woodland on cool,

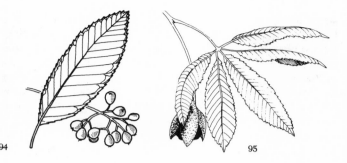

94

95

94. Toyon, *Heteromeles arbutifolia*. A shrub or small tree 5 to 15 ft (1.5 to 4.5 m) tall; evergreen leaves elliptical, pointed at both ends, with toothed margins, leathery, glossy green above, lighter below; flowers small, white, in terminal clusters; ripe red berries appear in late fall and winter. Toyon is also known as Christmas berry or California holly because of its red crop of winter berries, which are an important food source for birds and animals. It is common in both woodland and chaparral on the west slope below 3500 ft (1000 m).

95. California Buckeye, *Aesculus californica*. *Height:* 15 to 30 ft (4 to 8 m), sometimes shrubby. *Bark:* gray, smooth. *Leaves:* dark green above, paler below; compound palmate, with 5 to 7 lanceolate leaflets, 3 to 6 in (8 to 15 cm) long, 1½ to 2 in (4 to 5 cm) wide; deciduous—leaves drop in midsummer and reappear in late winter. *Flowers:* white, in long, showy spikes; very conspicuous in late spring. *Fruit:* round pods containing one, rarely two, shiny, dark brown seeds. *Range:* common in foothill woodland below 4000 ft (1200 m), west slope.

north-facing slopes, along with California laurel, *Umbellularia californica;* toyon, *Heteromeles arbutifolia;* red bud, *Cercis occidentalis;* and a number of other shrubs and trees. Blue oaks are usually absent from this mixed woodland, but scattered digger pines may be present. A good example of this particular association occurs along the steep, winding Old Priest Grade on Highway 120 a few miles west of the small village of Big Oak Flat. The opposite slope in this canyon, however, is covered largely by chaparral.

Slope aspect often affects the woodland–chaparral boundary in this way. Chaparral also replaces woodland on steep slopes with thin, dry, rocky soils, or on outcrops of serpentine, marble, and other sterile substrates. The boundary between woodland and chaparral may be distinct where changes in conditions are abrupt, but mixed formations intermediate to the two communities are also common, forming a sort of "chaparral savanna" in which widely spaced blue oaks, interior live oaks, and digger pines grow among a well-developed understory of common buckbrush, whiteleaf manzanita, and other shrubs.

Fire and Succession in the Foothill Woodland

Because of the openness of most woodland stands, as well as the sparseness of the understory brush, fire is a much less important factor in the foothill woodland than in chaparral. Grass fires seldom have much effect on mature trees, though seedlings are vulnerable. Some authorities believe that fires set by Indians, and later by ranchers, may have contributed to the openness of the oak savanna, but this remains speculation. Set against this idea is the fact that understory shrubs have failed to establish themselves in woodland stands that have gone unburned for decades.

All in all, little is known about the fire history of the foothill woodland, and substantial data is lacking on the ways in which the community and its members respond to fire. In recent times, at least, far greater changes have been wrought in the community as a result of clearing land for agriculture or suburban development. Valley oak savanna has particularly suffered in this regard because it grows on the flat, deep, alluvial soils also preferred by farmers and, now, housing contractors. The blue oak–digger pine woodland of the higher foothills has been much less affected.

Within the past 50 years a noticeable decline in seedling success has been observed among the valley oaks and, to a lesser extent, blue oaks. This has been attributed to heavy acorn and seedling losses to deer and cattle, which may be true but does not explain why interior live oaks have been less severely affected. Whatever the explanation, unless the rate of seedling survival greatly increases for blue and valley oaks, the mature specimens standing today may be among the last to grace the California hills. It is also feared that given the amount of understory brush that has accumulated in some woodland stands over the past decades, fu-

FOOTHILL PLANT COMMUNITIES

ture fires might be intense enough to eliminate many of the mature blue oaks. If this were to occur, the interior live oak might well replace the blue oak as the dominant broadleaf tree in the foothill woodland. After a fire the live oak sprouts vigorously from its root crown, and these sprouts, supported by a vast root system already in place, would enjoy a competitive advantage over blue oak seedlings with regard to obtaining moisture and nutrients.

Woodland Trees

The following species are common to abundant in some or most woodland stands.

Digger Pine, *Pinus sabiniana*, Fig. 92.
Valley Oak, *Quercus lobata*.
Blue Oak, *Quercus douglasii*, Fig. 90.
Canyon Live Oak, *Quercus chrysolepis*.
Interior Live Oak, *Quercus wislizenii*, Fig. 93.
Redbud, *Cercis occidentalis*.
California Buckeye, *Aesculus californica*, Fig. 95.

The following species are uncommon or of local occurrence in the foothill woodland. Species more common to other communities are so indicated.

Ponderosa Pine, *Pinus ponderosa*, mixed coniferous forest.
Incense Cedar, *Calocedrus decurrens*, mixed coniferous forest.
Knobcone Pine, *Pinus attenuata*.
MacNab Cypress, *Cupressus macnabiana*.
Piute Cypress, *Cupressus nevadensis*.
Tanbark Oak, *Lithocarpus densiflora*.
Black Oak, *Quercus kelloggii*, mixed coniferous forest.
Oregon Oak, *Quercus garryana*.
California Laurel, *Umbellularia californica*.
Bigleaf Maple, *Acer macrophyllum*, riparian woodland.

Woodland Shrubs

The following species are common in suitable habitats within foothill woodland.

Bitter Gooseberry, *Ribes amarum*.
Oak Gooseberry, *Ribes quercetorum*.

Chaparral Currant, *Ribes malvaceum.*
Toyon, *Heteromeles arbutifolia,* Fig. 94.
Pacific Ninebark, *Physocarpus capitatus.*
Silver Lupine, *Lupinus albifrons.*
Poison Oak, *Toxicodendron diversiloba,* Fig. 91.
Buckbrush, *Ceanothus cuneatus,* Fig. 108.
California Coffeeberry, *Rhamnus californica.*
Parry Manzanita, *Arctostaphylos manzanita.*
Whiteleaf Manzanita, *Arctostaphylos viscida,* Fig. 105.
Bush Monkeyflowers, genus *Mimulus.*
Coyote Brush, *Baccharis pilularis.*

The following species are either uncommon or of strictly local occurrence within the foothill woodland.

Scrub Oak, *Quercus dumosa,* common in chaparral.
Tree Anemone, *Carpenteria californica.*
Osoberry, *Osmaronia cerasiformis,* more common in riparian woodland.
Pacific Ninebark, *Physocarpus capitatus.*
California Blackberry, *Rubus ursinus,* more common in riparian woodland.
Hop Tree, *Ptelea crenulata.*
Squawbush, *Rhus trilobata.*
California Bladdernut, *Staphylea bolanderi.*
Chaparral Whitethorn, *Ceanothus leucodermis.*
Fremont's Globe Mallow, *Malacothamnus fremontii.*
Congdon's Silk-Tassel, *Garrya congdonii.*
Red Huckleberry, *Vaccinium parvifolium.*
Blue Elderberry, *Sambucus caerulea.*
Golden Fleece, *Haplopappus arborescens.*

Woodland Wildflowers

The following are a representative sample of the more common species and genera.

Larkspurs, genus *Delphinium.*
Carolina Geranium, *Geranium caroliniana.*
Chinese Caps, *Euphorbia crenulata,* Fig. 96.
Fan Violet, *Viola sheltonii.*
Tower Mustard, *Arabis glabra.*
California Milkmaids, *Dentaria californica,* Fig. 97.
California Indian Pink, *Silene californica,* Fig. 88.
Miner's Lettuce, *Montia perfoliata,* Fig. 103.
Wild Buckwheats, genus *Eriogonum.*

96

97

96. Chinese Caps, *Euphorbia crenulata*. Flowers without petals, with glands resembling devil heads or ancient Chinese caps, surrounded by clustered pairs of oval to spatula-shaped leaves; stem somewhat waxy, 5 to 20 in (13 to 50 cm) tall. Chinese caps are fairly common in partial shade below 5000 ft (1500 m) on the west slope.

97. California Milkmaids, *Dentaria californica*. Flowers white or pink with four petals; leaves on stem divided into 3 or more divided leaflets; a single, round fleshy leaf appears after first autumn rains and persists until flowering stem develops; stem 4 to 16 in (1 to 4 dm). California milkmaids grow in shady woods below 3000 ft (900 m) on the west slope.

Hansen's Shooting Star, *Dodecatheon hansenii*.
Star Flower, *Trientalis latifolia*.
Wild Heliotrope, *Phacelia distans*.
Chinese Houses, *Collinsia heterophylla*, Plate 2A (see description below).
Selfheal, *Prunella vulgaris*.
Blue Skullcap, *Scutellaria tuberosa*.
California Saxifrage, *Saxifraga californica*.
Lupines, genus *Lupinus*.
White Yarrow, *Achillea lanulosa*.
Mariposa Tulips, genus *Calochortus*, Fig. 87.
Irises, genus *Iris*, Plate 2B (see description below).

COLOR PLATES

Plate 2A. Chinese Houses, *Collinsia heterophylla*. Flowers in tiers around central stem, tubular with upper lip white or pale lilac, lower lip reddish violet; leaves lanceolate, opposite; stem erect, 8 to 20 in (2 to 5 dm). Common in shady foothill woodland below 4000 ft (1200 m). This species derives its name from the

Foothill Woodland

fancied resemblance of the slanted flower tiers to the roof of a pagoda.

Plate 2B. Bowl-Tubed Iris, *Iris macrosiphon*. Flowers pale yellow with blue tint or blue-purple; ovary sits 2½ to 7½ in (5 to 15 cm) *below* flower; stem below ovary short; leaves linear, growing from base. The similar Hartweg's iris, *I. hartwegii*, has only yellow flowers, a stouter and shorter ovary tube, and a much longer (2½ to 7½ in) stem below the ovary. Both occur in the foothill woodland and ponderosa pine forest, but the bowl-tubed iris is more common.

Riparian Woodland

Along foothill streamcourses a distinctive riparian woodland dominated by willows, genus *Salix*, poplars, genus *Populus*, and white alder, *Alnus rhombifolia*, extends from the coniferous forest downslope through woodland and chaparral and out onto the floor of the Central Valley. From Yosemite north, bigleaf maple, *Acer macrophyllum*, is a common member of the riparian woodland. South of Yosemite, western sycamore, *Plantanus racemosa*, may be locally common along some streams. Oregon ash, *Fraxinus latifolia*, and box elder, *Acer negundo*, are occasionally present in the riparian woodland. In addition, a number of shrubs uncommon elsewhere in the foothills are often found growing in the moist streamside soils. These include California pipe vine, *Aristolochia californica;* spice bush, *Calycanthus occidentalis;* osoberry, *Osmaronia cerasiformis;* Pacific ninebark, *Physocarpus capitatus;* California wild grape, *Vitis californica;* buttonbush, *Cephalanthus occidentalis;* and coyote brush, *Baccharis pilularis*.

As one moves upslope through the foothills, stream canyons become increasingly narrow and steepsided. The stream gradient increases, and rapids replace the lazy pools found downslope. Streams run faster and are able to carry more debris, and the steeper slopes are more subject to erosion. As a result, streambeds in the upper foothills are often choked with large boulders and deadwood. The steeper canyon walls drain rapidly, so that the riparian woodland is reduced to a thin margin of vegetation along the streambank, frequently losing its identity as a commu-

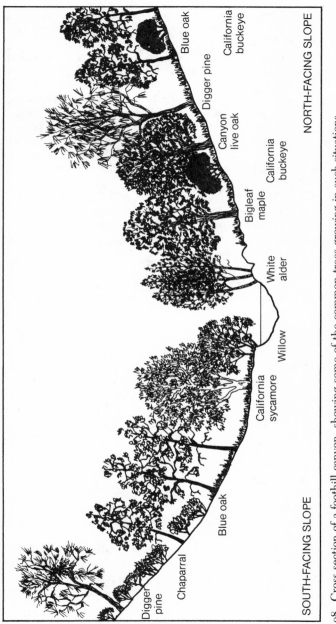

98. Cross section of a foothill canyon, showing some of the common trees growing in such situations.

nity to become merely a local mesophytic association within the foothill woodland or, even farther upslope, the mixed coniferous forest.

Alone among foothill plants, those of the riparian wood-land do not have to contend with summer drought because they occur only on soils where the water table remains high throughout the year. Consequently, they show few of the specialized adaptations—such as small, leathery leaves, deep roots, and summer dormancy—exhibited by various chaparral and woodland plants. All of the trees and several of the shrubs are winter-deciduous. Assured of moisture during the summer, they have little need to brave the rigors of winters even as comparatively mild as those of the foothills. Perennial herbs are also more plentiful in the riparian woodland than in drier foothill communities. Where moisture is readily available, as it is near streams, the main advantage of being an annual—rapid growth and seed production prior to the onset of summer drought—is less important than on drier sites. At the same time, peren-nials, which sprout from roots already in place, are better able than annuals, which must begin each year from seed, to secure available moisture and nutrients and to continue to hold the ground they already occupy.

The foothill riparian woodland is but a pale shadow of the luxuriant, jungle-like vegetation that once flourished on broad, well-watered flats bordering rivers and streams in the Central Valley. Now, pristine valley riparian woodland exists only in a few small, scattered stands, the most nota-ble being that along the Stanislaus River in Caswell Memo-rial State Park, near the town of Ripon. The foothill riparian woodland was never so extensive or well developed as that of the valley. Since foothill canyons are generally steep and narrow, the riparian woodland quickly gives way to foothill woodland within a few yards of a stream. Nor does it sup-port the stands of valley oak characteristic of pristine valley woodland. This oak requires soils that are deep and fertile as well as moist, and such are seldom found in the rocky canyon bottoms of the Sierra foothills.

Very little detailed information is available on the ecol-ogy of the riparian woodland because virtually no work has been done on the community, not even on such basic topics as stand structure and succession. Now the finest stands,

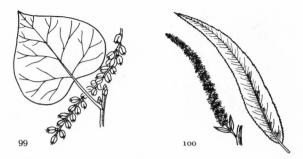

99. Fremont Cottonwood, *Populus fremontii*. *Height:* 40 to
90 ft (12 to 27 m). *Bark:* grayish white, roughly cracked. *Leaves:*
yellow-green, 1½ to 3½ in (4 to 9 cm) long, broadly heart-shaped,
deciduous, turning yellow in autumn. Flowering parts consist of
male and female catkins, the latter with dense long white hairs
forming cottony masses. *Range:* riparian woodland, west slope
below 2500 ft (750 m); scarcer on east slope along streams to 6500
ft (2000 m).

100. Willows, genus *Salix*. Five species of arborescent willows
occur along streams in the foothills and montane zone of the west
slope. They are very difficult to distinguish without the careful use
of botanical keys. All form large shrubs or small to medium-sized
trees, 10 to 40 ft (3 to 12 m) tall. The leaves tend to be linear or
narrowly lance-shaped, ranging in length from ¾ to 5 in (2 to 13
cm) and from less than ¼ to 1¼ in (6 to 30 mm) in width. The five
species are: Red Willow, *S. laevigata;* common below 5000.
Yellow Willow, *S. lasiandra;* common below 8000. Black Willow,
S. gooddingii; common below 2000. Arroyo Willow, *S. lasiolepis;*
common below 4000. Sandbar Willow, *S. hindsiana*; common
below 3000.

where such work could best have been carried out, no
longer exist. Any future studies will have to rely on the
small stands of valley woodland that remain and on the
poorly developed foothill riparian woodland, neither of
which constitutes a representative sample of what the
community was prior to the invasion of agriculture.

Riparian Woodland Trees

The following species are common or abundant in some
or most riparian woodland stands.

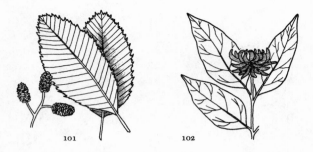

101   102

101. White Alder, *Alnus rhombifolia*. *Height:* 30 to 100 ft. *Bark:*
grayish brown, broken into irregular plates on older trees. *Leaves:*
deciduous; dark green above, yellow-green below and covered
with fine down; ovate with toothed margins; 2 to 4 in (5 to 10 cm)
long, 1½ to 2 in (4 to 5 cm) wide. *Fruit:* small brown woody cones.
Range: common along streams below 7000 ft (2150 m), west slope.

102. Spice Bush, *Calycanthus occidentalis*. *Height:* 4 to 12 ft (1 to
4 m); erect shrub; bark smooth, brown; deciduous leaves narrowly
oval-shaped, tapering to a point, fragrant when crushed; flowers
red, 1½ to 2½ in (4 to 6 cm), with many sepals and petals, growing
singly at ends of branches. The spice bush grows along streams,
mostly in the foothill zone below 3500 ft (1050 m) on the west
slope.

Fremont Cottonwood, *Populus fremontii*, Fig. 99.
Black Cottonwood, *Populus trichocarpa*.
Red Willow, *Salix laevigata*.
Yellow Willow, *Salix lasiandra*.
Black Willow, *Salix gooddingii*, Fig. 100.
Arroyo Willow, *Salix lasiolepis*.
Sandbar Willow, *Salix hindsiana*.
White Alder, *Alnus rhombifolia*, Fig. 101.
Valley Oak, *Quercus lobata*.
Canyon Live Oak, *Quercus chrysolepis*.
California Laurel, *Umbellularia californica*.
Western Sycamore, *Plantanus racemosa*.

The two following species are restricted to the riparian
woodland, but are nowhere common.

Flowering Ash, *Fraxinus dipetala*.
Oregon Ash, *Fraxinus latifolia*.

Riparian Woodland Shrubs and Vines

The following species are restricted to or more common in the riparian woodland than in other foothill communities.

Sandbar Willow, *Salix hindsiana*. (The willows listed as trees also often occur in shrubby forms.)
California Pipe Vine, *Aristolochia californica*.
Spice Bush, *Calycanthus occidentalis*, Fig. 102.
Osoberry, *Osmaronia cerasiformis*.
Pacific Ninebark, *Physocarpus capitatus*.
California Blackberry, *Rubus ursinus*.
Buttonbush, *Cephalanthus occidentalis*.
Blue Elderberry, *Sambucus caerulea*.
Honeysuckles, genus *Lonicera*, vines.
Common Snowberry, *Symphoricarpos rivularis*.
Douglas's Baccharis, *Baccharis douglasii*.

In addition to the above species, numerous shrubs more common to the foothill woodland are also found in the riparian woodland.

Riparian Woodland Wildflowers

The riparian woodland includes many wildflowers also common to other foothill communities. The following are a

103. Miner's Lettuce, *Montia perfoliata*. Flowers tiny, white; leaves fleshy, round, often surrounding stem entirely; stem with clasping leaves, 4 to 12 in (1 to 3 dm). Miner's lettuce is common in moist, springy places, often along streams, below 6000 ft (1800 m) on the west slope. Its leaves are excellent in salads, having a pungent, refreshing flavor.

representative sample of species and genera especially common to the riparian woodland.

Larkspurs, genus *Delphinium*.
Buttercups, genus *Ranunculus*.
Western Dog Violet, *Violet adunca*.
Watercress, genus *Rorippa*.
American Winter Cress, *Barbarea orthoceras*.
Miner's Lettuce, *Montia perfoliata*, Fig. 103.
Monkeyflowers, genus *Mimulus*, Plate 2C (see description below).
Bee Plant, *Scrophularia californica*.
White Hedge Nettle, *Stachys albens*.
Elk Clover, Aralia californica.
Stream Orchid, *Epipactis gigantea*, Plate 2D (see description below).

COLOR PLATES

Plate 2C. Common Monkeyflower, *Mimulus guttatus*. Flowers tubular with five petals partly fused to form an upper lip of two petals and a lower lip of three; flower bright yellow with reddish spots and some hairs on lower lip; leaves opposite and roughly elliptic, margins smooth or toothed; stems creeping and variable in length. Numerous species of monkeyflowers, including a few shrubby forms, grow throughout the Sierra, mostly in damp places. The common monkeyflower is the commonest type on such sites and ranges upslope to 10,000 ft (3000 m). Blooms March–August. Other streamside monkeyflowers found in the foothills include the Musk Monkeyflower, *M. moschatus*, and Scarlet Monkeyflower, *M. cardinalis*.

Plate 2D. Stream Orchid, or Giant Helleborine, *Epipactis gigantea*. Flowers orchidlike, yellow-green, with lower lip streaked with red; leaves broadly ovate with parallel veins; stem erect, 1 to 3 ft (3 to 9 dm). The stream orchid is found on steep banks near seeps and springs below 7500 ft (2300 m). Blooms May–August.

Chaparral

Dense, impenetrable brush thickets are scattered throughout the entire length of the Sierra foothill zone on hot dry slopes with thin rocky soils. Known as chaparral (Spanish, *chaparro*, scrub oak), this shrub community is characteris-

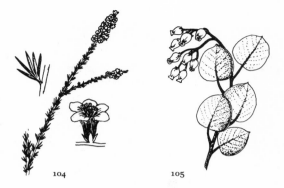

104

105

104. Chamise, or Greasewood, *Adenostoma fasciculatum*.
Height: 2 to 12 ft (6 to 30 dm); stems straight, much branched, and
densely covered with bundles of tiny leaves; leaves evergreen, ¼
inch (0.5 cm) long, needlelike with sharp points, resinous; flowers
white, tiny, clustered in dense terminal panicles; blooms February–July. Chamise is the most common and conspicuous chaparral shrub, often occurring in pure stands.

105. Whiteleaf Manzanita, *Arctostaphylos viscida*. *Height:* 4 to 12
ft (1 to 3 m); branches crooked with smooth, thin red bark;
branchlets whitish; leaves ovate, 1 to 2 in (2.5 to 5 cm) long;
flowers white to rose, bell-shaped, in loose, drooping clusters.
Whiteleaf manzanita is common and widespread below 5000 ft
(1500 m) on the west slope, occurring in both chaparral and
foothill woodland. Blooms February–April.

tic of the California foothills from south of the border to
southern Oregon. Chaparral is most extensive in Southern
California, becoming less common and more sporadically
distributed northward. This trend is also true in the Sierra
foothills, where the most extensive stands occur south of
the San Joaquin River. Farther north, as precipitation increases, chaparral, though not uncommon, is increasingly
replaced by foothill woodland.

From a distance, chaparral appears as a velvety mantle
rather uniform both in height (3 to 12 feet/1 to 4 meters)
and color (usually a drab brownish or grayish green). Many
stands, especially those on the hottest, driest slopes, consist mostly of but one species—chamise, or greasewood,
Adenostoma fasciculatum. Other stands may be dominated
by one or more species of manzanita or ceanothus, notably

Chaparral

whiteleaf manzanita, *Arctostaphylos viscida;* Indian manzanita, *A. mewukka;* common buckbrush, *Ceanothus cuneatus;* and chaparral whitethorn, *C. leucodermis.* On moister slopes, stands dominated by scrub oak, *Quercus dumosa,* and a shrubby form of interior live oak, *Q. wislizenii,* var. *fruticosa,* may contain a greater variety of species, including birchleaf mountain mahogany, *Cercocarpus betuloides;* flowering ash, *Fraxinus dipetala;* toyon, *Heteromeles arbutifolia;* chaparral honeysuckle, *Lonicera interrupta;* red bud, *Cercis occidentalis;* chaparral pea, *Pickeringia montana*; redberry, *Rhamnus crocea*; and poison oak, *Toxicodendron diversiloba.* Grasses and wildflowers are rare or absent in mature chaparral, as are seedlings of the dominant shrubs, but occur abundantly on recently burned areas.

Chaparral Fire

Chaparral has been characterized as one of the most fire-prone vegetation types in the world. Stems and leaves are exceedingly dry during the summer, and those of many species even contain volatile substances that turn the plants into torches. Large amounts of fuel are present in the form of dead lower branches and strips of sloughed bark. Chaparral fires are therefore extremely hot, ranging up to 2000° F (1100° C), and when driven by hot, dry summer winds often burn large areas rapidly.

Many wildfires in California start in chaparral, and a given stand can be expected to burn every 10 to 40 years. Chaparral shrubs are in various ways adapted to fire and within a few years reappear on burned sites. Recurrent fires are not only essential to the survival of many chaparral plants, but are necessary for the renewal of the entire community.

ADAPTATIONS TO FIRE Chaparral plants exhibit three main adaptations to fire: (1) crown-sprouting, (2) fire-resistant seeds, and (3) seed production at an early age.

About half of all chaparral shrubs reoccupy burned areas by sending up sprouts from root-crown burls located just below the surface of the ground. These enlarged organs, along with the supporting root systems, are not destroyed by fire. They generate new sprouts within weeks following a burn. Crown sprouts are not dependent on rain because they are supplied with water already present in the large root systems of chaparral shrubs, so they are among the first new green vegetation to be found on recently burned sites. Because their roots are already in place, sprouts do not have to face the difficulties encountered by seedlings, which includes not only moisture stress, but competition with other plants and the need to divert precious energy into root production. Sprouts also tend to grow more rapidly than seedlings and eventually shade them out. Common chaparral sprouters include chamise, scrub oak, toyon, redberry, and California coffeeberry, *Rhamnus californica*.

Chaparral plants that do not crown-sprout must rely on seeds as a means of re-establishing themselves on burned ground. Most species, including sprouters, produce abundant seed crops early in their lives as insurance against fire. The seeds can survive extremely hot fires if they are buried in but a thin layer of soil. Those of some species, such as chamise, are not fire resistant, but so numerous that a few manage to survive anyway. Many chaparral shrubs, such as various species of manzanita and ceanothus, produce seeds that are impervious to moisture until their tough coats are cracked or scarified by the heat of a fire. They remain dormant for decades, if necessary, until fire causes them to open and germinate.

FIRE SUCCESSION Mature stands of chaparral are characterized by comparatively few species and an absence of understory seedlings and herbs. The shrubs put on very little new growth at this stage, and most of their lower branches are dead. Soils are generally deficient in nutrients, which are bound up in the plants themselves. In addition, the soils commonly contain high levels of plant toxins, which are produced by both chamise and manzanitas in the normal course of metabolism. In the case of chamise the toxins accumulate on leaf surfaces and are washed into the soil by rains. Manzanitas concentrate similar substances in their leaves, roots, fruit, and bark. These toxins inhibit the germination and subsequent establishment not only of competing plants, but also of chamise and manzanita seedlings, constituting a form of plant interaction known as *allelopathy*. In this way, these dominant chaparral shrubs are able to prevent most other species, as well as potential competitors among their own seedlings, from becoming established in mature stands. Soil deficiency, competition for moisture, light, and nutrients, and the inability to germinate in thick litter are additional factors working to exclude herbs and shrub seedlings from mature chaparral.

Fire eliminates these obstacles and paves the way for seedling establishment and overall stand renewal in the following ways:

1. The destruction of shrub cover opens burned areas to sunlight and reduces competition for moisture and nutrients.

2. Plant toxins in the soil are destroyed by the intense heat.

3. Nutrients bound up in plant tissues are returned to the soil in the form of ash; though some nutrients may be vaporized by extremely hot fires, chaparral soils generally show marked increases in fertility following burns.

4. Removal of litter and duff, exposing the mineral soil beneath, creates optimal seedbed conditions for most plants.

5. Soil bacteria and fungi, which carry out decomposition of organic materials, are more active after fires; increased fungal activity is especially important to the many chaparral shrubs that rely on mycorrhizal symbiosis to obtain essential nutrients and water (see page 182).

Seeds that have lain dormant for years, even decades, germinate in the first wet season following a chaparral fire.

106. (*facing page*) Mature chaparral is dense, supports few or no understory herbs, and sustains only minimal growth. After a fire, annual herbs invade chaparral sites. Many of these plants sprout from long-dormant seeds and appear only on recently burned ground. At the same time, shrubs such as chamise send up new sprouts from massive root crowns, while others, such as whiteleaf manzanita, sprout from seeds that were in the soil prior to the fire. Herbs dominate postfire chaparral sites for a few years until they are forced out by the shrubs, which monopolize light, water, and nutrients, and in some cases—notably chamise—release growth-inhibiting substances into the soil. Eventually, nonsprouting shrubs may largely be crowded out by the longer-lived crown-sprouting species. After 20 years or so, the chaparral is once again mature and ripe for yet another fire.

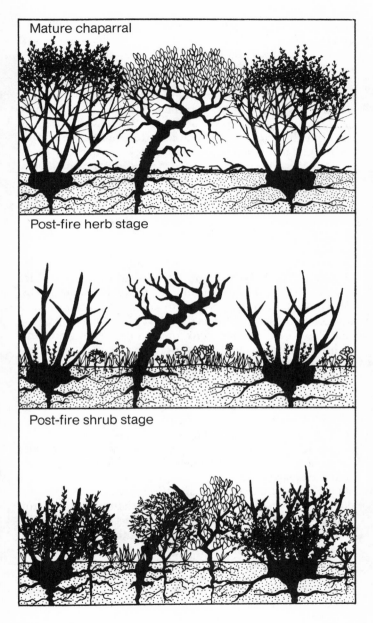

Mature chaparral

Post-fire herb stage

Post-fire shrub stage

Comparatively few are blown or carried in from adjacent areas. Annual herbs dominate chaparral sites for the first three years following a fire. Many of these herbs are fire endemics, that is, they are found only on recently burned ground. Others are plants that are able to thrive in a variety of disturbed sites—along roads, near buildings, in cultivated areas, and the like. Sprouts and seedlings of chaparral shrubs are also present during the first postfire season, but they are far outnumbered by annual grasses and forbs, and many seedlings die for lack of adequate moisture or for other reasons. The rapidly growing annual herbs fare much better on the whole. After three years forbs are largely replaced by grasses, which dominate burned chaparral sites through the fifth or sixth years following a fire.

Shrub sprouts, as well as seedlings that have survived the rigors of the first year or two, begin to dominate postfire sites after the sixth year, at which point herbs become rare or absent. As the shrubs grow taller and develop broader crowns, shade becomes a limiting factor for some herbs. Others are inhibited by competition for nutrients and moisture or by increasing concentrations of plant toxins in the soil. Poor seedbed conditions, owing to increasing amounts of litter and duff, and heavy usage by grazing and seed-eating animals no doubt also contribute to the decline of herb species. At any rate, shrubs replace grasses and forbs by the seventh to ninth year following a fire, at which point the stand can once again be described as chaparral, though it will be shorter, more open, and contain a different mix of species than a mature stand.

Young chaparral stands exhibit greater vitality than older ones, in terms of both productivity and variety of species. Many chaparral shrubs that are rare or absent in mature stands are common in the postfire years. These include coyote bush, *Baccharis pilularis;* rabbitbrush, genus *Chrysothamnus;* tree poppy, *Dendromecon rigida;* yerba santa, *Eriodictyon californicum;* goldenbush, genus *Haplopappus;* deerweed, *Lotus scoparius;* silver lupine, *Lupinus albifrons;* Fremont's globe mallow, *Malacothamnus fremontii;* and bush monkeyflowers, genus *Mimulus.* The most successful postfire shrubs are those such as deerweed, silver lupine, chaparral pea, and the several species

107. California Fremontia, *Fremontia californica. Height:* 6 to 16 ft (2 to 5 m); evergreen; leaf and flower buds borne on short, hairy spurs; leaves ovate, often three-lobed, ¼ to 1½ in (6 to 90 mm), dark green above, covered with whitish felt below; flowers lemon yellow, borne singly, 1½ to 2 in (4 to 5 cm), with five petal-like sepals united at base, but no petals. The California fremontia is often called flannel bush for its dense coating of white hairs. Its showy yellow flowers appear May–June.

of ceanothus, all of which contain nitrogen-fixing bacterial root nodes. Nitrogen-fixers often dominate the early shrub stage and, by increasing soil fertility, improve conditions for other species.

Chaparral shrubs grow much more vigorously during their early years than in old age, producing abundant seeds and adding significant new growth each year. This greater productivity is made possible by the increased sunlight and soil fertility of postfire sites, as well as by reductions in concentrations of plant toxins and decreased competition with

108. Common Buckbrush, *Ceanothus cuneatus. Height:* 3 to 8+ ft (1 to 3+ m); branches rigid, dense; leaves narrow, ¼ to 1 in (6 to 25 mm) long, wider at tips than at bases; flowers small, white, fragrant, in showy terminal clusters. Common buckbrush is one of the more common foothill shrubs, occurring both in chaparral and woodland. From March through May its abundant white flowers are conspicuous throughout the upper foothills.

other shrubs. As a stand matures, however, it becomes increasingly dominated by longer-lived sprouting species, which crowd out many of the pioneer shrubs. The latter must rely on seeds left behind in the soil to guarantee their return following the next fire. Eventually, 30 to 40 years after a burn, most stands are dominated by chamise and other sprouting species. Production declines, and the stand is ready once again for rebirth by fire.

Adaptations to Heat and Drought

Vegetation similar to chaparral is found along the shores of the Mediterranean, at the tip of South Africa, in central Chile, and in southwest Australia, all of which have cool, rainy winters and hot, dry summers. Mediterranean climates, as such regimes are known, pose two critical problems for plants growing away from permanent sources of water. First, the plants must somehow prevent dehydration during the dry summer months, when low humidity and high temperatures combine to increase moisture loss through evapotranspiration. Second, they must be able to grow and reproduce, at least to some degree, during the cooler months of the year, when soil moisture is available. Chaparral shrubs exhibit three major adaptive strategies for solving these problems: (1) evergreenness, (2) small, thick, leathery leaves, and (3) summer dormancy.

Chaparral shrubs commence growth in late fall or early winter. Since almost all of them are evergreens, they need not waste time putting on whole new sets of leaves, but are able to begin rapid photosynthesis as soon as conditions are favorable. Growth proceeds slowly during the cool winter months, but the shrubs only have to concentrate on producing new shoots. By March, when soils are still moist and air temperatures finally high enough to permit more rapid growth, chaparral shrubs are able to shift gears immediately, flowering and setting fruit within a month or two before declining soil moisture inhibits further activity.

By the first of June most chaparral shrubs have begun to enter dormancy, which will last through the summer and early fall, broken only by short spurts of activity during rare periods of rain. As rates of photosynthesis steadily decline from moist-season highs, growth slows and eventually stops. Yet since chaparral plants are able to carry out photosynthesis even when soils are extremely dry, they can sustain themselves at minimal levels throughout the summer. By reducing rates of photosynthesis they also reduce their need for water and carbon dioxide, the two principal ingredients in the process. The importance of reducing water consumption during the summer is obvious. Reducing the carbon dioxide requirement allows stomata to remain closed or only partly open for much of the time, thereby reducing water loss from leaf surfaces.

Many chaparral shrubs drop a few of their leaves during the summer in order to reduce the surface area at which photosynthesis and moisture loss can occur, as well as to reduce the bulk of tissues that must be provided with moisture and nutrients. Many species also abandon lower limbs in order to reduce their bulk. This self-pruning produces the picturesque, twisted trunks and branches common to many chaparral species. Manzanitas are notable as well for shedding their outer bark as a snake sloughs its skin. Like leaf-drop and self-pruning, this is thought to be a way of reducing plant bulk as much as possible. Manzanitas also point their leaves skyward to minimize exposure to the sun.

Chaparral shrubs are characterized as a group by small, thick, leathery leaves and are therefore classified as *sclerophylls*, or "hard-leaved plants." The shiny, waxy surface of such leaves is produced by a layer of cutin, which reduces moisture loss over the entire leaf surface and provides insulation against extremes of heat and cold. Since nighttime temperatures during the winter often fall below freezing in the foothills, chaparral plants, which are active during this season, must be frost hardy. Cutinized leaves are important in this regard, as well as in reducing heat and loss of moisture during the summer. Their shiny surfaces tend to reflect solar radiation, keeping their temperature down and thereby reducing evaporation. The light leaf color characteristic of many chaparral plants serves much the same purpose. Moreover, the leaves of many species are less than one-half inch (13 millimeters) long and thus offer a minimal surface area to the sun. They also have fewer stomata per area than the leaves of plants growing in cooler, moister habitats. Small leaf size also increases frost hardiness.

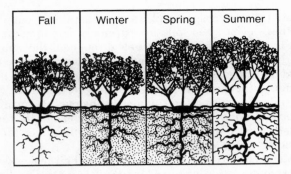

Fall	Winter	Spring	Summer

109. Chaparral shrubs begin to put on new growth in the fall after the first rains. Growth proceeds slowly during the cold winter, accelerating in the spring as soil and air temperatures increase. With the onset of summer drought, chaparral shrubs become dormant. Rates of photosynthesis, respiration, and transpiration drop radically, and the plants even slough some of their leaves and stems in order to cut down on the amount of living tissue to be supported.

Chaparral shrubs utilize all the moisture available to them during the year. Most have huge two-part root systems: deep taproots that help to sustain them during the dry season and extensive lateral root systems that absorb moisture near the soil surface. Chaparral plants are able to take advantage even of the sparse moisture delivered by occasional summer storms. Aside from the primary function of supplying moisture and nutrients, the large root systems of chaparral shrubs provide firm anchorage on the steep slopes favored by these plants. Chaparral is unsurpassed for promoting slope stability and reducing runoff. When heavy rains follow especially severe chaparral fires, destructive floods and mudslides often ensue.

Serpentine Chaparral

In the central and northern Sierra foothills chaparral may occur on outcrops of serpentine in areas that otherwise would support foothill woodland. Serpentine consists largely of magnesium silicate and contains large amounts of such heavy metals as chromium, nickel, and iron. Soils derived from serpentine are extremely hostile to plant growth, so vegetation on them tends to be stunted and sparse. Serpentine soils contain little calcium, an essential nutrient for growth, but a great deal of magnesium, a structurally analogous element that plants absorb instead. Magnesium inhibits calcium intake and therefore results in stunted growth. In addition, even small amounts of nickel and chromium are toxic to most plants. Serpentine soils also tend to be deficient in nitrogen and in such essential trace elements as molybdenum.

Common chaparral shrubs such as chamise and toyon, however, are able to tolerate serpentine soils and form a sparse cover on such sites, along with several herbs and shrubs that are largely or entirely restricted to serpentine outcrops. Leather oak, *Quercus durata*, and Congdon's silk-tassel, *Garrya congdonii*, are good indicators of serpentine soils in the Sierra foothills. Knobcone pine, *Pinus attenuata*, though not quite so restricted, is also common on serpentine. Its center of abundance in the Klamath Mountains of northwestern California corresponds to an extensive outcrop of peridotite, an igneous rock from which serpentine is derived. Outcrops of serpentine can generally be identified by the slick texture and gray-green color of the rock. Vegetation may be conspicuously sparser and more stunted than that of adjacent areas. Abrupt transitions from woodland to chaparral on otherwise uniform slopes may signal the boundary of a serpentine outcrop.

Abrupt vegetational changes also mark the sterile soils characteristic of the few marble outcrops in the Sierra foothills, as well as the lateritic clays and ironstone crusts found just east of the small town of Ione, in Amador County. The latter formation is particularly interesting to botanists because it hosts a few small patches of *Eriogonum apricum*, which is found nowhere else in the world and does not seem closely related to any of the dozens of other species of wild buckwheat found in the Sierra or the rest of California. Ione manzanita, *Arctostaphylos myrtifolia*, is similarly restricted to this spot and a few others like it to the north and south. This shrub dominates a dwarf chaparral-type brush community on the Ione clays, forming an abrupt border with taller, more typical chaparral on adjacent soils. Travelers on the Carson Pass highway (State Route 88) cross the

Ione Formation a few miles west of the Mother Lode town of Jackson. The Ione soils consist of extremely ancient acidic clays from which nutrients were removed by Eocene weathering in a wet, tropical climate. Today, they are leached by annual winter flooding followed by rapid drying during the early summer. Most chaparral shrubs cannot tolerate these difficult conditions, and those that can are sparsely distributed and usually stunted.

Chaparral Shrubs

The following species are common to abundant in many or most chaparral stands.

Spanish Bayonet, *Yucca whipplei*.
Scrub Oak, *Quercus dumosa*.
Interior Live Oak, *Quercus wislizenii*, shrubby form (see Woodland Trees, page 225).
Leather Oak, *Quercus durata*.
Chaparral Currant, *Ribes malvaceum*.
Chamise, *Adenostoma fasciculatum*, Fig. 104.
Birchleaf Mountain Mahogany, *Cercocarpus betuloides*.
Toyon, *Heteromeles arbutifolia*, Fig. 94.
Deerweed, *Lotus scoparius*.
Common Buckbrush, *Ceanothus cuneatus*, Fig. 108.
Chaparral Whitethorn, *Ceanothus leucodermis*.
California Coffeeberry, *Rhamnus californica*.
Redberry, *Rhamnus crocea*.
California Fremontia, *Fremontia californica*, Fig. 107.
Whiteleaf Manzanita, *Arctostaphylos viscida*, Fig. 105.
Bush Monkeyflowers, genus *Mimulus*.
Coyote Brush, *Baccharis pilularis*.

The following species are less common than the above.

Chaparral Virgin's Bower, *Clematis lasiantha*, vine.
Tree Poppy, *Dendromecon rigida*.
Bitter Gooseberry, *Ribes amarum*.
Canyon Gooseberry, *Ribes menziesii*.
Chaparral Pea, *Pickeringia montana*.
Squawbush, *Rhus trilobata*.
California Bladder Nut, *Staphylea bolanderi*.
Fremont's Globe Mallow, *Malacothamnus fremontii*.
Silk-Tassels, genus *Garrya*.
Golden Fleece, *Haplopappus arborescens*.

Formal lists of trees and herbs are not included for the chaparral because neither is characteristic of the community, though mixed chaparral—woodland stands are not uncommon.

FOOTHILL ANIMALS

FROM LATE FALL to early summer the Sierra Nevada foothills provide a particularly congenial environment for animal life. Food and water are normally abundant during this period, and moderate temperatures mean that most animals do not have to contend with rapid loss of body heat. Consequently, the region's animal population swells during the winter months as year-around residents are joined by downslope migrants and wintering birds from more northerly climes, both escaping seasonal cold and food shortages in their breeding habitats. Most foothill animals remain active throughout winter and spring, notable exceptions being reptiles and amphibians that hole up during occasional cold spells.

Summer is the most critical season for foothill animals. From late June through October, food and water are scarcer, and high daytime temperatures, combined with very dry air, make moisture loss a severe problem for animals as well as plants. Ways in which resident foothill animals have adapted to such conditions are discussed in Chapter IV (see page 201), but it is worthwhile to recall these strategies here.

First, most species breed during the spring, before the onset of summer drought. After breeding, many birds wander upslope into forest and meadow. Second, a few animals become inactive during the summer months, causing predator populations to decline as the latter are forced to wander upslope in search of food. Third, rodents and some birds obtain sufficient water through their food, and a few even conserve it by excreting "dry urine." Fourth, few foothill animals are active during the heat of the day. Fifth, many species seldom stray far from reliable sources of water such as streams, stock ponds, and reservoirs.

Each foothill plant community provides a limited set of options for obtaining food, water, and cover. Such limitations are greatest in the grassland and chaparral, which thus support fewer kinds of animals than the foothill and riparian woodlands. Each community houses animals rarely found elsewhere, as well as some species adapted to a variety of habitats and others able to utilize different habitats for different purposes. The following discussion surveys the four major foothill communities in terms of available habitats and the animals that utilize them.

Animal Life in the Grassland

The valley grassland exhibits relatively little diversity with respect to animal habitats and therefore supports fewer species than adjacent woodlands. Residents of the community must be specially adapted to life in the open as well as to the comparatively limited types of plant food. The extreme scarcity of green vegetation and water during the summer months also limits the types of animals able to utilize the community during this season.

Life Underground

Since the grassland affords few hiding places for small rodents and nesting birds, they are particularly vulnerable to predators, which consequently patrol this community in large numbers. Red-tailed hawks soar over the grasslands during the day searching for ground squirrels and other rodents. So do golden eagles, though in far fewer numbers. In some areas white-tailed kites and marsh hawks are major predators of meadow mice. At night the silent great horned owl is the scourge of jackrabbits, cottontails, pocket gophers, and various small rodents. Coyotes, gray foxes, and bobcats hunt both day and night in the grasslands, as do several species of snakes.

The ground itself provides the best available cover in the grassland, and a significant portion of animal activity in the community occurs beneath it. The broad-handed mole and valley pocket gopher occupy more or less permanent tunnel systems, complete with nesting chambers. Moles are entirely subterranean, but pocket gophers sometimes come partly out of their burrows to feed. Most other small grassland mammals—such as meadow mice, harvest mice, the California ground squirrel, pocket mice, and kangaroo rats—live in burrows, though they also spend much time above ground foraging for food. The western toad rests in rodent burrows from time to time, and the western spadefoot toad digs its own. The only resident owl in the grasslands—the burrowing owl—nests in abandoned ground-squirrel burrows, and the community's several species of snakes often rest in rodent burrows during the heat of the day. The western rattlesnake may hibernate in abandoned burrows from October to April. The only large mammalian predator to actually live in the community— the American badger—digs a shallow burrow for itself, the large entrance to which is not likely to be mistaken for the work of a small rodent.

Burrows are used for sleeping, escaping predators and hot weather, breeding, rearing young, and storing food. Though a particular animal species may not use them in all these ways, most small grassland mammals do. They appear above ground largely to forage, and except for the California ground squirrel do so almost entirely at night. Consequently, though mammals are numerous in the grassland, most species are seldom seen.

Predation and Survival

Although burrows provide a measure of protection from predators, they are not foolproof. Snakes, for example, enter them at will. In order to protect themselves from such invasion, some burrowing animals—the ground squirrel for one—create networks of tunnels, with dead ends and alternate entrances, and plug the entrance to their sleeping or nesting chambers during occupation. Such precautions, however, are of no avail against the badger, whose powerful forelegs and long digging claws enable it to excavate rodents, even in deep burrows, within a few minutes. Sooner or later, of course, all burrowers except the gopher

Animal Life in the Grassland

and the mole must venture above ground to forage, at which time they are exposed to the large number and variety of grassland predators.

Prey species—both birds and mammals—have developed various strategies for eluding or enduring heavy predation in the open grassland environment. Ground squirrels alert their neighbors to predators by uttering a high shrill whistle, and at the first sign of danger retreat to their burrows. Kangaroo rats and pocket mice, which can jump for distances up to several feet, execute a series of rapid zigzag leaps when fleeing predators. The black-tailed jackrabbit, which nests beneath brush adjacent to the grassland, relies on its great speed—up to 35 miles per hour (56 kilometers per hour)—to elude predators. When startled it bounds away in leaps of a yard or more. The California meadow mouse does not so much evade predators as compensate for them through an extraordinarily high rate of reproduction. Though averaging only four per litter, the female is able to mate again within 15 hours after giving birth, so several litters per year are typical.

Aside from the burrowing owl, only two species of birds—the western meadowlark and the kildeer—regularly nest in the foothill grasslands. This small number is understandable given the sparseness of trees and shrubs in the community. Nests placed on the ground in the open grassland are particularly vulnerable to predators, and comparatively few species of birds anywhere have evolved efficient ways of using this habitat. The western meadowlark, which is the most common and conspicuous grassland bird, conceals its nest through camouflage, building a domed saucer of grasses that is difficult to detect in the grasses surrounding it. The kildeer, a medium-sized grassland plover, lays its eggs in a shallow, bare or grass-lined depression on open ground. Both eggs and chicks are speckled, which makes them more difficult to spot than might be imagined. Adult kildeer take care not to give away the location of their nests and will run some distance away before taking flight. They are also known to feign injury as a way of distracting predators away from the nest.

FOOTHILL ANIMALS

Visitors

Most species of birds commonly seen in the grasslands are visitors from adjacent woodlands, where they nest. Among the more conspicuous are the turkey vulture, American kestrel (or sparrow hawk), mourning dove, western kingbird, western bluebird, common flicker, and—during the winter—the American robin, Brewer's blackbird, and the red-winged blackbird, which nests in marshy areas. Other visiting birds include the common predatory species mentioned earlier.

During the summer the grassland constitutes the hottest, driest, altogether most inhospitable community in the foothills. Days are hot, water is scarce, and green forage is largely confined to the borders of occasional streams, stock ponds, and reservoirs. In the shimmering heat of a summer day, animal activity seems almost to halt as rodents take to their burrows, predators sleep in the cool of the woodland, and birds hunker quietly in the sparse shade of grasses or occasional shrubs and trees. Some California ground squirrel and the western spadefoot toad spend much of the season estivating in their burrows, and since the squirrel is the primary food of the red-tailed hawk, the latter's population declines in the foothills as many individuals wander upslope to forage in mountain meadows.

Grassland Residents

The following species live in the grassland the year around. Asterisks after some entries refer to further discussion in Selected Foothill Animals, page 268. Species described in detail in other chapters are so noted.

AMPHIBIANS

Western Spadefoot, *Scaphiopus hammondi.* *
Western Toad, *Bufo boreas.*

REPTILES

Coast Horned Lizard, *Phrynosoma coronatum.* *
Western Whiptail, *Cnemidophorus hyperythrus.* *
Southern Alligator Lizard, *Gerrhonotus multicarinatus.* *
Racer, *Coluber constrictor.*

Striped Racer, *Masticophis lateralis*.*
Common King Snake, *Lampropeltis getulus*.*
Gopher Snake, *Pituphis melanoleucus*.*
Garter Snake, Genus *Thamnophis*.
Western Rattlesnake, *Crotalus viridis*.*

BIRDS

Kildeer, *Charadrius vociferus*.*
Mourning Dove, *Zenaida macroura*.*
Burrowing Owl, *Speotyto cunicularia*.*
Horned Lark, *Eremophila alpestris*.
Western Meadowlark, *Sturnella neglecta*, Fig. 114.*

MAMMALS

Ornate Shrew, *Sorex ornatus*.
Broad-Handed Mole, *Scapanus latimanus*.
California Ground Squirrel, *Otospermophilus beecheyi*.*
Valley Pocket Gopher, *Thomomys bottae*.
San Joaquin Valley Pocket Mouse, *Perognathus inornatus*.
Heerman's Kangaroo Rat, *Dipodomys heermanni*.
Western Harvest Mouse, *Reithrodontomys megalotus*.
California Meadow Mouse, *Microtus californicus*.

Regular Grassland Visitors

The following species of birds and mammals visit the grassland to forage or hunt, but they breed or roost elsewhere. Many range through various communities. Winter visitors are designated by WV.

BIRDS

Turkey Vulture, *Cathartes aura*.*
Red-Tailed Hawk, *Buteo jamaicensis*.*
Golden Eagle, *Aquila chrysaetos*.
White-tailed Kite, *Elanus leucarus*.
American Kestrel, *Falco sparverius*.*
Great Horned Owl, *Bubo virginianus*.
Common Flicker, *Colaptes auratus*.*
Yellow-Billed Magpie, *Pica nuttallii*.
American Robin, *Turdus migratorius*, WV.
Western Bluebird, *Sialia mexicanus*.*
Red-Winged Blackbird, *Agelaius phoeniceus*.
Brewer's Blackbird, *Euphagus cyanocephalus*.

Brown-Headed Cowbird, *Molothrus ater*.
Lesser Goldfinch, *Spinus psaltria*.
Savannah Sparrow, *Passerculus sandwichensis*, WV.
Lark Sparrow, *Chondestes grammacus*.

MAMMALS

Ornate Shrew, *Sorex ornatus*.
Broad-Handed Mole, *Scapanus latimanus*.
Bats, several species. Order *chiroptera*.
Black-Tailed Jackrabbit, *Lepus californicus*, Fig. 115.*
Audubon's Cottontail, *Sylvilagus audubonii*.
Gray Fox, *Urocyon cinereoargenteus*, Fig. 117.*
Coyote, *Canis latrans*. See Selected Forest Animals.
Bobcat, *Lynx rufus*, Fig. 120.*
Mule Deer, *Odocoileus hemionus*. See Selected Forest Animals.

Animal Life in the Foothill Woodland

The foothill woodland offers a wide variety of habitats for animals, including as it does an understory of grasses and scattered shrubs. Food is plentiful and varied, even during the summer. Water remains a problem from June through October, but the shade provided by woodland trees brings relief from hot daytime temperatures. Cover from predators is readily available, and the numerous nesting sites support many different kinds of animals. For example, more than 100 species of birds are commonly found in this community at various times during the year.

Woodland oaks dominate community life and in large measure determine the types of habitats available to animals. Their foliage provides shade and cover and supports an immense insect population that in turn attracts many different species of birds. Acorns form an important part of the diet for numerous woodland animals. Cavities in the trees provide nesting sites for both birds and mammals. Other species of birds build nests on limbs among the cover of leaves. Hawks and turkey vultures often roost on the uppermost branches of the trees. The shade cast by the oaks,

Animal Life in the Foothill Woodland

the amount and chemical composition of their leaf litter, and their role in depleting available soil moisture all influence soil conditions and largely determine the types of plants able to grow in the woodland. This, in turn, also affects the types of food and cover available to animals.

Acorn Eaters

The importance of the acorn as a food source in the foothill woodland cannot be overestimated. It is significant in the diets of such animals as the wood duck, band-tailed pigeon, scrub jay, yellow-billed magpie, Audubon's cottontail, California ground squirrel, Merriam's chipmunk, dusky-footed wood rat and raccoon. But the two animals most intimately associated with the acorn are the gray squirrel and acorn woodpecker, both among the most common and conspicuous residents of the foothill woodland.

The grizzled, bushy-tailed gray squirrel spends much of its time gathering acorns from the ground. It hides them in underground caches to which it later returns in time of scarcity, detecting the buried nuts by smell. The acorn woodpecker derives its name from its habit of storing acorns by the thousands in small, specially drilled holes—each containing a single acorn—in dead trees, telephone poles, fenceposts, and even the sides of buildings.

Seed Eaters

The seeds of understory herbs and shrubs feed a wide variety of birds and mammals, including many that cannot consume the large, hard-shelled acorn. Important seed eaters include white-footed mice, the dusky-footed wood rat, mourning dove, black-headed grosbeak, purple finch, house finch, rufous-sided towhee, brown towhee, dark-eyed junco, chipping sparrow, and fox sparrow.

The towhees are both large sparrows. The brown towhee is a drab, uniform brown in color, which serves to camouflage it while foraging in the open. In contrast, the rufous-sided towhee has striking plumage of black, white, and rusty red, and rarely forages in the open, preferring to search for seeds among the dense litter of forest brush or

254

chaparral, where its varicolored coat blends into the dappled light and shade. Both towhees uncover seeds from beneath dense litter by hopping back and forth vigorously on both feet, thus kicking the debris aside. Often the presence of these birds is revealed only by the loud characteristic rustle of litter emanating from dense brush.

Insect Eaters

The majority of birds found in the foothill woodland rely largely or entirely on insects for food. Competition among these species is largely avoided through different foraging behavior and habitats. On the broadest scale, winter and summer visitors to the woodland avoid competition by utilizing the habitat at different times of the year. Among the year-around residents, some—such as the western bluebird and common bushtit—spend a good deal of time foraging in adjacent communities, and others—such as the white-breasted nuthatch and Nuttall's woodpecker—have evolved in ways allowing them to exploit feeding opportunities denied to other species.

The ladder-backed Nuttall's woodpecker works its way along trunks and limbs in search of boring insects, which it pries loose or excavates with its sharp beak. The closely related downy woodpecker forages in similar fashion, but is largely restricted to riparian woodland and seldom frequents the open, drier woods preferred by Nuttall's woodpecker. Insects found on the surface of the bark are largely ignored by Nuttall's woodpecker, but form the bulk of the white-breasted nuthatch's diet. This sparrow-sized bird has a squat, almost stooped posture well suited to scooting along limbs and trunks. It often moves upside-down on the bottom of a limb and is the only foothill bird that regularly descends trunks head first.

Of the year-around resident woodland birds, the gray, crested plain titmouse is among the most common and conspicuous. It forages for insects in the outer foliage of oaks or in digger pines and brush on occasion. Upslope in the forest, where the plain titmouse does not occur, a similar *foraging niche* (method and place of feeding) is occupied by the related mountain chickadee, which is not found in the foothill woodland. A third member of the tit family (*Paridae*), the common bushtit, is, like the titmouse, a year-around woodland resident, though it forages in under-story brush and adjacent chaparral more often than in trees.

During the summer several additional species of birds search for insects in the foliage of woodland trees, though none of them is able to exploit the outermost branches preferred by the titmouse. The black-throated gray warbler specializes in the upper branches and crowns of canyon live oaks. The black-headed grosbeak pursues insect larvae and slow-moving adult insects in the upper branches of most any woodland tree. Hutton's vireo depends on similar prey, but prefers the lower portion of a tree.

Two wintering thrushes, the American robin and the hermit thrush, both feed on the ground, but the robin prefers more open areas—and specializes in earthworms—while the hermit thrush scratches among the litter beneath trees and woodland brush. The common flicker, a year-around resident, forages in various habitats, including grassland and chaparral, but specializes in ants and termites. Ground-dwelling invertebrates are also an important food source for woodland lizards and salamanders. The California slender salamander, for example, eats sowbugs, millipedes, spiders, insects, and other invertebrates, which it finds in damp places beneath logs and rocks. Gilbert's skink, the most colorfully marked Sierra lizard, forages in leaf litter or grass for insects.

Flying insects provide the major food source for flycatchers such as the western kingbird, western wood peewee, willow flycatcher, black phoebe, and ash-throated flycatcher. All but the phoebe are summer visitors. Flycatchers obtain insects by making aerial sallies from an exposed perch to which they repeatedly return, but each of the above species prefers a different type of hunting habitat. The western kingbird perches atop shrubs or fenceposts or on lower tree branches in relatively open areas where scattered trees, brush, and grassland occur together. The ash-throated flycatcher nests in trees, but hunts over chaparral, especially stands containing scattered digger pines and oaks. The western wood peewee forages beneath the woodland canopy, and the willow flycatcher among streamside vegetation. The black phoebe captures insects hovering over streams, ponds, or reservoirs, whether bordered by dense vegetation or not.

Swallows and swifts also subsist on flying insects, which they capture by means of continual acrobatic flight. Swallows forage near the ground, over water, or just above the woodland treetops, while swifts forage several hundred feet above the earth.

Bats capture flying insects in similar fashion, but are seldom abroad during the day, when swallows and swifts are active. Like birds, bat species also have preferred foods and foraging places. For example, the long-eared bat flies back and forth over treetops, where it feeds on flying insects frequenting the outer branches, while the pallid bat forages relatively close to the ground and may even swoop to earth to capture a Jerusalem cricket or other insect.

Omnivores

Given the wide variety of foods available in the foothill woodland—acorns, seeds, berries, green vegetation, insects and other invertebrates, small vertebrates, and eggs—it is understandable that several animals characteristic of the community are omnivores, feeding through the year on whatever is readily available. Two of the most common, if not always conspicuous, residents of the foothill woodland, the scrub jay and the dusky-footed wood rat, show no particular specializations for any single type of food. Both consume acorns, seeds, fruits, and insects and other invertebrates. In addition the scrub jay relishes birds' eggs, nestlings, and small reptiles and amphibians.

Among the larger woodland mammals, the raccoon, its relative the ringtail, and both the striped and spotted skunks eat a wide variety of animal and vegetable matter.

110. Striped skunk tracks.

All are fairly common species, and their success may well be due in part to their lack of discrimination with regard to most foods. Even the coyote and gray fox, which prefer meat, eat vegetable matter on occasion. The fox, for example, often eats the berries of toyon and manzanita.

Predators

Important predators in the foothill woodland include the coyote, gray fox, bobcat, ringtail, great horned owl, Cooper's hawk, and various snakes, including the western rattlesnake, gopher snake, and common kingsnake. The Cooper's hawk, unlike the red-tail, rarely leaves the cover of trees. It is the chief predator of small woodland birds, which it plucks from perches even in dense vegetation. The wings of this hawk are proportionally shorter than those of most other hawks, an anatomical feature enabling it to move with great agility through dense stands of trees.

The mountain lion is a scarce transient in the community, though owing to its great stealth and shyness it may be somewhat more common than supposed. Mule deer, the big cat's main prey, are most common in the winter and spring, when herds that spend the summer upslope move down into the foothills. No doubt the population of mountain lions increases accordingly.

Shelter

In terms of the variety and number of available nesting sites, the foothill woodland is the antithesis of the open grassland. The dense foliage of trees protects woodland residents from the summer sun and provides small birds with cover from most predators. Ground-dwelling birds and mammals often congregate near understory brush, which provides them with both cover and nesting sites.

Abandoned woodpecker holes provide nesting sites for an impressive number of foothill animals, including the plain titmouse, white-breasted nuthatch, western bluebird, starling (a common alien species), violet-green swallow, house wren, and Bewick's wren. The gray squirrel, rac-

FOOTHILL ANIMALS

coon, and ringtail occupy larger cavities. Several aboreal salamanders may share a tree cavity during hot weather.

Numerous birds, of course, construct saucer-shaped nests on tree branches. Some prefer the dense foliage of understory shrubs. The northern oriole weaves a long, pouchlike nest, which it suspends from a branch high in a tree. Hawks and magpies build large stick platforms in the treetops, and these nests may be occupied later by great horned owls. The turkey vulture, along with coyotes, foxes, bobcats, and ringtails, prefers crevices in cliffs or rock outcrops.

The dusky-footed wood rat constructs an elaborate domed nest from twigs, leaves, and miscellaneous debris. These "apartment houses" contain several passageways and chambers, some abandoned by the wood rat and later occupied by such tenants as mice, snakes, and even quail. The wood rat seems to add to its nest continually and may change living quarters frequently.

Woodland Margins

Many animals that nest or seek shelter in the foothill woodland forage in adjacent stands of grassland and chaparral. These include mule deer, most predators, and numerous species of insect-eating birds. Conversely, animals from the latter communities venture into the woodland for food or cover from predators. Consequently, woodland margins are particularly good places to observe wildlife, and from a good vantage point along this ecotone one may expect to see creatures characteristic of most or all foothill communities.

Unless one is willing and equipped to observe animals in the dead of night, the best time to see them abroad is from first light to about an hour after dawn. Many nocturnal animals will still be active, and diurnal creatures will have just begun to move about. During the middle of a hot summer day, when even the shade of the trees is not entirely adequate to mitigate the region's intense heat, comparatively few animals will be evident in the foothill woodland. A few birds may be abroad but most animals will be resting and waiting for dusk.

Woodland Residents

The following species live in the foothill woodland the year around. Asterisks after some entries refer to further discussion in Selected Foothill Animals. Species described in detail in other chapters are so noted.

AMPHIBIANS

Tiger Salamander, *Ambystoma tigrinum.*
California Newt, *Taricha torosa.* *
California Slender Salamander, *Batrchoseps attentuatus.* *
Ensatina, *Ensatina escholtzi.* See Selected Forest Animals.
Arboreal Salamander, *Aneides lugubris.*

REPTILES

Gilbert's Skink, *Eumeces gilberti.* *
Western Fence Lizard, *Sceloporus occidentalis.* See Selected Forest Animals.
Gopher Snake, *Pituphis melanoleucus.*
Common Kingsnake, *Lampropeltis getulus.* *
Western Rattlesnake, *Crotalus viridis.* *

BIRDS

Red-Tailed Hawk, *Buteo jamaicensis.* *
Cooper's Hawk, *Accipiter cooperii.*
Mourning Dove, *Zenaida macroura.* *
Screech Owl, *Otus asio.*
Great Horned Owl, *Bubo virginianus.* See Selected Forest Animals.
Long-eared Owl, *Asio otus.*
California Quail, *Lophortyx californicus.* *
Anna's Hummingbird, *Calypte anna.* *
Common Flicker, *Colaptes auratus.*
Acorn Woodpecker, *Melanerpes formicivorus*, Fig. 112. *
Downy Woodpecker, *Dendrocopos pubescens.*
Nuttall's Woodpecker, *Dendrocopos nuttallii.*
Scrub Jay, *Aphelocoma coerulescens*, Fig. 113. *
Yellow-Billed Magpie, *Pica nuttalli.*
Plain Titmouse, *Parus inornatus.* *
Common Bushtit, *Psaltriparus minimus.* *
White-Breasted Nuthatch, *Sitta carolinensis.*
Bewick's Wren, *Thyromanes bewickii.* *
Western Bluebird, *Sialia mexicana.* *

House Finch, *Carpodacus mexicanus.**
Rufous-Sided Towhee, *Pipilo erythrophthalmus.**
Brown Towhee, *Pipilo fuscus.*
Lark Sparrow, *Chondestes grammacus.*

MAMMALS

Ornate Shrew, *Sorex ornatus.*
Bats, order *Chiroptera.*
Gray Squirrel, *Sciurus griseus.**
Deer Mouse, *Peromyscus maniculatus.*
Gray Fox, *Urocyon cinereoargenteus,* Fig. 117.*
Coyote, *Canis latrans.* See Selected Forest Animals.
Raccoon, *Procyon lotor,* Fig. 118.*
Ringtail, *Bassariscus astutus,* Fig. 119.*
Spotted Skunk, *Spilogale putorius.*
Striped Skunk, *Mephitis mephitis,* Fig. 110.
Mountain Lion, *Felis concolor.* See Selected Forest Animals.
Bobcat, *Lynx rufus,* Fig. 120.*
Mule Deer, *Odocoileus hemionus.* See Selected Forest Animals.

Woodland Visitors: Migratory Birds

The following species are summer visitors to the foothill woodland, where they nest and rear their young.

Western Kingbird, *Tyrannus verticalis.**
Western Wood Peewee, *Contonpus sordidulus.*
Violet-Green Swallow, *Tachycinetta thalassina.*
House Wren, *Troglodytes aedon.*
Swainson's Thrush, *Catharus ustulatus.*
Blue-Gray Gnatcatcher, *Polioptila caerulea.*
Hutton's Vireo, *Vireo huttoni.*
Warbling Vireo, *Vireo gilvus.*
Black-Throated Gray Warbler, *Dendroica nigrescens.*
Northern Oriole, *Icterus galbula.**
Black-Headed Grosbeak, *Pheucticus melanocephalus.*
Chipping Sparrow, *Spizella passerina.*

The following species are winter visitors to the foothill woodland. Some species are downslope migrants; others come from distant regions to the north. For some species—the hermit thrush, for example—the winter population living in the foothills is different from the breed-

Animal Life in the Foothill Woodland

ing population found in montane and subalpine forests during the summer. In the following list, downslope migrants
are indicated by the initials *DM*.

Band-Tailed Pigeon, *Columba fasciata*, DM.
Red-Breasted Nuthatch, *Sitta canadensis*, DM.
American Robin, *Turdus migratorius*, some DM.
Hermit Thrush, *Catharus guttatus*. See Selected Forest Ani-
mals.
Golden-Crowned Kinglet, *Regulus satrapa*, DM.
Ruby-Crowned Kinglet, *Regulus calendula*, DM.
Cedar Waxwing, *Bombycilla cedorum*.
Yellow-Rumped Warbler, *Dendroica coronata*, some DM.
See Selected Forest Animals.
Purple Finch, *Carpodacus purpureus*, DM.
Dark-Eyed Junco, *Junco hyemalis*, some DM. See Selected
Forest Animals.
White-Crowned Sparrow, *Zonotrichia leucophrys*. See
Selected Forest Animals.
Golden-Crowned Sparrow, *Zonotrichia atricapilla.*
Lincoln Sparrow, *Melospiza lincolnii.*

Animal Life
in the Riparian Woodland

During the summer, streams draining the upper slopes of
the Sierra constitute the major source of water for foothill
animals. (Other reliable water sources include scattered
stock ponds, human settlements, and the several large reservoirs in the region.) The riparian woodland thus serves
as an oasis for animal life during the hottest, driest months
of the year. Even dry streambeds usually offer a few persistent pools to thirsty animals and provide ample subterranean moisture for streamside vegetation. Consequently,
riparian plants remain active during the summer, so in addition to water the community also provides green vegetation and ripe berries at a time when such foods are scarce or
unavailable elsewhere in the foothills.

The types and numbers of animals that frequent the riparian woodland during the summer exceed those of all
other foothill communities. Most predators regularly visit
streamsides during the summer, as do most other animals

from nearby communities. During the morning, bands of deer approach quiet pools to drink, and small songbirds frequently cool themselves with midafternoon baths.

The riparian woodland offers many of the same opportunities for food and shelter as the drier foothill woodland, so most animals found in the latter community also frequent the former in varying degrees. The main difference with regard to vegetation is that in the riparian woodland grasses are an insignificant element in the understory, which is dominated instead by numerous mesophytic shrubs and vines. Animals that frequent woodland thickets—wood rats and towhees, for example—are also found in riparian undergrowth, but those such as the chipping sparrow and western kingbird, which forage for food on open ground, are scarce or absent.

In addition to streamside visitors and animals also typical of adjacent woodlands and brush, the riparian woodland supports a number of creatures that are either less common or absent elsewhere. The wood duck, spotted sandpiper, black phoebe, yellow warbler, willow flycatcher, kingfisher, and downy woodpecker, for example, are more or less restricted in the Sierra foothills to streamside vegetation. The northern oriole, screech owl, Wilson's warbler, and song sparrow are more common there than elsewhere. So too are mammals such as the ornate shrew, raccoon, ringtail, and mink.

Steeper, rockier sections of foothill streams are inhabited by the dipper and canyon wren. Riparian woodland is poorly developed in such areas, but these birds are included here because both are commonly seen along streams. The dipper, in fact, almost never ventures away from running water. It nests on rocks washed by stream spray, forages for insects on streambed rocks and even beneath the water, and flies only along streamcourses, never taking shortcuts through the woods. The canyon wren also

111. Mink tracks.

occurs in rocky, steep-walled canyons devoid of running water, but is more abundant along active streams.

Streamsides and adjacent woodlands are excellent places to look for frogs and salamanders. The native red-legged frog and foothill yellow-legged frog both frequent moist streambanks and breed in quiet pools. The red-legged frog is largely restricted to quiet waters in the lower foothills. The yellow-legged frog also occurs along faster streams ranging upslope into the forest. The tiger salamander and California newt both breed in stream pools, ponds, and reservoirs but spend much of the year away from water. At such times they may be found in both the foothill and riparian woodlands, usually under rocks, logs, or other debris.

Streamside Animals

Since so many creatures visit the riparian woodland from adjacent communities, the following list includes only the following classes of species: (1) species rarely or never found away from streams; (2) species that only breed in or along streams; and (3) species more common along streams than elsewhere. Birds that winter outside the Sierra foothills are designated SV (summer visitor). Asterisks following some entries refer to further discussion in Selected Foothill Animals. Species described in other chapters are so noted.

AMPHIBIANS

Tiger Salamander, *Ambystoma tigrinum.*
California Newt, *Taricha torosa.* *
Red-Legged Frog, *Rana aurora.*
Foothill Yellow-Legged Frog, *Rana boylii.*

REPTILES

Ringneck Snake, *Diadophis punctatus.*
Sharp-Tailed Snake, *Contia tenuis.*
Western Aquatic Garter Snake, *Thamnophis couchi.*

BIRDS

Wood Duck, *Aix sponsa.*
Screech Owl, *Otus asio.*

FOOTHILL ANIMALS

Long-Eared Owl, *Asio otus.*
Spotted Sandpiper, *Actitus macularia.*
Belted Kingfisher, *Megaceryle Alcyon.*
Downy Woodpecker, *Dendrocopos pubescens.*
Black Phoebe, *Sayornis nigricans.*
Willow Flycatcher, *Empidonax traillii,* SV.
Dipper, *Cinclus mexicanus.* See Selected Forest Animals.
Canyon Wren, *Catherpus mexicanus.*
Yellow Warbler, *Dendroica petechia,* SV.
Common Yellowthroat, *Geothlypis tricha.*
Yellow-Breasted Chat, *Icteria virens,* SV.
Northern Oriole, *Icterus galbula.**
Song Sparrow, *Melospiza melodia.*

MAMMALS

Ornate Shrew, *Sorex ornatus.*
Raccoon, *Procyon lotor,* Fig. 118.*
Ringtail, *Bassariscus astutus,* Fig. 119.*
Mink, *Mustela vision.*

Animal Life in the Chaparral

Dense stands of chaparral provide excellent cover for numerous species of small birds and mammals, several of
which seldom or never occur in other types of vegetation.
Most of these animals are drab, inclining toward shades of
brown or gray that blend with the muted tones of most
chaparral shrubs. Resident animals tend to be elusive,
partly out of wariness, no doubt, but also because they are
very difficult to see—wary or not—in the dense brush. For
example, the wrentit, a small brown bird with a perky tail
and yellow eye, is abundant in chaparral—indeed, seldom
found elsewhere—yet even experienced birdwatchers
count themselves lucky to observe it. The wrentit's sustained, bouncy whistle, however, is one of the most characteristic sounds in the community during the breeding season in late winter and spring.

Owing to the denseness of the shrub cover, large predators have difficulty entering the community, which therefore may serve as a refuge for species from adjacent areas.

Snakes, however, can move through the brush easily and therefore constitute the most important type of predator in the community. Rattlesnakes take brush rabbits and small rodents on the ground. The striped racer climbs among the branches to feast on birds' eggs or nestlings. Scrub jays, which nest in both woodland and chaparral, also raid nests from time to time.

During the rainy season chaparral shrubs provide food in the form of young shoots and leaves, and at this time mule deer commonly feed along the margins of the community. Small rodents, such as the dusky-footed wood rat, brush mouse, and Merriam's chipmunk, eat green vegetation when available, then switch to berries and finally seeds as the year progresses. The brush rabbit feeds on green grasses and wildflowers found growing along the margins of the community during the rainy season, but turns to the branches of chaparral shrubs for food during the summer months.

The black-chinned sparrow, which is restricted largely to chaparral, is primarily a seedeater, as are the lazuli bunting and brown and rufous-sided towhees, which commonly nest in the community. The wrentit flits through the shrubbery gleaning small insects from leaves and stems, but also eats chaparral fruits when available. The brown thrasher, another characteristic chaparral bird, uses its long curved beak to pluck insects from leaves and probe for them in the soil. The ash-throated flycatcher, which usually nests in trees, prefers to capture flying insects near or over chaparral stands.

The scrub jay, lazuli bunting, and Bewick's wren commonly nest in chaparral as well as woodland brush, but also freely wander into adjacent communities. The beautiful turquoise bunting is easily the most brightly colored chaparral bird. Unlike most birds inhabiting the community, it is seen often, usually singing from the top of a shrub or branch of a nearby tree.

Animal populations are highest in fairly young stands of mixed chaparral, where a variety of shrub species provide a varied and ample menu. Mature stands of pure chamise contain very few resident animals, and many species, such as the black-chinned sparrow, which are common in mixed stands, may be absent. Recently burned stands characterized by abundant postfire herbs and scattered young shrubs also host a larger number and variety of animals than mature stands. Chaparral populations increase in response to abundant food and greater habitat diversity. They drop steadily in subsequent years in response to increased predation and the progressive homogeneity of vegetation as shrubs once again assert their dominance.

The ways in which chaparral animals survive the periodic fires characteristic of this community are discussed in Chapter IV, but it is worthwhile to review these strategies here. First, all species finish breeding before the fire season begins, so that the young are able to fend for themselves. (Early breeding also ensures an ample supply of water and both green vegetation and other foods for young animals.) Second, small chaparral mammals and snakes either flee to relatively safe areas or to burrows, where chances of survival are good. Third, birds merely fly to adjacent stands. Animal mortality as a result of chaparral fire is accordingly rather low. Indeed, some studies have shown no significant drop in populations on recently burned sites.

Chaparral Animals

The following animals are known to breed in or regularly frequent chaparral. The list does not include casual visitors or those that merely forage along the margins of the community. Asterisks refer to further discussion in Selected Foothill Animals. Species described in detail in other chapters are so noted.

REPTILES

Western Whiptail, *Cnemidophorus hyperythrus.*
Southern Alligator Lizard, *Gerrhonotus multicarinatus.* *
Striped Racer, *Masticophis lateralis.* *
Gopher Snake, *Pituophis melanoleucus.*
Common Kingsnake, *Lampropeltis getulus.* *
Western Black-Headed Snake, *Tantilla planiceps.*
Night Snake, *Hypsiglena torquata.*
Western Rattlesnake, *Crotalus viridis.* *

BIRDS

California Quail, *Lophortyx californicus.* *

Anna's Hummingbird, *Calypte anna.**
Ash-Throated Flycatcher, *Myarchus cinerascens.*
Scrub Jay, *Aphelocoma coerulescens*, Fig. 113.**
Common Bushtit, *Psaltriparus minimus.**
Wrentit, *Chamaea fasciata.**
Bewick's Wren, *Thryomanes bewickii.**
California Thrasher, *Toxostoma redivivum.**
Orange-Crowned Warbler, *Vermivora celata.*
Lazuli Bunting, *Passerina amoena.*
Rufous-Sided Towhee, *Pipilo erythrophthalamus.**
Brown Towhee, *Pipilo fuscus.*
Sage Sparrow, *Amphispiza bilineata.*
Black-Chinned Sparrow, *Spizella atrogularis.*

MAMMALS

Black-Tailed Jackrabbit, *Lepus californicus*, Fig. 115.**
Brush Rabbit, *Sylvilagus bachmani*, Fig. 116.**
Merriam's Chipmunk, *Eutamias merriami.*
California Pocket Mouse, *Perognathus californicus.*
Deer Mouse, *Peromyscus maniculatus.*
Brush Mouse, *Peromyscus boylii.*
California Mouse, *Peromyscus californicus.*
Dusky-Footed Wood Rat, *Neotoma fuscipes.**

Selected Foothill Animals

A description of every species of animal occurring in the
Sierra foothills is obviously impossible in a book of this
scope and size. The criteria used in making the following
selection are discussed in the introduction to this guide.

Amphibians

California Newt, *Taricha torosa. Length:* 2¾ to 3½ in (7
to 9 cm). *Color:* tan to reddish brown above, yellow to
orange below. *Food:* earthworms, slugs, snails, sowbugs,
insects. *Habitat:* open woodland; breeds in streams, ponds,
and reservoirs. *Distribution:* foothills and lower forest to
about 5000 ft (1500 m). The newt spends most of its time on
land, migrating toward water to breed beginning in midwinter. Males arrive at the breeding pond first and may

have to spend a good deal of time in the water prior to the arrival of the females. Consequently, around breeding time the body of the male undergoes several changes designed to aid its survival in water and assist it in mating. The skin, normally somewhat dry and rough on land, becomes smooth and swollen, presumably to prevent the animal from becoming waterlogged. The skin of amphibians, most of whom live in damp places to prevent dessication, is pervious to water. For the terrestrial newt the problem during the breeding season is one of preventing too much water from passing through the skin from the outside. Prior to breeding, the male newt also develops a fin on its tail to assist in swimming. The region of the vent becomes swollen, and rough areas develop on the bottoms of the feet to aid the male in grasping his slippery mate. When the females arrive, pairing begins. The male rides on the back of his partner—an embrace known as *amplexis*—rubbing her snout with his chin, which contains glands that release a substance that pacifies the female. The male deposits a gelatinous mound capped with sperm on the bottom of the pond and leads the female over it. She grasps the sperm cap with her vent and takes it inside her, so that fertilization is internal even though the male does not enter the female. This is the case not only with the newt, but with all California salamanders. Among frogs and toads, however, fertilization is external, the male depositing sperm over the eggs after they have been laid.

California Slender Salamander, *Batrachoseps attenuatus. Length:* up to 5 in (13 cm), no more than ⅜ in (1 cm) diam. *Color:* black, sometimes with narrow, rusty stripe down back. *Food:* sowbugs, millipedes, mites, spiders, slugs, snails, and insects. *Habitat:* damp places under logs, rocks, and other objects on the ground. *Distribution:* below forest on west slope. This small, wormlike salamander may wriggle violently if disturbed. Its legs are evident only upon close examination. It is also common to backyard gardens throughout much of California, where it provides valuable assistance in controlling plant pests.

Arboreal Salamander, *Aneides lugubris. Length:* to 7 in (18 cm); head is blunt and triangular. *Color:* dark brown, often with yellow spots. *Food:* insects, spiders, slender salamanders, fungus, various small invertebrates. *Habitat:*

rotting logs, beneath bark, under stones, logs, boards, and other objects. *Distribution:* foothills to lower margins of the mixed-coniferous forest. The arboreal salamander got its name because individuals have been found up to 30 ft (9 m) off the ground in cool, damp cavities in oaks. Its prehensile tail is no doubt useful for climbing. Males have enlarged, exposed teeth at the front of the upper jaw and can inflict a nasty wound if mishandled. This species is active from October through May.

Western Spadefoot, *Scaphiopus hammondi. Length:* 1½ to 2½ in (4 to 6 cm). *Color:* splotchy green or gray. *Food:* insects, worms, spiders, and other invertebrates. *Habitat:* open grassland or mixed woodland–grassland near vernal pools, temporary or permanent streams, other moist places. *Distribution:* Central Valley, Sierra foothills to about 4500 ft (1350 m). Toads begin life in the water, but are terrestrial thereafter. The spadefoot toads as a group are adapted to living in arid regions, burrowing during the hottest, driest parts of the year. The western spadefoot uses its back feet (hence the name) to burrow backward in loose soil to depths up to 3 ft. Here it spends most of the hot dry summer months, absorbing moisture from the surrounding soil through its permeable skin, emerging only in the fall or winter after heavy rains. Breeding occurs in spring, when rains form vernal pools in the grasslands. The eggs are laid and fertilized in these transient ponds, and the tadpoles metamorphose into adult toads within the brief space of a month.

Reptiles

Coast Horned Lizard, *Phrynosoma coronatum. Length:* to 3½ in (9 cm). *Color:* pale yellow to reddish above, with dark spots bordered partly by white; yellowish with brownish gray spots below. *Food:* insects. *Habitat:* open sandy ground; seeks shelter in burrows or rock crevices. *Distribution:* foothills of west slope. The "horny toad" is easily recognized by its flattish body, numerous pointed or keeled scales along its back, and pointed scales (or horns) behind its head.

Gilbert's Skink, *Eumeces gilberti. Length:* 2½ to 4 in (6 to 10 cm). *Tail:* to about 6 in (15 cm). *Color: adults*—yellow-brown above with coppery head and pinkish tail; pale below with perhaps a trace of blue-green on sides; *young*—two narrow yellow stripes run from head to tail on back; tail, blue; gray below; the scales of both young and adults are smooth and somewhat iridescent; the young assume adult coloration in the second or third year. *Food:* largely insects, obtained by foraging through leaf litter or herbaceous ground cover. *Habitat:* grassland, woodland, and open pine forest near rocks and water. *Distribution:* Sierra foothills, ranging into the lower montane zone. Among the most beautiful Sierra lizards, Gilbert's skink is seldom seen because it is largely nocturnal, spending the day, often in groups, under rock slabs. It wriggles like a snake to avoid pursuers, but walks on its short legs when hunting insects. If captured, the tail breaks off and continues to wiggle, providing a distraction that may allow the skink to escape.

Western Whiptail, *Cnemidophorus hyperythrus.* *Length:* to 14 in (35 cm), of which 10 in (25 cm) may be tail. *Color:* adults, blackish above with pale spots; young have pale lengthwise stripes instead of spots; dark blotches on legs and sides of head; white or tan below. *Food:* insects and other invertebrates. *Habitat:* open, dry, sandy or rocky areas. *Distribution:* Central Valley to lower margins of ponderosa pine forest. The whiptail is the fastest foothill lizard, often running in swift bursts of from 50 to 100 ft (15 to 30 m), sometimes on its hind legs. The tail, which is more than twice the length of the body, serves as a counterbalance.

Southern Alligator Lizard, *Gerrhonotus multicarinatus.* *Length:* 7 to 18 in (18 to 46 cm) the tail accounting for up to two-thirds this length. *Color:* brownish above, gray to yellowish below. *Food:* insects, spiders, young birds, young field mice, and other small mammals. *Habitat:* grassland, brush, rocky areas. *Distribution:* foothills of west slope; also along eastern base of Sierra from Independence south. Although the alligator lizard will thrash vigorously if held and may even bite its captor, its teeth are too small to inflict serious injury. And though its triangular head—similar in shape to that of the rattlesnake—has lead some people to think it poisonous, such is not the case. The similar northern alligator lizard, *G. coeruleus,* ranges throughout the montane zone to 9000 ft (2700 m). The southern species lays eggs; the northern bears live young.

Striped Racer, *Masticophis lateralis. Length:* 2½ to 5 ft (18 to 16 dm). *Color:* black or dark brown, with yellowish stripe on each side running length of body; lacks median stripes of the similar garter snakes. *Food:* toads, frogs, lizards, snakes, insects, small mammals, eggs, birds. *Habitat:* various, but especially chaparral and open, brushy areas. *Distribution:* foothills of west slope. The striped racer is one of the few predators able to prey effectively on chaparral birds and rodents. It can easily invade burrows and will commonly climb shrubs to raid birds' nests. Prey is held down by loops of the snake's body and then crushed in its jaws.

Common Kingsnake, *Lampropeltis getulus. Length:* 2½ to 7 ft (8 to 21 dm). *Color:* alternating "rings" of black and pale yellow. *Food:* snakes, including rattlesnakes, lizards, amphibians, birds, and eggs. *Habitat:* all communities. *Distribution:* foothills of west slope. The common kingsnake is one of the few predators of rattlesnakes, to whose venom it is largely immune. It will also climb shrubs to obtain young birds and eggs. It kills its prey by constriction.

Western Rattlesnake, *Crotalus viridis. Length:* 1½ to 5 ft (5 to 16 dm); body, thick and heavy, up to 5 in (13 cm) diam. *Color:* pale brown with large dark blotches down back and two rows of smaller blotches on each side. *Other identifying marks:* head is broad and roughly triangular, unlike that of any other Sierra snake; neck thinner than head or body; heat-sensing "pits" that resemble a pair of nostrils on the snout; bony rattles on tail (young rattlesnakes have a single "button"). *Food:* rodents, rabbits, lizards, and birds. *Habitat:* grasslands, brush, rocky areas; dens in rock crevices and on ledges; several snakes may spend the winter in a single den; rests during the day along trails, on rock ledges, near logs and boulders, among leaf litter. *Distribution:* west slope, mostly below 6000 ft (1800 m); most common in foothill zone; a few rattlesnakes have been found in the southern Sierra between 9000 and 10,000 ft (2700 and 3050 m) and one at 11,000 ft (3350 m), but rattlesnakes are very rare at such elevations; east slope south to vicinity of Lake Crowley in southern Mono County; replaced southward by the speckled rattlesnake, *Crotalus mitchelli;* absent from Tahoe Basin. This most feared of Sierra reptiles waits in ambush for its prey, which it kills by injecting venom. Heat-sensing pits on the snout help the rattler locate warm-blooded prey and direct its strike. Reptiles and amphibians are detected by eyesight. Rattlers also use their venom to protect themselves from hawks, owls, coyotes, mountain lions, and humans. The western rattlesnake is a retiring creature that will avoid human contact at all costs. It bites people only in self-defense. If unable to escape, it forms a coil and holds the forward part of its body in an erect, S-shaped curve in preparation for striking. At the same time, it rapidly shakes the bony rattles at the tip of its tail to produce a distinctive buzzing sound that once heard is instantly recognizable. If left alone at this point, it will eventually crawl off without striking. Foothill rattlesnakes hibernate in frost-free burrows from about October to April. Those occurring farther upslope hibernate for even longer periods.

Birds

Abbreviations used in the following descriptions: R = year-around resident; SV = summer visitor breeding in the foothills.

Turkey Vulture, *Cathartes aura. Length:* 26 to 30 in (66 to 76 cm). *Wingspread:* 6 ft (2 m). *Color:* black with red head, which is featherless. *Eggs:* 1 to 3. *Nest:* ledges and crevices in cliffs, among rocks, in holes in trees and hollow logs on ground. *Food:* carrion; does not prey on live animals. *Distribution:* common SV in foothills; very common R in Central Valley; some may wander upslope in summer. The turkey vulture is the common "buzzard" of the foothills, over which it soars gracefully on rising thermals, searching for dead animals. Roosts in trees at night. Easily distinguished from hawks and eagles by its black plumage, red head, and wing position while soaring. Hawks hold their wings straight out; vultures hold theirs upward at an angle, forming a V readily apparent from the ground.

Red-Tailed Hawk, *Buteo jamaicensis. Length:* 19 to 25 in (48 to 64 cm). *Wingspread:* 4 to 4½ ft (12 to 14 dm). *Color:* brown above, white breast; belly, white streaked with brown; tail, reddish brown. *Eggs:* 2 to 4. *Nest:* stick platform in top of tree or on rock ledge. *Food:* mostly small rodents, rabbits; does not take poultry or livestock. *Distribution:* common R in foothills; fairly common SV to near timberline; common R east of Sierra crest; may be seen soaring anywhere. This is the most common soaring hawk of the Sierra, easily recognized in adult plumage by its conspicuous reddish tail, which is often fanned out as it wheels and soars over the hills. When not soaring, the red-tailed hawk perches in treetops and on fenceposts and utility poles along highways.

American Kestrel (Sparrow Hawk), *Falco sparverius.* *Length:* 9 to 12 in (23 to 30 cm). *Wingspread:* about 2 ft (6 dm); wings pointed and swept back in flight. *Color: male* — head gray with reddish crown, black and white on cheeks; buffy orange extends from nape of neck around to breast and down to belly; sides spotted with black; wings gray; back reddish brown, barred; tail reddish brown with broad black band and narrow white band at tip; *female* — similar, but wings are reddish brown; tail lighter and faintly barred; breast buff with pale streaks on sides. *Eggs:* 3 to 5. *Nest:* tree cavity. *Food:* mostly insects, especially grasshoppers; small rodents; occasionally a small bird. *Distribution:* common R in foothills, wandering upslope in late summer to subalpine meadows. About the size of a jay, the kestrel is our smallest hawk and one of the most beautiful; does not soar, but hovers on flapping wings a few yards above the ground, looking for insects and mice; roosts on utility lines, fenceposts, shrubs, and low trees when not hunting; frequently attacks much larger hawks that venture into its hunting territory.

California Quail, *Lophortyx californicus.* *Length:* 9½ to 11 in (24 to 28 cm). *Color: male* —back and tail dark brown; sides, brown streaked with white; breast, bluish gray; belly, buff, scalloped with brown; nape of neck, bluish gray, scalloped; black bib with white border extending from eye and beak down onto the breast; black and white stripes over the eyes; forehead, cream-colored; crown, reddish brown with conspicuous, black topknot feather resembling a single quotation mark; *female* —duller, has light throat. *Eggs:* 10 to 17. *Nest:* grass-lined hollow on ground in brush. *Food:* seeds mostly, also green vegetation and insects. *Distribu-*

274

tion: common R of foothills amid woodland and near chaparral. Able to fly short distances when necessary, the California quail prefers to remain on the ground; a fast runner, often scurrying into dense brush when alarmed; forms pairs during nesting season, otherwise found in small flocks of males, females, and—after nesting—chicks; a favorite prey of bobcats, gray foxes, coyotes, and Cooper's hawks.

Mourning Dove, *Zenaida macroura. Length:* 11 to 13 in (28 to 33 cm). *Color:* head and back, light brown; buff below; tail, light brown bordered with white, pointed; wings, bluish gray. *Eggs:* 2. *Nest:* flimsy twig platform on ground or in shrubs and low trees. *Food:* seeds. *Distribution:* common R in foothills and in valleys east of crest, occasionally wandering upslope into the forest; found in open grassland, brushy areas, woodlands, around human settlements; often perched on utility wires. Mourning doves are named for the plaintive quality of their *oooah, cooo, cooo* call. In pairs most of the year, but form loose feeding flocks in winter; forage on the ground, walking with a distinctive head-bobbing gait.

Anna's Hummingbird, *Calypte anna. Length:* 3½ to 4 in (9 to 10 cm). *Color: male*—metallic red throat and crown; back of head and back, green; breast white; belly grayish; female lacks red on throat and crown. *Eggs:* 2. *Nest:* lichen-covered cup the size of half a walnut shell, placed in shrub or tree. *Food:* primarily nectar from flowers; some gnats. *Distribution:* common R in foothill woodland, riparian woodland, and chaparral; visits grassland when flowers are in bloom. During mid and late summer, when flowers are scarce throughout the foothills, Anna's hummingbird will wander upslope, venture into gardens, or retire to the riparian woodland, where flowers at this season are more abundant.

Acorn Woodpecker, *Melanerpes formicivorus.* Fig. 112. *Length:* 8 to 9½ in (20 to 24 cm). *Color:* back of head, chin, breast, back, wings, and tail, black; rump and belly, white; crown, bright red in female bordered in front with black; cream-colored band extends from forehead to shoulders and across upper breast in both sexes; yellow eyes, black beak. *Eggs:* 4 to 5. *Nest:* tree cavity. *Food:* acorns, grubs in tree bark, flying insects. *Distribution:* common R in foothills and among oaks of mixed-coniferous forest, west slope.

112. Acorn Woodpecker,
Melanerpes formicivorus.

The most common and conspicuous woodpecker of California's oak woodlands; noisy and social; its loud *jack-up, jack-up, jack-up* call is one of the commonest bird sounds of the foothills; often congregates in noisy, active groups in pines and oaks; stores acorns by the hundreds in holes drilled in dead trees, buildings, and telephone poles; captures flying insects in the manner of flycatchers, repeatedly flying out and back from the same perch; odd facial markings and antic behavior make it the clown among woodpeckers.

Western Kingbird, *Tyrannus verticalis. Length:* 8 to 9½ in (20 to 24 cm). *Color:* head, gray with inconspicuous orange crown; back, olive gray; wings and tail, brown; chin, whitish; breast, pale gray; belly, lemon yellow. *Eggs:* 3 to 5. *Nest:* woven bowl of twigs, grass, wool; placed on horizontal branch, pole or building. *Food:* flying insects. *Distribution:* common SV to foothills. This large flycatcher hunts in the classic manner of its clan: perching on fenceposts, shrubs, and other exposed spots, it periodically flies out to nab a flying insect and returns to the same perch; extremely aggressive in defending breeding territory against all comers, even much larger birds.

Scrub Jay, *Aphelocoma coerulescens.* Fig. 113. *Length:* 11 to 13 in (28 to 33 cm). *Color:* head, wings, rump, and tail, bright blue; back gray; black patch on cheeks; white throat; pale, buffy gray belly; no crest. *Eggs:* 3 to 6. *Nest:* bowl of twigs in shrubs. *Food:* acorns, nuts, seeds, berries, insects, eggs, small birds. *Distribution:* abundant R in oak woodlands and chaparral. Except during the spring, when breeding pairs are secretive, this noisy, raucous jay is one of the most conspicuous birds in the foothills, sometimes perching quietly on top of a shrub, but often flying here and there with a loud cry of *check-check-check-check-check* as it goes.

Plain Titmouse, *Parus inornatus. Length:* 5 to 5½ in (13 to 14 cm). *Color:* soft gray all over. *Eggs:* 6 to 9. *Nest:* hole in tree. *Food:* insects found among outer branches of oaks and other trees. *Distribution:* common R of foothill woodland. Unlike its close cousins the chickadees, the plain titmouse has a crest, which together with its small size and gray plumage is distinctive. Commonly heard in the foothill woodland; two calls: a high, raspy *chicka-dee-dee,* and a loud whistled *tee-wit, tee-wit, tee-wit.*

Common Bushtit, *Psaltriparus minimus. Length:* 4 to 4½ in (10 to 11 cm). *Color:* gray with brownish cap; slightly paler breast and belly. *Eggs:* 5 to 7. *Nest:* woven sack 8 to 9 in (20 to 23 cm) long, made of vegetation and placed usually in oaks. *Food:* small insects gleaned from plants. *Distribution:* common resident of foothill woodland and chaparral. This tiny relative of the titmouse forages in large, loose flocks, constantly chattering and flicking its wings as one bird after another darts from this shrub or tree to that. Like other members of the titmouse family, which includes chickadees, the common bushtit is rather tame and often clings upside-down to the outer tips of branches in its search for insects on the undersides of leaves.

Wrentit, *Chamaea fasciata. Length:* 6 to 6½ in (15 to 17 cm). *Color:* brown all over; eye, yellow. *Eggs:* 3 to 5. *Nest:* small cup in shrub. *Food:* insects and berries. *Distribution:*

113. Scrub Jay,
Aphelocoma coerulescens.

common R in foothill chaparral. This is the chaparral bird par excellence, only rarely leaving the dense brush and then not for long. Difficult to see even where common, for it is constantly on the move and seldom perches in plain view. More often heard than seen, its monotonous "ping-pong ball" song—*pip-pip-pip-pip-pip-pip-pip-pi-pi-p-p-p-p*—is distinctive. Found only in California and adjacent areas in Oregon and Mexico where coastal scrub and chaparral are found.

Bewick's Wren, *Thryomanes bewickii*. *Length:* 5 to 5½ in (13 to 14 cm). *Color:* brown above, whitish below; white stripe over eye; outer tail feathers tipped with white. *Eggs:* 5 to 7. *Nest:* twigs and plant stems lined with hair or other soft materials and placed among shrubs or in a tree cavity. *Food:* mostly insects. *Distribution:* Common R in chaparral and woodland brush.

California Thrasher, *Toxostoma redivivum*. *Length:* 11½ to 13 in (29 to 33 cm). *Color:* drab brown, somewhat paler below; whitish chin. *Eggs:* 2 to 4. *Nest:* lined bowl of twigs in shrubs. *Food:* insects. *Distribution:* fairly common R in foothill chaparral. The long downcurved bill of the California thrasher is distinctive, setting it apart from all other Sierra birds. Like the wrentit it is restricted almost entirely to chaparral, which it leaves only occasionally. Normally wary, the thrasher is most often seen in the early morning or near dusk, when males may sing from exposed perches on top of shrubs. Its song is highly varied, consisting of a rapid succession of whistles, chirps, trills, squawks, and scolding notes.

Western Bluebird, *Sialia mexicana*. *Length:* 6½ to 7 in (17 to 18 cm). *Color: male*—head, throat, lower back, wings, and tail, brilliant blue; upper back and breast rusty; *female*—pale bluish gray above, reddish brown below. *Eggs:* 4 to 6. *Nest:* hole in tree or birdhouse. *Food:* mostly insects. *Distribution:* common R in foothill woodlands and nearby open areas; ranges into lower forest. The western bluebird is frequently seen perched on fenceposts or hovering for insects in the manner of a sparrow hawk. Though it nests in woodland, most foraging is done in open, grassy areas.

Western Meadowlark, *Sturnella neglecta*. Fig. 114. *Length:* 8½ to 11 in (22 to 28 cm). *Color:* head, striped black and white with touches of yellow; back and wings, mottled brown; tail, brown with white borders; throat, breast, and belly, bright yellow; wide black necklace on throat; sides, white streaked with black. *Eggs:* 3 to 7. *Nest:* domed saucer made of grass and placed in grass. *Food:* insects and seeds; forages on ground. *Distribution:* grassland in foothills and in valleys east of the range; common R, often seen perched on fenceposts along roads. When facing the observer, the bright yellow breast and black V-shaped necklace are distinctive. When alarmed, flies low and directly disappears into the grass. The male's short rolling song is a familiar springtime sound in rural areas throughout the West.

Northern Oriole (Bullock's Oriole), *Icterus galbula*. *Length:* 7 to 8½ in (18 to 22 cm). *Color: male*—cheeks, breast, belly, rump, and outer tail feathers, brilliant yellow-orange; orange stripe above eye; black chin and throat, eyestripe, and crown, extending down back; wings black with large white patch; *female*—gray above, yellow-green head and breast; white belly; gray wings with two white stripes on each. *Eggs:* 4 to 6. *Nest:* deep pouch of woven plant fibers and hair suspended from end of branch, usually high in streamside trees. *Food:* insects, fruits. *Distribution:* common SV in foothill and, especially, riparian woodlands. The male northern oriole is the most brilliantly colored foothill bird and is not likely to be mistaken for any other; males arrive before the females in spring and depart before them in autumn, wintering from Mexico to Costa Rica. This is the western edition of the familiar Baltimore oriole of the east.

114. Western Meadowlark,
Sturnella neglecta.

Black-Headed Grosbeak, *Pheucticus melanocephalus.* *Length:* 6½ to 7¾ in (17 to 20 cm). *Color: male*—rusty ocher throat, breast, belly, and rump; head, black; wings, black spotted with white; tail mostly black; back, black and ocher stripes running lengthwise; *female*—head, striped with brown, white, and pale yellow; back, mottled brown; wings, rump, and tail, brown; breast, pale buffy orange. *Eggs:* 3 to 4. *Nest:* shallow saucer of stems and twigs in tree. *Food:* half insects, half seeds, buds, fruit. *Distribution:* common SV in foothill woodland, riparian woodland, and lower mixed-coniferous forest. The male's bold robinlike song is heard constantly from spring through early summer, but the bird itself can be difficult to see because it tends to keep to dense foliage high in the trees.

House Finch (Linnet), *Carpodacus mexicanus. Length:* 5½ to 6 in (14 to 15 cm). *Color: male*—red on forehead, throat, breast, and rump; belly, pale with prominent brown streaks; back, wings, and tail, brown: *female*—lacks red; breast and belly heavily streaked. *Eggs:* 4 to 5. *Nest:* sturdy cup of grasses or plant fibers in shrub, tree, rock crevice, residential vegetation. *Food:* seeds, fruits, berries, supplemented with some insects. *Distribution:* abundant R in foothills; also in valleys along the eastern base of the Sierra; frequents woodlands and brushy areas. This is the common "red finch" of the California lowlands, where it is frequently found in backyard gardens as well as in wilder areas. The male sings much of the year, often while in flight. Its rollicking warble, though lacking musical distinction, is bold and cheerful.

Rufous-Sided Towhee, *Pipilo erythrophthalmus. Length:* 8½ to 10 in (22 to 25 cm). *Color: male*—head, chin, and throat black; back, black with white spots; tail, black with outer feathers tipped white; sides, rusty red; breast and belly, white; *female*—similar except that the head is brown rather than black. *Eggs:* 3 to 4. *Nest:* lined bowl of grassses and bark placed on ground amongst dense shrubbery. *Food:* mostly seeds. *Distribution:* abundant R in chaparral and brushy areas in woods. Although the rufous-sided towhee is among the more boldly marked birds in the Sierra foothills, it is often inconspicuous in the dense brush it normally frequents. Most often its presence is revealed only by the rustle of litter as it scratches vigorously for seeds. The best time to see this large sparrow is near dawn or dusk, when males frequently sing from exposed perches.

Mammals

Black-Tailed Jackrabbit, *Lepus californicus.* Fig. 115. *Head and body:* 18 to 19 in (46 to 48 cm). *Tail:* 2 to 4 in (5 to 10 cm). *Ears:* 4 to 8 in (10 to 20 cm), very conspicuous. *Color:* buffy gray, black on tips of ears, tail, and rump. *Litter:* 7, twice a year; unlike the young of "true" rabbits, those of jackrabbits, which are actually hares, are born fully furred and alert. *Nest:* open ground beneath shrubs. *Food:* grasses, various herbs, leaves and stems of shrubs. *Enemies:* coyotes, bobcats, foxes, rattlesnakes, gopher snakes, owls, large hawks, eagles. *Habitat:* valley grassland, sagebrush, openings in woodland and chaparral. *Sign:* flattened pellets ⅜ in (1 cm) diam., runways through grass, resting areas, tracks. *Distribution:* Central Valley, foothill zone, pinyon–sagebrush zone.

Jackrabbits are mostly nocturnal, spending the day resting beneath shrubs. They rely on their great speed—up to 35 mph (56 km/hr)—to elude predators. If startled, they will bound away in great leaps of a yard or more. Their tracks usually show hindfeet in front of forefeet. Black-tailed jackrabbits can be told by their large size from cottontails, brush rabbits, and snowshoe hares, and by their black-tipped ears and darker tails from white-tailed jackrabbits.

115. Black-tailed jackrabbit tracks.

Audubon's Cottontail, *Sylvilagus audubonii. Head and body:* 12 to 15 in (30 to 38 cm). *Tail:* 2 in (5 cm). *Ears:* 2½ to 3 in (6 to 8 cm). *Color:* mixed black, blond, and brown above, white below; tail and tops of hindfeet white. *Litter:* 2 to 6; two or more per year; young born blind and furless. *Nest:* depression in ground lined with fur, grass, or both; sometimes in abandoned burrows. *Food:* grass, forbs,

Selected Foothill Animals 281

leaves, fallen fruit, acorns. *Enemies:* coyotes, foxes, bobcats, owls, hawks, eagles, snakes, dogs. *Habitat:* open, grassy areas with nearby brush. *Sign:* flattened pellets ¼ in (6 mm) diam. *Distribution:* Central Valley, foothills of west slope.

Brush Rabbit, *Sylvilagus bachmani.* Fig. 116. *Head and body:* 10 to 13 in (25 to 33 cm). *Tail:* 1 to 1½ in (2 to 4 cm). *Ears:* 2 to 3 in (5 to 8 cm). *Color:* dark brown above, grayish white below. *Litter:* 2 to 5, spring. *Food:* grass, rush, clover, various herbs, leaves of shrubs. *Enemies:* same as cottontail's. *Habitat:* chaparral and nearby openings. *Sign:* droppings similar to cottontail's. *Distribution:* foothill zone. This shy rabbit seldom ventures far from dense brush. Its comparatively low birthrate reflects the excellent protection from predators offered by chaparral.

California Ground Squirrel, *Otospermophilus beecheyi.* *Head and body:* 9 to 11 in (23 to 28 cm). *Tail:* 5 to 7 in (13 to 18 cm). *Color:* dappled gray above, light buff below; shoulders and back of head mantled with a wash of darker fur. *Litter:* 4 to 7 in May or June. *Nest:* dried vegetation in burrow; burrows 5 to 200 ft (2 to 61 m) long, often with several openings. *Food:* green vegetation, seeds, berries, acorns, pine nuts, insects, small birds, eggs; stores food in burrows. *Enemies:* red-tailed hawk is chief enemy; also coyotes, bobcats, weasels, badgers, foxes, owls, etc. *Habitat:* grassy slopes, forest openings; at higher elevations burrows beneath boulders or talus. *Sign:* burrow openings, runways through grass; call is a loud shrill whistle. *Distribution:*both slopes to 8000 ft (2500 m), though less common on east slope; most common in foothill zone.

At lower elevations the California ground squirrel avoids the heat and drought of summer by retiring to its burrow in July or August, where it estivates until midwinter, when green vegetation is once again plentiful. Above the snow

116. Brush Rabbit,
Sylvilagus bachmani.

line, the ground squirrel hibernates from late October through May. Predominantly a ground dweller, the California ground squirrel may occasionally climb trees to obtain acorns and other foods. It is known to rob chickarees and gray squirrels of cut pine cones that drop to the ground. As many as 2 or 3 breeding ground squirrels may occupy a single acre.

Gray Squirrel, *Sciurus griseus. Head and body:* 10 to 12 in (25 to 30 cm). *Tail:* 9 to 11 in (23 to 28 cm), very bushy. *Color:* grizzled gray above, white below; tail, gray with white margins. *Litter:* 3 to 5, spring. *Nest:* in oaks, abandoned woodpecker holes; in conifers, large globular nests of twigs placed high in the trees. *Food:* mostly acorns and pine nuts; also mushrooms, berries, seeds, insects, eggs. *Enemies:* coyotes, foxes, and other carnivores, which generally are able to take the squirrel only when it is foraging on the ground. *Habitat:* oak woodlands, mixed-coniferous forest where oaks are common. *Sign:* twig nests; remains of pine cones dismantled for seeds. *Distribution:* foothill and lower montane zones, west slope, to about 6000 ft (1800 m). Discussed further in Chapter IV, Elevational Ranges.

Dusky-Footed Wood Rat, *Neotoma fuscipes. Head and body:* 7 to 9 in (18 to 23 cm). *Tail:* 6 to 9½ in (15 to 24 cm). *Color:* brown to blackish above; white below and on bottoms of feet and tail. *Litter:* 2 to 4, spring. *Nest:* elaborate constructions of twigs, leaves, various debris, 2 to 3 ft (6 to 9 dm) tall, conical to rounded in shape; each with one or more nest chambers and connecting runways; placed on ground beneath shrubs or trees, also in rock crevices and several feet above ground in oaks; several entrances to permit easy access and escape. *Food:* acorns, roots, leaves, seeds, berries, some insects, etc. *Enemies:* legion; virtually all predatory mammals, birds, snakes, etc. *Habitat:* brush thickets and rock crevices. *Distribution:* foothill zone and lower forest; some on east slope; most common in chaparral and foothill woodland.

The dusky-footed wood rat is one of two species of pack rat inhabiting the Sierra. It may venture into camps or around human habitations, trading various articles for shiny objects, which are taken back and incorporated into its nest. Although quite common, it is rarely seen, owing to its nocturnal habits. The dusky-footed wood rat does not hibernate, but consistent with its acquisitive streak, stores food in its nest. Quail, snakes, California mice, salamanders, and other animals have been known to share the wood rat's ample and multichambered quarters.

Gray Fox, *Urocyon cinereoargenteus.* Fig. 117. *Head and body:* 23½ to 25 in (60 to 64 cm). *Tail:* 11 to 17 in (28 to 43 cm). *Color:* grizzled gray above, rusty on flanks and forelegs; white below; black "mane" running length of tail. *Litter:* 4; the young are driven from home when six months old. *Den:* rock piles and crevices. *Food:* gophers, rabbits, wood rats, mice, small birds, etc.; also manzanita and toyon berries, as well as other vegetable matter. *Enemies:* golden eagles and dogs. *Habitat:* various, including foothill woodland, chaparral, grassy and rocky areas, lower forest. *Sign:* doglike droppings ½ in (1 cm) diam.; doglike tracks 1 in (2 cm) diam. with claw marks. *Distribution:* foothill zone, ranging into lower forest, west slope.

Gray foxes are solitary and timid creatures and thus difficult to see in the field. The silvery gray fur brushed with orange and black, along with the conspicuous bushy tail, is distinctive. Gray foxes may be about both day and night. Gophers are their favorite food and they will wait patiently at the entrance of a gopher burrow for the rodent to appear. Unlike most members of the dog families, gray foxes are able to climb trees, where they may rest during the day.

Raccoon, *Procyon lotor.* Fig. 118. *Head and body:* 18 to 24 in (46 to 61 cm). *Tail:* 9 to 12 in (23 to 30 cm). *Color:* brown, tipped with black above, light gray below; black mask over eyes; tail with about 6 black rings. *Litter:* 3 to 7 in spring. *Den:* tree cavities, rock piles, large burrows. *Food:* omnivorous, including small rodents, birds, eggs, frogs, fish, shellfish, insects, fruits, berries, acorns, etc. *Enemies:* mostly dogs, occasionally great horned owls; may be quite tame around humans. *Habitat:* as varied as its food, but most commonly in woodland near water. *Sign:* handlike tracks in moist streambank soil; mournful *hooooo* call at night. *Distribution:* mostly in Central Valley and foothill zone; scarcer in forest and on east slope; found in Tahoe Basin.

Ringtail, *Bassariscus astutus.* Fig. 119. *Head and body:* 14 to 16 in (36 to 41 cm). *Tail:* 14 to 15 in (36 to 38 cm).

117. Gray fox tracks.   118. Raccoon tracks.   119. Ringtail tracks.

Color: brown washed with black above, whitish below; white around eyes; tail usually has 8 black rings, incomplete beneath. *Litter:* 3 to 4, late spring. *Den:* tree cavities, rock piles, caves, old cabins. *Food:* small rodents such as white-footed mice and wood rats, small birds, insects, wild fruits and other vegetable matter on occasion. *Enemies:* none to speak of. *Habitat:* woods, brush, rocky areas near water. *Sign:* round droppings 1 in (2 cm) diam.; barking call. *Distribution:* foothill zone, less commonly in forest to 7000 ft (2150 m), west slope.

The ringtail resembles a long, slim raccoon, but its face is noticeably foxlike and lacks a black mask. This animal is extremely agile both in trees and on the ground. Its long, bushy tail, which equals its body length, serves as a rudder and counterbalance as it leaps among boulders and in trees. The ringtail is normally a shy, retiring animal that emerges from its den long after dusk. For this reason it is seldom seen even though rather common throughout most of its range.

Bobcat, *Lynx rufus.* Fig. 120. *Head and body:* 23 to 27 in (58 to 69 cm). *Tail:* 4 to 8 in (10 to 20 cm), conspicuously small for body size. *Ears:* tufted. *Color:* light reddish brown in summer; buffy gray in winter; white below and on insides of legs; spotted with black overall; tail barred. *Litter:* 2 to 4, spring. *Den:* rock crevices, beneath boulders, hollowed-out places beneath trees. *Food:* rabbits and hares; gophers, wood rats, ground squirrels, and other rodents; seldom takes birds; occasionally may kill young deer stranded in snow. *Enemies:* none to speak of. *Habitat:* rocky, brushy, and wooded areas. *Sign:* catlike tracks smaller than those of

Selected Foothill Animals   285

mountain lion and larger than those of a house cat. *Distribution:* common on west slope chiefly in foothill zone, but also ranging into montane zone.

The bobcat is rather common and may be abroad during the day, but it is seldom seen. At night its blood-curdling scream may be thought to be that of the larger mountain lion. Quail hunters have cursed the bobcat for allegedly preying on this game species, but analysis of stomach contents of bobcats has shown this charge to be unfounded.

120. Bobcat tracks.

CHAPTER VI

Heart of the Mountains: Forest Belt Communities

ABOVE ELEVATIONS ranging from 2000 feet (600 meters) in the north to 5000 feet (1500 meters) in the south, the oak woodlands and chaparral of the western foothills give way to the Sierra conifer forest, a broad vegetational belt that spans three life zones—the lower montane, upper montane, and subalpine—and includes four distinct coniferous communities as well as montane chaparral and meadows. In the northern Sierra the forest extends upslope to about 8000 feet (2450 meters), covering most of the higher peaks and ridges north of Lake Tahoe. In the southern half of the range, where the climate is somewhat warmer, trees occur as high as 11,000 feet (3350 meters), ranging to 12,000 feet (3650 meters) in certain limited areas.

The lower limit of the forest is closely tied to precipitation. Ponderosa pine tolerates hotter and drier sites than any other important forest conifer, yet still requires a minimum of about 25 inches (63 centimeters) of rain a year. Its first appearance among the digger pines and chaparral of the upper foothill zone—usually on cool, relatively mesic north-facing slopes and sometimes in the company of incense cedar or Douglas-fir—is a sign that this amount has more or less been reached. On the east slope, where precipitation is less at all elevations, the forest begins about a thousand feet higher. East-side stands are seldom as dense as those of the west slope and nowhere form a cover of comparable extent, being largely restricted to moist canyon bottoms, north-facing slopes, and high, snowy lake basins.

The upper limit of the forest is largely a function of air temperature, coinciding more or less with the July 50° isotherm, the line above which average daytime temperatures during the month do not exceed 50° F (10° C). Above this line temperatures are too low and the growing season too short to enable trees to obtain enough energy through photosynthesis to fuel their annual cycles of growth and reproduction. Since air temperatures rise from north to south, timberline, or tree limit, occurs at progressively higher elevations as one moves south in the Sierra. North of Lake Tahoe even the highest peaks, which barely exceed 8000 feet (2450 meters), are well below climatic tree limit, and depending on local conditions may support dense forest stands. In the Tahoe region climatic tree limit occurs at about 10,000 feet (3050 meters), increasing to 10,500 feet

(3200 meters) in the Yosemite region and 11,000 feet (3350 meters) or more to the south.

Local variations in tree limit occur in response to varying topography, snow, wind, and soil. Trees often range somewhat higher on warm southern exposures than on cool north-facing slopes, though they also may be more stunted and widely spaced because of higher winds and greater soil aridity. Wind alone does not limit the upward distribution of trees, but its chilling effect makes mountain passes and ridgetops colder than sheltered areas at the same elevation. It also affects the distribution of trees by removing snow from some areas and depositing it in others. Areas where snowdrifts linger until late summer can seldom support trees because their soils are too cold and soggy and their growing season too short. At the other extreme, trees are also commonly absent from areas swept free of snow during the winter, since without the protection of the snowpack seedlings are exposed to severe cold, wind damage, and moisture stress. Absence of soil also precludes trees from occupying many sites in the High Sierra and locally may—as in Desolation Valley, where glaciers removed the soil mantle—affect their upward distribution.

Among temperate coniferous forests that of the Sierra is remarkable for the variety and stature of its trees. Twenty-four species of arborescent ("treelike") conifers as well as one shrubby form are found in the range. About a dozen of them reach record sizes. Although summer drought and abundant rock outcrops cause the Sierra forest to be less dense and lush than those of, say, the Cascades or northern Rockies, the Sierra's longer, warmer summers enable trees to attain maximum size on sites where sufficient moisture is available. Sheltered flats and gentle slopes underlain by deep, well-drained soils, which are able to absorb enough snowmelt to last the entire summer, provide optimum growing conditions for numerous conifer species, including white fir, sugar pine, ponderosa pine, red fir, lodgepole pine, and western juniper, all of which attain their greatest stature in the Sierra. The largest tree in the world, the giant sequoia, grows only in the central and southern Sierra on sites of precisely this type.

The unsurpassed variety of conifers found in the Sierra is largely attributable to its wide range of temperature and moisture regimes, which in turn reflects its great length and elevation, as well as its position with respect to marine and continental air masses. Trees from regions as climatically diverse as the Pacific Northwest, Southern California, the Southwest, and the Rocky Mountain states can be found in the Sierra. The east side of the range is dry enough to support desert and Great Basin species; the west slope, cool and moist enough in places to satisfy many northern and coastal species. Spanning five degrees of latitude (about 400 miles/650 kilometers), the Sierra marks the southern limit for six California conifers and the northern limit for four others.

Although shrubs, thickets of young saplings, and downed timber make the Sierra forest nearly impenetrable in places, for the most part it is characterized by more or less open stands through which one can walk with ease. From a distance the west slope seems almost entirely covered by trees, yet only 43 percent of the ground surface supports stands dense enough to be considered forest. The rest is given over to rock outcrops, brush, meadows, talus, lakes, streams, and land cleared by people for one reason or another. As elevation increases, so does the percentage of open ground in the forest. Rock outcrops become increasingly extensive, and lakes and meadows are more numerous. Meadows occupy soils too cold and moist to support trees. Brush occurs on sites that are too dry or where forest has recently been burned or logged. The landscape of the Sierra forest belt, then, is seldom monotonous, for continuous unbroken tracts of dense forest are rare. Instead, the terrain is characterized by an open, highly varied mosaic of diverse elements that change from place to place in response to local environmental conditions.

Primary Forest Succession

Following the retreat of the last Pleistocene glaciers about 10,000 years ago, much of the region now occupied by forest in the Sierra contained no vegetation whatsoever. Plants had to reinvade areas where glacial scouring had stripped the soil mantle away and thereby exposed the naked bedrock beneath. Reinvasion of the glaciated portions of the Sierra commenced in rock crevices and lake basins, where small particles of weathered rock could accumulate in the presence of enough moisture for chemical weathering—the process whereby rock particles are reduced to soil by the action of mild acids—to occur. That soil formation in the Sierra has been extremely slow is evidenced by the vast expanses of bare rock which remain. At the same time, the numerous meadows in glacial basins and the plants that everywhere cling to life in narrow crevices in bedrock or crannies among talus indicate that the invasion of bare ground by vegetation inexorably continues. Meadows and crevice vegetation constitute seres in the course of primary succession leading from bare rock to climax forest (see page 146). Given proper climate and enough time, trees will cover most of the outcrops and meadow basins below timberline. (Secondary succession due to fire or other disturbance is discussed in the context of the individual forest communities.)

Crevice Invasion

According to a recent estimate rock outcrops account for nearly a third of the land surface above 5000 feet (1500 meters) in the Sierra Nevada. As elevation increases so does the amount of land given over to bare or sparsely vegetated rock. Outcrops are widely scattered throughout the forest of the lower and upper montane zones and constitute the dominant element of the subalpine landscape. Above timberline, in the alpine zone, it is the vegetation rather than the rocks that form "outcrops," for here areas of continuous plant cover are for the most part small in extent and restricted to dependable sources of water.

Rock outcrops have persisted this long in the Sierra partly because soil formation is inhibited by California's Mediterranean climate. Chemical weathering, which proceeds most rapidly in warm, moist climates, slows down as temperatures drop and is impossible in the absence of moisture. Climates such as California's, where precipitation is sparse or absent during the warmest months of the year, are less than optimal for chemical weathering. In the Sierra the process is further retarded because most precipitation

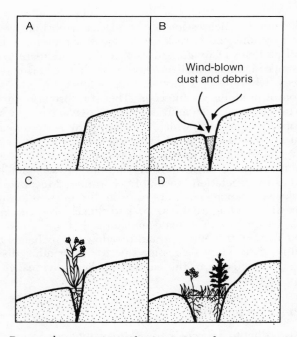

121. Bare-rock succession in the Sierra Nevada. Frost riving pries open joints in granitic rocks (A), which collect wind-blown dust and debris (B), as well as the seeds of many kinds of plants able to grow in such rudimentary soil (C). Pioneer plants contribute organic matter to the seedbed, thus creating suitable sites for still other plants (D), whose roots further probe and widen the crevice. Eventually, over a period of centuries, an entire rock surface may thus be reduced to soil.

falls as snow, in which form water is not chemically active.

Soil formation is further impeded by the nature of granitic rocks, which make up the overwhelming majority of rock outcrops in the Sierra. Composed of hard, fused mineral crystals, these rocks are exceptionally resistant to chemical weathering, even under optimal conditions. The deep forest soils of the middle and lower slopes of the Sierra have taken thousands of years to develop, and are deepest in areas that were not overrun by glaciers.

According to a classic model used to describe how plants colonize bare-rock surfaces, lichens form the vanguard, paving the way for mosses, followed by herbaceous species, and finally by shrubs and trees. Lichens obtain nutrients from rock by secreting mild acids that dissolve minerals, breaking down the rock surface in the process. Gradually a tiny patch of soil develops, and eventually enough accumulates so that mosses are able to colonize the rock, in time replacing the lichens. The mosses promote further soil development, thus enabling herbaceous species to take root, and these in turn prepare the ground for the eventual invasion by shrubs and trees.

Although this process has been widely hypothesized, it has not been analyzed and documented through careful observation of an ecologically well-defined site over a long period of time. Studies in 1941 of the very recent volcanic rocks in the Craters of the Moon National Monument in southern Idaho showed a quite different pattern of primary succession. So did a recent study of primary succession on granite outcrops in the Sierra Nevada.

According to the Sierra study, lichens and mosses often may be among the first plants to colonize granite outcrops in the range, but their work in weathering the rock surfaces is rarely if ever essential to the subsequent establishment of herbs, shrubs, and trees. Of much greater importance is the development of crevices, through chemical weathering and frost action, along joints in the granite (see Weathering, Chapter II). These crevices trap runoff and windblown debris, providing suitable seedbeds for vascular plants long before lichens or mosses have sufficiently worn down the rock surfaces.

Among the first herbaceous species to establish themselves in rock crevices are California fuschia, *Zauschneria californica*, Torrey's lomatium, *Lomatium torreyi*, pussypaws, *Calyptridium umbellatum*, shaggy hawkweed, *Hieracium horridum*, mountain jewel flower, *Streptanthus tortuosus*, and Wright's eriogonum, *Eriogonum wrightii*, all of which are able to tolerate minimal amounts of soil and moisture. In shadier, moister areas three ferns are characteristic of rock crevices: lip fern, *Cheilanthes gracillima*, Indian's dream, *Onychium densum*, and Bridges' cliffbrake, *Pellaea bridgesii*.

Shrubs and trees are able to occupy rock crevices even prior to the establishment of herbs if soil and moisture are

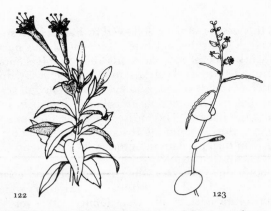

122   123

122. California Fuschia, *Zauschneria californica*. Flowers red-orange, tubular; 1 to 1½ in (2.5 to 4 cm); leaves elliptical, hairy, with toothed margins; stems woody at base, densely leaved, to 2 ft (6 dm) long. This is one of the first plants to colonize rock crevices and one of the latest to bloom during the year. Flowers appear August–September, when those of most other Sierra plants are long gone. California fuschia occurs in rocky areas 5000 to 10,000 ft (1500 to 3050 m).

123. Mountain Jewel Flower (Shieldleaf), *Streptanthus tortuosus*. Flowers yellow or purplish, tiny; leaves round or heart-shaped, clasping stem; stems 8 to 40 in (2 to 10 dm) long; plant covered with bluish, waxy bloom. Shieldleaf is a common plant of dry, thin, rocky soils, 1000 to 12,000 ft (300 to 3650 m), blooming May–August. Its clasping leaves are distinctive.

sufficient. Jeffrey pine, incense cedar, and greenleaf manzanita are notable in this regard among the shrubs and trees of the montane zones. Other, somewhat less commonly encountered outcrop invaders include ponderosa pine, black oak, canyon oak, whiteleaf manzanita, white fir, and snow bush. All subalpine conifers routinely invade rock crevices, since other sites are seldom available. Trees growing on rock outcrops in the Sierra are often arranged in orderly ranks and files that follow the checkerboard pattern of the joint crevices in which they are rooted.

Plants are able to occupy rock crevices through the services of birds, rodents, and winds, all of which transport seeds to such sites. Once established, plants further soil development by trapping additional windblown debris and

124. Rock Outcrop.

contributing organic matter in the form of their own remains. In addition, their roots may probe deeply into crevices, wedging them farther apart and thereby furthering
the disintegration of the bedrock. Plants growing in crevices are assured of a fairly dependable moisture supply and
a certain degree of shelter from the elements. They are
able, for example, to occupy sites in otherwise exposed,
windy areas even when lacking specific adaptations for such
conditions. Solar radiation reflecting off sheltered rock surfaces also provides a warmer microclimate than exists on
totally exposed sites.

The disintegration of bedrock proceeds most rapidly in
areas where joints are closely spaced. Continued chemical
weathering and frost action eventually reduces the rock surface to broken rubble. Plants already established in crevices
contribute to the process in the ways mentioned above.
Rocks are broken to gravel, and gravel to sand. Increasing
amounts of silt and clay may be present, along with additional organic matter.

When soils are one to two inches deep, spring annuals
such as mustang clover, *Linanthus montanus*, mountain
phacelia, *Phacelia orogenes*, and spurry eriogonum,
Eriogonum spurgulinum, may form a fairly thick cover,
along with perennials such as pussypaws, terebinth
pteryxia, *Pteryxia terebinthina*, and Sierra Nevada lotus,
Lotus nevadensis. As soils become even deeper and richer
in organic matter, species characteristic of drier sites in the

forest are able to invade an outcrop. Trees and shrubs are no longer dependent on crevices once soil development has progressed this far.

Lichen

The vast expanses of exposed rock in the Sierra offer ideal habitats for the numerous species of lichen that often coat their surfaces. Black flake lichens, genus *Umbilicaria,* may in places entirely obscure the faces of boulders or talus. Bright-orange jewel lichens, genus *Xantheria,* are common in rockslides, where animal wastes provide abundant nutrients. Map lichen, *Rhizocarpon geographicum,* with black dots on a field of pale green, is common on granite. Vivid chartreuse lichens, along with others in shades of brown and gold, occur on rocks throughout the Sierra. Gray soil lichens often inhabit soils too thin and dry for any other plants.

Lichens are symbiotic unions of fungi and algae. The fungus forms the body of the organism, providing shelter for colonies of microscopic algal cells. The latter contain chlorophyll and through photosynthesis provide carbohydrates for both partners. The fungus absorbs minerals from the surfaces to which the lichen is attached and moisture, which the alga requires for photosynthesis, from the air. Lichens are attached to rocks, trees, and other surfaces by threadlike fungal rhizoids, which grip so tightly that they often cannot be pried loose even with a knife.

Lichens occur in three forms: *crustose* lichens, which form the dense, crusty mats covering bare rocks and other surfaces; *foliose* lichens, leafy types that occur both on rocks and tree bark; and *fruticose* lichens, large branching types such as *Usnea,* which resembles Spanish moss in the way it festoons conifers, and staghorn lichens (genus *Letharia*), which commonly occur on red firs. Lichens reproduce both by spores and by fragmentation, wherein pieces broken off from the main body colonize new surfaces.

Lichens are exceptionally hardy, able to withstand greater extremes of cold and drought than other types of plants. Plastered against the rocks they are protected from the wind, and their tough skins inhibit moisture loss. They may persist indefinitely so long as they receive moisture

Crustose lichen

Foliose lichen

Fruticose lichen

125. Crustose lichen, such as the map lichen (*Rhizocarpon geographicum*) shown here, forms a dense, tough coating on Sierra rocks. Foliose lichens occur on rocks, living trees, and dead logs and stumps. Fruticose lichens, such as the bright-green staghorn lichen (*Letharia vulpina*) of the red fir forest, commonly grow on the trunks and branches of living and dead trees.

from time to time. When conditions are unfavorable they simply fall dormant, becoming active again only when the combination of available moisture and above-freezing air temperatures makes photosynthesis possible.

Meadow Formation

When the last major glaciers retreated from their high cirques some 10,000 years ago, they left behind thousands of small lakes dammed behind either moraines or resistant ridges of bedrock. At first the scoured, polished rocks around these glacial lakes were devoid of vegetation; today all but the highest are fringed at least in part by meadows, and many are even bordered by forest. Most Sierra meadows now lie in basins that once contained lakes, and most existing lakes will someday be replaced by meadows. The work is accomplished by vigorous snowmelt streams that deposit on the lake bottoms layer upon layer of sediments washed down from the slopes above.

Primary Forest Succession

When a tumbling mountain stream enters the quiet waters of a lake, the sudden reduction in stream velocity and turbulence allows suspended sediments to settle to the bottom, where they accumulate to form a fan-shaped wedge that spreads out from the point of entry. Gradually the delta grows larger, and near the mouth of the stream, where the wedge is thickest, begins to rise above the level of the water. In this way the shore gradually encroaches on the lake, which eventually is completely filled with sediments. The newly formed shore is first invaded by sedges and rushes able to withstand marshy conditions, later by willows, grasses, and other plants partial to moist—but not soggy—soils. As the shoreline continues to advance, older shores, now set back from the lake, gradually become drier, thus becoming available to entirely new groups of plants.

The process is extremely slow, as evidenced by the 2000 or so lakes in the Sierra—many of them a long way from disappearing—left over from the last major glacial episode 10,000 years ago. The amount of time required to complete the conversion from lake to meadow varies greatly according to numerous environmental factors, including the size and depth of the lake, local topography, the resistance of upstream rocks to erosion and weathering, precipitation as

Facing Page:
126. Lake–meadow–forest succession. (A) A glacial lake in a bare, rocky basin. Plants are sparse or absent around the shore. (B) Weathering may eventually produce a thin veneer of soil on the bedrock. Meadow plants invade the moister sites bordering the lake; conifers occupy drier soils well away from the shore. An inlet stream, or streams, has washed sediments into the lake. (C) The lake is now almost entirely filled with sediment, and the meadow plants have advanced into new areas as they have become available. Lodgepole pines now occupy the original shoreline, which is now much drier, followed by red fir. (D) The lake has now been completely filled in, and the meadow has been invaded by such trees as aspens, lodgepole pines, willows, and black cottonwoods. Red firs now occupy some of the ground formerly colonized by lodgepole pines. (E) Red firs have succeeded in shading out competing trees and now dominate the entire area. Each of the above successional stages—which are admittedly simplified—are well represented in the Sierra.

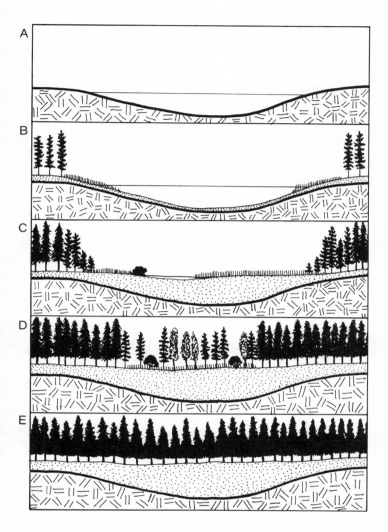

it affects the vigor and sediment capacity of the inlet
stream, and the nature and extent of local plant cover.
Lakes at various stages in their evolution toward meadows
are scattered throughout the Sierra. They range from tiny
remnant ponds surrounded by turf to rockbound tarns that
seem as permanent as the mountains themselves.

Primary Forest Succession

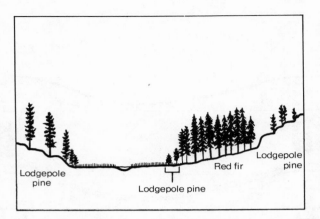

127. Cross section of upper-montane forest, showing lodgepole pines dominating dry, rocky slopes and moist meadow borders, while red fir is restricted to sites with intermediate moisture and deep, well-developed soils.

Meadow Invasion

Meadows below timberline are subject to gradual invasion by forest trees. Lodgepole pines, which can tolerate greater soil moisture than other Sierra conifers, usually lead the way, joined perhaps by quaking aspens, alders, cottonwoods and willows. Eventually, these pioneer trees may be replaced by red firs or other conifers, which shade them out and form a climax forest capable of occupying the site indefinitely in the absence of outside disturbance or pronounced climatic shifts.

The invasion of meadows by forest trees is still a rather poorly understood phenomenon. Little is known about why it happens at some times and places but not others. Since about the turn of the century, for example, lodgepole pines have vigorously advanced into numerous Sierra meadows, yet there is no agreement whether this recent spurt of activity was triggered by human activities or is merely part of a recurring natural cycle.

According to one view, sheep grazing in the High Sierra during the middle and late nineteenth century probably prevented lodgepole-pine invasions at that time, since young seedlings would presumably have been eaten as soon as they appeared. At the same time, grazing may have produced bare soils that could successfully be invaded by lodgepoles once the sheep were removed.

The suppression of wildfires during the twentieth century may also have contributed to the recent advance of lodgepole pines. It has also been suggested that lodgepole invasions may occur in cycles, with peaks occurring perhaps every 200 to 300 years. This could explain the occasional presence in meadows of isolated older trees, which might be remnants of earlier invasions. This hypothesis, however, does not explain why such cycles should occur in the first place. Moreover, not all meadows have been invaded during this century, and thus far no one is sure why some have escaped encroachment. Defoliation of pines by lodgepole needle-miners may be an important factor locally.

The presence of abundant moisture close to the soil surface is probably the most important factor inhibiting tree growth in meadows. Cold, soggy soils deficient in oxygen, combined perhaps with the presence of dense sod and abundant organic materials, may inhibit germination and subsequent seedling development among forest trees. Early-summer flooding followed by extreme drought later in the season, a fairly typical regime for many Sierra meadows, may also prevent tree growth. Once a tree is established in a meadow, however, it will probably thrive, reaching greater size in the rich, moist soil than it does on drier sites.

Forest Soils

The Sierra conifer forest is best developed on deep, well-drained soils derived mostly from granite, but also from metamorphic and volcanic rocks. Dark brown to reddish brown in color and crumbly in texture, the soil contains abundant organic material in its upper layers, or *horizons*. Soil, of course, is a mixture of organic materials derived from decaying matter on its surface and inorganic materials derived from the bedrock below. Decomposition reduces the organic matter to humus, and weathering breaks up the bedrock and reduces the resulting rock particles eventually to clay. Soil horizons reflect the degree to

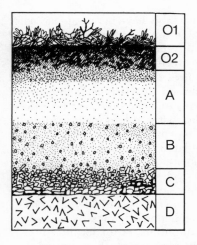

128. Profile of forest soil: O_1 horizon—forest litter, undecomposed; O_2 horizon—duff, partly decomposed; A horizons—true soil, derived from materials in O horizons; B horizons—fine rock particles mixed with clay; C horizon—slightly weathered bedrock; D horizon—unweathered bedrock.

which these two basic constituents of soil—organic matter and rock—are broken down and mixed. Each horizon is identified by a letter, and some are subdivided into several layers, each one identified by a number.

The O_1 horizon comprises the forest *litter*—undecomposed plant materials consisting mostly of conifer needles.

The O_2 horizon, or *duff*, consists of partly decomposed organic materials derived from the overlying litter. These materials, no longer identifiable as such, form a more or less uniform mass.

The several A horizons each consist of a mixture of mineral and organic materials derived from the duff and litter. They differ with respect to relative amounts of each component. The soil is dark and crumbly, becoming lighter and more compacted with depth. Most root activity is confined to these horizons.

The several B horizons each consist of fine rock particles mixed with clay particles leached down from above to form a dense mass inhospitable to most roots and soil organisms.

FOREST BELT COMMUNITIES

The B horizons differ with respect to relative amounts of rock particles and clay.

The C horizon consists of weathered bedrock with little or no organic matter. It lies on top of unweathered bedrock.

Forest soils tend to be moderately to highly acidic and deficient in important nutrients, some of which are leached from the A horizons and deposited in the B horizons, where they are largely inaccessible to shallow-rooted plants. In addition, a good deal of the nutrients remaining in the upper horizons are taken up by the trees, leaving little for other plants. Nutrients are returned to the soil through the decomposition of litter, largely by fungi, but this process is inhibited by the cool temperatures beneath the forest canopy, the lack of moisture during the warmest months, and the nature of the litter itself. Conifer needles, which make up the bulk of the litter, contain *lignin*, a chemically complex substance that decomposes very slowly. The needles also contain substances that react with water to form acids. Acidity is characteristic of forest soils in temperate regions, especially when they are derived, as in the Sierra, from granitic rocks rich in silica and feldspars.

FOREST PLANT COMMUNITIES

THE SIERRA FOREST can be divided into four distinct communities more or less arrayed according to elevations.

The *mixed coniferous forest* dominates the lower montane zone, ranging in elevation from 2000 to 6000 feet (600 to 1800 meters) in the north and from 4000 to 8000 feet (1200 to 2450 meters) in the south. It consists of three easily distinguished subtypes—ponderosa pine forest, white fir forest, and Jeffrey pine forest. (Some sources treat these subtypes as separate communities; this guide follows the classification proposed by Griffin and Critchfield in *The Distribution of Forest Trees in California*, USDA Forest Service Research Paper PSW-82, 1972.)

The *red fir forest* dominates the upper montane zone, occupying deep, well-drained soils from 6000 to 7000 feet

(1800 to 2150 meters) elevation in the northern Sierra and from 8000 to 9000 feet (2450 to 2700 meters) in the south.

The *lodgepole pine forest* is typical of glacial basins in the lower subalpine zone, forming open stands at elevations ranging from 6000 to 8000 feet (1800 to 2450 meters) in the north and from 8000 to 11,000 feet (2450 to 3350 meters) in the south.

The *subalpine forest* consists of scattered stands and individual trees, often dwarfed or shrubby, occupying rocky slopes in the upper subalpine zone above 8000 feet (2450 meters) in the central Sierra and 9500 feet (2900 meters) in the south. North of Lake Tahoe the community is present only as isolated stands on a few of the higher peaks. Dominated by whitebark pine, mountain hemlock, and in the southern Sierra, foxtail pine, the subalpine forest is the uppermost forest community.

Although these four forest communities are more or less arrayed according to elevation, their shared boundaries are seldom distinct. The mixed coniferous forest merges gradually with the red fir forest above, the latter, in turn, with the lodgepole pine forest, and so on. As a general rule the communities tend to range higher on warm south-facing slopes and ridgetops and lower on northern exposures and in canyon bottoms. Other factors strongly affecting community boundaries include soil development, snow depth, fire history, and human activities.

Mixed Coniferous Forest

The Sierran mixed coniferous forest contains more than a dozen species of conifers as well as several types of broadleaf trees. The community is best developed between 3000 and 7000 feet elevation on the west slope, where as many as five or six different conifers are found in some stands. Ponderosa pine, *Pinus ponderosa*, and white fir, *Abies concolor*, dominate most west-slope stands, the former on lower, hotter, drier sites, the latter on higher, cooler, moister ones. Incense cedar, *Calocedrus decurrens*, sugar pine, *Pinus lambertiana*, and black oak, *Quercus kelloggii*,

FOREST PLANT COMMUNITIES

129. Mixed Coniferous Forest.

are important associates in most stands. Although these five species range into southern Oregon, well-developed stands containing all of them are found only in California and are best represented in the Sierra. Douglas-fir, *Pseudotsuga menziesii*, giant sequoia, *Sequoiadendron giganteum*, and Jeffrey pine, *Pinus jeffreyi*, are also present in many west-slope stands and even dominate some.

The mixed coniferous forest also occurs on the east side of the Sierra, primarily between 6000 and 8000 feet elevation but ranging farther downslope along streams. Fewer species occur in east-slope stands, and the community is poorly developed south of Sonora Pass. White fir or Jeffrey pine dominates most stands. South of Carson Pass ponderosa pine is absent and incense cedar is uncommon. Black oak occurs only very sparingly along streams emptying into Owens Valley. Douglas-fir, sugar pine, and giant Sequoia are missing on the east side of the Sierra. In the Tahoe Basin the mixed coniferous forest is dominated by white fir and Jeffrey pine, with red fir, *Abies magnifica*, and incense cedar as important associates.

Of the more than two dozen broadleaf trees and treelike shrubs found in the mixed coniferous forest, black oak is by far the most common. Ranging between 1000 and 8000 feet (300 and 2450 meters) on the west slope, it is a characteristic tree on open, dry ridges, where it typically occurs in mixed stands with ponderosa pine and incense cedar. Canyon live oak, *Quercus chrysolepis*, ranges up to 8000 feet elevation on canyon slopes and rocky stream bottoms. In Yosemite Valley canyon live oak occupies weathered talus at the bases of the cliffs; black oak, the flat valley floor. Big-leaf maple, *Acer macrophyllum*, white alder, *Alnus rhombifolia*, mountain alder, *Alnus tenuifolia*, Fremont cottonwood, *Populus fremontii*, black cottonwood, *Populus trichocarpa*, mountain dogwood, *Cornus nuttallii*, California hazelnut, *Corylus californica*, and several species of willows form an irregular streamside woodland in the mixed coniferous forest. Mountain dogwood also occurs well away from streams on moist, shady sites beneath white fir, incense cedar, giant sequoia, and other conifers. Above 5000 feet (1500 meters) elevation, quaking aspen, *Populus tremuloides*, forms pure, dense stands on old, well-watered talus slopes and moist flats and along streams. The individual trees making up an aspen stand all sprout from and share a common network of roots. Only rarely do aspen reproduce from seeds.

Ponderosa Pine Forest

Ponderosa pine dominates forest stands on dry, sunny sites ranging in elevation from 2000 to 6000 feet (600 to 1800 meters) in the northern Sierra and from 4000 to 7000 feet (1200 to 2150 meters) in the south. This community ranges lower than any other forest type in the range, occurring immediately above the foothill woodland and chaparral. Along this boundary foothill and montane vegetation interfinger in response to local topography, with foothill communities extending upslope on hot, dry, south-facing slopes and on ridgetops, and pine forest ranging downward on cool, mesic northern exposures and in canyon bottoms. In El Dorado County ponderosa pines range as low as 500 feet (150 meters) along streams. Ponderosa pine is replaced in the forest above 5000 feet (1500 meters) in the northern Sierra and 6000 feet (1800 meters) in the south by Jeffrey pine, a closely related species able to withstand lower air temperatures and deeper snows. Although the deep roots of ponderosa pine make it extremely drought resistant, the Jeffrey pine is even more so and consequently

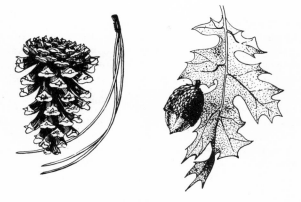

130. Ponderosa Pine, *Pinus ponderosa*. *Height:* 60 to 225 ft (15 to 70 m). *Bark:* light yellow-brown, scaly, divided into large plates separated by darker furrows; on young trees, dark, brown, closely furrowed. *Leaves:* needles, yellow-green, 5 to 10 in (12.5 to 25 cm) long, in bundles of 3. *Fruit:* cones, 2 to 5 in (5 to 12.5 cm) long, reddish brown; each scale armed with a sharp, out-turned prickle. *Range:* abundant, mixed-coniferous forest of lower montane zone, west slope, 3500 to 7000 ft (1000 to 2150 m); less common on east slope north of Carson Pass.

131. Black Oak, *Quercus kelloggii*. *Height:* 30 to 80 ft (9 to 24 m), with spreading branches and broad crown. *Bark:* dark, smooth. *Leaves:* deciduous, dark green above, paler below; 4 to 7 in (10 to 18 cm) long, 2 to 4 in (5 to 10 cm) wide, with sharply pointed lobes. *Fruit;* acorns, 1 to 1½ in (3 to 4 cm) wide, cups wide and fairly shallow. *Range:* common associate of ponderosa pine, 1000 to 8000 ft (300 to 2450 m), west slope; local on east slope of the southern Sierra.

also replaces it along the east side of the Sierra from Carson Pass south.

The structure and composition of the ponderosa pine forest varies widely according to the amount of soil moisture available during the summer, when precipitation is virtually nil. Black oak and incense cedar are common associates of ponderosa pine throughout most of the Sierra. Sugar pine, Douglas-fir, and white fir join it on moister sites. The driest sites may be dominated by black oaks, perhaps with a smattering of pines and incense cedars. On moister—though still xeric—sites the pine becomes dominant, with the other two species as common associates. A

Mixed Coniferous Forest

variety of understory shrubs occurs throughout the ponderosa pine forest, some ranging up from the foothills, some downslope from higher forest communities. Among the more common understory shrubs in the ponderosa pine forest are greenleaf manzanita, *Arctostaphylos patula;* buckbrush, *Ceanothus cuneatus;* deer brush, *C. integerrimus;* birchleaf mountain mahogany, *Cercocarpus betuloides;* bitter cherry, *Prunus emarginata;* service berry, *Amelanchier alnifolia;* mountain misery, or kit-kit-dizze, *Chamaebatia foliosa;* whitesquaw, *Ribes cereum;* and common rabbit bush, *Chrysothamnus nauseosus.* These form dense thickets in sunnier areas, on rocky slopes, and in places recently burned or logged. On shadier, undisturbed sites dense thickets of young incense cedars commonly dominate the understory, often to the exclusion of shrubs. Few young pines and oaks are present in such stands.

On still moister sites, sugar pine, Douglas-fir and white fir become increasingly common associates of ponderosa pine. Understory vegetation includes the shrubs listed above, along with increasing numbers of shade-tolerant and moisture-loving species, including willows of several kinds; Sierra wax myrtle, *Myrica hartwegii;* California hazelnut, *Corylus californica;* spice bush, *Calycanthus occidentalis;* various gooseberries and currants, genus *Ribes;* wild roses, genus *Rosa;* thimbleberry, *Rubus parviflorus;* dogwoods, genus *Cornus;* western azalea, *Rhododendron occidentale;* red huckleberry, *Vaccinium parvifolium;* snowberries, genus *Symphoricarpos;* and many others. Often, however, the understory may be dominated by dense thickets of young white fir, in which shrubs are few in number and kind. As sites become increasingly moist white fir replaces ponderosa pine as the dominant conifer, and between 4000 and 5000 feet (1200 and 1500 meters) elevation the ponderosa pine forest and white fir forest divide the terrain between them, forming a mosaic based largely on available moisture. Above this zone the latter community becomes dominant, and increasingly Jeffrey pine replaces ponderosa pine in most stands.

Prior to this century the ponderosa pine forest typically consisted of open parklike stands in which the understory was at once less dense yet composed of a greater variety of

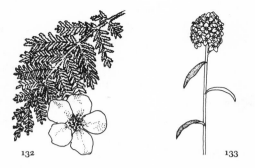

132   133

132. Mountain Misery (Kit-kit-dizze), *Chamaebatia foliosa.*
Height: 1 to 2 ft (3 to 6 dm); spreading, many-branched shrub;
bark smooth and brown; evergreen; leaves lacy or fernlike, mi-
nutely divided into tiny, elliptical leaflets; foliage sticky, hairy;
flowers white, to ½ in (13 mm). Mountain misery forms dense,
low thickets in the mixed coniferous forest of the west slope,
where it is widespread and abundant below 6000 ft (1800 m). Its
dense growth and sticky leaves make walking difficult in areas
where it occurs, hence the name mountain misery. The Miwok
Indians, who made a medicinal tea from its leaves, called the
shrub *kit-kit-dizze.*

133. Western Wallflower, *Erysimum capitatum.* Flowers orange,
sometimes yellow, in loose terminal clusters; leaves lance-shaped
with toothed margins, gray-green; stem 8 to 32 inches (2 to 8 dm).
Western, or Douglas' wallflower is common in dry, open, often
disturbed areas below 8000 ft (2450 m), commonly occurring
along roads or in rocky areas. The sierra wallflower, *E. perenne,*
which has green leaves and bright yellow flowers, occurs on similar sites about 7000 ft (2150 m). Western wallflower commonly
blooms March–July.

shrubs than exist in many stands today. Young white fir and
incense cedar were much less common in the forest understory. This primeval ponderosa pine forest, which is gradually disappearing from the Sierra, was produced by
periodic, comparatively cool groundfires, which every few
years burned much or all of the accumulated litter, understory shrubs, and young trees while leaving the mature
ponderosa pines and blue oaks largely unscathed. In this
way the forest was kept more or less open. The policy of
suppressing wildfires, which began near the turn of the
century, has prevented this periodic housecleaning, largely

at the expense of ponderosa pine, black oak, and understory shrubs. The forest has become both denser and more uniform.

Black oak and ponderosa pine both require full sunlight in their younger stages and definitely prefer it even when mature, as indicated by the widely spaced trees in older stands. The suppression of wildfires has produced a denser, shadier forest over the years, one in which white fir and incense cedar, both tolerant of shade, have become increasingly common. Black oaks produce numerous seedlings each year, but the great majority die because they are overshadowed by dense thickets of young cedars and firs. Ponderosa pine seedlings and those of many forest shrubs also stand little chance of surviving unless they are located in full sunlight. As older shrubs die fewer young ones survive to replace them, and throughout the Sierra the composition of the ponderosa pine understory is shifting from shrubs to fir and cedar saplings. Since ponderosa pines and black oaks live much longer than the shrubs, the number of mature trees on undisturbed stands has not declined sharply in response to the invasion of firs and cedars, but it can be expected to do so in the future if fire suppression continues.

The ponderosa pine forest is a fire-adapted community in the Sierra, able to hold its own in the face of potential plant invaders largely, and in some cases perhaps entirely, through the recurrent agency of fire. Some typical understory shrubs—whiteleaf manzanita, deer brush, and buckbrush, for example—are able to reproduce abundantly only after their dormant seeds, produced over a period of years, are cracked open by the heat of the flames. Within a few years following a fire, burned sites are covered in the summer with white, sweet-smelling flowers, owing to the proliferation of deer brush, but this stage only lasts 20 years or so before trees, usually the available hardwoods, shade out the shrubs. Fire produces an ideal seedbed for such plants, as well as for ponderosa pine and black oak, one consisting of exposed mineral soil enriched by nutrients contained in the ashy residue of forest litter and understory plants. Seeds produced by mature pines and oaks subsequent to a fire germinate more readily than before, and the seedlings stand a better chance of survival because the competing understory vegetation has been removed. More-

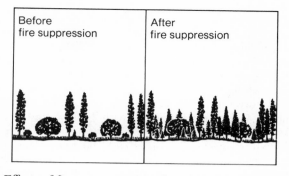

Before fire suppression	After fire suppression

134. Effects of fire suppression on the ponderosa pine forest. Before the policy of fire suppression was instituted early in this century, periodic burning cleaned out the forest understory, producing open, parklike stands like that shown on the left. Widely spaced ponderosa pines and black oak dominated such stands, which also included a wide variety of understory shrubs. Following the suppression of natural fires, shade-tolerant white firs and incense cedars began to proliferate, shading out many understory shrubs, as well as the sun-loving seedlings of ponderosa pine and black oak. The result has been a denser but less varied forest like that on the right, one in which firs and cedars are gradually replacing pines and oaks as the dominant trees in many stands.

over, black oaks, along with many species of shrubs found in the ponderosa pine forest, regenerate quickly by crown-sprouting after a fire.

White Fir Forest

The white fir forest is the dominant type on cool, mesic sites from 4000 to 7000 feet (1200 to 2150 meters) elevation on the west slope of the Sierra. In typical stands white firs may account for 80 percent of the large trees. Common associates include sugar pine, incense cedar, Douglas-fir, and on drier sites, ponderosa or Jeffrey pines. Giant sequoia is an important member of the community on moist, unglaciated flats in the central and southern Sierra, where it is often the dominant species. Sites intermediate in composition between the ponderosa pine forest and white fir forest are common at lower elevations and on xeric sites.

Along its upper boundary the white fir forest often blends imperceptibly with the red fir forest. The community is poorly developed on the drier eastern flank of the Sierra, though white fir is fairly common from Mammoth Pass north. Appropriate sites become scarcer southward, however, so white fir becomes increasingly restricted to moist canyons between 6500 and 8000 feet (2000 to 2450 meters) elevation. Individual firs occur with Jeffrey pine at lower elevations along streams.

The white fir forest receives 40 to 60 inches (100 to 150 centimeters) of precipitation a year, about half of it falling as snow. The elevational belt occupied by this community is moister than the ones below and enjoys a longer, warmer growing season than those above. It forms a broad transitional zone in which the ranges of plants from zones above

135. Incense Cedar, *Calocedrus decurrens*. *Height:* 75 to 150 ft (23 to 46 m). *Bark:* cinnamon-brown, fibrous. *Leaves:* yellow-green, 1/8 to 3/16 in (3 to 5 mm) long; flat and scalelike, pressed tightly against branchlets in alternate, overlapping pairs. *Fruit:* rudimentary "cones" consisting of 2 flat, winglike, seed-bearing scales. *Range:* common, mixed coniferous forest, 2000 to 7000 ft (600 to 2150 m), west slope; fairly common on east slope south to Sonora Pass.

136. Sugar Pine, *Pinus lambertiana*. *Height:* 100 to 200+ ft (30 to 60+ m), with long horizontal branches and a flattened crown. *Bark:* deeply furrowed, dark reddish brown to purplish. *Leaves:* needles, blue-green, 3 to 4 in (8 to 10 cm) long, in bundles of 5. *Fruit:* cones, 13 to 18 in (33 to 45 cm) long, 4 to 6 in (10 to 15 cm) wide, hanging from the ends of the uppermost branches. *Range:* common associate on sunny, mesic sites in the mixed coniferous forest, 3500 to 9000 ft (1050 to 2700 m), west slope.

135   136

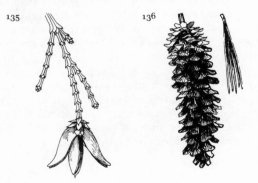

137. White Fir, *Abies concolor*. *Height:* 60 to 200 ft (18 to 60 m).
Bark: dark gray, deeply furrowed, but smooth and whitish on
young trees. *Leaves:* needles, blue-green, 1 to 2 in (2 to 5 cm)
long, grooved above, keeled below with 2 whitish lines, twisted at
base. Branches radiate from trunk in horizontal whorls. *Fruit:*
cones, barrel shaped, 2 to 5 in (5 to 12 cm) long, erect on upper
branches; they disintegrate in place, so are seldom seen on the
ground intact. *Range:* abundant, west slope 2500 to 8000 ft (750
to 2450 m); dominant conifer in the mesic aspect of the mixed
coniferous forest; less common on the east slope, especially south
of Sonora Pass.

and below overlap. Consequently, the white fir forest
exhibits greater floral variety, not only in trees, but also in
shrubs and herbs, than any other forest community in the
Sierra. It has a lusher appearance and is the only forest
community in the range to display a well-developed multi-
layered structure. The top layer, or canopy, is formed by
the dominant conifers. A second layer includes broadleaf
trees such as black oak, bigleaf maple, mountain dogwood,
white alder, and madrone, *Arbutus menziesi,* as well as
younger conifers. Below this is the shrub layer, which on
lower, drier sites is dominated by species characteristic of
the ponderosa pine forest and on higher, moister sites by
young firs and cedars, along with California hazelnut;
Scouler's willow, *Salix scouleriana;* golden chinquapin,
Chrysolepis sempervirens; bitter cherry; ground rose, *Rosa
spithamia;* and various species of gooseberries and currants.

The lowest understory layer consists of herbaceous
ground cover, which varies greatly in species and density
according to soil moisture, available light, fire history, litter
depth, and other factors. On mesic sites that receive
sufficient sunlight the ground cover may be nearly total,
but in most areas it is rather sparse. The most common
herbs on moist sites within the forest include white-

138. Cross section of the white fir forest, showing the layered understory characteristic of many stands.

flowered hawkweed, *Hieracium albiflorum;* bedstraw, *Galium sparsifolium;* trail plant, *Adenocaulon bicolor;* Hooker's fairy bell, *Disporum hookeri;* and mountain sweet cicely, *Osmorhiza chilensis.* In sunnier spots, sedges, genus *Carex;* pine violet, *Viola lobata;* and bracken fern, *Pteridium aquilinum,* may be common. Several herbaceous species that occur in the ponderosa pine forest and white fir forest up to 6000 feet (1800 meters) are absent above, including bride's bonnet, *Clintonia uniflora;* California straw-

139. Mountain Dogwood, *Cornus nuttalli. Height:* 10 to 40 ft (3 to 10 m). *Bark:* smooth, ashy brown or reddish. *Leaves:* deciduous, bright green and somewhat hairy above, paler and downy below; turn dusty rose in autumn; 3 to 5 in (8 to 13 cm) long, 1½ to 3 in (4 to 8 cm) wide, heart-shaped. *Flowers:* small, yellow-green, surrounded by large, showy, white bracts. *Fruit:* cluster of red drupes. *Range:* moist places, mixed coniferous forest, 2500 to 6000 ft (750 to 1800 m), west slope.

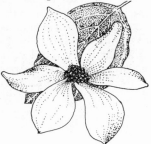

berry, *Fragaria californica;* rattlesnake orchid, *Goodyera oblongifolia;* Hartweg's ginger, *Asarum hartwegii;* and Hartweg's iris, *Iris hartwegii.*

Douglas-fir sometimes replaces white fir as the dominant conifer on cool, moist sites between 4000 and 5000 feet (1200 and 1500 meters) in the Sierra north of Lake Tahoe. Southward, as the climate becomes warmer and drier, Douglas-fir becomes progressively less common. In the Yosemite region it is still an important member of the mixed coniferous forest, but only 20 miles (32 kilometers) south, in the drainage of the San Joaquin River, it reaches the southern limit of its range.

Climatic conditions in the region occupied by the Sierra Douglas-fir forest are similar to those of portions of the northern Coast Ranges of California. Consequently, the community resembles a cross between the coniferous forest of those ranges, in which Douglas-fir is often a dominant member, and the Sierra white fir forest to the south. The understory of the Sierra Douglas-fir forest is especially well developed, like that of its coastal counterpart, and includes a number of plants common to the latter community but rare or absent farther south in the range. These include madrone; tanoak, *Lithocarpus densiflora;* California nutmeg, *Torreya californica;* and western yew, *Taxus brevifolia.* These are joined by understory trees also common farther south in the white fir forest: bigleaf maple, white

140. Douglas-fir, *Pseudotsuga menziesii. Height:* 70 to 125 ft (21 to 38 m); in the Pacific Northwest, may exceed 300 ft (90 m). *Bark:* dark brown and deeply furrowed on older trees; grayish brown and smoother on young trees. *Leaves:* needles, blue-green above, paler below, with two gray lines running the length of the needle; flattish, slightly twisted at the base. *Fruit:* cones, brown, 1¾ to 3 in (3 to 8 cm) long; bracts protrude between scales. *Range:* common, mixed coniferous forest south to the San Joaquin River, 1000 to 6000 ft (300 to 1800 m), west slope.

alder, and mountain dogwood. Even the maple, however, is more characteristic of the coastal forest and becomes increasingly scarce and local as one moves southward in the Sierra. The southern limit of the yew is in Calaveras County near Calaveras Big Trees State Park, the only place where the yew and the giant sequoia occur together. The southern limit of the madrone occurs in the same general area. Tanoak ranges south to Yosemite.

Giant Sequoia Groves

Seventy-five groves of giant sequoias, or "big trees," *Sequoiadendron giganteum*, are scattered through the white fir forest of the west slope from Placer County to southern Tulare County. The giant sequoia is the dominant tree within these groves, though in other respects they are similar in structure and ecology to the white fir forest, of which they may be considered a part. The same understory herbs and shrubs are present, along with white fir, sugar pine, incense cedar, and other trees common to the white fir forest. Sequoia groves are restricted to moist, unglaciated ridges between 4500 and 8400 feet (1370 and 2560 meters) elevation. All but eight groves occur south of the Kings River in a belt some 60 miles (95 kilometers) long in which no two groves are more than 4.5 miles (7.25 kilometers) apart. In contrast, the eight groves north of the Kings River are scattered over a distance of nearly 200 miles (320 kilometers).

The giant sequoia is native only to the west slope of the Sierra, though it has been planted widely throughout America and Europe as a park and garden tree. About 60 million years ago, when winters were warmer and summers cooler and moister than they are today, species ancestral to the present giant sequoia, as well as to its only close living relatives, the coast redwood of northern California and the dawn redwood, or metasequoia, of southern China, were prominent members of a mixed deciduous–conifer forest that extended over much of northern Europe and North America. Over the next 50 million years or so winters gradually became cooler and summers warmer and drier. Many species of trees disappeared from the forest, and

141. Giant Sequoia, *Sequoiadendron giganteum*. *Height:* 150 to 250+ ft (45 to 75+ m); trunk, 5 to 30+ ft (1.5 to 9+ m) diameter, depending on available moisture and age. *Bark:* cinnamon-red, with broad ridges and deep furrows, fibrous. *Leaves:* awl-shaped, ⅛ to ½ in (3 to 12 mm) long, overlapping and lying flat; blue-green. *Fruit:* cones, oblong, 2 to 3 in (5 to 7.5 cm) long, with woody scales. *Range:* scattered groves, 4500 to 8400 ft (1370 to 2560 m), west slope, from Placer County south to Tulare County; rather common south of the Kings River, scarce and strictly local northward; endemic to the west slope of the Sierra.

others were increasingly restricted to areas with reliable summer moisture. The forest was replaced over vast areas by more drought-resistant communities. By the beginning of the Pleistocene epoch, about 2.5 million years ago, the giant sequoia had vanished from all of its former range save the west slope of the Sierra. The tree was then probably more common there than today. Its present scattered distribution resulted from the subsequent intrusion of glaciers in many areas, particularly in the northern Sierra, and from the episode of climatic warming that followed the close of the Ice Age 10,000 years ago.

Today the largest groves are those at Redwood Mountain in Kings Canyon National Park and Giant Forest in Sequoia National Park, which was established to protect the finest remaining stands of giant sequoias. Each grove covers about 2500 acres (1000 hectares) and contains some 20,000 mature sequoias. The northernmost grove in the Sierra, which is located in Placer County 25 miles (40 kilometers) west of Lake Tahoe and nearly 60 miles (100 kilometers) from the next grove to the south, covers less than three acres and contains only a half-dozen trees. The next grove south, however, the Calaveras Grove, is the largest north of the Kings River, comprising about 1100 mature sequoias spread over 415 acres (165 hectares). Altogether there are about 36,500 acres (14,600 hectares) of giant sequoias remaining in the Sierra, most of this land protected under state and federal jurisdictions. Prior to 1950 some 10,000 acres (4000 hectares) were logged for timber, but the wood is too brittle for first-rate lumber, and this, combined with the protected status of most remaining groves, makes further logging unlikely.

In age and stature the giant sequoia is the unrivalled monarch of the Sierra forest. Not even the massive sugar pine, which may be more than 200 feet (60 meters) tall and seven feet (2.1 meters) thick at the base, even closely approaches the giant sequoia in size. Mature sequoias average 15 feet (4.5 meters) thick at the base and about 250 feet (75 meters) tall. Exceptional trees exceed 300 feet (90 meters) in height and 30 feet (9 meters) in diameter, though the thickest trees are not the tallest. The dimensions of the three largest giant sequoias, all found in Sequoia or Kings Canyon national parks, are:

General Sherman Tree, 272.4 feet (83 meters) tall, 36.5 feet (11.1 meters) thick at base

General Grant Tree, 267.4 feet (81.5 meters) tall, 40.3 feet (12.3 meters) thick at base

Boole Tree, 268 feet (81.7 meters) tall, 35 feet (10.7 meters) thick at base

The General Sherman tree may be the largest living thing in the world, weighing perhaps 6000 tons and containing 50,000 cubic feet (4250 cubic meters) of wood, an amount comparable to the yield from more than five acres (2 hectares) of virgin white fir, enough to build 40 five-room houses. The lowest branch of the General Sherman would itself dwarf many forest trees, being seven feet (2.1 meters) in diameter at its base and about 125 feet (38 meters) long. It branches off the trunk some 130 feet (40 meters) above the ground, at which point the trunk is 15 feet (4.5 meters) thick.

The General Sherman tree is estimated to be about 2500 years old, though nobody knows for sure because core samplers long enough to penetrate to the center of the larger trees have not been developed. The oldest known giant sequoia is a fallen tree with about 3300 annual growth rings, and some standing trees may even be older. The longevity of the giant sequoia is attributable to its resistance to fire, insects, and disease. The fibrous, reddish brown bark contains no sap, which is usually very flammable. In addition, the great thickness of the bark—two to four feet (60 to 120 centimeters) in mature trees—protects the inner wood from heat and flames. Furthermore, even when fire does manage to penetrate the bark, the tree will continue to live so long as some bark and living wood remains intact. Fire-hollowed giants are common in most groves, not only attracting amazed visitors but also providing favored winter dens for black bears.

The giant sequoia's resistance to insects and disease is largely due to the presence of tannin in the bark, which inhibits wood-boring insects and destructive fungi. Since these organisms are also responsible for the decomposition of dead timber, whether standing or fallen, toppled sequoias may remain virtually intact for decades or even centuries.

Unlike most trees, which eventually succumb to insects, fire, or fungal activity, the giant sequoia, being highly resistant to all three, is instead undermined from below. Giant sequoias are supported by vast but, for such large trees, remarkably shallow root systems that are vulnerable to undercutting by floodwater, thus causing the trees to fall. This is believed to be the most important factor contributing to the eventual demise of these extremely long-lived trees.

The size of a giant sequoia is not a function of age so much as soil moisture. Sequoia groves receive between 45 and 60 inches (115 and 150 centimeters) of precipitation a year—which is typical for the white fir forest as a whole—but they are restricted to sites where soil moisture is ample throughout the dry summer months. Mature giant sequoias on well-favored sites grow at a rate unexcelled by any other kind of tree. Annual growth rings one-half inch (13 millimeters) thick are typical of large sequoias on good sites, amounting to an increase in trunk diameter of one inch a year. Over the past 40 years, the General Sherman tree has added about 40 cubic feet of wood, enough to build a suburban tract home.

In the seedling stage, growth of the above-ground stem is slow while that of the roots proceeds rapidly. Less drought-resistant than other Sierra conifers, a sequoia seedling must rapidly establish its root system in order to survive the first rainless summer. During the first couple of years, root growth is primarily downward, but thereafter lateral extension of the roots predominates. Those of a mature sequoia commonly extend 100 to 150 feet (30 to 45 meters) from the tree, sometimes more than 200 feet (60 meters), so that the entire root system may affect from two to four acres of ground. The roots lie only four to five feet (1.2 to 1.5 meters) beneath the ground, however, so that great lateral extension is required to support the huge bulk of the tree. At the same time, the tree's vast shallow root system allows it to obtain surface moisture as it becomes available, especially following the melting of the snowpack.

Sequoia seeds are extremely light, averaging about 90,000 per pound (200,000 per kilogram), and despite the production of abundant seed crops each year, the reproduction rate of giant sequoias is extremely slow. The restricted distribution of the tree suggests that as a species it is merely hanging on, that environmental conditions at present are far from optimal for its survival. This is borne out by the extremely poor success rate for sequoia seedlings in the wild. Conditions of light, soil temperature, and moisture must be just right for germination to occur in the first place, Seedlings must then be able to tap reliable moisture during the first summer, compete successfully with shrubs and trees for both moisture and light, and survive the rigors of snow the following winter. Of course, so must the seedlings of other forest conifers, but those of the giant sequoia are less able to do so. Whether conditions change in favor of the giant sequoia over the next several centuries is impossible to predict, but at the moment its reproduction rate is insufficient to maintain present numbers over the long run. Still, the trees are likely to be around at least for another thousand years, even if conditions do not improve.

Bare mineral soil is essential for successful germination, for sequoia seeds are too light to sift down through the deep forest litter characteristic of most groves. The seeds must lie within a half-inch of the soil surface in order to survive. Periodic fires, which destroy litter and open up the forest to more sunlight, are essential to the giant sequoia's sustained reproductive success. Fire suppression in this century has certainly not helped the giant sequoia in this regard, but present grove boundaries are determined by available soil moisture rather than local fire regimes, and evidence suggests these boundaries have remained more or less constant for the past 500 to 1000 years.

Jeffrey Pine Forest

The Jeffrey pine is more or less a cold-weather edition of the ponderosa pine, replacing the latter on the east side of the Sierra and above 5000 to 7000 feet (1500 to 2150 meters) on the west slope. At the southern end of the Sierra, on the Kern Plateau, large stands of Jeffrey pine are found at elevations that farther north on the west slope would be dominated by ponderosa pine. The Jeffrey pine is apparently even more drought resistant than its cousin, which probably explains its wider distribution in the mountains of Southern California.

Ponderosa and Jeffrey pines are closely related, and where their ranges overlap may prove rather difficult for beginning students to distinguish. Hybrids exhibiting characteristics of both species are not uncommon, making identification even more tentative. The most obvious differences between the two pines are in their bark and cones.

142. Jeffrey Pine, *Pinus jeffreyi. Height:* 60 to 170 ft (18 to 50 m). *Bark:* rich reddish brown, divided into plates separated by darker furrows. *Leaves:* needles, blue-green, 5 to 10 in (13 to 25 cm) long, in bundles of 3. *Fruit:* cones, 5 to 10 in (13 to 25 cm) long, with prickles turned inward. *Range:* 5000 to 9000 ft (500 to 2700 m), mixed coniferous forest, both slopes; dominates many east-slope stands.

The bark of the Jeffrey pine is usually reddish brown, that of the ponderosa, golden. Nevertheless, variations in color are great enough that this criteria may not always prove reliable. Guidebooks to Sierra trees invariably point out that the bark of Jeffrey pine emits a fragrance similar to vanilla or pineapple, while that of the ponderosa does not. Yet the latter is also fragrant, and given the subjectivity of such labels, as well as personal differences in olfactory sensitivity, this distinction may not prove useful to some people. Cones offer perhaps the most reliable clue. The cones of the ponderosa pine are armed with sharp, readily felt, outward-turned prickles. Those of Jeffrey pine cones are turned inward, so the cones are smoother to the touch. Moreover, the Jeffrey pine cone is much larger than that of the ponderosa, ranging in length from 5 to 12 inches (13 to 30 centimeters), while the latter are only 2 to 5 inches (5 to 13 centimeters) long.

On the west slope of the Sierra Jeffrey pine occurs in mixed stands with incense cedar, black oak, white fir, and sugar pine on drier, rockier sites from 5000 to 7000 feet (1500 to 2150 meters). West-slope stands dominated by Jeffrey pine are largely confined to the Kern Plateau and, farther north, to the drainage of the south fork of the San Joaquin River. In Plumas County, at the northern end of the range, Jeffrey pine forest occurs in three isolated stands north of Sierra Valley. Here ample precipitation has produced a lusher, denser Jeffrey pine forest than is found southward in the range. By and large, understory vegetation is rather sparse in west-slope stands. It generally consists of herbs and shrubs characteristic of the more widespread white fir and red fir forests.

At the upper elevational limits of its range, Jeffrey pine commonly associates with western white pine, red fir, and lodgepole pine. On rocky outcrops it may occur with western juniper, *Juniperus occidentalis*. In the Tahoe Basin Jeffrey pine dominates most of the forest below 8000 feet (2450 meters), occurring with red fir on mesic sites and western juniper on xeric ones. White fir, ponderosa pine, and incense cedar are also present. Jeffrey pine is the only one of the main conifers of the mixed coniferous forest that regularly colonizes rock outcrops and serpentine soils, the latter primarily from Plumas County south to El Dorado County. Jeffrey pines on rock outcrops are often stunted and twisted by adverse soil and moisture conditions, as well as exposure to the wind. The best known Jeffrey pine in the world is probably the oft-photographed tree atop Sentinel Dome, overlooking Yosemite Valley. On deep forest soils, on the other hand, Jeffrey pines range from 60 to 180 feet (18 to 55 meters) in height and from four to seven feet (1.2 to 2.1 meters) in trunk diameter. They commonly live 300 to 400 years. Jeffrey pines prefer coarse, well-drained, sandy soils, and while somewhat tolerant of shade when young usually form open, sunny stands when mature. Abundant seeds are produced by older trees at irregular intervals. The seeds germinate readily, even in moderate shade; if conditions are not suitable, they can remain viable for many years.

Jeffrey pine is restricted to the Pacific coast, from southern Oregon south into Baja California. The largest known stand occurs on the east slope of the Sierra between Mono Lake and Long Valley, occupying the volcanic ridge crossed by U.S. 395 at Deadman Summit. From this ridge the forest extends southward sparingly through Long Valley to the vicinity of Sherwin Grade. White fir, western juniper, lodgepole pine, and quaking aspen are scattered through this nearly pure stand only in small numbers. The existence of this forest in a region otherwise dominated by sagebrush and pinyon woodland is largely due to local topography. The stand lies east of the only significant gap in the Sierra crest from north of Lake Tahoe to south of Mt. Whitney. Storms push their way through this gap to bring the Mammoth Lakes region considerably more precipitation than any other area on the east side of the southern Sierra. Understory vegetation is rather sparse in the forest, consisting mostly of grasses with scattered shrubs and broadleaf herbs. Understory shrubs are largely those of the adjacent sagebrush steppe—Great Basin sagebrush, *Artemisia tridentata;* curl-leaf mountain mahogany, *Cercocarpus ledifolius;* granite gilia, *Leptodactylon pungens;* antelope bitterbrush, *Purshia tridentata,* and Parry's rabbitbrush, *Chrysothamnus parryi.* Sagebrush also dominates openings in the forest that presumably are too dry for trees. The most common wildflowers in the community are moun-

143. Mountain Pennyroyal, *Monardella odoratissima*. Flowers purple in dense, round heads; leaves linear; stems woody at base, 6 to 14 inches (15 to 35 cm). Mountain pennyroyal is also known as coyote mint, and its leaves do have a strong mintlike fragrance. It is common in open forest below 11,000 ft (3350 m) on both slopes, blooming June–August.

tain mule ears, *Wyethia mollis;* mountain pennyroyal, *Monardella odoratissima;* and white-veined wintergreen, *Pyrola picta.*

Mixed Coniferous Forest Trees

WEST SLOPE

The following species are common or abundant in the mixed coniferous forest on the west slope of the Sierra. No single species, however, will be found in all stands. The giant sequoia becomes increasingly rare and local north of the Kings River watershed and is absent north of Donner Pass. Species more or less restricted to streamsides are not included.

> Ponderosa Pine (Western Yellow Pine), *Pinus ponderosa*, Fig. 130.
> Jeffrey Pine, *Pinus jeffreyi*, Fig. 142.
> Sugar Pine, *Pinus lambertiana*, Fig. 136.
> Douglas-fir, *Pseudotsuga menziesii*, Fig. 140.
> White Fir, *Abies concolor*, Fig. 137.
> Giant Sequoia, *Sequoiadendron giganteum*, Fig. 141.
> Incense Cedar, *Calocedrus decurrens*, Fig. 135.
> Black Oak, *Quercus kelloggii*, Fig. 131.
> Mountain Dogwood, *Cornus nuttallii*, Fig. 139.

The following species are more or less restricted to cool, moist canyons or streamsides. Many become increasingly uncommon southward through the Sierra.

Western Yew, *Taxus brevifolia*.
California Nutmeg, *Torreya californica*.
Quaking Aspen, *Populus tremuloides*, Fig. 234.
Black Cottonwood, *Populus trichocarpa*.
Red Willow, *Salix laevigata*.
Yellow Willow, *Salix lasiandra*.
Arroyo Willow, *Salix lasiolepis*.
Scouler's Willow, *Salix scouleriana*.
MacKenzie Willow, *Salix mackenziana*.
White Alder, *Alnus rhombifolia*, Fig. 101.
Mountain Alder, *Alnus tenuifolia*.
Canyon Live Oak, *Quercus chrysolepis*.
Bigleaf Maple, *Acer macrophyllum*.
California Laurel, *Umbellularia californica*.
Oregon Ash, *Fraxinus latifolia*.

The following species are uncommon or extremely local in the mixed coniferous forest of the west slope of the Sierra.

Singleleaf Pinyon, *Pinus monophylla*, Fig. 232.
Western Juniper, *Juniperus occidentalis*, Fig. 158.
Tanbark Oak, *Lithocarpus densiflora*.
Interior Live Oak, *Quercus wislinzenii*, Fig. 93.
Cascara Sagrada, *Rhamnus purshiana*.
Madrone, *Arbutus menziesii*.

EAST SLOPE

The following species are common or abundant in most stands of mixed coniferous forest on the east slope of the Sierra.

Jeffrey Pine, *Pinus jeffreyi*, Fig. 142.
White Fir, *Abies concolor*, Fig. 137.

The following species are more or less restricted to cool, moist canyons or streamsides.

Quaking Aspen, *Populus tremuloides*, Fig. 234.
Fremont Cottonwood, *Populus fremontii*, Fig. 99.
Black Cottonwood, *Populus trichocarpa*.
Water Birch, *Betula occidentalis*, Fig. 235; Owens Valley streams only.

Mixed Coniferous Forest

The following species occur in stands of east-slope mixed coniferous forest north of Carson Pass, but are rare or absent in the community southward.

Ponderosa Pine, *Pinus ponderosa*, Fig. 130.
Washoe Pine, *Pinus washoensis*.
Red Fir, *Abies magnifica*. Fig. 144.
Incense Cedar, *Calocedrus decurrens*, Fig. 135.
Western Juniper, *Juniperus occidentalis*, Fig. 158.

Shrubs and wildflowers of the mixed coniferous forest: see page 351.

Red Fir Forest

Dense, stately forests dominated by red fir, *Abies magnifica*, occur on fairly deep, well-drained soils at elevations ranging from 5000 to 8000 feet (1500 to 2450 meters) in the northern Sierra and from 7000 to 9000 feet (2150 to 2700 meters) in the south. Mature stands often contain no other conifer because red firs form such a dense canopy on favored sites that competitors are shaded out. For the same reason, understory shrubs and herbs are largely confined to forest openings, which occur on logged or burned sites, rocky outcrops, or where soils are too moist, thin, or rocky to support red firs. Except for thin shafts of sunlight, constantly shifting through the day, the red fir forest is a realm of deep shade. Animal life is scarce because the forest provides comparatively few sources of food. Most of the resident birds feed high in the canopy, their occasional calls or the distant tapping of a woodpecker being the only sounds to break the profound silence. Cool, moist, dark, silent— these attributes give the red fir forest a somber, almost sepulchral quality shared by no other forest community in the Sierra. In this respect the red fir forest is most reminiscent of the dense forests of the Pacific Northwest.

The "Snow Forest"

The red fir forest is often called the "snow forest" of the Sierra because it occupies the zone of the greatest reported

144. Red Fir, *Abies magnifica*. *Height:* 60 to 180 ft (18 to 55 m). *Bark:* dark reddish brown, with rough ridges and deep, diagonal furrows; gray or whitish and smooth on young trees. *Leaves:* needles, blue-green, ¾ to 1½ in (2 to 4 cm) long, somewhat 4-sided and *not* twisted at base (as are those of the white fir). Branches sweep down and curve up at their ends. *Fruit:* cones, barrel-shaped, 4 to 8 in (1 to 2 dm) long, erect on upper branches; disintegrate in place, so are seldom seen on ground intact. *Range:* dominant tree in the upper montane zone, most often forming nearly pure stands on mesic sites; common on west slope south to northern Kern County, 5000 to 9000 ft (1500 to 2700 m); common in Tahoe region and near Mammoth Lakes, elsewhere on east slope confined to smaller stands in cool, moist canyons and basins.

snowfall. The depth of the winter's snowpack is indicated on the trunks of red firs by the lower limit of the fruticose staghorn lichens, *Letharia vulpina* and *L. columbiana*, which form a bright chartreuse mantle over both trunk and limbs. The red fir forest receives 35 to 65 inches (90 to 165 centimers) of precipitation a year, 80 percent of which— between 400 and 500 inches (10 to 13 meters)—is snow (ten inches of snow equals one inch of rain). Rainfall is almost entirely confined to the spring and fall, with small amounts falling during summer thunderstorms. Red firs are extremely vulnerable to lightning because they are the tallest trees in the area of greatest thunderstorm activity. Lightning-blasted crowns, burnt stumps, and scattered sections of trunks lying on the ground are common sights in almost any stand of red firs. Lightning fires play an important role in opening up the forest to young trees and understory herbs and shrubs.

Average winter snow depths in the red fir forest range

Red Fir Forest

from 10 to 15 feet (3 to 5 meters), and because so little sunlight filters down to the forest floor, the community is among the last to be free of snow. Patches commonly persist as late as mid-July. The slow rate of melting allows deep forest soils to absorb large amounts of runoff and shortens the period during the late summer and fall when soil moisture is limited. Extremely cool temperatures in the red fir forest, resulting from both shadiness and high elevation, reduce evaporation from both plants and soil, thereby further decreasing the possibility of moisture stress.

Red fir requires soils that are neither too wet nor too dry during the summer months, and its distribution in the Sierra is more closely tied to local moisture conditions than to air temperature. Mature stands are best developed on gently sloping uplands or old, highly weathered glacial moraines, where soils are deep enough and of the proper texture to absorb ample moisture without becoming soggy. In swales, canyon bottoms, and glacial basins that have filled with soil, red firs give way to meadows and moisture-loving trees such as quaking aspen and lodgepole pine. Thin, rocky soils, however, dry out too quickly for red fir, and where these occur the tree is replaced by xerophytic herbs and shrubs, as well as by Jeffrey pine, western white pine, lodgepole pine, and western juniper. If slopes are too steep, soils may be too shallow and poorly developed, and runoff too rapid to support red fir. Southern exposures present an additional difficulty since warmer air temperatures will not only speed up the melting of the snowpack but increase subsequent evaporation rates as well.

Soil moisture is the primary factor governing the upper and lower elevational limits of the red fir forest. Below 5000 to 7000 feet (1500 to 2150 meters), depending on latitude, decreased snowfall and warmer summer temperatures result in drier soils than red fir can tolerate. Above 8000 to 9000 feet (2450 to 2700 meters) soils are usually either too wet or too dry. Well-developed soils in the subalpine zone are largely restricted to glacial basins and canyon bottoms, where deep snows combine with minimal runoff to produce soggy conditions suitable mainly for meadow plants. The rest of the terrain consists either of bare rock stripped of soil by glaciers, or thin, gravelly soils better suited to lodgepole pine and other subalpine trees. Air temperature has little to

145. Western White Pine (Silver Pine), *Pinus monticola. Height:* 50 to 150 ft (15 to 45 m). *Bark:* mature trees, brownish, broken into small, square, scaly plates. *Leaves:* needles, blue-green, 2 to 4 in (5 to 10 cm) long, in bundles of 5. *Fruit:* cones oblong, 6 to 8 in (15 to 20 cm). *Range:* upper montane and subalpine zone, 6000 to 11,000 ft (1800 to 3350 m), both slopes.

do with the present upper boundaries of the red fir forest, for where soil is suitable red fir may range up to nearly 11,000 feet (3350 meters) elevation.

The red fir forest is most widespread and best developed in the northernmost section of the Sierra, where glaciation was limited and precipitation is greatest. Deep, well-drained soils and abundant snowfall are characteristic of the region north of Lake Tahoe, and here red firs often form dense stands even on steeper slopes and exposed ridgetops. Southward in the range stands become less extensive and more sporadic in distribution as suitable terrain becomes scarcer. Here the red fir forest is largely confined to sheltered, gently sloping uplands such as that traversed by the Tioga Pass Road through Yosemite National Park. Travelers along this road pass through miles of magnificent red fir forest, which gives way on drier, rockier sites to mixed coniferous forest at lower elevations and lodgepole pine forest on the higher slopes. The red fir forest is less well developed on the east slope of the Sierra, where south of Sonora Pass it is largely confined to small stands in moist canyons above 8000 feet (2450 meters). The community is also poorly developed in the extreme southern part of the range, where precipitation is least and air temperatures highest. The southernmost occurrence of red fir is in northern Kern County.

Red Fir Forest

The red fir forest lies immediately above the white fir forest, and mixed stands containing both trees occur along their shared boundary. Mature specimens of the two firs are easily distinguished by the color of their bark: red fir, as the name implies, has deep reddish purple bark that has led some people to mistake it for the much larger giant sequoia; the bark of white fir is ashy gray. The needles of the two firs are also somewhat different and provide the best means of distinguishing young firs, which otherwise are very similar. The differences are enumerated in the captions beneath Figures 137 and 144. Sugar pine and incense cedar are often present in mixed fir stands, but like white fir are confined to the lower reaches of the red fir forest. Jeffrey pine and western white pine range higher, occupying exposed, rocky sites inhospitable to red fir.

Lodgepole pine is the most characteristic associate of red fir in the Sierra, especially at higher elevations, where the pine grows on sites either too moist or too dry for the fir. The association is so consistent throughout the Sierra that the zone between 5000 and 8000 feet (1500 and 2450 meters) in the north and 7000 and 10,000 feet (2150 and 3050 meters) in the south is often called the "lodgepole pine–red fir belt." Here the lodgepole pine forest and the red fir forest divide the terrain suitable for trees between them, forming a vegetation mosaic that also includes meadows, montane chaparral, and rock-outcrop communities as conspicuous elements.

Small islands of lodgepole pines occur within the red fir forest on wet soils near lakes, streams, and meadows, and on areas where lightning fires have removed the firs. The pines grow rapidly on the bare, mineral soil characteristic of burned ground and for a time dominate such sites. Eventually, however, young firs growing in the dappled shade of the pines will overshadow their predecessors and reclaim the ground. A similar process occurs at meadow edges, which are invaded first by lodgepole pines and later, when the meadows have dried further, by red firs, which again eventually shade out the pines. It takes 400 to 500 years for a stand of red fir to mature.

Most red fir stands appear to be—in the jargon of foresters—"even aged," that is, the dominant trees belong to the same generation more or less. Even-aged stands

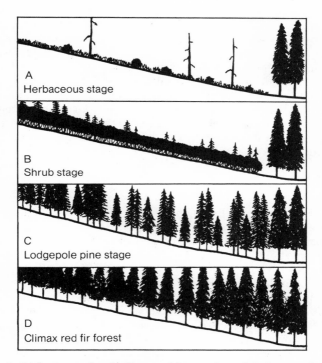

146. Lightning is the chief cause of fires in the red fir forest. After a burn, the site is invaded first by herbs and shrubs, whose seeds are blown in from adjacent areas (A). Eventually, shrubs such as huckleberry oak, bush chinquapin, and pinemat manzanita crowd out the herbaceous species to form a dense stand of montane chaparral (B). After a time, lodgepole pines, a common pioneer tree on burned sites, shade out the shrubs (C), only to be replaced in turn by red firs (D), which will dominate the site until a future fire (or logging operation) starts the cycle anew.

occur because the first firs to colonize an open area create conditions unfavorable to the establishment of subsequent seedlings. Younger trees are shaded out by the older ones or die because they are unable to compete successfully for soil moisture. Because of low daytime temperatures, summer drought, and the relatively brief period during which the ground is free of snow, the decomposition of litter is extremely slow in the red fir forest. Thick layers of needles compacted into dense mats by heavy snow cover are characteristic of the forest litter. They provide a formidable obstacle to germination, since most seeds require either mineral soil, or at the very least, no more than a third of an inch of litter, to germinate successfully. As a result of inhospitable conditions red fir seedlings and saplings, as well as those of most other plants, are scarce or absent from many mature stands, a situation very different from that of the mixed coniferous forest, where the understory is often thick with young trees.

Understory Plants

Few species of herbs and shrubs are able to endure the dense shade and deep litter in mature stands of red fir. Shrubs are especially scarce and often confined to areas where at least a little sunlight is available sometime during the day. Those which have managed to establish themselves in shadier areas tend to be low and spindly. The most common shrubs within the red fir forest are sticky currant, *Ribes viscosissimum;* double honeysuckle, *Lonicera conjugalis;* huckleberry oak, *Quercus vaccinifolia;* and mountain snowberry, *Symphoricarpos vaccinioides.*

Herbaceous vegetation, while not abundant, is better developed and characterized by a larger number of species. The most common herbs in the red fir forest are Brewer's golden aster, *Chrysopis breweri;* white-flowered hawkweed, *Hieracium albiflorum;* mountain pennyroyal, *Monardella odoratissima;* white-veined wintergreen, *Pyrola picta;* western prince's pine, *Chimaphila umbellata;* snow plant, *Sarcodes sanguinea;* spotted coralroot, *Corallorhiza maculata;* and pinedrops, *Pterospora andromedea.*

Snow plant, spotted coralroot, and pinedrops are *saprophytes,* plants lacking chlorophyll that obtain carbohydrates not through photosynthesis, but from forest humus. Snow plant is supplied with nutrients by soil fungi that form mycorrhiza with its roots. Coralroot and pinedrops have no fungi of their own and instead parasitize those of adjacent plants. Snowplant and pinedrops are members of the wintergreen family, which also includes other saprophytes, such as sugar stick, *Allotropa virgata;* pityopus, *Pityopus californica;* and fringed pinesap, *Pleuricospora*

FOREST PLANT COMMUNITIES

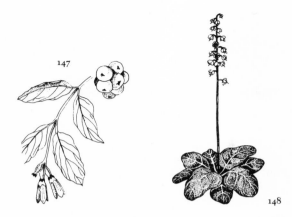

147

148

147. Mountain Snowberry, *Symphoricarpos vaccinioides. Height:*
3 to 5 ft (1 to 2 m); leaves dark green, elliptical, to 1 in (2.5 cm)
long; flowers pinkish, bell-shaped, hanging from tips of stems;
fruit a white berry in tight clusters. Mountain snowberry is common on rocky slopes, 5000 to 10,000 ft (1500 to 3000 m). Of three
other species of snowberry found in the Sierra, two are sprawling shrubs and the third is largely confined to moist streambanks
below 3000 ft (900 m).

148. White-veined Wintergreen, *Pyrola picta.* Flowers greenish
or white in terminal cluster; leaves broadly elliptical, dark green
with white veins; stem 4 to 8 inches (1 to 2 dm). The white-veined
wintergreen is one of the few Sierra wildflowers that prefers dense
shade. It occurs on both slopes below 9500 ft (2900 m), blooming
June–August. The one-sided wintergreen, *P. secunda,* which
grows in similar places, lacks white leaf veins, and has yellowish
or greenish flowers, all on one side of the stalk.

fimbriata. This family seems to have specialized in symbiotic relationships with fungi, for even members such as
white-veined wintergreen, which normally contains
chlorophyll (one form lacks chlorophyll), are known to rely
to some degree on mycorrhiza for their nutritional needs.
Spotted coralroot, striped coralroot, *Corallorhiza striata,*
and phantom orchid, *Eburophyton austinae,* are saprophy-
tic members of the orchid family. It is notable that both the
orchid and wintergreen families have specialized in developing strategies for coping with deep shade and that
their representatives in the Sierra are seldom found in

Red Fir Forest 333

sunny or xeric habitats. The large number of saprophytes found in both the red fir forest and mixed coniferous forest suggest that Sierra soils permit a high level of fungal activity.

Montane Chaparral

Brush thickets occur on dry, rocky slopes, weathered talus, and recently burned areas within the red fir forest. Dominated by huckleberry oak, *Quercus vaccinifolia;* golden chinquapin, *Chrysolepis sempervirens;* and pinemat manzanita, *Arctostaphylos nevadensis,* this community is known as montane chaparral. Unlike foothill chaparral and the brush stands found in similar habitats in the mixed coniferous forest, montane chaparral consist of species adapted to the colder temperatures, deeper snows, shorter growing seasons, and other conditions characteristic of

149. Huckleberry Oak, *Quercus vaccinifolia. Height:* 2 to 4 ft (6 to 12 dm); low, spreading shrub; branches thin, flexible, with terminal tufts; bark smooth, gray; leaves elliptical or narrower, sometimes with spiny margins; acorn ½ × ¼ in (15 × 20 mm). The huckleberry oak, which never occurs as a tree, is a common and widespread shrub on dry, open sites, 5000 to 10,000 ft (1500 to 3000 m). It is one of the dominant shrubs in montane chaparral.

150. Bush, or Golden, Chinquapin, *Chrysolepis sempervirens. Height:* to 8 ft (2.5 m); rounded, spreading shrub; bark gray or brown, smooth; leaves elliptical, 1½ to 3 in (4 to 5 cm), yellowish green above, brownish or gold below; fruit like a spiny chestnut. Bush chinquapin occurs on open dry or rocky slopes above 6000 ft (1800 m), often along with huckleberry oak. Both are especially common on recently burned sites.

149   150

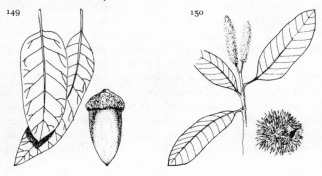

higher elevations. Most of its species are either rare or absent below 5000 feet (1500 meters) and many extend upwards to 10,000 or 11,000 feet (3050 to 3350 meters).

Montane chaparral is more compact and lower to the ground than brush communities downslope, typically forming a dense thicket less than six feet (two meters) tall. Understory herbs are absent from well-developed stands, which may cover entire hillsides or form small understory elements in open forest stands. Following a fire, ground formerly occupied by forest is first invaded by herbs from nearby areas. These are eventually forced out by shrubs, which are succeeded in turn by lodgepole pines and ultimately, red firs or other climax conifers. In addition to the three shrubs mentioned above, montane chaparral commonly includes the following species: greenleaf manzanita, *Arctostaphylos patula;* snow bush, *Ceanothus cordulatus;* Coville's ceanothus, *Ceanothus pinetorum;* bitter cherry, *Prunus emarginata;* Parish's snowberry, *Symphoricarpos parishii* (southern Sierra); and mountain snowberry, *Symphoricarpos vaccinioides.*

Red Fir Forest Trees

The only species that is characteristic of and abundant in all stands of red fir forest is the red fir itself:

Red Fir, *Abies magnifica,* Fig. 144.

The following species, however, are widely scattered throughout the red fir forest on appropriate sites and may be locally common.

Lodgepole Pine, *Pinus contorta,* var. *murrayana,* Fig. 152.
Jeffrey Pine, *Pinus jeffreyi,* Fig. 142.
Western White Pine (Silver Pine), *Pinus monticola,* Fig. 145.
Mountain Hemlock, *Tsuga mertensiana,* Fig. 157.
Western Juniper, *Juniperus occidentalis,* Fig. 158.
Quaking Aspen, *Populus tremuloides,* Fig. 234.

Shrubs and wildflowers of the red fir forest: see page 351.

151. Lodgepole pine forest.

Lodgepole Pine Forest

Anyone who has spent much time in the High Sierra is familiar with the lodgepole pine, *Pinus contorta*, var. *murrayana*, the slender campsite pine with the "cornflake" bark. Lodgepole pine occurs in several plant communities from 6000 to 8000 feet (1800 to 2450 meters) elevation in the northern Sierra and from 8000 to 11,000 feet (2450 to 3350 meters) in the south. It is the dominant conifer of glacially scoured ridges, valleys, and basins in the lower subalpine zone, where it forms an extensive, open forest of scattered, often pure stands intermingled with lakes, meadows, and outcrops of polished granite. On higher, rockier slopes lodgepole pine is a prominent associate of whitebark pine and mountain hemlock, ranging upward to tree limit in some areas. Throughout the lower portion of its range in the Sierra, lodgepole pine is a locally common associate in the red fir forest and upper mixed coniferous forest, where it occupies burned areas and moist sites along streams and meadow borders. Intolerant of deep shade, however, it rarely occurs among dense stands of red fir, which tends to replace it on sites where soils are deep, moderately moist, and rich in humus. The scarcity of such

336

sites in the subalpine zone partly accounts for the lodgepole pine's dominance in the region. Among the more versatile of Sierra conifers, it is able to thrive both in damp meadow loams and thin, poorly developed soils of disintegrated granite, the two most common soil types in the subalpine zone. Red fir tolerates neither type. Nevertheless, as soil development has progressed in the High Sierra red firs have made inroads into the lodgepole pine forest and no doubt will continue to do so in the centuries to come. North of Lake Tahoe, where glaciation was less widespread, red firs have already replaced lodgepole pines over large areas. On higher slopes and in rocky basins, however, lodgepole pine is probably a climax species that will persist indefinitely as an integral part of the subalpine forest. This is an exceptional circumstance for the pine, which throughout most of its range—from Alaska south to Baja California and east to the Black Hills of South Dakota—is largely confined to disturbed areas, such as burns, which it occupies only for a time before being shaded out by other conifers. The ability of lodgepole pine to tolerate a wide range of soil and moisture conditions is largely responsible for its notable success in the Sierra. It is able to alter the rate at which moisture is absorbed and transpired according to soil conditions, speeding up the process in damp soils, slowing it down in dry ones.

152. Lodgepole Pine, *Pinus contorta*, var. *murrayana*. *Height:* 50 to 100 ft (15 to 30 m) tall, often shrubby or prostrate near timberline. *Bark:* light orange-brown or pale gray to buff, extremely flaky. *Leaves:* the only native Sierra pine with 2 needles per bundle; needles yellow-green, 1 to 2½ in (2.5 to 6 cm) long. *Fruit:* cones, nearly round, 1 to 1¾ in (2.5 to 4.5 cm) long, armed with sharp points. *Range:* abundant in lodgepole pine forest, subalpine forest, and red fir forest, both slopes, 5000 to 11,000 ft (1500 to 3350 m); often bordering meadows.

A slender, tapering tree from 50 to 80 feet (15 to 25 meters) tall and 6 to 20 inches (15 to 50 centimeters) thick, the average lodgepole pine well deserves its name, which reportedly refers to its use by northern Plains Indians to make teepees. In the Sierra the size and shape of the pine, as well as the density of individual stands, varies greatly according to local conditions of soil and moisture. On sheltered sites with deep, moist, well-developed soils lodgepole pines may grow to be 100 feet (30 meters) tall and from three to five feet (90 to 150 centimeters) thick or larger, forming a shady forest with little or no understory herbs or shrubs. On exposed slopes near timberline, where winds are strong and nearly constant and soils thin and poor, lodgepoles grow as dwarfed, sometimes prostrate shrubs no more than four or five feet tall.

Understory vegetation is sparse or absent in the lodgepole pine forest, where sparse sunlight combined with especially wet or dry soils often create conditions inhospitable to most shrubs and herbs. Understory plants are therefore often confined to sunny openings or moist soils near lakes and streams. In this latter situation red mountain heather, *Phyllodoce breweri,* and Labrador tea, *Ledum glandulosum,* commonly form dense shrubby cover around the bases of the pines. Alpine prickly currant, *Ribes montigenum;* pinemat manzanita, *Arctostaphylos nevadensis;* black elderberry, *Sambucus melanocarpa;* tobacco brush,

153. Red Mountain Heather, *Phyllodoce breweri.* Low shrub with stems 4 to 12 in (1 to 3 dm) branching from base near ground; leaves evergreen, needlelike, densely clustered on stems; flowers rose. Red mountain heather commonly occurs 6500 to 12,000 ft (2000 to 3650 m), both slopes, in moist, soggy soils, often near lakes or streams. It blooms shortly after snowmelt.

Ceanothus velutinus; willows; and several other shrubs are commonly found in the lodgepole pine forest, but seldom form a dense cover. On the east side of the Sierra, Great Basin sagebrush, *Artemisia tridentata,* and curl-leaf mountain mahogany, *Cercocarpus ledifolius,* range upslope into the lodgepole pine forest. Understory herbs are sparse and generally consist of species common to adjacent rock, meadow, and forest communities.

Lodgepoles are vulnerable to lightning strikes during the summer, as evidenced by numerous snag-topped trees. Their thin bark and highly flammable sap makes them susceptible even to fairly cool groundfires. Mature lodgepoles destroyed by fire, however, are quickly replaced by dense stands of seedlings. In the absence of fires a large number of lodgepole pine cones remain on a tree for many years, their bracts sealed by resin. The cones open when the seal is melted by the heat of fire, at which time the numerous minute seeds are released. Lodgepoles are prolific seeders and though some of the seeds may be destroyed by fire, more than enough will survive to regenerate the stand. Recently burned ground provides an ideal seedbed, for lodgepole seeds germinate most readily in bare, mineral soil, and the young trees grow most rapidly in full sunlight. Large stands of even-aged lodgepoles are common in the Sierra and may represent successful crops of fire seedlings. Fire may prevent lodgepoles from invading meadows, and their notable success in doing so during the past 70 years may be due in part to the policy of fire suppression that has prevailed during this period. Nevertheless, lodgepole pines, in the Sierra at least, do not require fire in order to reproduce successfully.

Lodgepole Needle-Miners

The large stands of dead, bleached lodgepole pines ("ghost forests") found in the upper basins of the Tuolumne River watershed, and to a smaller extent elsewhere in the Sierra, are not the result of fire but of defoliation caused by the caterpillar of a tiny quarter-inch moth, the lodgepole needle-miner, *Coleotechnites milleri.* During the first three weeks of August in odd-numbered years the moths lay their minute, lemon-yellow eggs in old, previously mined needles, or near new needles and buds, on mature lodgepole pines. They less commonly choose younger trees and only rarely those of other species. Upon hatching, the tiny caterpillars migrate and bore into needles two or more years old, feeding on them until the onset of winter, when the larvae become dormant. They recommence feeding the following spring, seeking out new foliage in midsummer and again in the fall. After migrating to new needles one last time during the second spring, they enter the pupal stage, emerging as adult moths in early summer. A week to ten days later the moths begin to mate and lay eggs, initiating the two-year cycle once again.

Most of the time needle-miner populations are kept under control by more than 40 parasitic insects, most of them small wasps whose larvae eat those of the moths, and by mountain chickadees and several other birds, which eat enormous quantities of needle-miner larvae, especially during the winter, when other foods are scarce. Every few years, however, a population explosion occurs among needle-miners, lasting a decade or more and resulting in the defoliation of thousands of lodgepole pines. The largest known outbreak in the Sierra occurred near Tuolumne Meadows in Yosemite National Park between 1947 and 1965, during which time more than 50,000 acres (20,000 hectares) were infested. Past campaigns to control needle-miner outbreaks, first with DDT and later with Malathion, not only failed but in the process killed a number of the moth's parasites and predators, including a large number of birds. Today researchers are investigating biological controls.

It seems likely that needle-miner outbreaks occur in response to the development of local imbalances in the normal system of control. Although thousands of lodgepoles may be destroyed during major infestations, it is unlikely that the needle-miner represents a long-term threat to the pine's welfare in the Sierra, for pine and moth have evolved together over thousands of years. Moreover, needle-miners may be instrumental, along with periodic fires, in preventing the invasion of meadows by lodgepole pines and thereby help to maintain the mosaic of rock, meadow, and forest characteristic of the High Sierra.

The large-scale destruction of lodgepole pines during needle-miner outbreaks is not the work of the larvae alone, for weakened mature trees are also attacked by bark beetles, genus *Dendrocotonus*, whose larvae feed on the cambium layer just below the bark. Normally healthy trees literally drown the beetle larvae with resin exudates; weakened trees cannot. The depredations of the bark beetles, together with the defoliation caused by needle-miners, rather than just the latter alone, are usually responsible for the bulk of pine deaths during a prolonged moth infestation.

Lodgepole Pine Forest Trees

The only species that is characteristic of and abundant in all stands of lodgepole pine forest is the lodgepole pine itself:

Lodgepole Pine, *Pinus contorta*, var. *murrayana*, Fig. 152.

The following species, however, are commonly associated with lodgepole pines on appropriate sites.

Western White Pine, *Pinus monticola*, Fig. 145.
Whitebark Pine, *Pinus albicaulis*, Fig. 155.
Red Fir, *Abies magnifica*, Fig. 144.
Quaking Aspen, *Populus tremuloides*, Fig. 234.

Lodgepole pine is also a common member of the subalpine forest, in which it associates with the characteristic trees of that community.

Shrubs and wildflowers of the lodgepole pine forest: see page 351.

Subalpine Forest

The subalpine forest forms an open woodland of small groves and scattered individual trees on both slopes of the Sierra from 8000 to 10,000 feet (2450 to 3050 meters) in the north and from 9500 to 12,000 feet (2900 to 3650 meters) in the south. The community is poorly represented north of

154. Subalpine landscape.

Lake Tahoe and occupies a narrower belt on the steep eastern flank than on the broad western slope of the range. The community is virtually absent south of Mineral King and the Mt. Whitney region. The upper limit of the subalpine forest constitutes timberline, above which lies the treeless alpine zone. Along its lower limit the community merges with the lodgepole pine forest in most areas, less commonly with stands of red fir or Jeffrey pine.

The subalpine forest is one element in a spectacular, open, high-mountain landscape that also includes lakes, meadows, vast rocky slopes, and high peaks as conspicuous elements. Meadows occur on moist flats in lake basins, along streams, and below lingering snowbanks—sites where soils are too wet, cold, and poorly aerated to support trees, or where snow melts so late in the season that the time available for growth is too short. Subalpine conifers prefer sites characterized by moderate snow depths and moisture—benches and rock crevices, well-drained flats, old glacial moraines, weathered talus, and higher ground near lakes, meadows, and streams. Trees are able to invade rocky areas primarily by means of frost-riven crevices, which in granitic terrain correspond to structural joints in the rock.

Summer days in the subalpine zone are fairly warm, reaching a peak around noon, after which increasing cloud-

FOREST PLANT COMMUNITIES

iness results in cooler temperatures. Winds are nearly constant, and on overcast afternoons their chilling effect can be pronounced. Overall precipitation during the summer is slight, and late-season soil drought is a limiting factor for many plants. Summer nights are usually cool, and just before dawn the temperature commonly drops below freezing. Snow arrives early in the fall and melts early in the summer, remaining on the ground for eight or nine months. Annual snowfall ranges from 250 to 400 inches (6 to 10 meters), somewhat less on the east side of the Sierra. The growing season, which is only seven to nine weeks, is determined primarily by the date of snowmelt in the early summer and by falling soil-moisture levels later in the season.

Composition of the Subalpine Forest

The most common and characteristic trees of the subalpine forest are whitebark pine, *Pinus albicaulis;* lodgepole pine, *P. contorta,* var. *murrayana;* mountain hemlock, *Tsuga mertensiana;* and foxtail pine, *P. balfouriana.* Limber pine, *P. flexilis;* western white pine, *P. monticola;* and western juniper, *Juniperus occidentalis,* are locally important associates. Although lodgepole pine is sometimes omitted from the list of species making up the subalpine forest, it occurs so commonly in mixed stands with other subalpine trees, in many places even ranging to timberline, that including it in the community seems essential. The open stands of lodgepole pines that occupy rocky slopes and basins along the boundary between the lodgepole pine and subalpine forests form an ecotone between the two communities, and for most purposes there is little need to assign such stands to one or the other.

Whitebark pine is the characteristic timberline tree throughout most of the Sierra, commonly forming a sprawling shrub on high slopes and ridges that are too cold, rocky, and windblown for other conifers. In more sheltered areas downslope it often occurs in mixed stands with lodgepole pine, foxtail pine, or mountain hemlock, where it grows as an erect multitrunked tree from 30 to 50 feet (9 to 15 meters) tall. Although confined largely to thin, rocky soils, whitebark pines occasionally occur in deeper, moister soils, where erect single-trunked specimens up to 80 feet (25 meters) tall have been recorded. The most extensive stands of whitebark pine are found in the central Sierra from Ebbetts Pass south to the Mammoth Lakes region and in the high country of northern Kings Canyon National Park. Southward, small stands occur sporadically to the Mt. Whitney region. North of Ebbetts Pass whitebark pine is largely confined to the higher peaks around Lake Tahoe, becoming exceedingly scarce from there north to Lake Almanor.

In the central and southern Sierra open stands composed entirely of foxtail pine commonly form a timberline on exposed southern slopes and high ridges. Foxtail pines, which remain erect regardless of conditions, never occur as timberline shrubs. On the most exposed sites the windward side of the tree may be stripped entirely of bark and foliage, while on the leeward side sparse clumps of needles are kept alive by a thin strip of living wood extending down to the rocky soil. Yet these battered giants of the timberline may endure a thousand years or more before they finally succumb to the elements. Downslope, foxtail pines occur in both pure and mixed stands. Common associates in the latter include whitebark pine, lodgepole pine, and on the east slope of the Sierra, limber pine.

The foxtail pine is found only in California and has a curious, disjointed range. It occurs in two widely separated locations: (1) the Scott, Salmon, and Yolla Bolly mountains in the northwestern part of the state; and (2) the central and southern Sierra Nevada from Monache Mountain north to the south fork of the San Joaquin River. Three hundred miles apart, these two populations are remnants of the richer, more extensive subalpine forest that existed in the late Miocene and Pliocene epochs, when a good deal of summer rainfall in California permitted the widespread development of coniferous and mixed hardwood forests. As time passed rainfall became increasingly restricted to the winter months, as it is today, and species dependent on summer precipitation either died out or retreated northward. Foxtail pine was apparently able to hang on in the central and southern Sierra because summer thundershowers occur more frequently in this part of the range, owing to its greater height and closer proximity to summer tropical

155. Whitebark Pine, *Pinus albicaulis. Height:* 20 to 50+ ft (6 to 15+ m), but often shrubby or many-trunked on exposed sites near timberline; forms sprawling mats on high, windswept ridges. *Bark:* pale gray or whitish, smooth or somewhat scaly; bark on branches reddish brown. *Leaves:* needles, dark green, 1 to 2½ in (2.5 to 6.5 cm) long, in bundles of 5, clustered at tips of branchlets. *Fruit:* cones, 1 to 3 in (2.5 to 8 cm), purplish; disintegrate on the tree. *Range:* the dominant timberline tree of the central Sierra, especially west of the main crest; 7500 to 11,000+ ft (2300 to 3350+ m), both slopes from the Tahoe region south.

156. Foxtail Pine, *Pinus balfouriana. Height:* 20 to 45 ft (6 to 14 m), remaining erect even on high, exposed ridges at timberline. *Bark:* fissured, somewhat flaky or checked, reddish brown to tan; smooth and gray on young trees. *Leaves:* needles, ¾ to 1½ in (2 to 4 cm) long, curved, blue-green above, pale below, in bundles of 5 densely clustered around branchlets. *Fruit:* cones, 2 to 5 in (5 to 13 cm) long, scales purplish and armed with prickles. *Range:* the dominant timberline tree of the southern Sierra, 6000 to 11,500 ft (1800 to 3500 m), both slopes in Tulare and Inyo counties.

storms that from time to time stray north from Mexico.

Mountain hemlock dominates the subalpine forest of the northern Sierra, typically forming extensive, dense stands quite unlike the sparse cover of pines characteristic of the community in the central and southern parts of the range. Mountain hemlock prefers cool, moist, sheltered sites, often near lakes, streams, and meadows. On northern and eastern exposures it sometimes ranges to timberline along with lodgepole and whitebark pines. Occurring mostly as an erect single-trunked tree, it may also form a huge sprawling shrub on the highest, windiest sites. In more sheltered locations mountain hemlock often occurs in mixed stands with lodgepole pine, western white pine, and red fir. Hemlock stands are best developed from Yosemite north to Ebbetts Pass, though the tree is fairly common all the way to the Sierra Buttes some 40 miles (65 kilometers) north of Lake Tahoe. South of Yosemite mountain hemlock becomes increasingly scarce and confined to high, well-watered basins on north- and east-facing slopes.

Western white pine is a fairly common associate of red fir, lodgepole pine, and mountain hemlock, forming small, rather open stands on dry, rocky upland flats, though it also can be found near lakeshores. In the southern Sierra small stands dominated by western white pine range as high as 11,000 feet (3350 meters). It is most abundant in the central and northern Sierra, however, from Kings Canyon National Park to the Tahoe region.

Limber pines occur on the east slope of the Sierra from the Yosemite region south, forming open stands on steep, dry slopes. Their distribution is spotty, the trees being rather common in some areas—Onion Valley, for example—but absent from others. Foxtail pine and lodgepole pine are present in some stands. Whitebark pine is not common on the eastern flank of the Sierra south of Yosemite, and in its absence limber pine often forms a timberline.

Western juniper is a locally common member of the subalpine forest, but only rarely occurs at timberline. It typically grows as an erect but twisted tree on steep, arid slopes and high ridges. Shrubby forms are known to occur only in the higher basins west of Lake Tahoe. Hikers entering the Desolation Wilderness via Rockbound Pass, for example, will find dwarfed junipers along the steep trail. Of all the subalpine conifers, western juniper has the widest elevational range, occurring in several plant communities down to 6000 feet (1800 meters) on both slopes of the Sierra.

Aside from quaking aspen, *Populus tremuloides*, which may range as high as 10,000 feet (3050 meters) on sheltered sites, deciduous trees are conspicuous by their absence from the subalpine forest. Evergreens have a distinct advantage in the subalpine zone because they do not need to waste precious growing time putting on a new crop of leaves each year. In fact, subalpine conifers typically retain

157. Mountain Hemlock, *Tsuga mertensiana. Height:* 15 to 100+ ft (4 to 30+ m); forms a large shrub on exposed timberline sites. *Bark:* dark gray to deep reddish brown, deeply furrowed. *Leaves:* needles, dark blue-green, grooved above, rounded below, curved and twisted at base; up to 1 in (2.5 cm) long; grow from all sides of branchlet. *Fruit:* cones, brown, 2 to 5 in (5 to 13 cm) long. *Range:* subalpine forest south to Sequoia National Park; most common, Yosemite north; typically found in cool, moist sites, but may also range on rocky slopes nearly to timberline; 6000 to 11,000 ft (1800 to 3350 m), both slopes.

158. Western Juniper, *Juniperus occidentalis. Height:* 20 to 60 ft (6 to 18 m). *Bark:* rich reddish brown, fibrous. *Leaves:* flat, scalelike, closely pressed on branchlets in overlapping ranks of 3; yellow-green. *Fruit:* berrylike "cones" ¼ to ⅓ in (6 to 8 m) diameter, blue-black with whitish bloom; leaves and berries have pungent aroma reminiscent of gin, which contains juniper as a flavoring. *Range:* 4000 to 11,000 ft (1200 to 3350 m), east slope, rocky sites and dry soils; dominant tree in northern juniper woodland south to Mono County; less common southward; also widespread on west slope, 6500 to 11,000 ft (2000 to 3350 m).

their needles even longer than those growing at lower elevations, an energy-conserving measure essential near timberline. Foxtail pines, for example, may retain their needles for up to 17 years.

Since subalpine conifers retain their needles for long periods, litter tends to be scarce. What exists breaks down into humus very slowly because of low air and soil temperatures and marked aridity during the summer, all of which retard the efforts of soil fungi. Consequently, subalpine forest soils tend to be rather rudimentary, consisting largely of disintegrated granite with little humus and minimal horizon development. Such soils are called *lithosols*—literally, "rock soils." Deeper, better-developed soils occur in lake

Subalpine Forest

basins and along watercourses, but are often too moist for trees. Most forest soils in the subalpine zone are poor in nutrients and rather acidic.

The subalpine forest lacks a characteristic understory of herbs and shrubs, though species found in nearby meadows and open, rocky areas commonly associate with the scattered conifers. For the most part, of course, the trees are so widely separated that to speak of an understory seems to be stretching the meaning of the term. Locally, sagebrush, *Artemisia tridentata*; whitesquaw, *Ribes cereum*; creambush, *Holodiscus discolor*; alpine prickly currant, *Ribes montigenum*; and other shrubs may be scattered among the trees. At timberline sprawling coniferous mats and thickets may serve in much the same way as large rocks to protect herbaceous species from wind and cold.

Growth Habits of Timberline Trees

Whitebark pines are able to colonize high, windblown ridges primarily by forming prostrate thickets known as *krummholz* (German for "twisted wood"), or elfinwood, thereby taking advantage of warmer air temperatures and less severe winds near the ground. Lodgepole pine and mountain hemlock also assume dwarfed, shrubby forms on exposed sites near timberline. Do such dwarfed trees constitute distinct genetic races that developed in response to the harsh timberline environment? Or are their prostrate forms shaped entirely by the environment—wind, cold, and thin, dry, impoverished soils? Would the same trees grow as tall, single-trunked specimens on sheltered sites with better soils?

Whitebark, lodgepole, and mountain hemlock all exhibit great variety of form: elfinwood, erect single-trunked trees up to 80 feet (25 meters) high, and intermediate types characterized by multiple trunks that often rise above a dense skirt of shrubby branches. Although the taller forms tend to be restricted to sheltered sites farther downslope, the presence on a single site of all three forms of the same species has led some observers to suggest that these variations are largely inherited traits. According to this hypothesis, a given population of, say, whitebark pines would contain

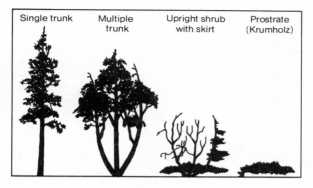

159. Growth forms of timberline trees. Whitebark pine, lodge-pole pine, and mountain hemlock may occur in all four forms shown here. Foxtail pine is always an erect single-trunked tree. Western juniper occurs as krummholz only in the high country west of Lake Tahoe.

genes for erect single-trunked forms and for sprawling, prostrate forms. On sheltered sites, where cold and wind are less critical, tall forms would be more common than in exposed locations farther upslope, where dwarfed forms would be favored. Intermediate forms would arise as hybrids between the other two. The hereditary hypothesis remains unproved, however, and some botanists believe the several forms displayed by timberline trees are merely variable responses to different habitats.

A close correlation exists between snow depth and the height of krummholz trees, since shoots that extend above the snow during the winter are killed back by frost damage, moisture stress, and abrasion by windblown snow. Intermediate forms might result from variable snow depths during successive winters, with taller branches surviving during years of deeper snow. Later these same branches might die back during less snowy winters, or become flagged, with foliage surviving only on the leeward sides of the trunks. Upright branches stand a better chance of surviving if they put on enough growth during the summer to extend well above the snow surface during the winter. Foliage extending just barely above the surface quickly succumbs to abrasion from blowing snow. Elfinwood often creates its own protection from the elements by trapping windblown snow that otherwise would not stick to the ground. In this way krummholz can also afford protection to smaller herbs and shrubs nearby. Snow and wind, however, are not the only factors that contribute to stunted tree growth at timberline. Impoverished soils, inadequate moisture, and low air temperatures all contribute to slow growth rates during the summer, making the elaboration of large trunks and extensive branch systems impossible for most species. Krummholz may spread laterally, however, through a process known as *layering*. A seedling established in the lee of, say, a boulder, where wind velocity is reduced, extends its branches outward parallel to the ground and at certain points sets down new roots. Eventually the older portion of the plant may die, leaving the youngest part separated from the site where the plant was originally established.

Subalpine Forest Trees

The following species are the dominant members of the subalpine forest of the Sierra Nevada. None occurs in all community stands. The primary area of dominance for each is indicated.

Whitebark Pine, *Pinus albicaulis*, Fig. 155; central Sierra.
Foxtail Pine, *Pinus balfouriana*, Fig. 156; southern Sierra.
Mountain Hemlock, *Tsuga mertensiana*, Fig. 157; northern Sierra.

The following species are common associates in some stands.

Lodgepole Pine, *Pinus contorta*, var. *murrayana*, Fig. 152.
Western White Pine, *Pinus monticola*, Fig. 145.
Limber Pine, *Pinus flexilis*.
Western Juniper, *Juniperus occidentalis*, Fig. 158.

In addition, quaking aspen, *Populus tremuloides*, is present locally along streams or on moist talus slopes.

Shrubs and wildflowers of the subalpine forest; see the following section.

Forest Shrubs, Wildflowers, and Ferns

Few shrubs, wildflowers, or ferns are restricted to a particular forest community in the Sierra. Instead they typically range through several communities wherever appropriate habitats occur. Available light and moisture, soil conditions, and the length of the growing season are the most important factors governing the distribution of understory shrubs and wildflowers, and these factors are primarily determined by forest density, local topography, and elevation. The *kind* of trees growing in a particular place is rarely—and then only incidentally—important to the distribution of a particular shrub, wildflower, or fern, so the following lists are arranged by type of habitat rather than by community, and the elevational range of each species is indicated. Plants found only in meadows are not included in these lists because montane meadow constitutes a distinct community in terms of type of plant cover, characteristic flora, and physical environment. Meadow shrubs and wildflowers are listed on page 370.

Forest Shrubs

The following species are characteristic of, but not necessarily restricted to, the habitats under which they are listed. Elevational ranges are given in feet. Very common species are so indicated. Those found locally in the forest but more common in montane meadow, foothill woodland, chaparral, and sagebrush scrub are not included.

DRY SHADY FOREST   Moderate to dense shade; soil well developed but often dry near the surface. Shrubs sparse or absent in denser stands. No shrub species is particularly common in this habitat.

> Gooseberry and Currant, genus *Ribes;* several species ranging to timberline.
> Mountain Misery (Kit-kit-dizze), *Chamaebatia foliosa,* Fig. 132; 3000–7500; more common here than most.
> Sierra Coffeeberry, *Rhamnus rubra;* 4000–7000.

160. Greenleaf Manzanita, *Arctostaphylos patula*. *Height:* 3 to 7 ft (1 to 2 m); stems several, usually swollen at base; bark smooth, reddish brown, sometimes greenish yellow on branchlets; flowers pink ¼ in (13 mm), in dense drooping clusters. Greenleaf manzanita is one of the most common shrubs in the mixed coniferous forest. It prefers open stands and often forms a dense cover on recently burned areas. It occurs below 5000 ft (1500 m) in the north and 9000 ft (2700 m) in the south.

Deer Brush, *Ceanothus integerrimus;* 2500–7000.
Small-Leaved Ceanothus, *Ceanothus parvifolius;* 4000–9000.
Tobacco Brush, *Ceanothus velutinus;* 3000–10,000.
Pinemat Manzanita, *Arctostaphylos nevadensis;* 5000–10,000.
Greenleaf Manzanita, *Arctostaphylos patula,* Fig. 160; 2000–11,000.
Snowberry, genus *Symphoricarpos;* several species ranging to timberline.

OPEN FOREST   Moderate to ample sunshine; soil well developed but often dry near the surface; includes areas cleared of trees by fire or logging. Shrubs may form dense thickets in this habitat. Numerous species are common to abundant.

Huckleberry Oak, *Quercus vaccinifolia,* Fig. 149; 5000–10,000; very common.
Bush Chinquapin, *Castanopsis sempervirens,* Fig. 150; 4000–11,000; very common.
Gooseberry and Currant, genus *Ribes;* several species ranging to timberline; very common except where extirpated by the U.S. Forest Service as a measure for controlling white pine blister rust.

Mountain Misery, *Chamaebatia foliosa*, Fig. 132; 3000–7500; very common.

Bitter Cherry, *Prunus emarginata;* 4000–9000.

Sierra Coffeeberry, *Rhamnus rubra;* 4000–7000; common.

Squaw Carpet, *Ceanothus prostratus;* 3000–7000.

Deer Brush, *Ceanothus integerrimus,* 2500–7000; very common.

Small-Leaved Ceanothus, *Ceanothus parvifolius;* 4000–9000.

Snow Brush, *Ceanothus cordulatus;* 3500–9000; very common.

Fresno Mat, *Ceanothus fresnensis;* 3000–7000.

Pinemat Manzanita, *Arctostaphylos nevadensis;* 5000–10,000; very common.

Greenleaf Manzanita, *Actostaphylos patula,* Fig. 160; 2000–11,000; very common.

Mountain Snowberry, *Symphoricarpos vaccinioides,* Fig. 147; 5000–10,000; common.

STREAMSIDES OR DAMP FOREST FLOOR   Soil well developed and damp; light conditions ranging from partly sunny along some streams, lakes, or ponds to mostly shady in the forest understory.

Willows, genus *Salix,* Fig. 100; several shrubby species at all elevations; very common.

Sierra Wax Myrtle, *Myrica hartwegii;* 4000–7500.

California Hazelnut, *Corylus californica;* below 7000; common.

Western Virgin's Bower, *Clematis lingustifolia;* below 7000.

Spice Bush, *Calycanthus occidentalis,* Fig. 102; below 6000.

161. Western Azalea, *Rhododendron occidentale. Height:* 2 to 10 ft (0.6 to 3 m); deciduous; leaves elliptical, 1 to 4 inches (2.5 to 10 cm), in clusters at ends of twigs; flowers white or pinkish, with yellow tinge on upper lobe, in clusters. The western azalea is one of the showiest blooming shrubs in the Sierra, where it usually occurs along streams between 3500 and 7500 ft (1050 and 2300 m) on the west slope. Blooms May–July.

Gooseberry and Currant, genus *Ribes;* several species ranging to timberline; very common locally.

Serviceberry, *Amelanchier alnifolia;* 2500–9000; common.

Bitter Cherry, *Prunus emarginata;* 4000–9000; common.

Sierra Plum, *Prunus subcordata;* 2500–4500.

Western Chokecherry, *Prunus demissa;* 1500–7000.

Wild Roses, genus *Rosa;* several species below 7000; common.

Thimbleberry, *Rubus parviflorus;* 3000–7000; common.

Mountain Maple, *Acer glabrum;* 5000–9000.

Mountain Ash, *Sorbus sitchensis;* 7000–10,000.

Creek Dogwood, *Cornus stolonifera;* 5000–7000.

Labrador Tea, *Ledum glandulosum,* 6000–10,000; common.

Western Azalea, *Rhododendron occidentale,* Fig. 161; 3500–7500; common.

Red Mountain Heather, *Phyllodoce breweri,* Fig. 153; 6500–12,000; common.

Double Honeysuckle, *Lonicera conjugalis;* below 10,000.

Twinberry, *Lonicera involucrata;* 6000–10,000.

Red Elderberry, *Sambucus microbotrys;* 6000–11,000; common.

ROCKY HABITATS Soil development rudimentary; full sun or at most partial shade; moisture variable, ranging from damp to very dry. Includes talus slopes, open rocky or gravelly flats, and rock crevices.

Huckleberry Oak, *Quercus vaccinifolia,* Fig. 149; 5000–10,000; very common.

Bush Chinquapin, *Castanopsis sempervirens,* Fig. 150; 4000–11,000; very common.

Alpine Gooseberry, *Ribes lasianthum;* 7000–10,000.

Alpine Prickly Currant, *Ribes montigenum;* 7000–12,000; common.

Whitesquaw, *Ribes cereum;* 5000–13,000.

Sierra Plum, *Prunus subcordata;* 2500–3500.

Pinemat Manzanita, *Arctostaphylos nevadensis;* 5000–10,000; very common.

Granite Gilia, *Leptodactylon pungens;* 4000–13,000; common.

Red Elderberry, *Sambucus microbotrys;* 6000–11,000; common.

Mountain Spray (Creambush), *Holodiscus microphyllus;* 5500–11,000; common.

Forest Wildflowers and Ferns

The following wildflowers are a representative sample of some of the more common species and genera. Ferns, which are not listed elsewhere in this guide, are included here because they form a common and conspicuous element in the forest, mostly on moist ground or in rock crevices. Only the common species are listed.

DRY SHADY FOREST   Moderate to dense shade; soil well developed but often dry near the surface. Comparatively few species of wildflowers grow in this habitat. The most common and widespread species are saprophytes (see page 332).

California Indian Pink, *Silene californica*, Fig. 88; below 6000.
White-Veined Wintergreen, *Pyrola picta*, Fig. 148; below 7500; partial saprophyte.
One-Sided Wintergreen, *Pyrola secunda;* below 11,000; partial saprophyte.
Little Prince's Pine, *Chimaphila menziesii;* below 8000; saprophyte.
Western Prince's Pine, *Chimaphila occidentalis;* below 10,000; saprophyte.
Sugar Stick, *Allotropa virgata;* below 10,000; saprophyte.
Snow Plant, *Sarcodes sanguinea*, Fig. 162; below 8000; saprophyte.
Pinedrops, *Pterospora andromedea;* below 8500; saprophyte.
California Waterleaf, *Hydrophyllum occidentale;* below 9000.
Pine Woods Lousewort, *Pedicularis semibarbata;* below 11,000.
California Skullcap, *Scutellaria tuberosa;* below 7000.
Sierra Nevada Pea, *Lathyrus nevadensis;* below 7000.
Hartweg's Ginger, *Asarum hartwegii;* below 7000.
California Harebell, *Campanula prenanthoides;* below 7000.
False Solomon's Seal, *Smilacina tuberosa;* below 7000.
Washington Lily, *Lilium washingtonianum;* below 7000.
Humboldt Lily, *Lilium humboldtii;* below 7000.
Hartweg's Iris, *Iris hartwegii;* below 6000.
Rattlesnake Orchid, *Goodyear oblongifolia;* below 8000.
Spotted Coralroot, *Corallorhiza maculata;* below 9000; saprophyte.
Striped Coralroot, *Corallorhiza striata;* below 9000; saprophyte.
Heartleaf Arnica, *Arnica cordifolia;* 3500–10,000.

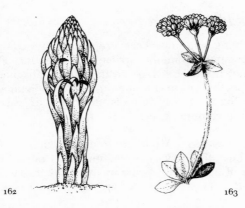

162   163

162. Snow Plant, *Sarcodes sanguinea*. Flowers reddish, small;
leaves and stem bright red; 6 to 12 inches (15 to 30 cm). The
snowplant lacks chlorophyll and is therefore incapable of photosynthesis. Instead, it obtains nutrients from decayed matter
in the forest soil. The bizarre red spike of this plant pokes through
the forest litter shortly after snowmelt; the small red flowers
bloom May–August. It occurs on shady sites, 4000 to 8000 ft (1200
to 2400 m), both slopes.

163. Sulfur-Flowered Eriogonum, *Eriogonum umbellatum*. Flowers bright sulfur-yellow, in terminal heads; leaves gray-green,
spoon-shaped; plant cushionlike with flower stems 8 to 18 in
(2 to 6 dm) tall. Sulfur-flowered eriogonum is common in dry,
rocky places, 2500 to 10,000 ft (750 to 3050 m), both slopes.
Blooms May–August, depending on elevation. Numerous other
eriogonums, or wild buckwheats, occur in similar habitats in the
Sierra. This species is among the most common and widespread. A
number of other wild buckwheats in the Sierra closely resemble
this species and can be distinguished only by carefully using a
botanical key.

OPEN FOREST   Moderate to ample sunshine, soil well developed but often dry near the surface; includes areas
cleared of trees by fire or logging.

Larkspurs, genus *Delphinium;* mostly below 9000.
Wild Peony, *Paeonia brownii;* 4000–8000.
Sidalceas, genus *Sidalcea;* below 9000.
Pine Violet, *Viola lobata;* 1000–6500.
Campions, genus *Silene;* forest species range to timberline.
Naked-Stemmed Eriogonum, *Eriogonum nudum;* below 8000.

Sulfur-Flowered Eriogonum, *Eriogonum umbellatum*, Fig. 163; 2500–10,000.

Wright's Eriogonum, *Eriogonum wrightii;* all elevations.

Common Knotweed, *Polygonum aviculare;* most communities.

Green Gentian, *Frasera speciosa;* 6500–10,000.

Waterleaf Phacelia, *Phacelia hydrophylloides;* 5000–10,000.

Pretty Nemophila, *Nemophila pulchella;* below 6000.

Showy Penstemon, *Penstemon speciosus;* 3500–8000.

Indian Paintbrush, *Castilleja applegatei,* Plate 3D (see description below); 2000–11,000.

Mountain Pennyroyal, *Monardella ordoratissima,* Fig. 143; below 11,000.

Brewer's Lupine, *Lupinus breweri;* above 4000.

Anderson's Lupine, *Lupinus andersonii;* 4000–8500.

Fireweed, *Epilobium angustifolium,* Plate 4A (see description below); below 11,000.

Bedstraw, *Galium aparine;* below 7500.

Mountain Mule's Ears, *Wyethia mollis,* Plate 8D (see description on page 478); below 10,000.

Singlestem Butterweed, *Senecio integerrimus,* var. *major;* below 11,000.

Short-Beaked Agoseris, *Agoseris glauca,* var. *monticola;* 5000–11,000.

White-Flowered Hawkweed, *Hieracium albiflorum;* below 11,000.

Brewer's Golden Aster, *Chrysopis breweri;* 4500–11,000.

Bear Grass, *Xerophyllum tenax;* below 7000.

Sierra Onion, *Allium companulatum;* 2000–9000.

FERNS

Bracken, *Pteridium aquilinum;* below 7500.

Desert Cliffbrake, *Pellaea compacta;* 4500–8500.

STREAMSIDES AND DAMP FOREST FLOOR   Soil well developed and damp; light conditions ranging from partly sunny along some streams, lakes, or ponds to mostly shady in the forest understory.

Larkspurs, genus *Delphinium;* several species below 11,000.

Columbia Monkshood, *Aconitum columbianum,* 4000–10,000.

Crimson Columbine, *Aquilegia formosa,* Plate 3B (see description below); 4000–10,000.

Plantainleaf Buttercup, *Ranunculus alismaefolius;* 4500–12,000.

Waterfall Buttercup, *Ranunculus hystriculus;* 3000–6000.

Forest Shrubs, Wildflowers, and Ferns   357

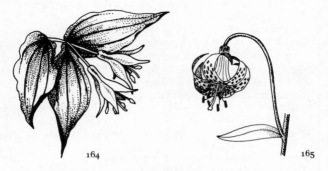

164

165

164. Hooker's Fairybell, *Disporum hookeri*. Flowers white, bell-like; leaves broadly elliptical, with parallel veins; stems arching, 12 to 32 in (3 to 8 dm). Fairly common and widespread in damp, shady areas 4000 to 8000 ft (1200 to 2400 m) on the west slope. Blooms April–July.

165. Leopard Lily, *Lilium pardalinum*. Flowers orange with darker spots, petals curved back; leaves oblong and lance-shaped, in whorls around upper portion of stem; stem 3 to 8 ft (1 to 2.5 m). The leopard lily is common in moist, springy places, below 6500 feet, where it often occurs in masses. The similar Sierra lily, *L. kelleyanum*, has fragrant flowers, unlike those of the leopard lily. The leopard lily blooms May–July.

Fendler's Meadow Rue, *Thalictrum fendleri;* 3000–10,000.
Geraniums, genus *Geranium;* below 9000.
Stream Violet, *Viola glabella;* below 8000.
MacCloskey's Violet, *Viola mackloskeyi;* 3500–11,000.
Western Dog Violet, *Viola adunca;* 5000–11,500.
Bleeding Heart, *Dicentra formosa,* Plate 3A (see description below); below 7000.
Watercresses, genus *Rorippa;* in shallow quiet streams below 10,000.
Alaska Whitlow Grass, *Draba stenoloba;* 7000–12,000.
Chamisso's Starwort, *Stellaria crispa;* below 11,000.
Miner's Lettuce, *Montia perfoliata,* Fig. 103; below 6000.
Shooting Stars, genus *Dodecatheon;* all elevations.
Sierra Nemophila, *Nemophila spatulata;* 4000–10,500.
Common Monkeyflower, *Mimulus guttatus,* Plate 2C (see description on page 234); below 10,000.
Primrose Monkeyflower, *Mimulus primuloides;* above 4000.
Scarlet Monkeyflower, *Mimulus cardinalis;* below 8000.
Speedwell, *Veronica americana;* below 12,000.
Great Red Paintbrush, *Castilleja miniata;* below 11,000.

358

White Hedge Nettle, *Stachys albens;* below 8000.
Bud Saxifrage, *Saxifraga bryophora;* 7000–11,000.
Broad-Petaled Strawberry, *Fragaria platypetala;* 4000–10,000.
Broadleaf Lupine, *Lupinus latifolius,* Plate 3C (see description below); below 7000.
Narrowleaf Lotus, *Lotus oblongifolius;* below 9000.
Hooker's Evening Primrose, *Oenothera hookeri;* below 6000.
Elk Clover, *Aralia californica;* below 7000.
California Coneflower, *Rudbeckia californica;* 5000–8000.
Arrowhead Butterweed, *Senecio triangularis;* 4000–12,000.
Hooker's Fairy Bell, *Disporum hookeri,* Fig. 164; 4000–8000.
Leopard Lily, *Lilium pardalinum,* Fig. 165; below 6000.

FERNS

Brittle Fern, *Cystopteris fragilis;* 2000–10,000.
Lady Fern, *Athyrium filix-femina;* 4000–8000+.
Bracken, *Pteridium aquilinum;* below 7500.

ROCKY HABITATS Soil development rudimentary; full sun or at most partial; moisture variable, ranging from damp to very dry. Includes talus slopes, open rocky or gravelly flats, and rock crevices.

Pasque Flower, *Anemone occidentalis;* 6000–11,000.
Mountain Violet, *Viola purpurea;* 2000–6000.
Steer's Head, *Dicentra formosa;* above 1500.
Mountain Jewel Flower, *Streptanthus tortuosus,* Fig. 123; below 12,000.
Rock Cresses, genus *Arabis;* numerous species, all elevations.
Western Wallflower, *Erysimum capitatum,* Fig. 133; below 8000.
Sierra Wallflower, *Erysimum perenne;* 7000–12,000.
Drabas, genus *Draba;* numerous species, above 7500.
Sandworts, genus *Arenaria;* several species, above 5000.
Campions, genus *Silene;* several species, below 12,000.
Pussypaws, *Calyptridium umbellatum,* Fig. 214; above 2500.
Bitterroot, *Lewisia rediviva,* Plate 4D (see description below); below 10,000.
Eriogonums, genus *Eriogonum,* Fig. 163, and Plate 7D (see description below); numerous species, all elevations.
Mountain Sorrel, *Oxyria digyna,* Fig. 222; above 8000.
Sierra Primrose, *Primula suffrutescens,* Fig. 221; above 8000.
Green Gentian, *Frasera speciosa;* 6500–10,000.
Showy Polemonium, *Polemonium pulcherrimum;* 8000–11,000.
Collomia, genus *Collomia;* several species, below 10,500.

Forest Shrubs, Wildflowers, and Ferns

166. Mountain Pride, *Penstemon newberryi*. Flowers bright pink to rose, tubular; leaves leathery, egg-shaped, with toothed margins; stems woody at base, 6 to 12 in (15 to 30 cm). Mountain pride forms a low, spreading mat over rocks on both slopes, 5000 to 11,000 ft (1500 to 3350 m). Masses of bright pink or rose flowers form one of the most conspicuous floral displays to be seen along Sierra highways. Blooms June–August.

167. Spreading Phlox, *Phlox diffusa*. Flowers, white, pink, or pale lavender; leaves needlelike, densely clustered along stems; stems prostrate and spreading, 4 to 12 in (1 to 3 dm) long. The showy flowers of spreading phlox appear shortly after snowmelt, often in masses so dense that the underlying leaves are obscured. This species forms dense, low mats in open rocky areas above 3000 ft (900 m) and is perhaps the most conspicuous late-spring or early-summer wildflower in the high country.

Spreading Phlox, *Phlox diffusa*, Fig. 167; above 3000.
Sierra Cryptantha, *Cryptantha nubigena;* 8000–12,500.
Davidson's Penstemon, *Penstemon davidsonii;* 9000–12,000.
Sierra Penstemon, *Penstemon heterodoxus;* 8000–12,000.
Mountain Pride, *Penstemon newberryi*, Fig. 166; 5000 to 11,000.
Gray Paintbrush, *Castilleja pruinosa;* below 8000.
Narrowleaf Stonecrop, *Sedum lanceolatum;* 6000–12,000.
Rosy Stonecrop, *Sedum rosea*, Plate 4C (see description below); 7500–13,000.
Brewer's Lupine, *Lupinus breweri;* above 4000.
Lotuses, genus *Lotus;* several species, below 9000.
Locoweed, genus *Astragalus;* several species, all elevations.
California Fuschia, *Zauschneria californica*, Fig. 122.
Fireweed, *Epilobium angustifolium*, Plate 4A (see description below); below 11,000.
Rock Fringe, *Epilobium obcordatum*, Plate 4B (see description below); 7000–13,000.

FOREST PLANT COMMUNITIES

Terebinth Pteryxia, *Pteryxia terebintha;* below 10,000.

Mountain Mule's Ears, *Wyethia mollis,* Plate 8D (see description on page 478); below 10,000.

Loose Daisy, *Erigeron vagus;* above 1000.

Cutleaf Daisy, *Erigeron compositus,* Plate 6D (see description on page 453); above 8000.

Hulseas, genus *Hulsea;* several species, above 6000.

Butterweeds, genus *Senecio;* several species, all elevations.

Shaggy Hawkweed, *Hieracium horridum;* 5000–11,000.

Rosy Everlasting, *Antennaria rosea;* below 12,000.

Low Everlasting, *Antennaria dimorpha;* 4500–9500.

Greenleaf Raillardella, *Raillardella scaposa,* Fig. 220; 6500–11,000.

Chaenactises, genus *Chaenactis;* several species, below 12,500.

Leichtlin's Mariposa Tulip, *Calochortus leichtlinii;* 4000–11,000.

FERNS

Brittle Fern, *Cystopteris fragilis;* below 12,000.

Licorice Fern, *Polypidium vulgare;* below 4000.

Rock Brake, *Cryptogramma acrostichoides;* 5500–12,000.

Cliff Brakes, genus *Pellaea;* several species, 4500–12,000.

Indian's Dream, *Onychium densum;* 6000–8500.

Lip Fern, *Cheilanthes gracillima;* 2500–9000.

COLOR PLATES

Plate 2C. Common Monkeyflower, *Mimulus guttatus.* Description, page 234.

Plate 3A. Bleeding Heart, *Dicentra formosa.* Flowers pale pink or purplish in drooping terminal clusters; leaves fernlike and lacy; stems 8 to 18 in (2 to 4.5 dm), leafless. Bleeding heart is found in moist, shady woodlands below 7000 ft (2150 m), blooming March–July. Golden ear drops, *D. chrysantha,* occurs in dry places below 5000 ft (1500 m); steer's head, *D. uniflora,* which is named for the distinctive shape of its flowers, frequents rocky places below 10,000 ft (3050 m).

Plate 3B. Crimson Columbine, *Aquilegia formosa.* Flowers crimson with backward-pointing hollow spurs; leaves palmshaped, 3-parted, deeply lobed; stems branching, 20 to 40 in (5 to 10 dm). The crimson columbine is commonly found near streams and seeps in partial shade or full sun. Its flower shape is distinctive, separating it from all other Sierra wildflowers except for the Alpine columbine, *A. pubescens,* which has pale yellow flowers. Alpine columbine frequents sheltered rock crevices at or above

Forest Shrubs, Wildflowers, and Ferns   361

timberline. Crimson columbine ranges from 4000 to 11,000 ft (1200 to 3350 m). Blooms May–July, depending on elevation.

Plate 3C. Broadleaf Lupine, *Lupinus latifolius*. Flowers deep blue or purple, often tinged with pink, in terminal whorls; leaves palmlike, 4 to 8 in (1 to 2 dm) long, with 5 to 12 lance-shaped leaflets; stems 20 to 60 in (5 to 15 dm). This large, showy lupine is most common in damp soils amid the forest, often near streams, seeps, or lakes and in roadside ditches that collect runoff. Numerous species of lupines occur throughout the Sierra, and some type or another is found in virtually every habitat on both slopes from the adjacent lowlands to above tree limit.

Plate 3D. Indian Paintbrush, *Castilleja applegatei*. Flowers small and inconspicuous, sheathed in showy scarlet—and sometimes partly yellow—bracts, which form dense terminal clusters; leaves lance-shaped, with wavy margins; stems 8 to 20 in (2 to 5 dm). This common paintbrush frequents dry open places to timberline. Blooms May through August, depending on elevation. Many species of paintbrush are partial root parasites of neighboring plants. Numerous species occur in various habitats throughout the Sierra (see Plates 5B and 8C).

Plate 4A. Fireweed, *Epilobium angustifolium*. Flowers pink to rose, borne in terminal spike; bottom flowers open first, terminal flowers last; 4-sided seed pods up to 3 in (7.5 cm); leaves lance-shaped, 4 to 6 in (1 to 1.5 dm), with wavy margins; stem 1½ to 6 ft (5 to 18 dm). Fireweed grows commonly along roadsides and in dry open areas within the forest. Its name refers to its being one of the first plants to reinvade recently burned sites, where it may cover large areas with masses of pink bloom. Rock fringe, *Epilobium obcordatum*, is a much smaller plant that is largely restricted to open rocky areas (See Plate 4B).

Plate 4B. Rock Fringe, *Epilobium obcordatum*. Flowers red or rose, 1 in (25 mm) or more across; leaves oval, opposite; stems to 6 in (15 cm). Rock fringe occurs in rock crevices and at the bases of boulders from 7000 to 13,000 ft (2150 to 2950 m), but is most common near tree limit. Stems often form a dense, low mat on rock surfaces. The related fireweed, *E. angustifolium*, is widespread in the Sierra on dry, open sites (see Plate 4A).

Plate 4C. Rosy Stonecrop, *Sedum rosea*. Flowers rose-red or purple, tiny, borne in terminal clusters; leaves oval, fleshy, to ½ in (13 mm), growing densely up stem; stem 2 to 6 in (5 to 15 cm). Rosy stonecrop is most common in moist rocky crevices from 7000 to 13,000 ft (2150 to 3950 m) and often occurs among wet rocks along snowmelt streams. Several other stonecrops occur in the Sierra, but none have dark red or purple flowers. Rosy stonecrop blooms June–August, depending on elevation.

Plate 4D. Bitterroot, *Lewisia rediviva*. Flowers pale pink to rose, 1 in (2.5 cm) or more long, appear prior to leaves; leaves fleshy, narrow, 1 to 2 in (2.5 to 5 cm), in basal cluster; stems leafless, 1 to 3 in (2.5 to 7.5 cm). The showy, conspicuous flowers of the bitterroot enliven dry rocky places on both slopes below 10,000 ft (3050 m). Several other species of *Lewisia* occur in the Sierra, both on rocky sites and in meadows (see Figure 215).

Plate 6D. Cutleaf Daisy, *Erigeron compositus*. Description, page 453.

Plate 8D. Mountain Mule's Ears, *Wyethia mollis*. Description, page 478.

Montane Meadows

Meadows ranging in size from plots of turf a few yards across to large open flats covering several square miles are scattered throughout the Sierra near lakes and streams, in forest openings, and on moist slopes and benches. Although meadows range from wet to dry types, as a group they occur where moisture is abundant in the upper few inches of soil at least during part of the growing season. This factor more than any other accounts for the persistence of meadows on sites that otherwise might be covered by forest (see earlier section on Meadow Invasion, this chapter). At the same time, forest trees have invaded many Sierra meadows and continue to do so.

168. Montane meadow.

Sedge and Grass

Often called "grasslands," which they superficially resemble, meadows are actually dominated by sedges of the
genus *Carex*. The sedge family, which also includes the familiar tule, or bulrush, includes some 60 genera of which
the largest, *Carex*, contains more than 1000 species. About
145 of these occur in California and nearly 100 are found in
the Sierra Nevada, mostly in meadows.

Sedge and grass look very much alike. Both have narrow,
spearlike leaves and small, often inconspicuous flowers.
Both may form dense turfs, depending on the species in-
volved. The easiest way to distinguish a sedge from a grass
is to roll the stem between the fingers. Grass stems are
round and roll easily; sedge stems are triangular and the
angles can be felt. Closer examination of the plants reveals
that grass leaves grow in ranks of two; sedge leaves, in ranks
of three. The flowers of grass and sedge resemble each
other in being clusters of tiny florets, but they also show
important structural differences. Grass florets are "perfect," that is, they contain both male and female parts.
Sedge florets, while occasionally "perfect," usually consist
either of male or female parts entirely. Moreover, a sedge
flower head may consist of male florets, female florets, or a
mixture of both. To detect these differences requires close
scrutiny with a hand lens and not a small degree of famil-
iarity with plant anatomy. If anything, the members of the
genus *Carex* are even more difficult to distinguish from one
another than they are as a group from grasses. Many of the
differences among the species are clearly visible only under
magnification, and even then may not be evident to someone without professional training.

Although sedges dominate most montane meadows,
rushes, genus *Juncus* and a variety of grasses—tufted hairgrass, *Deschampsia caespitosa*, shorthair grass, *Calamagrostis breweri*, spiked trisetum, *Trisetum spicatum*, various bluegrasses, genus *Poa*, and others—are common
associates and in some cases locally dominant. Numerous
broad-leaved herbs, along with a few shrubs, complete the
meadow flora. From late June to mid-August meadow
wildflowers provide the most spectacular displays of massed
color found in the Sierra, the hues ever shifting through the
summer as different groups of species come into flower.

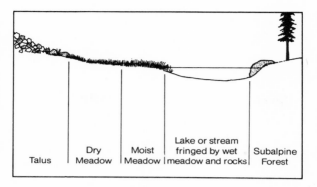

	Dry	Moist	Lake or stream fringed by wet	Subalpine
Talus	Meadow	Meadow	meadow and rocks	Forest

169. Cross section of a subalpine lakeshore, showing the gradual progression from wet meadow to talus on the left and an abrupt transition to rock and forest on the right.

Meadow Distribution

The largest meadows in the range occur on the west slope in glacially scoured basins and canyons in the subalpine zone. These vast lawns, of which Tuolumne Meadows in Yosemite National Park is the largest, are usually bordered at least in part, but sometimes entirely, by dense stands of lodgepole pine. Islands of trees may also occur on or near rock outcrops within the meadows. Willows are almost always found along meadow streams, and aspens or cottonwoods may be scattered in small groves on higher ground. Extensive meadows of this type, while fairly common on the west slope of the Sierra, are virtually absent from the east slope, where large flats are rare and moisture less plentiful. Slow soil formation limits meadow development in the alpine zone, though meadowlike turfs commonly occur in alpine lake basins, along streams, and near lingering snowbanks and seeps.

Although meadows are most numerous and extensive in the subalpine zone, they also occur downslope in the red fir and mixed coniferous forests. Their lower limit—4000 feet (1200 meters) in the northern Sierra and 6000 feet (1800 meters) in the south—roughly coincides with that of reliable winter snow cover. Farther downslope, precipitation averages less than 30 inches (75 centimeters) a year, much of it falling as rain. Snowfall is irregular and melts quickly. Numerous grassy flats known locally as "meadows" are scattered throughout the lower montane zone, but they are composed largely of drought-tolerant, winter-active foothill grasses and forbs. These plants die back by early summer, when the drought season begins, and when true montane meadows upslope, freed at last from snow cover, commence their seasons of growth. Meadow plants are geared to summer activity and therefore depend on melting snow, rather than rain, to provide adequate moisture. Unlike the valley grasslands, which are now dominated by annuals, montane meadows contain mostly perennials, which are better adapted to shorter growing seasons because they do not have to start from seed each year.

Meadow Types

Immediately after the snowpack has melted, all meadows are more or less soggy. They dry out at different rates, however, depending on the depth and texture of the soil, the slope of the terrain, and the proximity of dependable sources of moisture—lakes, streams, springs, and lingering snowbanks. Several types of meadows have been identified in the Sierra on the basis of moisture regimes and the species of plants associated with each.

WET MEADOWS These develop on sites where soil moisture is abundant throughout the growing season. They occur near lakes and streams on poorly drained soils where dependable supplies of additional water are available continuously. Water tables may even be above ground level in places, receding perhaps only in late summer, if at all. Soils consist of soggy, organic muck, high in acids and low in oxygen, a black ooze that may freeze during the winter and warms up very slowly during the summer. Few plants can withstand this rigorous environment, so certain species of sedges, rushes, and grasses have it all to themselves. Sphagnum is well adapted to such conditions but is found only in a few places in the Sierra.

Plant growth in wet meadows begins rapidly, fueled by starches stored through the winter in underground parts, then tapers off before midsummer and continues at a slower pace thereafter. Needle ice and peat hummocks commonly

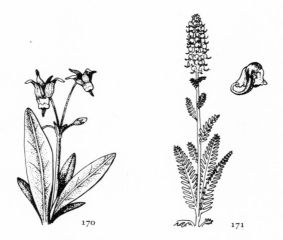

170. Subalpine Shooting Star, *Dodecatheon subalpinum*. Flowers drooping, several to a stem; 5 petals, pink to white, joined at base and folded backward to expose maroon corolla tube with yellow ring at base; leaves oblong, in basal clusters; stem 2 to 6 in (5 to 15 cm) tall. The subalpine shooting star occurs in moist places, both slopes, 7000 to 13,000 ft (2150 to 3950 m). Several other species of shooting stars occur on moist sites in the Sierra, ranging from the foothills and sagebrush slopes to above timberline.

171. Greater Elephant's Head, *Pedicularis groenlandica*. Flowers pink to deep rose, clearly resembling an elephant's head in shape, clustered at end of stem; leaves fernlike, much divided and subdivided; stem hairless, 12 to 24 in (3 to 6 dm) tall. Greater elephant's head occurs in moist to soggy soils above 6000 ft (1800 m). The similar little elephant's head, *P. attolens*, has woolly, rather than smooth, stems. It grows in similar places. Greater elephant's head blooms June–August.

develop on bare, waterlogged soils within wet meadows. Such frozen-ground phenomena occur most typically in the subalpine and alpine zones (see page 159).

MOIST MEADOWS These occur on sites where soils are moist—but not soggy—throughout the growing season, (though moist-meadow soils may be waterlogged for a week or two following snowmelt). The pace of plant activity throughout the growing season is comparable to that of wet meadows.

Moist meadows occur on well-drained, dark brown, sandy loams, usually on flats or gentle slopes near lakes and

172   173

172. Wandering Daisy, *Erigeron peregrinus*. Ray flowers pink to purple, occasionally white, numerous; disk flowers yellow; leaves narrowly oblong and lance-shaped, sprouting from basal cluster; stem to 21 in (7 dm). The wandering daisy is among the more common and widespread of the several members of the genus *Erigeron* occurring in the Sierra. It occurs in meadows on both slopes, 5500 to 11,000 (1700 to 3350 m), blooming July–September.

173. White Mountain Heather, *Cassiope mertensiana*. Low shrub, 4 to 12 in (1 to 3 dm); flowers white, ¼ inch (6 mm), bell-shaped, drooping from end of stems; leaves needlelike, ⅛ in (3 mm), tightly pressed in overlapping rows along length of stem. White mountain heather most commonly occurs in rocky crevices near timberline, where it may form a low, spreading mat. The tiny white flower bells appear July–September.

streams. These moist, friable soils support dense turfs dominated by several species of sedges, grasses, and rushes. Moist meadows support more species of plants than any other type, and during the summer successive waves of wildflowers put on the showiest displays of bloom in the Sierra. Asters, paintbrushes, irises, shooting stars, elephant heads, gentians, saxifrages, corn lilies, lupines, buttercups, cinquefoils, pussytoes, and many other kinds of wildflowers commonly occur in moist meadows from July through September. Late July and early August are the best times to witness the floral displays.

Willows commonly line streams and lakes in and around moist meadows, and several dwarf shrubs are often present within the meadows themselves, especially on higher ground or near rocks, where soils are somewhat drier. Common meadow shrubs in addition to willows include alpine laurel, *Kalmia polifolia,* var. *microphylla;* red mountain heather, *Phyllodoce breweri;* white mountain heather, *Cassiope mertensiana;* western blueberry, *Vaccinium occidentale;* and Sierra bilberry, *V. nivictum.*

DRY OR SHORTHAIR MEADOWS These are the most common and extensive type in the Sierra (Tuolumne Meadows is an example), occurring widely above 8000 feet (2450 meters) elevation on rapidly draining, gravelly soils. Shorthair sedge, *Carex exserta,* the dominant plant in the community, forms a sparse but tough, resilient, and frost-resistant sod. Shorthair grass, *Calamagrostis breweri,* which is also prominent in moist meadows, spiked trisetum, *Trisetum spicatum,* and various kinds of bluegrass, genus *Poa,* are frequent associates. On very dry sites shorthair meadows may consist of small plugs of turf scattered like islands in a sea of bare gravel. Moister areas support denser turf, as well as a large number of wildflowers.

Dry-meadow soils are usually saturated for a short period after snowmelt but drain rapidly, becoming completely dry by mid-August. As a result, most plants in dry meadows grow rapidly throughout the summer until soil aridity forces them into dormancy. Most perennial forbs flower in mid-July, set fruit by early August, and disperse their seeds by the middle of the month. Shorthair sedge follows a similar schedule. Shallow-rooted annuals grow even faster, setting flowers by the last week in June and beginning to die back three weeks later.

174. Sedge scarps on dry-meadow slopes, where the wind has blown soil away from the exposed ground in front of each tuft of sedge.

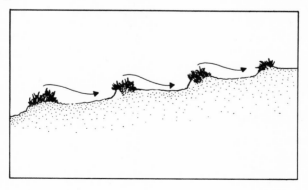

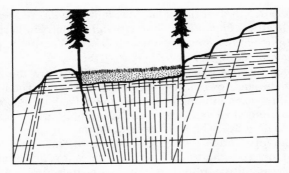

175. Cross section of a bench meadow produced by weathering in closely jointed granite. Conifers and other plants are often able to exploit rock crevices prior to meadow establishment.

WOODLAND MEADOWS These consist of several species of grasses and wildflowers beneath scattered lodgepole pines, quaking aspens, and black cottonwoods. Woodland meadows are scattered throughout the forest above 6000 feet (1800 meters) and are presumed to be transitional communities in the gradual conversion of meadow to forest.

Meadow Plants

The meadow flora comprises numerous kinds of sedges, grasses, and forbs. Few shrubs are found in the community, and except for willows, which may be fairly common along the borders of lakes and streams, meadow shrubs tend to be prostrate, widely scattered, and inconspicuous. Trees occur only incidentally during the community, mainly along its margins or in later stages of succession. Since meadows are rarely found below 6000 feet (1800 meters) or above timberline, elevations for the following species are omitted.

Meadow Sedges and Grasses

These are the dominant plants in montane meadows. Grasses and sedges can rather easily be distinguished as

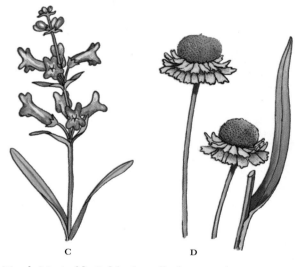

A. Marsh Marigold, *Caltha howellii* (page 373)
B. Lemmon's Paintbrush, *Castilleja lemmonii* (page 373)
C. Meadow Penstemon, *Penstemon rydbergii* (page 373)
D. Bigelow's Sneezeweed, *Helenium bigelovii* (page 374)

PLATE 5

A. Corn Lily, *Veratrum californicum* (page 374)
B. Alpine Laurel, *Kalmia polifolia*, var. *microphylla* (page 374)
C. Alpine Buttercup, *Ranunculus eschscholtzii* (page 446)
D. Cutleaf Daisy, *Erigeron compositus* (page 452)

PLATE 6

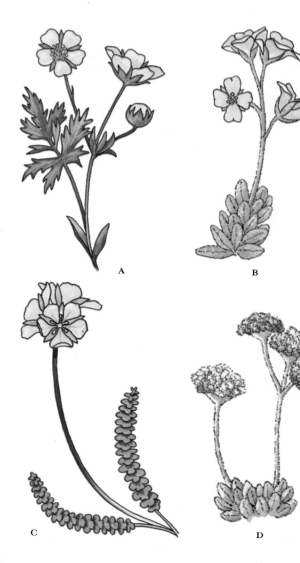

A. Drummond's Cinquefoil, *Potentilla drummondii* (page 446)
B. Lemmon's Draba, *Draba lemmonii* (page 453)
C. Club-Moss Ivesia, *Ivesia lycopodioides* (page 453)
D. Oval-Leaved Eriogonum, *Eriogonum ovalifolium* (page 453)

PLATE 7

A. Stansbury's Phlox, *Phlox stansburyi* (page 478)
B. Bridges' Penstemon, *Penstemon bridgesii* (page 478)
C. Desert Paintbrush, *Castilleja chromosa* (page 478)
D. Mountain Mule's Ears, *Wyethia mollis* (page 478)

PLATE 8

groups (see page 364), but the identification of individual species is quite difficult. The following species are among the most common.

SEDGES

Black Sedge, *Carex nigricans*.
Naked-Stemmed Sedge, *Carex gymnoclada*.
Shorthair Sedge, *Carex exserta*.
Narrowleaf Sedge, *Carex festivella*.
Brewer's Sedge, *Carex breweri*.
Alpine Sedge, *Carex subnigricans*.
Beaked Sedge, *Carex rostrata*.

GRASSES

Brewer's Shorthair Grass, *Calamagrostis breweri*.
Hairgrass, *Deschampsia caespitosa*.
Spiked Trisetum, *Trisetum spicatum*.
Squirreltail, *Sitanion hystrix*.
Hansen's Bluegrass, *Poa hanseni*.
Columbia Needlegrass, *Stipa columbiana*.
Western Needlegrass, *Stipa occidentalis*.
Alpine Fescue, *Festuca brachyphylla*.
Gray Wild Rye, *Elymus glaucus*.

Meadow Wildflowers

Dozens of species of native wildflowers are found in montane meadows, making a complete listing impossible in a book of this size and scope. The following are examples of the more common species and genera.

Marsh Marigold, *Caltha howellii*, Plate 5A (see description below).
Buttercups, genus *Ranunculus*.
Creeping Sidalcea, *Sidalcea reptans*.
Geraniums, genus *Geranium*.
Starworts, genus *Stellaria*.
Knotweeds, genus *Polygonum*.
Shooting Stars, genus *Dodecatheon*, Fig. 170.
Gentians, genus *Gentiana*.
Hiker's Gentian, *Gentianopsis simplex*.
Monkeyflowers, genus *Mimulus*.
Blue-Eyed Mary, *Collinsia torreyi*.

Meadow Plants 371

176. Leichtlin's Camas, *Camassia leichtlinii*. Flowers pale blue to violet, consisting of 3 petals and 3 sepals that look almost identical, in terminal cluster; leaves linear; stem leafless, 1 to 3 ft (3 to 9 dm) tall. This member of the lily family is common in moist meadows below 10,000 ft (3050 m), blooming June–August. The similar common camas, *C. quamash*, which may occur alongside, can be distinguished by its asymetrical flowers, which consist of 5 horizontal or upright sepals and petals and 1 drooping one. Those of Leichtlin's camas are symmetrical.

Sierra Penstemon, *Penstemon heterodoxus.*
Meadow Penstemon, *Penstemon rydbergii*, Plate 5C (see description below).
Little Elephant's Head, *Pedicularis attolens.*
Greater Elephant's Head, *Pedicularis groenlandica*, Fig. 171.
Lemmon's Paintbrush, *Castilleja lemmonii*, Plate 5B (see description below).
Brewer's Paintbrush, *Castilleja breweri.*
Bud Saxifrage, *Saxifraga bryophora.*
Grass of Parnassus, *Parnassia palustris.*
Slender Cinquefoil, *Potentilla gracilis.*
Drummond's Cinquefoil, *Potentilla drummondii.*
Sierra Lupine, *Lupinus confertus.*
Coville's Lupine, *Lupinus covillei.*
Carpet Clover, *Trifolium monanthum.*
Nuttall's Gayophytum, *Gayophytum nuttallii.*
California Valerian, *Valeriana capitata.*
Anderson's Alpine Aster, *Aster alpigenus*, var. *andersonii.*
Wandering Daisy, *Erigeron peregrinus*, Fig. 172.
Bigelow's Sneezeweed, *Helenium bigelovii*, Plate 5D (see description below).
Sierra Butterweed, *Senecio scorzonella.*
Camas (Quamash), *Camassia quamash.*

Leichtlin's Camas, *Camassia leichtlinii*, Fig. 176.
Death Camas, *Zigadenus venenosus*.
Corn Lily (False Hellebore), *Veratrum californicum*, Plate 6A
(see description below).
Swamp Onion, *Allium validum*.
Western Blue Flag, *Iris missouriensis*.

Meadow Shrubs

The following are the only shrubs consistently found in
Sierran montane meadows.

Willows, genus *Salix;* several low or dwarfed species; difficult
to distinguish.
Bush Cinquefoil, *Potentilla fruticosa*.
Alpine Laurel, *Kalmia polifolia*, var. *microphylla*, Plate 6B (see
description below).
Sierra Bilberry, *Vaccinium nivictum*.
Western Blueberry, *Vaccinium occidentale*.
White Mountain Heather, *Cassiope mertensiana*, Fig. 173.

COLOR PLATES

Plate 5A. Marsh Marigold, *Caltha howellii*. Flowers white or
cream colored, one per stem; leaves fleshy and round or kidney
shaped, growing in dense basal cluster; stems 4 to 12 in (1 to 3
dm). The marsh marigold is a harbinger of spring, appearing in
wet ground immediately following snowmelt, 4000 to 11,000 ft
(1200 to 3350 m). Blooms May–July, depending on elevation.

Plate 5B. Lemmon's Paintbrush, *Castilleja lemmoni*. Flowers
purplish, inconspicuous among larger purplish-red bracts; leaves
narrow, 1 to 2 in (2.5 to 5 cm), sometimes divided; stems 4 to 8 in
(1 to 2 dm). The most common and widespread paintbrush in
moist meadows. Numerous other species of paintbrush are found
both in meadows and other habitats throughout the Sierra (see
Plates 3D and 8C). Blooms July–August. 7000 to 12,000 ft (2150
to 3650 meters).

Plate 5C. Meadow Penstemon, *Penstemon rydbergii*. Flowers
reddish or bluish purple, tubular, arranged in whorls on upper
portion of stem; leaves linear, bright green mostly in basal cluster;
stem 4 to 28 inches (1 to 7 dm). The meadow penstemon is most
common in damp areas within meadows, blooming May–August,
depending on elevation. The very similar Sierra penstemon, *Penstemon heterodoxus*, prefers drier meadow margins. Leaves are
deeper green than those of the meadow penstemon. Flowers are

less densely clustered and rather sticky (the best identifying characteristic). Stems are only 4 to 8 inches tall (1 to 2 dm). Numerous other species of penstemon are found throughout the Sierra, especially on rock outcrops and dry open areas (see Fig. 166 and Plate 8B).

Plate 5D. Bigelow's Sneezeweed, *Helenium bigelovii*. Like other members of the sunflower family (*Compositae*), has composite flower heads consisting of central disc flowers and radiating petal-like ray flowers. Disc flowers burnt gold or brownish, arranged in dense, domelike cluster; ray flowers yellow and numerous around central disc; leaves lance-shaped, growing alternately on stem; stems single or in clump, 1 to 3 ft (3 to 9 dm). Common in damp places in mid-elevation meadows, blooming June–August. 3000 to 10,000 ft (900 to 3050 m). The similar subalpine sneezeweed, *Helenium hoopesii*, ranges higher—7500 to 11,000 ft (2300 to 3350 m)—blooming immediately after snowmelt and later where moisture persists. Its ray flowers are orange rather than yellow.

Plate 6A. Corn Lily (False Hellebore), *Veratrum californicum*. Flowers small white 6-petaled stars in numerous, densely clustered terminal spikes; leaves 6 to 12 in (1.5 to 3 dm) long and 4 to 8 in (1 to 2 dm) wide, oval with pointed tips and parallel veins; numerous and densely clustered on stem; stem 3 to 6 feet (1 to 2 m). The corn lily, which often occurs in dense clusters of several plants, is one of the most common and easily the most conspicuous wildflower in Sierra meadows and other open damp places. In late spring and early summer its shoots can be seen poking through the snow surface. Blooms June–August in meadows below 11,000 ft (3350 m).

Plate 6B. Alpine Laurel, *Kalmia polifolia*, var. *microphylla*. Flowers bowl-shaped, pink to rose-colored, less than 1 in (2.5 cm), in terminal clusters; leaves narrow and oblong with edges often rolled back; stems woody, prostrate, and spreading. The alpine laurel is common in boggy places within meadows above 6500 ft (2000 m), where it blooms June–August. It is the western, high-country cousin of the mountain laurel, *K. latifolia*, a large shrub common to eastern mountain forests.

FOREST BELT ANIMALS

WITHIN the Sierra forest belt extensive stands of conifers dominate a vegetation mosaic in which rocky areas, meadows, and streams or lakes may be locally important elements. In the upper montane and subalpine zones, in fact, these other elements often are more widespread than the forest itself. Each element in the mosaic provides different sorts of opportunities for obtaining food and shelter, which accounts in part for the numerous kinds of animals found in the Sierra forest belt.

A few animals are rather closely restricted to a single type of habitat: the dipper to streams, for example, or the pika to rockslides. At the other extreme, some species—notably the mule deer and most large predators—are truly cosmopolitan and range throughout the forest belt wherever food is to be found. Most forest animals fall somewhere between these two extremes, preferring one type of habitat but making frequent forays, mostly for food, into adjacent ones.

Lowland and Montane Animals

In terms of elevational distribution, the majority of forest-belt animals fall into two broad groups: lowland species and montane species. Montane animals are seldom found away from high mountains and in the Sierra are more or less restricted to the upper montane and subalpine zones. Lowland animals frequent lower mountain slopes and adjacent valleys and in the Sierra are largely confined to the lower montane zone and adjacent foothill or pinyon–sagebrush zones. In effect, these two groups divide the forest belt between them. Most montane animals reach their lower limit somewhere between 6000 and 7000 feet (1800 and 2150 meters) on the west slope of the central Sierra (somewhat lower to the north and higher to the south and on the east slope). Conversely, few lowland species range much above this elevation.

The various factors governing the upper or lower range limits of individual animal species vary from one to the next (see Elevational Ranges, Chapter IV). But the fact that so many species of animals—and plants too—reach their up-slope or downslope limits within this thousand-foot belt suggests that it reflects a rather profound environmental shift.

Among the several environmental factors that change with elevation, the one that undergoes the greatest shift between 6000 and 7000 feet is snowfall. Above this belt, snow accounts for the majority of precipitation and forms a deep, persistent cover from late autumn to early summer. Below 6000 feet, snowfall is lighter and more sporadic. The snowpack is often rather shallow and patchy. Intermittent rains and periods of relative warmth cause rapid melting, and many areas in the lower montane zone may be free of snow for much or most of the winter. The role of heavy snow cover in limiting the upward range of the gray squirrel has been discussed at some length (see Elevational Ranges, Chapter IV). Snow probably inhibits the ranges of other lowland animals in comparable ways.

Meadows and open rocky areas become increasingly prominent elements in the forest mosaic above 6000 feet, and animals more or less dependent on such habitats are scarce or absent below this elevation. The prevalence of both rocks and meadows in the upper forest can be traced ultimately to the action of Pleistocene glaciers (see Chapter II), which extended below 6000 feet only in a few river canyons (such as Yosemite Valley).

Many lowland animals have ecological counterparts at higher elevations. Some examples were given in Chapter IV; others include the valley pocket gopher in the foothill and lower montane zones, the mountain pocket gopher above; Swainson's thrush below 6500 feet (2000 meters), the hermit thrush above; and the purple finch in the lower forest, Cassin's finch in the upper. Each form is better adapted to conditions in its own zone or zones and in some cases may restrict the upslope or downslope range of its counterpart.

Many animals do not fall neatly into these two broad categories and may be found within the forest at virtually any elevation, though not necessarily during all seasons of the year. The mule deer, bighorn, and several species of birds, for example, are seasonal migrants that move upslope in the spring and downslope in the fall. The black bear roams wherever there is food to be found, though it is most common at middle elevations. The deer mouse occurs in all Sierra life zones except the alpine, though three closely related species have more restricted ranges. The dipper is found along swift, rocky streams on both slopes from lowland canyons to timberline—and occasionally above. Many forest birds, including the mountain chickadee, mountain quail, calliope hummingbird, hairy woodpecker, whiteheaded woodpecker, Steller's jay, western tanager, and dark-eyed junco, occur in both the upper and lower montane zones and in some cases the subalpine zone as well.

Animal Life in the Mixed Coniferous Forest

The mixed coniferous forest, which dominates the lower montane zone (see Figure 61), provides a congenial environment for animals. Well-developed stands are fairly open, contain several types of trees—broadleaf types as well as conifers—and have a well-developed understory of herbs and shrubs. Such stands provide food and shelter in great abundance and variety and therefore can accommodate substantial populations of many different kinds of animals. Grassy forest openings, outcrops, and streamsides scattered through the forest provide additional opportunities for food and shelter and attract still other animals.

The climate, too, is congenial. Though summers are nearly as hot as in the foothills, cover is ample and moisture somewhat more available, largely in the form of an increasing number of tributary streams draining higher parts of the range. Winters are milder than at higher elevations and, as discussed above, snow is for the most part neither deep nor persistent. Spring arrives earlier in the year than in the upper forest zones, and autumn lasts longer.

Seasonal Activities

Winter is still the most difficult time of year for animals in the mixed coniferous forest, but it is less stressful than at higher elevations. Plant food is normally more plentiful, and shallow, intermittent snow cover in many places makes obtaining food somewhat easier. Animals spending winters in the lower montane zone may require fewer calories than their counterparts upslope because warmer air temperatures in the lower forest may reduce the rate at which body heat is lost.

Plant foods available in the mixed coniferous forest during the winter include conifer seeds from several species of trees, acorns, bark, conifer needles, the leaves of numerous kinds of evergreen shrubs, and berries provided by these same plants. These feed such winter-active animals as the gray squirrel, northern flying squirrel, deer mouse, dusky-footed wood rat, bushy-tailed wood rat, and American porcupine, which subsists on bark alone during the winter. Berries are especially important to the mountain quail and the Townsend solitaire, a rather small gray thrush that spends summers at higher elevations and moves into the lower montane zone during the winter. Loose bands of mountain chickadees, golden-crowned kinglets, brown creepers, and both white- and red-breasted nuthatches forage for overwintering grubs and dormant adult insects found among trees and shrubbery. The white-headed and hairy woodpeckers subsist, as they do in the summer, largely on insects in and beneath the bark of trees.

Animal activity in the lower montane zone begins to pick up in early spring. In some years snow may have largely disappeared by this time from the lower portion of the mixed coniferous forest, and tender young grasses and plant shoots may begin to appear for the first time in months. Mule deer move into the forest from their winter ranges downslope in the foothill and pinyon–sagebrush zones. Black bears, ground squirrels, chipmunks, snakes, lizards, toads, frogs, and salamanders emerge from their winter sleeping quarters to feed on fresh green vegetation, newly active insects, or in some cases on one another. Resident birds set about establishing breeding territories and choos-

378   FOREST BELT ANIMALS

ing mates, joined from mid-April through early June by more than two dozen migratory species.

Most animals bear their young in early summer, when food is most abundant. A notable exception is the black bear, whose young are born during the winter and emerge in spring with their mothers to learn the ways of foraging and survival. Mule deer mate in late autumn and early winter, but the fawns are not born until June, when food and cover are abundant. After the fawns are able to fend for themselves, some deer wander upslope in search of browse. The animal population of the mixed coniferous forest reaches a peak in late June, at which time losses in predation are outweighed by increases in recently born young.

By late summer, migratory birds throughout the forest belt begin to depart for winter quarters, though some from the lower montane zone may wander upslope for a time before heading southward. Hibernating rodents often remain active until the first heavy snows, and some black bears may still be prowling about come the new year. Autumn and early winter also see the arrival of birds moving downslope from the upper forest zones—species such as the mountain quail, golden-crowned kinglet, red-breasted nuthatch, and Townsend's solitaire.

Seed Eaters

Opportunities for food and shelter in the mixed coniferous forest are comparable to those in the foothill woodland, but with one important addition: several species of conifers. The seeds of pines, incense cedar, white fir, and giant sequoia are an important element in the diets of numerous birds and mammals, including the gray squirrel, California ground squirrel, deer mouse, dusky-footed and bushy-tailed wood rats, Steller's jay, and the red crossbill. The latter is a rather uncommon and irregularly distributed finch whose crossed upper and lower mandibles allow it to pry pine seeds from their protective cone bracts.

The chipping sparrow, a summer visitor to the forest, and the dark-eyed junco, a year-round resident and the most abundant bird in the Sierra, both feed on smaller plant seeds found among the forest litter. Both commonly frequent campgrounds, where they also forage for tidbits left by campers and picnickers. Chipmunks also gather large quantities of seeds, as well as other foods, from the forest floor, and since they forage during the day, these small rodents are among the most familiar and conspicuous forest residents. Deer mice and wood rats are also common, but they forage mostly at night.

Omnivores

The raucous, crested Steller's jay is also a frequent campsite visitor. It feeds on a variety of plant and animal matter, including eggs and young birds, which it ranges from treetops to forest floor to obtain. Other forest omnivores include the raccoon, which is most common near streamsides, two species of skunk—the striped and spotted—and the familiar, indeed somewhat notorious, black bear. The black bear's diet is just about as catholic as that of humans, and what the latter carry with them into the woods the former often relishes. Numerous visitors to Sierra campgrounds, particularly those in the national parks, have been rudely surprised by bears ambling into camp during the day to help themselves to lunch. Frequent nighttime raids by "camp bears" are perhaps the most common cause of insomnia and consternation among Sierra campers. Wild bears, which have had little contact with humans, are normally rather shy, and one must be counted fortunate to see a black bear in the backcountry.

Insect Eaters

Insects and other invertebrates form the major part of the diet of the ensatina, a common salamander of the forest floor, Gilbert's skink, the northern alligator lizard, and numerous species of birds. The most common lizard on rock outcrops is the western fence lizard, also an insect eater, which is conspicuous for its bright blue sides and belly. Males often perform a rapid series of push-ups upon the approach of intruders, including humans.

Several species of woodpeckers occur in the mixed coniferous forest, most of them ranging into the upper montane zone as well. The most conspicuous is probably the
common white-headed woodpecker, which can readily be
distinguished from all other woodpeckers by its completely
white head. Most woodpeckers feed largely on insects obtained by boring into trees. A notable exception is the
yellow-bellied sapsucker, which as its name implies feeds
on sap, largely that of willows, cottonwoods, aspens, and
oaks, but also pines and incense cedars on occasion. It obtains the sap by drilling a ring of holes around the trunk of a
tree, which "bleeds" as a result. The sapsucker also eats
small flying insects that happen to become stuck in the sap.
In the upper montane and subalpine zones, Williamson's
sapsucker does the same thing but prefers lodgepole pines,
perhaps the most common and widespread tree in the
upper forests. As elsewhere throughout the Sierra, abandoned nesting cavities drilled by woodpeckers in dead
limbs or snags provide an important source of nesting sites
for numerous other species of birds.

ECOLOGICAL SEGREGATION AMONG WARBLERS
The several species of warblers found in the mixed coniferous forest—insect eaters all—have often been cited as particularly good examples of ecological segregation by foraging behavior and habitat. Each species forages in a different
part of the forest.

Orange-crowned warbler—brush in open woods
Nashville warbler—foliage of oaks or maples
Yellow warbler—streamside deciduous trees
Yellow-rumped warbler—outer foliage of conifers
Black-throated gray warbler—upper foliage of canyon oaks
Hermit warbler—middle portion of firs and pines
MacGillivray's warbler—dense, low shrubbery in damp areas
Wilson's warbler—shrubbery near lakes and streams

The birds are not restricted solely to these foraging
areas, of course, and some overlapping occurs; but by
largely confining their foraging activities to different places
these species on the whole avoid competing with each other
for food.

177. Long-tailed weasel tracks.   178. Badger tracks.

Predators

Most of the large predators common to the foothill zone range upslope into the mixed coniferous forest. The gray fox and bobcat reach the upper limits of their ranges at from 6000 to 7000 feet (1800 to 2150 meters). The mountain lion ranges somewhat higher, but is even less common in the upper forest than elsewhere in the Sierra. The red-tailed hawk, great horned owl, American badger, and coyote all commonly occur in the lower montane zone.

In addition to the above species, several predators not found at lower elevations occur in the forest belt. Most are largely confined to the upper forest, but the long-tailed weasel ranges everywhere from the foothills to timberline. It is a voracious predator of small rodents and to a lesser extent of birds and their eggs. The weasel hunts both day and night, and along with the great horned owl it is one of the two most important instruments of rodent control in the Sierra.

Snakes also take a large number of rodents, as well as lizards, frogs, toads, birds, and in some cases, other snakes. Common foothill snakes such as the western rattlesnake, gopher snake, and common king snake all range into the lower montane zone. In addition, several snakes scarce or absent at lower elevations range through the mixed coniferous forest. Two of the most common are the California mountain king snake and the rubber boa.

The mountain king snake is boldly patterned with alternating red, black, and pale yellow rings along the entire length of its body, leading some observers to mistake it for the poisonous coral snake, which does not occur either in the Sierra or the rest of California. The mountain king

FOREST BELT ANIMALS

snake is completely harmless to humans. It is perhaps most commonly seen basking on sunny rocks near the banks of streams, where it forages for rodents, lizards, young birds, and other snakes.

The rubber boa, which somewhat resembles a huge earthworm, frequents forested areas where the soil is loose enough to permit burrowing. Though seldom seen, the rubber boa is rather common. It feeds mostly on rodents and lizards, which it kills by constriction. This snake's unusual appearance is effected by its small eyes, which make its head and tail difficult to tell apart, and by its loose, tiny-scaled skin.

Mixed Coniferous Forest Residents

The following species live in the mixed coniferous forest the year around. Residents more commonly found in the upper forest communities are listed separately on page 392. Habitats are indicated only for species characteristic of streamsides, forest openings, or other special areas. Habitats are not indicated for wide-ranging species or for those characteristic of wooded areas. Asterisks after some entries refer to further discussion in Selected Forest Animals. Species described in detail in other chapters are so noted.

AMPHIBIANS

Ensatina, *Ensatina eschscholtzi.**
Western Toad, *Bufo boreas;* moist grassy openings.
Pacific Treefrog, *Hyla regilla;* streamsides.

REPTILES

Western Fence Lizard, *Sceloporus occidentalis;* rocky areas.*
Gilbert's Skink, *Eumeces gilberti.* See Selected Foothill Animals.
Western Whiptail, *Chemidophorus tigris;* dry openings.
Northern Alligator Lizard, *Gerrhonotus coeruleus.*
Rubber Boa, *Charina bottae.**
Racer, *Coluber constrictor.*
Gopher Snake, *Pituophis catenifer.*

California Mountain King Snake, *Lampropeltis zonata;* streamsides.*

Garter Snakes, genus *Thamnophis;* streamsides, moist areas.

Western Rattlesnake, *Crotalus viridis.* See Selected Foothill Animals.

BIRDS

Sharp-Shinned Hawk, *Accipiter striatus.*

Cooper's Hawk, *Accipiter cooperii.*

Red-Tailed Hawk, *Buteo jamaicensis.* See Selected Foothill Animals.

Great Horned Owl, *Bubo virginianus.**

Pygmy Owl, *Glaucidium gnoma.*

Long-Eared Owl, *Asio otus;* streamsides.

Belted Kingfisher, *Megaceryle alcyon;* streamsides.

Common Flicker, *Colaptes auratus.*

Acorn Woodpecker, *Melanerpes formicivorus,* Fig. 112; among oaks. See Selected Foothill Animals.

Hairy Woodpecker, *Dendrocopus villosus.*

White-Headed Woodpecker, *Dendrocopus albolarvatus,* Fig. 185.*

Stellar's Jay, *Cyanocitta stelleri,* Fig. 186.*

Mountain Chickadee, *Parus gambeli,* Fig. 188.*

Brown Creeper, *Certhia familiaris.*

Dipper, *Cinclus mexicanus,* Fig. 189; streamsides.*

Brewer's Blackbird, *Euphagus cyanocephalus.*

Dark-Eyed Junco, *Junco hyemalis.**

MAMMALS

Trowbridge Shrew, *Sorex trowbridgii.*

Broad-Handed Mole, *Scapanus latimanus.*

Bats, order *Chiroptera.*

California Ground Squirrel, *Otospermophilus beecheyi.* See Selected Foothill Animals.

Chipmunks, genus *Eutamias,* Fig. 196.*

Gray Squirrel, *Sciurus griseus.* See Selected Foothill Animals.

Northern Flying Squirrel, *Glaucomys sabrinus.*

Pocket Gophers, genus *Thomomys;* open, grassy areas.

Deer Mouse, *Peromyscus maniculatus,* Fig. 179.*

Dusky-Footed Wood Rat, *Neotoma fuscipes.* See Selected Foothill Animals.

Porcupine, *Erethizon dorsatum,* Fig. 203.*

Gray Fox, *Urocyon cinereoargenteus,* Fig. 117. See Selected Foothill Animals.

Coyote, *Canis latrans,* Figs. 204 and 205.*

Black Bear, *Eurarctos americanus*, Figs. 206 and 207.*

Raccoon, *Procyon lotor*, Fig. 118; streamsides. See Selected Foothill Animals.

Ringtail, *Bassariscus astutus*, Fig. 119. See Selected Foothill Animals.

Long-Tailed Weasel, *Mustela frenata*, Fig. 177.

Spotted Skunk, *Spilogale putorius*.

Striped Skunk, *Mephitis mephitis*, Fig. 110.*

Mountain Lion, *Felis concolor*, Fig. 209.*

Bobcat, *Lynx rufus*, Fig. 120. See Selected Foothill Animals.

Mule Deer, *Odocoileus hemionus*, Figs. 210 and 211.*

Mixed Coniferous Forest Visitors: Migratory Birds

The following species are summer visitors to the mixed coniferous forest, where they nest and rear their young.

Blue Grouse, *Dendragapus obscurus*, Fig. 184.*

Mountain Quail, *Oreortyx pictus*.

Spotted Sandpiper, *Actitus macularia*; streamsides.

Band-Tailed Pigeon, *Columba fasciata*.

Poor-Will, *Phalaenoptilis nuttallii*.

White-Throated Swift, *Aeronautes saxatalis*.

Calliope Hummingbird, *Stellula calliope*.

Yellow-Bellied Sapsucker, *Sphyrapicus varius*.

Willow Flycatcher, *Empidonax trailii*; streamsides.

Western Flycatcher, *Empidonax difficilis*.

Western Wood Peewee, *Cantopus sordidulus*.

Olive-Sided Flycatcher, *Nuttallornis borealis*.

Violet-green Swallow, *Tachycinetta thalassina*.

American Robin, *Turdus migratorius*.

Swainson's Thrush, *Catharus ustulatus*; streamsides.

Solitary Vireo, *Vireo solitarius*; oak–conifer stands.

Warbling Vireo, *Vireo gilvus*; streamsides.

Nashville Warbler, *Vermivora ruficapilla*; deciduous trees.

Yellow Warbler, *Dendroica petechia*; streamsides.

Yellow-Rumped Warbler, *Dendroica coronata*, Fig. 191.*

Black-Throated Gray Warbler, *Dendroica nigrescens*.

Hermit-Warbler, *Dendroica occidentalis*.

MacGillivray's Warbler, *Oporornis tolmiei*; damp areas in shrubs.

Wilson's Warbler, *Wilsonia pusilla*; vegetation near streams, lakes, and meadows.

Western Tanager, *Piranga ludoviciana*, Fig. 192.*

Animal Life in the Mixed Coniferous Forest

Black-Headed Grosbeak, *Pheucticus melanocephalus*.
Purple Finch, *Carpodacus purpureus*.
Pine Siskin, *Spinus pinus*.
Chipping Sparrow, *Spizella passerina*.

Animal Life in the
Upper Forest Communities

The upper forest communities include the red fir forest, lodgepole pine forest, and subalpine forest. They are here considered as a group because in the main they offer comparable animal habitats and are therefore frequented by many of the same animal species. The differences among the communities with regard to animal habitats are largely a matter of degree rather than kind, and this less often affects the kinds of species occurring in each community than it does the numbers present of those many species they contain in common.

In the upper montane and subalpine zones meadows and open, rocky areas are an important and often dominant element in the forest mosaic. A few animals are more or less restricted to rocky areas or meadows, but in general it is difficult to talk about the fauna of these areas separately from that of forest stands, with which they often intermingle. Most animals in the upper montane and subalpine zones range through all three major habitats, if only occasionally in some cases.

The greater part of the upper-forest fauna consists of montane species, along with a smaller number—notably mule deer, black bear (which is most abundant in the upper montane zone), long-tailed weasel, coyote, and several types of forest birds—also commonly found at lower elevations. Some, like the black bear, which prefers rather extensive forest, become increasingly uncommon toward timberline (though black bear are by no means absent from the subalpine zone, as numerous backpackers can attest).

Birds common to both the upper and lower forest zones include the blue grouse, mountain quail, great horned owl, Steller's jay, mountain chickadee, brown creeper, and dark-eyed junco. Several of these species become rather scarce in the subalpine forest, though not necessarily for the same reasons. Mountain quail, for example, require shrubby cover, which is sparse in the subalpine zone. The brown creeper, which spirals up tree trunks in search of insects, prefers rather dense stands of tall conifers, which are scarce near timberline. In both cases, of course, other factors may also help set their upper range limits. The Steller's jay is replaced in the subalpine zone by its relative, the Clark's nutcracker, whose ecological role and overall behavior is similar.

Clark's nutcracker is one of several birds largely confined to the upper forests. Others include Williamson's sapsucker, the black-backed three-toed woodpecker, hermit thrush, mountain bluebird, pine grosbeak and Cassin's finch. A few of these wander downslope during the winter, even into adjacent lowlands, but the upper forests constitute their primary summer range.

Seasonal Activities

Animals remaining in the upper forest zones during the winter—and this accounts for the majority—must contend with food shortages resulting from the region's deep persistent snowcover. The various ways which upper-forest animals have contrived to endure the long snowy winters have already been discussed in some detail (see page 196). In brief, some animals hibernate, some den up with food supplies stored during the late summer and autumn, and some remain active but switch to such foods as bark or conifer needles that remain plentiful during the winter. Predators feed largely on the various small birds and rodents that remain active all year long.

Spring is a brief and ephemeral season in the upper forest zones, for even though the weather becomes warmer and less stormy after mid-March, snow remains on the ground until mid-June through mid-July. Food continues to remain scarce during the spring months, becoming more plentiful only as vegetation begins growth on snow-free areas. Because open meadows are free of snow long before the shady forest, they are especially important sources of food during the late spring and early summer.

Summers are short and begin somewhat later than in the lower montane zone, but foods are plentiful during the four or five snow-free months. Meadows remain green for much or all of the season, depending on available moisture, and provide forage not only for numerous small rodents, but to a lesser degree also for mule deer ranging upslope following the birth of their young. Late in the summer the berries of such shrubs as the several species of snowberry, elderberry, gooseberry, and currant are an important source of food for certain birds and mammals.

Migratory birds begin to leave their nesting grounds in the upper forest zones by the end of summer, wandering southward along the crest of the range, where food and water are then more abundant than in the adjacent lowlands. Mule deer and bighorns also move downslope in autumn to winter ranges. Deer winter in the foothill and pinyon–sagebrush zones. The comparatively few bighorns remaining in the Sierra all wander down the east side of the range to spend their winters in the sagebrush scrub.

Forest Foragers

Forest stands in the upper montane zone often consist of a single tree species, either red fir or lodgepole pine, depending on soil and moisture. Such stands are typically dense, monotonous, and lacking in understory vegetation. Available plant food, therefore, is neither abundant nor various, so relatively few species are present. Among the most frequently seen is Cassin's finch, a small rosy-breasted sparrowlike bird that is the upslope counterpart of the purple finch of the lower montane zone. The pine grosbeak, a larger reddish finch, is also a regular resident in such stands, though in far fewer numbers. Most upper-forest animals prefer open woods adjacent to rocky areas and meadows, varied habitats that provide abundant food during the summer months. Such stands often include Jeffrey pines, mountain hemlocks, and western white pines in addition to lodgepole pines and/or red firs.

As in the lower montane zone, conifer seeds are an important food source for several upper-forest animals, including the chickaree, northern flying squirrel, lodgepole chipmunk, golden-mantled ground squirrel, bushy-tailed

179. Deer Mouse, *Peromyscus maniculatus.*

wood rat, pine grosbeak, and Clark's nutcracker. The chickaree, like its lowland counterpart, the gray squirrel, spends much of its time snipping cones from pines and firs and then racing down trees to retrieve them on the ground. It stashes part of them in piles for use during the winter but eats the majority on the spot. The golden-mantled ground squirrel and the various chipmunks occurring in the upper forests have special cheek pouches for storing seeds and other food. They carry stashes to their dens for use during the following spring, when they emerge from hibernation, and for occasional midwinter snacks upon temporarily awakening from their torpid state.

The most abundant small rodent, as elsewhere in the Sierra, is the deer mouse, which prefers open forest near rocks and meadows, where debris litters the forest floor and both shrubs and herbs are plentiful. Such habitats provide the deer mouse with cover and nesting sites as well as the green shoots, seeds, and berries on which it feeds. Most visitors seldom see the deer mouse, for it is strictly nocturnal, but many campers have heard it rustling outside their tents. The larger bushy-tailed wood rat prefers rocky areas in the forest and like the deer mouse is nocturnal. The wood rat also visits campsites and may carry off a shiny object that has not been put away for the night, perhaps leaving in its place a small rock or some other object. The bushy-tailed wood rat belongs to the same genus as the pack rats of the desert and shares their penchant for midnight barter.

Meadows and Rocky Places

Meadows and rocky places host several kinds of animals that are less common or absent in dense forest stands.

Those that do range into the forest are less conspicuous there and are most often seen in the open. In the subalpine zone, where the forest becomes sparse, open places constitute the primary habitat.

Clark's nutcracker most commonly occurs in high, open basins with scattered timber, where it feeds mostly on the seeds of whitebark pine, the principal subalpine tree through much of the Sierra. In this habitat it is often joined by the gray-crowned rosy finch, which feeds on smaller seeds as well as insects. Rarely occurring below 10,000 feet (3050 meters) in the summer, the rosy finch is one of the few species to range into the alpine zone. It is often seen near lingering patches of snow searching for stunned insects, but also visits lake margins and timberline meadows on occasion.

Many of the bird species nesting in the upper forests choose sites near meadows, where they spend a good deal of time foraging for food. Even the yellow-rumped warbler, for example, which nests and forages in the tops of conifers, frequently visits meadows to hunt for insects among the shrubby willows bordering streams and lakes. The dark-eyed junco, which primarily forages for seeds on the forest floor, also visits meadows to feed on the seeds of herbaceous plants.

The white-crowned sparrow and mountain bluebird feed almost exclusively in meadows. The white-crown breeds either in trees or shrubs at the meadow's edge or in willows within the meadow. The mountain bluebird nests in abandoned woodpecker holes in low trees adjacent to meadows, where it forages for insects, often hovering on rapidly beating wings in the manner of its lowland cousin, the western bluebird. It also feeds on flying insects among the low conifers growing along meadow–forest borders. The American robin also nests near meadows or other open areas, where it hunts for earthworms and other invertebrates in the same fashion as it does in suburban gardens.

The most conspicuous meadow mammal in most parts of the High Sierra is Belding's ground squirrel, also called the "picket pin" for its habit of standing bolt upright next to its burrow openings. These rather small, grayish brown ground squirrels are especially numerous in Tuolumne Meadows in Yosemite National Park, but are widely scattered in meadows throughout the central and northern Sierra. Like the California ground squirrel in the foothill grassland, Belding's ground squirrel relies on burrows for cover, as do other meadow rodents, such as the mountain pocket gopher, long-tailed vole, and montane vole. Small meadow rodents subsist primarily on green herbage and plant seeds.

The yellow-bellied marmot also feeds primarily on meadow vegetation, but dens in adjacent rock piles, which provide excellent cover from most predators. It often shares its rocky habitat with the pika, a small member of the rabbit clan that rarely occurs elsewhere, and the bushy-tailed wood rat, the upslope counterpart of the dusky-footed wood rat of the foothill and lower montane zones. The marmot and pika are rather shy animals, but because of their habit of perching on lookout rocks during the day, they are among the more conspicuous mammals of the subalpine zone. The bushy-tailed wood rat builds a nest of twigs either beneath boulder piles or inside hollow logs, the latter being less common near timberline, more so downslope in the forest. It spends the day sleeping in its nest, emerging to forage only after dark.

Predators

Above 6000 feet (1800 meters) several predators common at lower elevations become scarce or absent. These include the gray fox, American badger, mountain lion, bobcat, and all snakes but the garter snakes, which commonly frequent moist meadows and the margins of lakes and streams. The coyote, long-tailed weasel, red-tailed hawk, and great horned owl, however, range upslope to timberline or above. The black bear may also be considered a predator since it does from time to time take small rodents, lizards, nestlings, and even an occasional sick or young deer, but it is essentially an omnivore and eats great quantitites of vegetable matter of all kinds. Its hunting—if it can even be called that—is largely opportunistic. Given the chance, it won't hesitate to feast on meat, but it rarely goes out of its way to obtain it.

The upper forests also contain several predators not

180. Fisher tracks.   181. Wolverine tracks.

found at lower elevations. The most important of these in terms of numbers and its effect on rodent populations is the pine marten, a cat-sized member of the weasel family. During the summer the marten commonly frequents open forest adjacent to rockslides and meadows, where rodents are abundant. Its great speed and agility make it one of the most efficient predators in the forest. During the summer it may wander upslope to timberline, but it keeps to denser forest during the winter. There, its great agility in the treetops allows it to chase down chickarees.

The fisher, a larger cousin of the marten, is present in small numbers in the upper forest. It was formerly more common, but was widely hunted for its excellent fur. The fisher is even swifter and more agile than the marten, which it has been known to capture in the treetops. The fisher is also the only animal known to specialize in the capture and consumption of porcupines, which are seldom preyed upon by other large predators.

The wolverine, the largest and most indomitable member of the weasel family is also a scarce hunter of open rocky areas near and above timberline. Rather common in the far north, the wolverine is rare anywhere in the contiguous United States, and the High Sierra from Lake Tahoe south is one of its last refuges.

Upper Forest Residents

The following species live in the red fir forest, lodgepole pine forest, or subalpine forest the year around. Residents more commonly found in the mixed coniferous forest are not included. Habitats are indicated only for species characteristic of meadows or rocky places. Habitats are not indicated for wide-ranging species or for those characteristic of wooded areas. Asterisks after some entries refer to further discussion in Selected Forest Animals. Species described in detail in other chapters are so noted.

AMPHIBIANS

Long-Tailed Salamander, *Ambystoma macrodactylum;* ponds, streams, open forest.
Mt. Lyell Salamander, *Hydromantes platycephalus;* under rocks.
Western Toad, *Bufo boreas;* moist areas and meadows.
Yosemite Toad, *Bufo canorus;* moist areas and meadows.*
Pacific Treefrog, *Hyla regilla.*
Mountain Yellow-Legged Frog. *Rana mucosa.* Fig. 183; streams and lakes.*

REPTILES

Sagebrush Lizard, *Sceloporus graciosus;* open forest near rocks and brush.
Western Fence Lizard, *Sceloporus occidentalis;* rocky areas.*
Northern Alligator Lizard, *Gerrhonotus coeruleus.*
Garter Snakes, genus *Thamnophis,* moist areas and meadows.

BIRDS

Goshawk, *Accipiter gentilis;* uncommon.
Sharp-Shinned Hawk, *Accipiter striatus.*
Red-Tailed Hawk, *Buteo jamaicensis.* See Selected Foothill Animals.
Blue Grouse, *Dendragapus obscurus,* Fig. 184.*
Great Horned Owl, *Bubo virginianus.**
Belted Kingfisher, *Megaceryle alcyon;* streams and lakes.
Common Flicker, *Colaptes auratus.* See Selected Foothill Animals.
Pileated Woodpecker, *Drycopus pileatus.*
Black-Backed Three-Toed Woodpecker, *Picoides arcticus;* uncommon.
Williamson's Sapsucker, *Sphyrapicus thyroideus.*
Hairy Woodpecker, *Dendrocopus villosus.*
Steller's Jay, *Cyanocitta stelleri,* Fig. 186.*
Clark's Nutcracker, *Nucifraga columbiana,* Fig. 187.*
Mountain Chickadee, *Parus gambeli,* Fig. 188.*
Red-Breasted Nuthatch, *Sitta carolinensis.*
Brown Creeper, *Certhia familiaris.*
Dipper, *Cinclus mexicanus,* Fig. 189; streamsides.*

Cassin's Finch, *Carpodacus cassinnii*.*
Pine Grosbeak, *Pinicola enucleator;* uncommon.
Gray-Crowned Rosy Finch, *Leucosticte tephrocotis*, Fig. 223.
See Alpine Animals.
Dark-Eyed Junco, *Junco hyemalis*.*

MAMMALS

Shrews, genus *Sorex*, Fig. 193.*
Broad-Handed Mole, *Scapanus latimanus*.
Bats, order *Chiroptera*.
White-Tailed Jackrabbit, *Lepus townsendii*.
Pika, *Ochotona princeps*, Fig. 194; rocky areas.*
Mountain Beaver, *Aplodontia rufa*, Fig. 182; streamsides.
Yellow-Bellied Marmot, *Marmota flaviventris*, Fig. 197; rocky
areas and meadows.*
Belding Ground Squirrel, *Citellus beldingi;* meadows.
Sierra Nevada Golden-Mantled Ground Squirrel,
Callospermophilus lateralis, Fig. 195.*
Chipmunks, genus *Eutamias*, Fig. 196.*
Chickaree, *Tamiasciurus douglasii*, Figs. 199 and 200.*
Northern Flying Squirrel, *Glaucomys sabrinus*.
Pocket Gophers, genus *Thomomys;* meadows.
Deer Mouse, *Peromyscus maniculatus*, Fig. 179.
Bushy-Tailed Wood Rat, *Neotoma fuscipes*, Fig. 201; rocky
areas.*
Voles, genus *Microtus*, Fig. 202.*
Porcupine, *Erethizon dorsatum*, Fig. 203.*
Coyote, *Canis latrans*, Figs. 204 and 205.*
Red Fox, *Vulpes fulva;* rare.
Black Bear, *Eurarctos americanus*, Figs. 206 and 207.
Long-Tailed Weasel, *Mustela frenata*, Fig. 177.
Ermine, *Mustela erminea;* rare.
Pine Marten, *Martes americana*, Fig. 208.
Fisher, *Martes pennanti*, Fig. 180; rare.
Wolverine, *Gulo luscus*, Fig. 181; rare.
Badger, *Taxidea taxus*, Fig. 178.
Mule Deer, *Odocoileus hemionus*, Figs. 210 and 211.*
Sierra Bighorn, *Ovis canadensis*, Figs. 239 and 240. See
Selected Pinyon–Sagebrush Animals

182. Mountain beaver tracks.

Upper Forest Visitors: Migratory Birds

The following species are summer visitors to the red fir forest, lodgepole pine forest, and subalpine forest, where they nest and rear their young.

Common Merganser, *Mergus merganser;* lakes.
Mountain Quail, *Oreotyx pictus.*
Spotted Sandpiper, *Actitus macularia;* stream and lake borders.
Calliope Hummingbird, *Stellula calliope.*
Hammond's Flycatcher, *Empidonax hammondii.*
Dusky Flycatcher, *Empidonax oberholseri;* montane chaparral.
Western Wood Peewee, *Cantopus sordidulus.*
Olive-Sided Flycatcher, *Nuttallornis borealis.*
American Robin, *Turdus migratorius.*
Hermit Thrush, *Catharus guttatus,* Fig. 190.*
Mountain Bluebird, *Sialia currocoides,*
Townsend Solitaire, *Myadestes townsendii.*
Golden-Crowned Kinglet, *Regulus satrapa.*
Ruby-Crowned Kinglet, *Regulus calendula.*
Yellow-Rumped Warbler, *Dendroica coronata,* Fig. 191.*
Hermit Warbler, *Dendroica occidentalis.*
Wilson's Warbler, *Wilsonia pusilla;* streamsides, lakesides, meadows.
Brewer's Blackbird, *Euphagus cyanocephalus.*
Western Tanager, *Piranga ludoviciana,* Fig. 192.*
Pine Siskin, *Spinus pinus.*
Green-Tailed Towhee, *Chlorura chlorura.* See Selected Pinyon–Sagebrush Animals.
Vesper Sparrow, *Pooecetes gramineus.*
Chipping Sparrow, *Spizella passerina.*
White-Crowned Sparrow, *Zonotrichia leucophrys.*
Fox Sparrow, *Passerella iliaca;* montane chaparral.
Lincoln Sparrow, *Melospiza lincolnii.*

Selected Forest Animals

A description of every species of animal occurring in the Sierra forest belt is obviously impossible in a book of this scope and size. The criteria used in making the following selection are discussed in the introduction to this guide.

Amphibians

Ensatina, *Ensatina eschscholtzi.* Length 1½ to 3 in (4 to 8 cm). *Color:* orange spots on darker background; in central Sierra foothills, mostly below 6000 ft (1800 m), individuals may be mostly brownish orange with few or no spots. *Food:* earthworms, sowbugs, centipedes, spiders, insects, etc. *Habitat:* damp woodland or forest, with abundant litter and rotting logs, often near streams. *Distribution:* lower montane and foothill zones, west slope. The ensatina is often found beneath rotting logs. If disturbed, it may arch its back and thrash its tail. Strictly terrestrial, it does not even enter water to breed. Eggs are laid on land in late winter or spring. The female surrounds them with her body to keep them moist and protect them from other animals. Ensatinas in the Sierra are active April through September.

Yosemite Toad, *Bufo canorus. Length:* 1¾ to 3 in (4.5 to 8 cm); female larger than male. *Color: female*—many large black blotches on gray or greenish background; *male*—yellow-green to dark olive with only a few small blotches. *Food:* insects, spiders, other invertebrates. *Habitat:* moist meadows near streams, lakes, snowmelt ponds. *Distribution:* central Sierra, from just north of Ebbetts Pass south to Evolution Basin, 6000 to 11,000 ft (1800 to 3350 m); elsewhere it is replaced by the western toad, whose range it overlaps only at Blue Lakes, in Alpine County. Most of the year Yosemite toads hibernate in burrows beneath the snowpack, emerging April through June, when meadows are soggy with meltwater. Males congregate near ephemeral snowmelt ponds or other quiet waters and sing to attract females, which are far fewer in number. The song is a long melodious trill consisting of 10 to 20 notes. Unlike toads at lower elevations, which sing mostly at night, the Yosemite toad sings in broad daylight because nights are too cold in the high country for toads to be abroad. Where toads are numerous the singing males may sound like a chorus of birds. Breeding commences immediately after snowmelt, and the young tadpoles grow rapidly. They tend to congregate in warm shallows, and their black color absorbs light and heat readily. If summers are warm, the tadpoles will metamorphose into adult toads the same season. If summers are cool, tadpoles in ephemeral pools may die,

183. Mountain Yellow-Legged Frog, *Rana mucosa.*

before reaching adulthood, and those in lake shallows or quiet streams may overwinter beneath the ice, changing to adults the following summer.

Mountain Yellow-Legged Frog, *Rana mucosa.* Fig. 183. *Length:* 2 to 3¼ in (5 to 8 cm). *Color:* brown with darker spots above; yellow to orange below. *Food:* insects and other invertebrates. *Habitat:* margins of lakes and streams, often bordered by meadows. *Distribution:* Lake Tahoe to Mt. Whitney, 7000 to 11,500 ft (2150 to 3500 m). Approaching the shoreline of a subalpine lake, one is frequently greeted with a rapid series of *kerplops* as mountain yellow-legged frogs leave their damp shoreline seats for the relative safety of the water. They are difficult to spot against the rocks and debris of lake bottoms, where they will sit patiently, waiting for intruders to leave. They breed from June through August; tadpoles overwinter beneath ice-covered lakes and transform into adult frogs the following year. Adults hibernate in lake-bottom mud.

Reptiles

Western Fence Lizard, *Sceloporus occidentalis.* *Length:* 2½ to 3½ in (6 to 9 cm). *Color:* dark brown, gray, or blackish above; throat and sides of belly, blue; whitish to yellowish below; insides of hind legs distinctly yellowish; resembles sagebrush lizard, which is more whitish below, has rusty spots on flanks, and has smoother scales. *Food:* insects, spiders, and other invertebrates. *Habitat:* rock outcrops and open, dry areas. *Distribution:* entire Sierra, both slopes to 10,000 ft (3050 m). Active from April to October, depending on elevation, the western fence lizard spends most of its time on rock outcrops, where it may be easily seen. Males often display their blue throats during courtship and perhaps to drive off other males. This lizard has the somewhat comical habit of doing push-ups. The young hatch between July and September and along with adults spend the winter hibernating below ground or in rotting logs.

Rubber Boa, *Charina bottae. Length:* 14 to 30 in (3.5 to 7.5 dm). *Color:* dull greenish or yellowish brown. *Food:* small mammals and lizards, which it kills by constriction. *Habitat:* forested areas, especially where soils are loose enough for burrowing. *Distribution:* montane zone to about 9000 ft (2700 m). The rubber boa is a rather lethargic, harmless snake that resembles a huge worm. Its tail and head are similar in shape, and its small eyes—a feature typical of burrowing animals—often make it difficult to distinguish the two ends at first glance. The rubber boa is seldom seen, but may be more common than once supposed, owing to its retiring habits. Completely unaggressive, it does not bite even when handled and seldom attempts to escape. Occasionally, it may roll itself into a tight ball when picked up.

California Mountain King Snake, *Lampropeltis zonata. Length:* 20 to 40 in (5 to 10 dm). *Color:* red, white, and black bands, usually completely encircling snake for entire length of body; black bands alternate with red and white; nose, black; some specimens in the central Sierra may lack red bands. *Food:* lizards, snakes, young birds, small mammals; kills its prey by constriction. *Habitat:* moist forest, often near rocks or brush; often found along rocky streams littered with fallen timber. *Distribution:* mostly lower montane zone, a few ranging somewhat higher. This snake resembles the poisonous coral snake of the southern United States, but it is completely harmless and under no circumstances should be molested. Being rather uncommon and somewhat secretive, it is seldom seen.

Birds

Abbreviations used in the following descriptions: R = year-around resident; SV = summer visitor breeding in the forest.

Blue Grouse, *Dendragapus obscurus.* Fig. 184. *Length:* 15½ to 21 in (4 to 5 dm). *Color:* dusky gray, finely mottled; light yellow spot above each eye; light band at tip of tail. *Eggs:* 5 to 10. *Nest:* lined depression on ground among cover of shrubs, young trees, or forest debris. *Food:* chiefly needles of pines and firs; some berries in summer. *Distribution:* R to 11,000 ft (3350 m), especially in fir forests. The blue grouse winters in the upper montane zone, mostly in red firs, where it spends the season feeding on needles. In June blue grouse move downslope to mate. Males sit high in conifers and attempt to attract a mate through hooting, or "booming," after which they spread their tails, hold them erect, and strut about on their high perches. The deep, sonorous hoot of the male is produced by inflating air sacs in the throat. After mating, males move upslope in bands; females and young follow a few weeks later. Though quite common, the dark mottled plumage and retiring habits of blue grouse make them difficult to spot.

Great Horned Owl, *Bubo virginianus. Length:* 18 to 25 in (4.5 to 6 dm). *Color:* dark and light brown; back streaked, breast and belly barred; large yellow eyes and white throat; large ear tufts, or "horns"; much larger than similar long-eared owl. *Eggs:* 2 to 3. *Nest:* tree cavities, rock ledges, deserted hawk or magpie nests. *Food:* rodents, rabbits, snakes, lizards, squirrels, birds, even larger prey; owl pellets—small balls of undigested matter regurgitated after a meal—have shown that the great horned owl regularly takes skunks; pellets have also included remains of bobcats, raccoons, foxes, and even red-tailed hawks. *Distribution:* widespread and common R to timberline. The great horned owl is primarily nocturnal, resting during the day in trees. The deep *hoo hu-hoo hoo hoo* call, commonly heard at night, but sometimes on overcast days as well, is well-known and distinctive. Great horned owls patrol well-defined hunting territories from which others of their kind are usually excluded. The hoots may serve to announce territorial occupation.

184. Blue Grouse, *Dendragapus obscurus.*

White-Headed Woodpecker, *Dendrocopus albolarva-*
tus. Fig. 185. *Length:* 8 to 10 in (20 to 25 cm). *Color:* black
with white head and wing patches. *Eggs:* 3 to 7. *Nest:* hole,
often in dead tree. *Food:* insects and their larvae. *Distribu-*
tion: common R, conifer forest, lower montane zone and
lower margins of upper montane zone. The white-headed
woodpecker is unmistakable, for no other Sierra woodpecker
has a white head. It is rather common in the mixed coniferous forest and often may be seen foraging on the lower
trunk and branches of pines and firs, though it also ranges
higher up. The white-headed woodpecker is very common
along trails and in campgrounds in Yosemite Valley.

Stellar's Jay, *Cyanocitta stelleri.* Fig. 186. *Length:* 12 to
13½ in (30 to 34 cm). *Color:* head, crest, back, and breast,
black; wings, belly, rump, and tail, deep blue; tail lightly
barred. *Eggs:* 3 to 5. *Nest:* bowl of twigs, rootlets, and mud
lined with softer materials; placed in conifers. *Food:* seeds,
acorns, berries, insects, eggs, small birds and rodents. *Dis-*
tribution: common R, conifer forests of montane zones. Steller's jay is the most conspicuous, if not the most common,
bird in the Sierra forest, boldly venturing into camps to
feed on scraps, hopping from limb to limb through the
trees, uttering its harsh cry continually, except when nesting.

Clark's Nutcracker, *Nucifraga columbiana.* Fig. 187.
Length: 12 to 13 in (30 to 33 cm). *Color:* gray, with black and
white wings and tail; beak, black. *Eggs:* 2 to 4. *Nest:* bowl
of twigs and bark in conifers. *Food:* the nuts of the whitebark pine are its favorite food; also those of singleleaf pinyon
during the winter; seeds, insects, carrion, small birds. *Dis-*
tribution: common R above 9000 ft (2700 m); prefers open
subalpine slopes and basins with scattered timber. Clark's
nutcracker is the large, noisy gray and black bird of timberline, and anyone who has visited the High Sierra has surely
seen it. During the summer the nutcracker's raucous
kraaaaaa is often the only sound heard at timberline.
Breeding occurs in March and April, when snow is still
deep. The young are fed through late May, but continue to
harass their parents for food well into midsummer.

Mountain Chickadee, *Parus gambeli.* Fig. 188. *Length:*
5 to 5¾ in (13 to 15 cm). *Color:* top and back of head, chin
and throat, and stripe through eye, black; cheeks, stripe

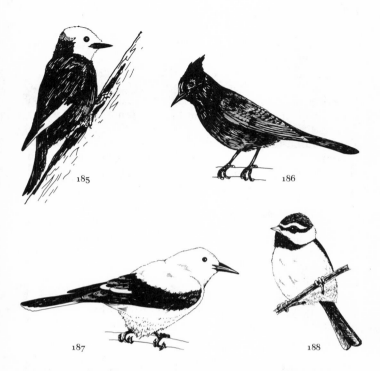

185. White-Headed Woodpecker, *Dendrocopus albolarvatus*.
186. Steller's Jay, *Cyanocitta stelleri*.
187. Clark's Nutcracker, *Nucifraga columbiana*.
188. Mountain Chickadee, *Parus gambeli*.

over eye, and breast, white; body, gray. *Eggs:* 7 to 9. *Nest:* lined with hair and feathers, usually in old woodpecker hole. *Food:* mostly insects gleaned from the outer branches of conifers; snips open lodgepole-pine needles to obtain larvae of needle-miner moths within. *Distribution:* common R, forest, both slopes to timberline; often in open forest and near meadows. The mountain chickadee is one of the most common and conspicuous forest birds. It is frequently observed as it forages among the outermost tips of lower conifer branches. Like other chickadees, it is an acrobatic feeder, often hanging upside-down as it forages. The mountain chickadee is bold and active, entering campsites to feed on scraps of bacon fat or other tidbits. In winter it wanders widely in large, loose flocks that may also include nut-hatches, kinglets, and creepers.

Dipper, *Cinclus mexicanus.* Fig. 189. *Length:* 7 to 8½ in (18 to 22 cm). *Color:* dark gray. *Eggs:* 3 to 6. *Nest:* ball of moss placed among rocks near enough to rushing stream that spray keeps the moss moist and green; often behind water-falls and cascades. *Food:* insects and other invertebrates along and on the bottom of streams. *Distribution:* common R, both slopes, along streams and sometimes lakes from 2000 ft (600 m) to timberline. The dipper, or water ouzel, spends all of its time near water. When flying it follows the streamcourse rather than taking shortcuts. The dipper for-ages among streamside rocks, in shallow water, or even on the bottoms of streams. Its dense feathers shed water read-ily. Its name is derived from the habit of bobbing up and down when perched on streamside rocks. The dipper re-mains at high elevations in the winter wherever open water is available.

Hermit Thrush, *Catharus guttatus.* Fig. 190. *Length:* 6 to 7 in (15 to 18 cm). *Color:* head and back, brown; chin and breast, whitish with brown speckles; rump and tail, red-dish brown. *Eggs:* 3 to 5. *Nest:* cup of twigs, mosses, shred-ded bark in low tree. *Food:* mainly insects on the ground—ants, caterpillars, beetles, spiders, etc. *Distribu-tion:* common SV, mainly upper montane and subalpine zones, both slopes; a different population winters in the western foothills and Central Valley. The hermit thrush is considered by many people to be the finest singer among North American birds. During the spring and early sum-mer the males sing throughout much of the day, repeatedly proclaiming their nesting territories to others of their kind. Later in summer, when mating and nesting have been completed, they become much less vocal. The song consists of three or four haunting, flutelike passages of varying pitch, each preceded by a long falling note and followed by a distinct pause.

Mountain Bluebird, *Sialia currucoides. Length:* 7 to 7¾ in (18 to 19 cm). *Color: male* —bright turquoise blue above; pale blue-gray below; *female*—brownish above with touches of blue on wings, rump, and tail; whitish below. *Eggs:* 4 to 8. *Nest:* old woodpecker holes or other cavities in trees. *Food:* insects, especially grasshoppers and crickets,

190

189

189. Dipper, *Cinclus mexicanus.*
190. Hermit Thrush, *Catharus guttatus.*

make up 90 percent of the mountain bluebird's diet. *Distribution:* common SV, subalpine meadows and bordering forest. In the summer the mountain bluebird seldom ventures far from meadows and commonly perches on young lodgepole pines at their borders. It hovers above the turf looking for grasshoppers and other insects and also catches flying insects on the wing.

Yellow-Rumped Warbler (Audubon's Warbler), *Dendroica coronata.* Fig. 191. *Length:* 4¾ to 5¼ in (12 to 13 cm). *Color: male in summer*—head, blue-gray with yellow patches on crown and chin; back, blue-gray with darker streaks; breast and sides, black; belly, white; yellow on rump and shoulders; tail, dark gray; *male in winter*— brownish above, white with faint brown streaks below; touches of yellow on rump, chin, and shoulders; *female*— in summer similar to male, but breast mottled with black and white; indistinguishable from male in winter. *Eggs:* 3 to 5. *Nest:* feather-lined cup of twigs and bark in conifers. *Food:* small insects, mostly obtained in the outer branches of conifers; sometimes flutters in air capturing flying insects; occasionally forages on the ground. *Distribution:* common SV, coniferous forest and adjacent meadows and brush to timberline; WV, lower elevations on west slope. This is the largest and most common Sierra warbler, often seen among the lower branches of pines and firs, particularly when it ventures into camps.

Selected Forest Animals

191. Yellow-Rumped (Audubon's) Warbler, *Dendroica coronata*.
192. Western Tanager, *Piranga ludoviciana*.

Western Tanager, *Piranga ludoviciana*. Fig. 192.
Length: 6¾ to 7¾ in (17 to 20 cm). *Color: male* —bright yellow with red head and throat and black wings and tail; *female* —yellowish green. *Eggs:* 3 to 5. *Nest:* lined saucer of needles, twigs, stems, etc., placed on limbs of conifers amidst dense foliage. *Food:* insects supplemented in late summer by berries. *Distribution:* common SV, montane zone of west slope; less common on east slope. The male western tanager ranks with the northern oriole of the foothill zone as one of the most strikingly colored Sierra birds. Nevertheless, the tanager is often difficult to spot among the foliage, where it forages for insects.

Cassin's Finch, *Carpodacus cassinnii*. *Length:* 6½ to 7 in (17 to 18 cm). *Color: male* —rump and breast, pale pink; crown, bright crimson; nape of neck and back, brown with darker streaks; wings and tail, brown; belly, white; larger and rosier than the house finch of the foothills; separated from the similar purple finch of the lower montane zone by the clear separation between the red crown and brown neck of the Cassin's finch; *female* —similar to house finch and purple finch: back, wings, tail, and head brown; breast and belly, whitish with numerous brown streaks. *Eggs:* 4 to 5. *Nest:* cup of grass, twigs, stems, etc., in horizontal branch of pine. *Food:* new buds, wild fruits, seeds, some insects. *Distribution:* common R, upper montane and subalpine zones, especially in open lodgepole pine forests; some downslope movement in winter. Cassin's finch is one of three similar red finches found in the Sierra. The purple finch occurs in the lower montane zone and the house finch in the western foothills.

Dark-Eyed Junco (Oregon Junco), *Junco hyemalis*. *Length:* 5½ to 6 in (14 to 15 cm). *Color:* head, neck, and upper breast, black; lower breast and belly, white, often with buffy sides; back, reddish brown; rump, brown; tail, black with white outer feathers; females similar, but head gray. *Eggs:* 4 to 5. *Nest:* lined cup of fine grasses and moss in depression in ground. *Food:* mostly seeds found on the forest floor. *Distribution:* abundant SV, conifer forests and adjacent meadows and brushy areas to timberline, both slopes; WV, lower elevations. During the summer, this small, boldly patterned sparrow is the most common bird in the Sierra and is frequently seen around campsites foraging in the forest litter.

White-Crowned Sparrow, *Zonotrichia leucophrys*. *Length:* 5¾ to 7 in (15 to 18 cm). *Color:* brown above with gray streaks on back; chin, throat, and breast, gray; belly whitish; two white bars on each wing; black and white stripes on crown; on immature birds, crown stripes are brown and gray. *Eggs:* 3 to 5. *Nest:* cup of twigs, rootlets, and sedges and grasses placed on ground among dense shrubbery or higher up in clumps of willows. *Food: summer*—meadow insects primarily; *winter*—mostly seeds. *Distribution:* very common SV, subalpine meadows; WV, lower elevations, both slopes, mostly below snowline. The conspicuous black-and-white crown of this species is diagnostic. It is seldom seen away from willow thickets in meadows during the summer but wanders widely at lower elevations in winter. Its song—a plaintive series of slurred whistles followed by a husky trill—may be heard at all hours of the day and well into the evening. Males may sing during the night.

Mammals

Shrews, genus *Sorex*

Seven species of shrews are found in the Sierra, all but two of which—the ornate shrew of the western foothills and Merriam's shrew of the pinyon–sagebrush zone—frequent the forest belt. Although shrews are fairly common in the Sierra and are often active during the day, they are seldom seen, being the smallest of mammals and easily hidden even in dense swards of grass and sedge. Moreover, even if one is lucky enough to see a shrew, identification will prove difficult, for there is little in either their appearance or habits to distinguish them. The sole exception in this regard is the water shrew, which can readily be identified by its aquatic habits. The following data applies to shrews as a group and is not intended as a guide for distinguishing the several species.

Head and body: 1½ to 3 in (4 to 8 cm). *Tail:* 1½ to 3¼ in (4 to 9 cm). *Color:* various shades of brown and gray; water shrew, black. *Litter:* 2 to 9, spring; may breed twice a year. *Food:* insects, earthworms, other invertebrates, mice, some vegetable matter. *Enemies:* most predators avoid shrews; owls may take some. *Habitat:* moist meadows, swards, streamsides; some are found in drier areas. *Distribution:* all zones but alpine.

1. **Dusky Shrew,** *Sorex obscurus.* Fig. 193. Moist meadows and turfs in the upper montane and subalpine zones. Color: rusty brown above, ashy gray below.

2. **Vagrant Shrew,** *Sorex vagrans.* Moist meadows in upper montane and subalpine zones. Color: grayish to reddish brown above; grayish or reddish below.

3. **Water Shrew,** *Sorex palustris.* Streamsides and lakesides in montane and subalpine zones. Color: black with gray hairs above; whitish tinged with brown below. This is the largest shrew, occasionally ranging to 6 in (15 cm) from tip of nose to end of tail. It is the only shrew that may be seen swimming in lakes or streams. Aquatic insects make up the largest portion of its diet; also tadpoles and minnows. The water shrew may occasionally fall victim to large trout. The shrew is ingeniously equipped for life in the water. Its thick fur prevents water from reaching the animal's skin. A fringe of stiff hairs on the hind feet serve as flippers while swimming. Water shrews have been observed skittering across the *surface* of a pool and even tapping bubbles of air while swimming. The dark upper side of the shrew renders it inconspicuous to predators overhead; its pale underside, to large trout below. Eyesight seems to

193. Dusky Shrew, *Sorex obscurus.*

play little part in navigation underwater. Some other sense organ seems to allow the water shrew to pursue its prey with assurance.

4. **Mount Lyell Shrew,** *Sorex lyelli.* Rare resident in meadows or beneath streamside shrubs in subalpine zone of the central Sierra. Color: olive-brown above; gray below.

5. **Trowbridge Shrew,** *Sorex trowbridgii.* Meadows; also litter of forest floor. Color: light to dark brown all over.

Shrews are so small that they must eat almost constantly in order to avoid death through loss of body heat (see Animal Mobility, Chapter IV). When they are not hunting or eating they are sleeping in order to conserve energy. The water shrew has 1½-hour activity cycles: a half hour of feeding followed by an hour of deep sleep. The dusky shrew hunts three times a day: once in the early morning, when insects, still dazed from the cold night, begin to crawl up plant stems to warm up in the sun; again after dusk, when termites and other nocturnal insects appear in great numbers; and a final time in the coldest hours of the morning, when insects are still inactive. In other words, periods of frenzied hunting are keyed to times of the day when insects and other high-calorie foods can be obtained most easily. Since shrews must eat every two to three hours, dozens of insects are captured and stunned for use throughout the long intervening periods of rest. Some shrews have poisonous saliva for this purpose. The home range of a dusky shrew is about 4000 sq ft (370 sq m), and though two neighboring shrews fight viciously when they meet, their home ranges often overlap. As many as 11 shrews have been found in a single area less than an acre in size. Shrews do not hibernate, but subsist during the winter on insect larvae and other invertebrates. An occasional mouse may also supplement their diet. Shrews seldom live more than 18 months, and many fail to survive even the first winter.

Pika, *Ochotona princeps.* Fig. 194. *Head and body:* 6½ to 8½ in (17 to 22 cm); no visible tail. *Color:* buffy gray to brown, ears tipped with white. *Litter:* 3 to 4, May to September. *Nest:* lined chambers in rockslides. *Food:* grasses, sedges, various herbs, tender shoots of red elderberry, creambush, and other shrubs found among boulders and talus. *Enemies:* primarily pine martens and weasels. *Hab-*

194. Pika, *Ochotona princeps.*

itat: rockslides. *Sign:* small, round droppings on rocks, white urine streaks; large piles of cut vegetation. *Distribution:* 7700 ft (2350 m) to above timberline; most common in the subalpine zone.

Although the pika resembles a small rodent, particularly with its round mouselike ears, it is actually a distant cousin of rabbits and hares. Its small size and drab coloring make the pika difficult to spot among the rockslides it inhabits. Moreover, it is usually quite wary of humans and quickly scurries for cover at their approach. Consequently, pikas are more often heard than seen. Their call consists of a high-pitched nasal bark that seems extraordinarily loud for such a small animal. When a predator approaches a rockslide the entire colony of pikas will set up quite a racket as each animal sounds the alarm.

Pikas spend much of their time beneath rockslides, where they build their nests, rear their young, and pass the winter. They seldom venture far beyond the rocks even to forage. During the day pikas often perch on protected rock shelves that serve as lookout posts. These are liberally marked with abundant pellets, like those of rabbits, as well as by white urine streaks. Pikas usually wait for the morning to warm up before emerging for the day and disappear in the afternoon if temperatures drop as a result of cloudiness. Pikas do not hibernate, but remain active in their rocky lairs throughout the winter, feeding on hay gathered and cured the previous summer and autumn. Small "haystacks" of various herbaceous plants are placed on rocky shelves out of the sun and protected from moisture. As they cure, these plant clippings retain their color and moisture and have the fresh sweet smell of real hay. Pikas usually hole up for the winter beginning in late October or early

FOREST BELT ANIMALS

November, when the first lasting snow arrives. They emerge late the following spring or early summer after snow has melted and the weather has warmed up.

Belding Ground Squirrel, *Citellus beldingi. Head and body:* 7½ to 9 in (19 to 23 cm). *Tail:* 2½ to 3 in (6 to 7 cm). *Color:* brown or gray above; buff on sides and belly; bottom of tail reddish. *Litter:* 8, early summer. *Nest:* lined chambers in burrows. *Food:* primarily grasses and sedges. *Enemies:* badgers, coyotes, foxes, weasels, hawks, and eagles. *Habitat:* grassland and meadows. *Sign:* burrows in meadows. *Distribution:* central Sierra, 6500 ft (2000 m) to timberline from Tahoe region south to Kings Canyon National Park.

Although Belding ground squirrels form loose colonies of sorts, each animal occupies its own burrow, and a good deal of scolding and squabbling commonly goes on among neighbors. A favorite prey of badgers and coyotes, the Belding ground squirrel is ever alert, frequently standing on its hind legs to survey the surrounding terrain, a habit that has earned it the affectionate name "picket pin." At any given time a number of these squirrels can be seen standing upright in subalpine meadows, uttering a series of high shrill whistles at the first sign of alarm, at which point all members of a colony quickly disappear down their burrows. Badgers often move into a meadow and proceed to dig out one ground squirrel after another, moving on only when the population has been so reduced that further hunting becomes too difficult. Populations of Belding ground squirrels recover rapidly, however, owing to their high reproductive rate. They enter hibernation by late September or early October, emerging in May, when meadows begin to be free of snow.

Sierra Nevada Golden-Mantled Ground Squirrel, *Callospermophilus lateralis.* Fig. 195. *Head and body:* 6 to 7½ in (15 to 19 cm). *Tail:* 3¼ to 4 in (8 to 10 cm). *Color:* head and shoulders, golden brown; back, grizzled brown, on each side one white stripe bordered by two black stripes; tail, black bordered with buff. *Litter:* 4 to 6 young, early summer. *Nest:* burrows lined with bark and hair, dug beneath rocks or fallen logs. *Food:* grasses, sedges, green leaves, blossoms, berries, pine nuts, bulbs, roots, truffles and other fungi, some insects. *Enemies:* weasels, coyotes, pine

195. Sierra Nevada Golden-Mantled Ground Squirrel,
Callospermophilus lateralis.

martens, hawks, owls, other carnivores. *Habitat:* forest
floor near brush, meadows, rocky slopes, fallen timber.
Sign: burrows. *Distrbution:* 6000 ft (1800 m) to timberline,
both slopes, in several forest communities.

Many campers and hikers have unknowingly seen the
golden-mantled ground squirrel, thinking it to be a chipmunk, which it closely resembles. Chipmunks, however,
are smaller, less plump and have stripes along the sides of
their heads, which the ground squirrel lacks. The stripes
down the backs of both the golden-mantled ground squirrel
and chipmunks serve to camouflage the animals from their
numerous predators, blending with the irregular textures
and broken patterns of light characteristic of the forest
floor. The golden-mantled ground squirrel prefers open
forest, where trees grow among rocks, fallen logs, and
sunny meadows. The most common ground squirrel in the
Sierra, it occurs above 6000 feet wherever such habitats are
found. Nevertheless, it seldom climbs trees nor ventures
far into open meadows, where it would be exposed to predators. Golden-mantled ground squirrels are typically bold
around humans, however, and are commonly seen in camp
begging for food or scurrying about looking for scraps. They
will also invade untended picnic baskets or backpacks. In
the fall the golden-mantled ground squirrel begins to prepare its den for winter hibernation, which usually lasts from
October to April. During this time body temperature drops
and metabolism slows down, though the squirrel may
awaken from time to time to urinate. While hibernating it
subsists on fat stored up the previous summer. In addition,
it caches foods for use the following spring, when deep
snows make foraging difficult.

Chipmunks, genus *Eutamias*. Fig. 196.

Of the eleven species of chipmunks found in the Pacific states, eight occur in the Sierra. All are found in some part of the forest, though three also occur in adjacent zones. Identification of a species depends on rather subtle distinctions in size, color, voice, and habitat, which may not be readily apparent to a casual observer in the field. The following data applies to the group as a whole.

Head and body: 4 to 6 in (10 to 15 cm). *Tail:* 3 to 4 in (8 to 10 cm). *Color:* reddish or yellowish brown with nine alternating light and dark stripes on back and five on sides of head. *Litter:* 3 to 6, spring and early summer. *Nest:* burrows, abandoned woodpecker holes, tree stumps, rock crevices, lined with sedges, lichens, feathers, hair, other materials. *Food:* mostly seeds, also nuts, berries, green vegetation, fungi, some insects and other animal matter. *Enemies:* weasels are the chief foe, also coyotes, snakes, hawks, and other carnivores. *Habitat:* forest conifers, forest floor near rocks, brush, meadow edges, fallen timber. *Sign:* nests; "pugholes," which are small depressions in the ground that once contained seed caches laid down by chipmunks. *Distribution:* all zones, both slopes, entire length of the Sierra.

1. **Yellow-Pine Chipmunk,** *Eutamias amoenus.* Open conifer forests, 4400 to 9400 ft (1340 to 2870 m); west slope south to Interstate 80, east slope south to Mammoth Pass. Spends most of its time on the ground.

2. **Montane Chipmunk,** *Eutamias umbrinus.* Subalpine forest, mainly on east slope from Mammoth Lakes south.

3. **Lodgepole Chipmunk,** *Eutamias speciosus.* Upper montane and subalpine zones, both slopes from Mt. Lassen south; the most common Sierra chipmunk; an agile climber, often in trees; also found among rocks and fallen timber.

4. **Townsend Chipmunk,** *Eutamias townsendii.* In thickets and near fallen timber in upper montane zone south to Fresno County; occasionally climbs trees.

5. **Long-Eared Chipmunk,** *Eutamias quadrimaculatus.* Open brushy forest or rocky areas in montane zone, 3200 to

196. Lodgepole Chipmunk,
Eutamias speciosus.

7500 ft (980 to 2290 m) on west slope south to Madera County, ranging east to Carson Range in Alpine County.

6. **Alpine Chipmunk**, *Eutamias alpinus*. Rocky areas or places with fallen timber, 7600 to 12,600 ft (2320 to 3840 m), both slopes, Yosemite region south to Olancha Peak; chiefly in subalpine zone, some above timberline; rarely climbs trees.

7. **Sagebrush Chipmunk**, *Eutamias minimus*. Sagebrush scrub, east slope, 6400 to 10,500 ft (1950 to 3200 m); also in conifer forest (mostly Jeffrey pine) with sagebrush understory or along forest–sagebrush scrub ecotone.

8. **Merriam's Chipmunk**, *Eutamias merriamii*. Rocky areas, chaparral, and brush, west slope, 1000 to 6500 ft (300 to 2000 m); sagebrush scrub and pinyon–juniper woodland below 8500 ft (2600 m), east slope north to Onion Valley, west of Independence.

As if it were not difficult enough to distinguish the various chipmunks from one another, as a group they are often confused with the golden-mantled ground squirrel, which is larger, fatter, lacks cheek stripes, and has fewer stripes on its back. The ground squirrel and chipmunks are also similar in having internal cheek pouches, storing food, hibernating, and being active during the day. During the summer chipmunks spend much of their time storing seeds into their ample cheek pouches (one was found to contain more than 1100 tiny seeds). After a time the chipmunks bury the gathered seeds in small holes in the ground, which are then filled with earth. These seed caches will provide food during brief periods of wakefulness during the winter, as well as after emerging from hibernation the following spring, when deep snows make food gathering difficult. Chipmunks begin to hibernate in October and become active once again in late March or April. Although they are torpid during most of this period, chipmunks are only partial hibernators, awakening from time to time to eat and urinate. Unlike golden-mantled ground squirrels, which subsist during hibernation on body fat stored during the summer, chipmunks rely on their seed caches to carry them through the season. Emerging from their nests during warm periods, they dig through the snow to one of their caches, eat their fill, and return to their nests for another round of sleep. Bold and playful, chipmunks are among the favorite forest mammals, and though the temptation to feed them by hand may be great, it should be resisted. First, chipmunks are wild creatures and may inflict a painful bite if upset for some reason; second, human foods are seldom appropriate for wild animals; third, constant feeding can make the chipmunks fat and lazy, making them easier prey for weasels and other carnivores; and fourth, chipmunks in the northern Sierra sometimes host fleas bearing bubonic plague, a serious, painful disease at best, a fatal one at worst.

Yellow-Bellied Marmot, *Marmota flaviventris.* Figs. 197 and 198. *Head and body:* 14 to 20 in (36 to 51 cm). *Tail:* 5 to 8 in (13 to 20 cm). *Color:* grizzled gray or brown above; dull yellow below; white around eyes; dark band above nose. *Litter:* 3 to 8, early summer. *Nests:* located in dens beneath rock piles, less commonly under tree roots. *Food:* sedges, grasses, and various other herbs; tender shoots of shrubs; some insects. *Enemies:* pine martens, weasels, badgers, coyotes, and predatory birds. *Habitat:* rockslides, outcrops, and nearby forest and meadows. *Sign:* burrow openings 5 to 6 in (13 to 15 cm), beneath boulders or trees; tear-shaped black droppings to ½ in (1 cm). *Distribution:* 6200 ft (1900 m) to timberline, both slopes.

Marmots are essentially large ground squirrels, though they lack the cheek pouches of that clan. They are among the more commonly sighted mammals of the High Sierra, often seen scurrying over rocks and adjacent meadows, but seldom allow a close approach. In spring and early summer,

197. Yellow-Bellied Marmot,
Marmota flaviventris.

198. Marmot tracks.

however, when food is scarce and snow still covers much of the ground, marmots may abandon their usually retiring ways to venture into camps for scraps. They are often seen at this season begging for food at the well-known Olmsted Point turnout overlooking Tenaya Canyon, along the Tioga Pass Road through Yosemite National Park.

Occurring throughout much of the western United States, the yellow-bellied marmot is one of five marmot species in North America, the best known being the eastern woodchuck, *Marmota monax*. The yellow-bellied marmot is also called a "woodchuck," hence such Sierra place names as the Woodchuck Country in the John Muir Wilderness. Marmots weigh from 5 to 10 lb (2.25 to 4.5 kg), half of this consisting of fat accumulated through the summer. This fat sustains the marmot during winter hibernation, which begins in early October and ends in late April or early May. Mating occurs shortly thereafter, and the young are born in early summer. Strictly diurnal animals, marmots prefer the warmer hours of the day and usually retire to their dens on cool, cloudy summer afternoons. When not feeding they spend a good deal of time sunbathing on boulders, each animal having a favorite spot of its own. When alarmed, marmots utter a loud shrill whistle and quickly disappear beneath the rocks. Periods of hectic activity are uncommon, for this would not promote the thick accumulation of fat on which marmots depend during hibernation. Despite their weight and rather indolent habits, however, marmots are extremely agile on rocky terrain.

Chickaree, or Douglas Squirrel, *Tamiasciurus douglasii*. Fig. 199. *Head and body:* 7½ to 8¼ in (19 to 21 cm). *Tail:* 4½ to 5½ in (11 to 14 cm). *Color:* dark reddish or olive brown above; dark stripe on each side divides upper parts from white or buffy fur below and on inside of legs; tail bordered with white. *Litter:* 5, early summer. *Nest:* usually old woodpecker holes high in pines or firs; lined with grass, twigs, lichen, and other materials; may build globular nest on branch if tree cavities unavailable. *Food:* mostly seeds of pines and firs, and of giant sequoia; fungi, which is placed on tree limbs to dry. *Enemies:* the pine marten is its chief predator; also Cooper's hawk, red-tailed hawk, goshawk, and great horned owl. *Habitat:* coniferous forest. *Sign:* piles of cones in hollows at bases of trees; dismantled cones

FOREST BELT ANIMALS

199. Chickaree, or Douglas Squirrel, *Tamiasciurus douglasii.*   200. Chickaree tracks.

on ground; scolding call. *Distribution:* 5000 to 11,000 ft (1500 to 3350 m), both slopes, entire Sierra; most numerous in white fir forest, red fir forest, and lodgepole pine forest; seldom ventures downslope into ponderosa pine forest.

Bushy-Tailed Wood Rat, *Neotoma cinerea.* Fig. 201. *Head and body:* 6½ to 9¾ in (17 to 25 cm). *Tail:* 4¾ to 8¾ in (12 to 22 cm). *Color:* light brown above, white below. *Litter:* 3 to 5, July. *Nest:* loose accumulation of bark and twigs in rock crevice, fallen log, or rockslide; more substantial quarters may be constructed for winter use. *Food:* fruits, nuts, and berries during the summer; mostly bark in winter. *Enemies:* pine martens, owls, and other nocturnal predators. *Habitat:* chiefly open, rocky terrain and nearby areas. *Sign:* piles of twigs and other debris along with black cylindrical droppings, usually among rocks. *Distribution:* both slopes, 5000 ft (1500 m) to timberline; most common in upper montane and subalpine zones.

The long bushy tail of this native "pack" rat resembles that of a chipmunk more than it does those of other mice and rats, and it is a sure way of distinguishing this species from its cousin the dusky-footed wood rat, which may occur together with the bushy-tailed wood rat in the lower forest. The long, dense, silky fur and bushy tail of the latter species are adaptations to cold weather, for the bushy-tailed wood

201. Bushy-Tailed Wood Rat, *Neotoma cinerea.*

rat, despite its preference for the higher slopes, is a nocturnal animal and remains active throughout the winter. Like its foothill cousin, the bushy-tailed wood rat is in the habit of trading bits of debris for shiny objects—such as utensils—left about campsites and cabins.

Voles, subfamily *Microtinae.* Fig. 202.

Long-Tailed Vole, *Microtus Longicaudus. Head and body:* 4 to 5 in (10 to 13 cm). *Tail:* 2 to 3¾ in (5 to 8 cm). *Color:* grayish on sides and below; reddish brown band along top of back. *Litter:* 2 per summer, 3 to 8 each. *Nest:* shallow burrows lined with grasses. *Food:* chiefly grasses and sedges. *Enemies:* badgers, coyotes, weasels, foxes, hawks, owls, and other carnivores. *Habitat:* moist grassy areas in forest and sagebrush; mountain meadows. *Sign:* small black droppings, burrow openings. *Distribution:* montane, pinyon–sagebrush, and subalpine zones to near timberline.

The very similar montane vole, *Microtus montanus,* also inhabits wet grassy areas and meadows, but feeds on succulent herbs rather than grasses. Runways in grass or sedge leading to burrow openings indicate the presence of this species.

Voles are prolific breeders, and the young born early in the season are sometimes able to bear litters later in the same year. Spending much of their time above ground during the day, voles constitute a staple item in the diets of many carnivores, and their prodigious reproductive rate is a response to heavy predation. Every few years, however, vole populations—for reasons as yet uncertain—increase far beyond normal levels, and meadows may seem to be alive with these small rodents. When such increases occur the population is quickly reduced not only by predators, which converge on affected meadows, but through death from overcrowding. Apparently the hormonal balance of voles is disrupted when the population exceeds a certain density, but the process leading to death has yet to be worked out.

202. Montane Vole, *Microtus montanus.*

203. Porcupine tracks.

Porcupine, *Erethizon dorsatum.* Fig. 203. *Head and body:* 20 to 26 in (51 to 66 cm). *Tail:* 7 to 12 in (18 to 31 cm). *Color:* yellowish to black above, with stiff quills up to 7 in (18 cm) long, especially on back, rump, and tail; quills are modified hairs that harden shortly after birth. *Litter:* 1 to 2, late spring or early summer; young are large and active, nurse only one week before fending for themselves. *Nest:* dens in rock crevices and tree cavities; during winter may spend entire season in a single tree. *Food:* herbs and shrubs in summer, inner bark of conifers in winter. *Enemies:* mainly the fisher, also coyotes, mountain lions, bobcats, and wolverines. *Habitat:* coniferous forest, often near rock outcrops. *Sign:* gnawed bark; oval droppings resembling pressed sawdust; tracks to 3 in (8 cm) with canvaslike texture from rough skin on bottoms of paws. *Distribution:* 4000 to 11,000 ft (1200 to 3350 m), especially in red fir and lodgepole pine forests.

Among North American rodents, the porcupine is second in size only to the beaver. The porcupine is the only native North American representative of a large group of South American rodents that includes guinea pigs, nutrias, capybaras, and chinchillas. Like most armored animals, porcupines are plodders and rather stupid, for their long barbed quills obviate the need for speed and wit. Once embedded in the flesh, the quills work their way deeper, causing infection and sometimes puncturing a vital organ. A number of predators have learned to grab the porcupine by the nose and quickly flip it over to expose its soft, unprotected belly. The fleet, powerful fisher which seems to be immune to the effects of the porcupine's quills, is its chief enemy; most other predators prefer to concentrate on simpler prey. When attacked, the porcupine puts its head between its legs, rears the spines on its back, and slaps its tail about. The porcupine is an agile climber of trees, and when descending, it does so rear first, thus presenting its least vulnerable part to predators that might be waiting below. Although active mostly at night, the porcupine is also commonly abroad during the day. Fond of the tender inner bark of young trees, the porcupine is a natural pruner of the forest, killing saplings that would die anyway from competition with older trees. During the winter it commonly spends much of its time in the trees, feeding on bark and resting in tree cavities.

Coyote, *Canis latrans.* Figs. 204 and 205. *Head and body:* 27 to 36 in (7 to 9 dm). *Tail:* 11½ to 15¾ in (3 to 4 dm). *Color:* buffy gray and black, or rusty above, paler below; tail, dark tipped. *Litter:* 3 to 11, spring or early summer. *Den:* may also enlarge rodent burrows or dig their own. *Food:* omniverous; rodents, such as mice, squirrels, and gophers, gophers, along with rabbits, hares, and pikas, form the bulk of its diet; carrion; also insects, tadpoles, frogs, birds, eggs, among rocks; may enlarge rodent burrows or dig its own. *Food:* omnivorous; rodents, such as mice, squirrels, and when other foods are scarce; may occasionally take a young, sick, or wounded deer, but this is uncommon; deer have been observed driving coyotes away from fawns with a few well-placed kicks. *Enemies:* other than humans, none to speak of. *Habitat:* grassland, woodland, rocky areas, forest, meadow, sagebrush, open desert. *Sign:* doglike tracks and droppings. *Distribution:* entire Sierra, all zones.

On most any night in the High Sierra a wild, eerie chorus of barks and howls may announce the presence of coyotes, which are common throughout the range at most any elevation. No sound in these mountains better sums up their wildness. Persecuted since the coming of Europeans to North America, the coyote has displayed greater resilience than any other large predator on the continent, not only surviving, but extending its range to areas where it was once rare or absent, even to the outskirts of many cities. The disappearance of wolves and other large carnivores

204. Coyote, *Canis latrans.*

205. Coyote tracks.

from many areas has apparently created an ecological vacancy that the coyote has been able to fill. The animal's success is due in part to its intelligence and healthy reproductive rate, but also to its catholic taste in foods, which allows it to scratch out a living in virtually every conceivable habitat.

Unlike wolves, coyotes do not run in packs. They tend to hunt alone, but occasionally two may team up to ambush a jackrabbit or other swift animal. Females tend the young alone, though the males may bring food to their mates. Not so swift as jackrabbits, the coyote relies on stealth and cunning to capture its prey. It is an excellent digger, a talent it uses to capture gophers, ground squirrels, and other rodents. Coyotes remain active all winter, digging out rodents, capturing birds, subsisting on available vegetation. It may hole up for a spell during bad weather or move downslope for a time.

Two subspecies of coyotes are found in the Sierra. The valley race ranges in the Central Valley and lower foothills; the mountain race occurs at higher elevations and along the east side. The mountain coyote is larger and has thicker fur than its lowland cousin. Because of its large size, many untrained observers mistake it for a wolf. While there is a remote chance that a few wolves may still survive in the high central and southern Sierra, reported sightings are very likely of the mountain coyote. One good way to distinguish the two animals is to observe how they hold their tails while running: the coyote holds it low; the wolf, high.

Black Bear, *Eurarctos americanus.* Figs. 206 and 207. *Head and body:* about 5 ft (15 dm); 40 in (10 dm) tall at shoulders; weight to 300 lb (140 kg) or more. *Tail:* 6 in (15 cm) or less. *Color:* two phases in the Sierra, both of which may occur in the same litter—cinnamon brown, the most common Sierra phase, and black. *Litter:* usually 2, born in winter den January or February; cubs about 8 oz (0.25 kg) at birth, growing rapidly in following months. *Den:* in the Sierra, rotted-out white fir trunks or burnt-out sequoias; also fallen logs, caves, rock crevices. *Food:* omnivorous, but mostly vegetable matter (see below); some honey, bees, other insects, fish, small mammals and birds; "camp bears" raid garbage cans, food lockers, ice chests, etc. *Enemies:* none. *Habitat:* mostly coniferous forest; ranges at times into

206. Black Bear, *Eurarctos americanus.* 207. Black bear tracks.

open high country. *Sign:* scratches on trees; large, black droppings; large 5-toed tracks, that of the hind paws resembling human footprints with claws. *Distribution:* 1200 to 9000 ft (370 to 2700 m), occasionally higher; most common between 5000 and 8500 ft (1500 and 2600 m) on west slope; uncommon in Tahoe Basin, scarcer southward along the east slope.

Though classed as a carnivore, the black bear subsists largely on vegetation. Upon emerging from its winter den in the spring, it feeds on bulbs, leaves, newly green grasses, and other herbs, supplementing this fare with insects and perhaps a few mice, squirrels, or even young birds. As summer draws to a close the bear turns to fattening foods such as nuts, berries, grubs, and acorns, adding about 30 percent of its weight in fat in preparation for winter sleep. Contrary to popular belief, black bears do not hibernate in the true sense of the word. Hibernation is a state of dormancy or suspended animation characterized by greatly reduced body temperature and metabolic processes. Though black bears spend much of the winter sleeping in dens, their body temperature remains close to normal and the sleep is light. They may even periodically emerge from their dens during warm periods. Food is scarce during the winter, however, so black bears rely largely on their accumulated fat to carry them through the season.

Females give birth to cubs—usually two—every other year. These are born in the winter, and both mother and cubs spend the next three months or so in their den. The male bear takes no part in rearing the young and will even kill and eat them if given the opportunity. The female defends her cubs vigorously from such attacks, first driving them to the safety of a tree, then turning on the male bear, whom she usually succeeds in vanquishing. This same protective instinct is unleashed with equal enthusiasm against humans who attempt to approach the cubs, and one does so only at great peril. The cubs spend their entire first summer with the mother and den up with her the following winter. After emerging in the spring of the second year the mother drives the cubs off to forage on their own while she resumes for a few months her own solitary way.

The black bear is the largest mammal in the Sierra and while rather common is seldom encountered outside developed campgrounds, especially those in the national parks. One can wander for days through known bear country without seeing one of these elusive animals, for truly wild bears—those which have not become accustomed to the soft life of a campground scrounger—are retiring, usually avoiding human contact. One may often encounter large bear tracks, however, in the fine dust of a trail or in moist soil near streams. So-called bear trees, which are scratching posts, are also fairly common and easily recognized by the shredded bark and pronounced claw marks. Some biologists believe these bear trees may serve the same function as scent posts do for some other animals—dogs being the most familiar example. Bears are normally silent, but may grunt and growl if angry or alarmed. Though largely nocturnal, black bears may also be about during the day, especially in the early morning.

Camp bears display little of the shyness of their backcountry cousins, having been emboldened by the ease with which they can obtain a variety of foods from garbage cans and picnic tables. Countless campers in Sequoia, Kings Canyon, and Yosemite national parks have been rudely surprised by bears ambling into camp in broad daylight to help themselves to lunch, not to mention their nightly forays, anticipation of which is perhaps the most common cause of insomnia among Sierra campers. The resulting bear incidents, as such confrontations are called, are sometimes unfortunate for the bear, sometimes for the people, often for both. Every year numerous injuries from bear attacks are reported from the Sierra, virtually all involving camp bears and almost invariably attributable to either human carelessness or stupidity. Unprovoked, black bears very rarely molest humans, as the grizzly sometimes will, and if one treats them with due respect there is little to fear from them.

Pine Marten, *Martes americana.* Fig. 208. *Head and body:* 14 to 19 in (36 to 48 cm). *Tail:* 7 to 9½ (18 to 24 cm). *Color:* light brown above, yellowish on throat and chest. *Litter:* 4, spring. *Den:* tree cavity or rocky bank. *Food:* pikas, marmots, wood rats, mice, voles, ground squirrels, chipmunks, tree squirrels, woodpeckers. *Enemies:* occasionally, the fisher. *Habitat:* rockslides and nearby areas in summer; forest in winter. *Distribution:* 7000 to 10,300 (2150 to 3140 m); usually winters in the red fir forest.

Although the pine marten is rather common in the Sierra, it is a swift, elusive animal that relatively few visitors are lucky enough to see. A low-slung mammal with a long bushy tail, the marten is essentially a large weasel. Like other members of the weasel family, it is a skilled and ferocious hunter and along with the coyote and great horned owl is primarily responsible for controlling rodent populations in the upper montane and subalpine zones. It relies on speed and agility to capture its prey and can run down any squirrel in a race through the treetops. Martens are solitary during the summer, but judging by tracks through the snow may sometimes hunt in small bands during the winter. (Either that, or several individual martens may use the same hunting route at different times.) In a single night a marten may travel 10 to 15 mi (16 to 24 km) over an irregular but definite hunting course which is used for a few nights in succession then abandoned for a time. Each marten has its own hunting territory that consists of several such routes. The marten tends to be nocturnal, but may also hunt during the day, especially in early morning

208. Pine Marten, *Martes americana.*

422

and late evening. Active all winter, it spends the colder months in the upper montane zone feeding on chickarees, flying squirrels, and woodpeckers in the red fir forest. During rough weather the marten usually seeks shelter in tree cavities, which also serve as nests for its young. The only animal with which the marten is likely to be confused is the much larger fisher, which is a rare forest resident in the Sierra.

Mountain Lion, *Felis concolor.* Fig. 209. *Head and body:* 3 to 6 ft (9 to 18 dm). *Tail:* 2 to 3 ft (6 to 9 dm). *Color:* reddish brown above; white on chin, throat, and belly; ears, nose, tail, and feet tipped with black. *Litter:* 2 to 3, spring. *Den:* cave or crevice in rocks; beneath boulders. *Food:* half of adult diet consists of mule deer; smaller animals make up the balance. *Enemies:* none, except man and his dogs. *Habitat:* forested, brushy, and rocky areas. *Sign:* large catlike tracks and droppings. *Distribution:* west slope from foothill to upper montane zone.

Formerly rather common in the Sierra, the mountain lion is now uncommon to scarce in most of the range, its numbers having been reduced by hunters intent on bounty or sport. Even where mountain lions are still fairly common, they are seldom seen, being retiring animals with a healthy aversion to humans. Unprovoked attacks on humans are so rare that no one need fear the large cat. Only a very few mountain lions develop the habit of killing livestock. Campers have claimed to hear the mountain lion scream at night, but the call is usually that of the bobcat. The mountain lion is quiet most of the time, though capable of growling and hissing much in the fashion of a house cat. The mountain lion is usually solitary, and the male does not assist in rearing the kittens.

Ranging from the foothills to near timberline, the mountain lion follows the seasonal migration of mule deer, which constitute half of its diet. The large cat is most common in the lower montane zone, where deer are also most abun-

209. Mountain lion tracks.

dant. A single mountain lion kills about 36 deer each year, relying on smaller game when hunting is poor. Each cat has a particular hunting territory ranging in size from 25 to 36 sq mi (65 to 93 sq km). Following an established circuit, the mountain lion may require a week to cover the entire route. Lacking the speed to run down a deer in open country, the mountain lion relies on stealth instead, slowly sneaking up on its prey and staking all on one final charge. Usually the deer escape, but research has shown conclusively that the health of deer herds depends in large measure on the mountain lion's periodic pruning of the population. The large, twitching ears and sensitive, moist nose of the mule deer have evolved over thousands of years as means for detecting its stealthy foe. Mother lions take considerable time teaching their kittens the technique of the hunt, and the young remain with her for more than a year.

Mule Deer, *Odocoileus hemionus.* Figs. 210 and 211. *Head and body:* 4 to 6 ft (12 to 18 dm); 32 to 42 in (8 to 11 dm) tall at shoulders; weight may exceed 200 lb (90 kg). *Tail:* small and slender near base. *Antlers:* on bucks only; short spikes in second summer, becoming branched in following years; antlers shed in March; new growth begins in April; antlers covered in "velvet" until September, hard and hornlike thereafter. *Color:* reddish or yellowish brown in summer; gray in winter; white on chin and throat and around tail, which is tipped in black; fawns, reddish brown with numerous white spots. *Litter:* usually 2 in June. *Nest:* among dense shrubbery. *Food:* mostly leaves and stems of shrubs and trees; also grasses, sedges, and most other herbs; wild fruits. *Enemies:* primarily the mountain lion; coyotes sometimes take old, sick, or young deer, as well as those stranded in deep snow. *Habitat:* forests, grasslands, meadows, brushy areas; prefers varied terrain with ample browse and cover. *Sign:* pointed, sheeplike tracks; oval droppings about ½ in (1 cm) long. *Distribution:* both slopes to timberline; most common in lower montane zone between 2000 and 5000 ft (600 and 1500 m); some herds migrate downslope in winter to foothill and pinyon–sagebrush zones; others remain in the lowlands year-round.

Mule deer are the most abundant and frequently seen of the large mammals inhabiting the Sierra. As many as 150,000 deer may live in the range from Yosemite south,

210. Mule Deer, *Odocoileus hemionus.*

211. Mule deer tracks.

though populations fluctuate greatly from season to season and year to year. Deer are most numerous in the summer after the birth of fawns, least numerous in early spring following the autumn hunting season and winter food shortages. Mortality among deer is high from starvation, disease, accident, hunting, and predation—mostly by mountain lions—yet probably more deer reside in the Sierra today than before the coming of European settlers to California. Grizzly bears were once common in the western foothills and lower forests of the Sierra and must have taken a large number of deer each year. Wolves roamed the higher slopes and took their share as well. Both of these predators, however, are now extinct in the Sierra (a few wolves may persist in the southern part of the range), leaving only the mountain lion, always the mule deer's chief predator, but now sadly reduced in numbers. Hunters in particular should note that mountain lions do not exterminate deer, for the relationship between the two animals is one that has evolved over thousands of years and was working quite well before humans instituted their current "management" programs. Killing off too many deer would not be in the lion's best interest since it would then die off itself for lack of food. The numbers of deer and lions occurring in the Sierra and elsewhere prior to the arrival of the white man were the results of prolonged evolutionary "negotiation."

Hunters have replaced the large carnivores as the chief predator of mule deer in the Sierra and elsewhere, yet despite the thousands of animals shot in the range each fall, deer populations often tend to increase beyond the capacity of the land to support them. Hunting could control deer overpopulation if does were allowed to be taken, rather than only bucks. After all, the mountain lion has never discriminated in this fashion, and it is the most successful "manager" of deer herds we know of. State and federal officials have repeatedly tried to institute doe hunts, but with little success, for such attempts have routinely been opposed by local authorities who apparently do not understand the mating behavior of mule deer.

The mating season or rut occurs in late autumn and early winter, after the hunting season is over. Beginning in October, bucks contend with each other for the right to service harems of does. These contests involve charging, kicking, nipping, and head-on confrontations in which antlers are interlocked and each buck tries to force the other to give ground. Old males commonly sport a variety of scars from these contests. Only the victors will mate, and these, of course, will be the largest, strongest, and most aggressive bucks, the animals most likely to produce healthy young. The vanquished bucks retire to small bachelor groups to wait out the mating season. Hunting bucks but not does only means that there will be fewer contestants in these annual tournaments, while the number of impregnated does will remain more or less the same. Only by reducing the number of does in a population can one hope to keep it under control.

The mule deer population of the Sierra is divided into a number of herds, each of which occupies a single watershed. A few of the herds are nonmigratory, remaining the year around on ranges in the western foothills or valleys along the east slope. Most are migratory, spending the winter at lower elevations and moving upslope into the forest come spring. The number of animals per herd ranges from less than 5000 in some of the small nonmigratory herds to more than 15,000 in the largest migratory ones. Summer ranges may be more than 1000 sq mi (2600 sq km) or less than 200 sq mi (520 sq km) depending on the size of the herd. Winter ranges are substantially smaller, seldom more than 500 sq mi (1300 sq km) and sometimes less than 100 sq mi (260 sq km). Migratory herds may travel as much as 50 mi (80 km) each way between their summer and winter ranges. During the summer, deer populations are highest in the mid-elevation forest, where more than 10 animals per square mile are common. Some deer may be seen upslope nearly to timberline.

Sierra herds are composed of small, scattered bands, for mule deer are not herd animals in the sense that, say, bison or caribou are. Seldom are more than a dozen mule deer seen together, and smaller family groups or bands of bucks are more common. Females establish "activity centers" that they will defend from other does, particularly when the fawns are young, but bucks show no comparable territorial behavior. The home range of mule deer in the Sierra is between one-half and three-quarters of a square mile. Deer are most active during the early morning and near dusk, bedding down for much of the day in cleared depressions beneath shrubs or, in the case of bucks, sometimes on high ridges commanding good views in all directions. Deer feed by taking a few bites and moving on, their ears and noses ever alert for the feared mountain lion. This habit also helps to prevent overbrowsing of individual shrubs and may limit the spread of disease.

Although mule deer are browsers—feeding largely on shrubs and trees—rather than grazers, they consume a large amount of grass in the spring, when it constitutes the first good source of nutrients in several months. Grass is largely abandoned in favor of shrubs as summer approaches, though small amounts continue to be eaten throughout the season. The favorite browse of Sierra mule deer are buckbrush, deer brush, and snow bush on the west slope—all species of *Ceanothus*—and bitterbrush on the east. Deer are not finicky eaters, however, and readily take a variety of plants, including sedges, clovers, dogwoods, wild roses, snowberries, some species of sagebrush, poison oak, chokecherry, bracken, acorns, lichens, mushrooms, assorted wild fruits and nuts, mistletoe, a wide variety of herbs, and the tender shoots of oaks, willows, alders, aspens, cottonwoods, and other trees. If other foods are not available, they will even eat conifer needles.

Bucks lose the previous year's antlers by March, just as the spring trek upslope begins. New antlers sprout in April as short spikes covered with "velvet," a furry coat of skin supplied with blood vessels. The antlers continue to grow through the summer, fed by the blood flowing through their velvet cover. By September they have hardened and the blood flow is cut off. The bucks then rub the velvet off, exposing the hard, sharp prongs beneath, which are then ready for use in the annual mating jousts. Although the antlers of mature bucks have more "points" than those of young males, the number is no indication of age beyond the first year or so. Bucks and does alike acquire their reddish summer coats in June, their gray winter ones the following September.

Does give birth to two, or sometimes more, fawns in June, remaining with them until the birth of new young the following year. Mother deer are extremely aggressive in defense of their fawns, which should be avoided for this reason. Does have even been known to drive off predators such as coyotes with a few well-placed kicks. Newborn fawns seem to have a natural instinct for hiding themselves. While the mother is away, they remain absolutely still, hidden in dense undergrowth and camouflaged by their spotted coats, which are lost at summer's end. They also have little or no odor that might attract predators.

CHAPTER VII

Roof of the Range:
Alpine Communities

THE SIERRAN ALPINE ZONE extends from tree limit to the summits of the highest peaks in the range. It is a cold, often desolate region devoid of trees and dominated by great expanses of bare or sparsely vegetated rock. Some people would call the alpine zone forbidding, yet others find great beauty in its starkness and seek comfort in its remote, still largely untrammeled reaches. It is a region accessible only to hikers, for no Sierra highway enters the alpine zone, though several—especially those over Sonora and Tioga passes—wind just below it.

The air is so thin, dry, and transparent at the roof of the range that the sky appears almost purple and the light shines with a pure, unsullied brilliance unknown at lower elevations. In this fiercely illuminated landscape middle tones disappear as forms are either flooded with a sharp, white light or plunged into deep shadow. Hundreds of glacial tarns nestled in rocky basins sparkle with sunspray and everywhere mirror ranks of lofty peaks sculpted by snowmelt and ice.

Vegetation in the alpine zone is sparse and consists almost entirely of dwarf perennial herbs hunkered close to the earth, where winds are gentler and rock faces warm with the sun. Alpine plants range downslope into the subalpine zone on moist, shady slopes, in low-lying basins where cold air collects, below lingering snowpatches, in avalanche tracks, and on xeric sites with thin soil and little or no winter snow cover. Some authorities include the dwarfed timberline trees in the alpine zone; others do not. If they are excluded—as they are in this discussion—the alpine zone occurs above 9900 feet (3000 meters) near Lake Tahoe, 10,500 feet (3200 meters) in the Yosemite region, and 11,000 feet (3350 meters) in the southern Sierra. From Sonora Pass south to Trail Pass and the peaks above Mineral King, a distance of about 150 miles (240 kilometers), alpine vegetation occupies a largely continuous zone encompassing not only the main crest, but also higher secondary ridges and intervening basins. South of this region, one small island of alpine plants occurs on the summit of Olancha Peak. From Sonora Pass northward to Donner Pass scattered islands of alpine vegetation occur on the higher peaks, including Highland Peak, Round Top, Freel Peak, Pyramid Peak, Jack's and Dick's peaks, and Mt.

ALPINE COMMUNITIES

212. Alpine landscape.

Rose. North of Lake Tahoe alpine vegetation is absent altogether from the Sierra, reappearing on the summit of Mt. Lassen, at the southern tip of the Cascade Range.

The Alpine Environment

Alpine climates are characterized by cold, snowy winters and cool, cloudy summers. Winds are nearly constant and often swift, especially during winter storms. Frosts may occur any day of the year, and often do. Although average snow depths may be greater downslope beneath forest cover, drifts may be 30 feet (9 meters), and they melt slowly because of lower spring and summer air temperatures. As a result, the alpine growing season is the shortest in the Sierra, ranging from six to eight weeks, depending on when a site is released from snow cover and how much moisture is available thereafter.

Alpine Climate

The Sierran alpine zone is warmer and sunnier than that of most other mountain ranges in North America. During July and August, maximum daytime temperatures may range into the 60s by noon, though they commonly drop thereafter as upslope winds and cloud cover increase.

Nevertheless, while scattered cumulus clouds and occasional thunderstorms are characteristic of summer afternoons in the High Sierra, the air masses moving over the range during this season are generally drier and generate less cloud cover than is typical, for example, of the northern Rockies, Cascades, or Olympic Mountains. By the same token, the Sierra also receives less summer precipitation, which accounts for the more desertlike aspect of its alpine landscape.

As environmental conditions grow more extreme the number of organisms able to tolerate them decreases. This is true not only of alpine areas, but of all habitats dominated by too much or too little of one or more environmental commodities. Consequently, the Sierran alpine flora comprises fewer species than those of the downslope communities. Some plants, on the other hand, are for various reasons more or less restricted to the alpine zone. In any case, about 600 plant species make up the Sierran alpine flora, of which some 200 are rarely found below timberline.

The two most hostile habitats for plant growth in the alpine zone are (1) areas beneath or just downslope from snow drifts that linger well into midsummer, and (2) exposed areas where high winds remove much or all of the snow cover during the winter. Too much snow produces cold, wet soils and growing seasons that are brief even by alpine standards. Too little snow exposes plants to wind and frost damage during the winter and severe soil drought during the summer. Between these two extremes lie numerous intermediate habitats, all of which are more congenial to vegetation. The distribution of snow, then, is a critical factor governing the distribution of alpine plants, since it profoundly affects local growing seasons and moisture regimes.

Although several factors combine to signal alpine plants when to break winter dormancy, the disappearance of snow cover is a prerequisite for most. Plant growth begins first on warm, exposed, south-facing slopes, which may be free of snow by mid-June. Snow disappears last from north- and east-facing slopes, sheltered basins, and shady areas, where it may linger until mid-July, or in some years even longer. Although basins sheltered from the wind usually receive heavy snowfall, they often may be free of snow fairly early thanks to prolonged exposure to sunlight. Even so, plant growth may be retarded for a week or two by cold, wet soils caused by poor drainage. Abundant soil moisture, however, may permit these same plants to continue to grow well into September, while those on drier sites are forced by soil aridity to enter dormancy by mid-August.

Alpine Soil

Although the Sierra receives a large amount of snow during the winter, desertlike conditions characterize much of the alpine zone during the summer months. Scarce rainfall during this season is primarily responsible, but two other factors are also important in this regard: first, warm summer air temperatures tend to discourage the lingering snowfields common to most other North American alpine areas; second, a large amount of land surface is given over to rock outcrops, where soils are thin or absent.

Meltwater flows rapidly down steep, exposed bedrock, and though some is caught by rock crevices, the greater portion by far flows into discrete channels. Basins and benches carved by glaciers interrupt the downslope movement of both water and rock particles, and therefore tend to have the deepest, moistest, best-developed soils. Such sites are generally dominated by turf and are often found near lakes or meandering streams.

On drier slopes, soil has been slow to develop because of cold air temperatures and inadequate moisture—both retard the decomposition of organic materials—combined with the extreme resistance of granite to chemical weathering. Xeric sites in the alpine zone are therefore characterized by rocky soils, or *lithosols*—when they have soil at all—composed of sands and gravels derived from granite by means of nearly continuous frost action. These soils drain rapidly and are often arid by midsummer. They contain little humus, which would increase moisture retention, partly because of slow decomposition of organic materials, but also because the plants growing on them, being tiny and scattered, provide little to begin with. Soils are often better developed in volcanic or metamorphic terrain because these rocks tend to weather more rapidly than granite.

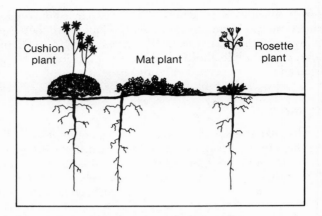

213. Most alpine perennial herbs bear their leaves close to the ground in compact cushions, sprawling mats, or tiny basal rosettes. The leaves are thus protected from the wind and are able to benefit from warmer air temperatures near the ground. Alpine species occupying dry soils also have extremely deep taproots (compared to the height of their above-ground parts). These long roots anchor the plants firmly to windy slopes and enable them to reach deep sources of moisture.

Plant Adaptations

Alpine plants have developed a number of strategies for coping with cold temperatures and short growing seasons. Species inhabiting open rocky areas have developed, in addition, ways of avoiding or minimizing the chilling, moisture loss, and abrasion resulting from exposure to wind. Although no single process or adaptation can by itself account for the success of alpine species, the two features most apparent to casual observers are a severe reduction in plant height and the absence or minimal development of woody stems. Though dwarfed shrubs do occur above timberline, most alpine species are perennial herbs only an inch or two high. There is simply not time or energy enough to permit the growth of large plants or the formation of much wood. Small size and prostrate growth habits largely eliminate the need for woody stems, which in larger plants are needed to provide support and elevation for leaves.

Structural Adaptations

In rocky areas the sun's rays hitting the dry earth create a warmer environment than exists just a few inches overhead. Prostrate and dwarf plants take advantage of this warm microclimate, avoiding the wind at the same time. Moreover, they require less moisture than larger plants simply because they have less tissue to supply. Some alpine plants, such as cutleaf daisy, *Erigeron compositus* (Plate 6D), form dense sprawling mats, with numerous roots anchored firmly in rock crevices or thin gravelly soils. Others, such as oval-leaved eriogonum, *Eriogonum ovalifolium* (Plate 7D), form tiny cushions, their rounded, streamlined shapes being the optimum compromise for obtaining the greatest amount of sunlight with the least exposure to the wind and cold. Cushion plants are able to inhabit windier, more desertlike sites than other alpine forms. Their dense foliage traps windblown soil, which stabilizes their hold on rocky slopes and retains moisture longer than the exposed sands and gravels around them. Mat plants, while generally restricted to more hospitable sites than cushion plants, are able to cover larger areas by means of creeping stems capable of putting down new roots.

Many alpine plants, such as pussypaws, *Calyptridium umbellatum* (Figure 214), form basal rosettes just an inch

214. Pussypaws, *Calyptridium umbellatum.* Flowers white or pink, borne in dense fuzzy terminal clusters on horizontal stems radiating from basal rosette of spatula-shaped leaves; reddish stems 2 to 10 in (5 to 25 cm) long. Pussypaws forms a prostrate rosette on bare, gravelly soils above 2500 ft (750 m) on both slopes of the Sierra. It is common and widespread on such sites, blooming May–August, depending on elevation.

or two high. As with cushion plants, radial symmetry allows rosette plants to obtain sunlight from all directions, and the outer rings of leaves afford some protection from wind and cold to the inner ones. Rosette plants are among the tiniest alpine species, yet their flowers may crown wiry stalks several inches high. After seeds have been produced, stalk and flowers will die back.

Alpine species often produce large, showy blooms that dwarf the tiny plants producing them, and great masses of flowers sometimes completely obscure the foliage. Big, bright flowers are important to minute, widely scattered plants that might otherwise be overlooked by wandering butterflies and bees. Moreover, by thrusting their blooms several inches into the air, alpine plants can take advantage of the wind for pollination and the scattering of seeds, without concurrently exposing their leaves to it.

The rocky slopes of the alpine zone are cold deserts characterized by minimal soil moisture, intense sunlight, and drying winds. The plants that occupy these slopes not surprisingly share a number of adaptive features in common with desert plants, among them a tendency toward miniaturization. Many species of both alpine and desert plants are covered with dense coats of hair, giving their foliage a frosted or silvery appearance.

Intense sunlight, a characteristic of both regions, decomposes chlorophyll, so plants living in full sun must either produce chlorophyll at a sufficiently fast rate to replace that which is lost or possess ways of reducing the amount of sunlight absorbed by their leaves. Thick coats of hair do just this by reflecting excess sunlight away from the plant surfaces. They also insulate alpine plants from cold and desert plants from intense heat. Furthermore, they protect plants from wind and reduce evaporation.

Some alpine plants, such as dwarf lewisia, *Lewisia pygmaea* (Figure 215), resemble certain desert plants in having waxy, succulent leaves and stems in which they store water. The tough cutin reduces evaporation to a minimum, so succulents are commonly able to survive long periods of drought.

Leafy-stemmed plants are also common both to deserts and alpine areas. An example from the Sierra is sky pilot, *Polemonium eximium* (Figure 216). Numerous tiny leaves

ALPINE COMMUNITIES

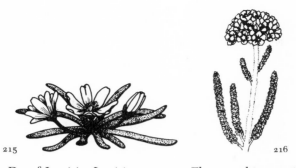

215. Dwarf Lewisia, *Lewisia pygmaea*. Flowers white or pink, with 6 to 8 petals, ½ in (13 mm); leaves linear, in basal cluster; stem 1 to 3 in (2.5 to 7.5 cm). The tiny pygmy lewisia prefers moist soils fed by snowmelt. It occurs mostly above timberline, blooming July–September, depending on available moisture.

216. Sky Pilot, *Polemonium eximium*. Flowers blue, fragrant, densely clustered in terminal globelike head; leaves basal, 1 to 4 inches (2.5 to 10 cm) long, crowded with numerous leaflets surrounding central vein; stem 4 to 12 inches (1 to 3 dm) tall. Sky pilot is strictly an alpine plant, rarely growing below 10,000 ft (3050 m). It is usually found in rock crevices or among boulders on high ridges. Blooms June–August.

tightly clustered around flowering stalks provide insulation, offer fewer exposed surfaces to the wind, and eliminate the need to grow additional stems merely to support leaves.

Alpine and desert plants both form long taproots and spreading surface roots in response to pronounced soil aridity and in order to provide firm footing in regions regularly harassed by winds. The weight of the underground parts of alpine plants may be six to ten times greater than that of the leaves and stems.

Physiological Adaptations

PERENNIALITY Almost all alpine and subalpine plants are perennials, since the need to produce an entirely new plant each year would be a decided handicap in the short growing season near timberline. With root systems and shoot and flower buds already developed, perennials are ready to begin new leaf and flower growth as soon as

Plant Adaptations

possible after snowmelt. Furthermore, perennials need not produce viable seed every year.

Annuals, on the other hand, must not only produce seeds each summer, regardless of conditions, but these seeds must, first, survive cold winters and, second, be suitably situated for germination the following spring or early summer. Then, in the brief space of six to ten weeks, roots, stems, and leaves must form; flowering must occur, and the blossoms must be pollinated; seeds must ripen and at least some must be situated on suitable ground—all before soil drought kills the plant or an early snow buries its chances.

Only one to two percent of all arctic and alpine species are annuals, and most of these grow in meadowy areas, where soil moisture is assured for most or all of the summer. The Sierran alpine flora, however, contains an unusually high percentage of annuals, probably because Sierra summers are warmer and sunnier than those of other alpine regions. Six percent, or about 40, of the alpine species in the Sierra are annuals, most of them derived from desert ancestors that were able to migrate up the range's dry, sunny eastern slope.

BREAKING DORMANCY Arctic and alpine perennial herbs are capable of commencing photosynthesis at air temperatures down to freezing, though the rate of photosynthesis increases as temperatures rise. This ability, combined with their perenniality, means that alpine plants are ready to begin growth almost immediately after snowmelt. However, in order to prevent a premature break in winter dormancy, say, during a year of little snowfall, when some sites may be free of snow a month or two ahead of schedule, alpine plants also require that other conditions be met, though these vary from species to species. Most require that soil temperatures exceed certain minimums. Some are finicky about air temperatures as well. Many cannot begin growth until moisture levels have dropped from the soggy highs immediately following snowmelt. Most require a minimum number of daylight hours before breaking dormancy.

CARBOHYDRATE STORAGE When conditions are just right, alpine plants begin their race against time. Carbohydrates stored over winter in underground roots, bulbs, and corms are quickly sent to shoot and flower buds that

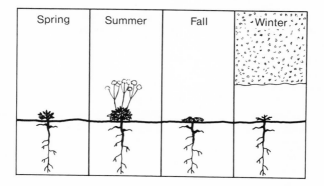

| Spring | Summer | Fall | Winter |

217. Alpine herbs commence growth as soon as possible in the late spring, rapidly putting on new shoots and leaves. By mid-summer most have already flowered, the blooms developing from buds set the preceding summer. After flowering, the plants become dormant in late summer or early fall. They remain dormant through the winter, but their roots contain abundant carbohydrates to fuel rapid growth once more the following spring.

were formed during the preceding season. Photosynthesis begins as soon as leaves are formed, but proceeds slowly at first as the plant concentrates on pouring its energy reserves into new growth.

Some of the stored carbohydrates are converted into reddish pigments called *anthocyanins,* which are pumped into tender young leaves as protection against the intense sunlight characteristic of high altitudes. Anthocyanins account for the reddish tinge characteristic of alpine vegetation in early summer; as leaves mature these pigments are largely or entirely masked by chlorophyll.

PHOTOSYNTHESIS AND RESPIRATION The rapid utilization of stored carbohydrates at the onset of the growing season is made possible by the ability of alpine plants to carry on respiration at low nighttime temperatures. During the first part of the summer more energy is being metabolized through respiration at night than is being supplied through photosynthesis during the day, but once growth is 75 to 90 percent complete, respiration slows down. Photosynthesis will continue to increase, however, as long as air temperatures continue to rise and sufficient moisture is available. It normally reaches a maximum during the flowering period. Excess energy obtained by the plant after growth and flowering are finished is stored as starches in underground parts for use the following year.

FLOWERING   Alpine plants must grow stems and leaves before flowering takes place, but these parts are developed so quickly that alpine plants are among the earliest to set blossoms. Early flowering allows ample time for seeds to mature and is especially important for some species occupying xeric sites, where the absence of moisture by midsummer may initiate premature dormancy. The advantage of miniaturization is once again apparent in that much less time is needed to complete the growth shoots.

Alpine flowers are produced by buds formed the previous year and, in some species, the previous two or more years. As a result the amount of bloom during any given summer is determined largely by conditions of growth during preceding summers. If summers are too cold, which is seldom the case in the Sierra, flowers may not set or, if they do, seeds may not ripen before the onset of winter. Seed production, however, is crucial only to alpine annuals.

The onset of dormancy occurs in late summer or early fall largely in response to shorter days and cooler temperatures, though many plants, as mentioned above, may become dormant as early as mid-August in response to insufficient soil moisture. By late September High Sierra meadows have turned from green to bronze, and most alpine plants have died back to a few hardy stems bearing buds from which the leaves and blossoms of the following summer will develop.

VEGETATIVE REPRODUCTION   Many alpine perennials reproduce vegetatively—by sprouting from bulbs, corms, and rhizomes or by setting down new roots from above-ground stems. Vegetative reproduction eliminates the need to produce viable seeds each year, though it has the disadvantage of prohibiting the introduction of invigorating traits through cross-breeding among several strains of the same species. It is especially advantageous for plants occupying moist sites where the onset of the growing season may be delayed by cold, wet soils. Since many meadow areas are cold and soggy early in the season only to dry out a few weeks later, seed production becomes a risky proposition, and many meadow plants seem to have abandoned it entirely.

The *graminoid*, or grasslike, plants—sedges, rushes, true grasses—typically form dense sods through rhizomatous reproduction (see page 142). Their moisture-loving associates, the *monocots*—such as lilies, orchids, irises, onions, and amaryllis—rely on bulbs and corms. In addition, mat plants, which rarely grow in meadows, reproduce by means of creeping stems which venture into adjacent areas and set down new roots. Eventually, older portions of the plant may die. This process, known as *layering*, is also characteristic of sprawling timberline trees (see page 350).

REPRODUCTION FROM SEED   Except for mat plants, most alpine perennials growing on gravelly or rocky sites reproduce from seed. When temperatures drop in the autumn, seeds produced during summer become dormant and will remain so until air temperatures once again rise to acceptable levels. Seed dormancy among alpine species ensures that young seedlings do not make the mistake of beginning life late in the growing season, when temperatures and moisture levels are both declining. Winter dormancy allows alpine seeds to germinate at the beginning of the following growing season if conditions are right, thereby giving the young seedlings the entire summer in which to establish themselves.

The germination temperatures for alpine plants are surprisingly high, ranging in the Sierra from 68° to 86° F (20° to 30° C). In requiring such warmth, however, alpine plants guarantee that their seeds will not germinate too early in the season or during a summer that may be abnormally cold. Tropical and temperate-zone plants generally germinate at lower temperatures since they can be assured of warm weather during the growing season. If the proper conditions of temperature and moisture are not met, the seeds of alpine plants may remain dormant for several years. If preserved in ice or frozen soil, they remain viable indefinitely.

The young seedling faces a more difficult task during the growing season than an already-established plant. It has only a few weeks to develop a root system and to produce and store enough carbohydrates to fuel the onset of growth the following year. It must rapidly develop roots deep enough to reach a supply of moisture sufficient to carry it through the late-season drought, so many seedlings put on only a few leaves and no flowers during their entire first summer.

Alpine Plant Communities

Detailed studies of the alpine plant communities of the Sierra Nevada are few, and ones designed to identify distinctive vegetation associations and their characteristic habitats are even rarer. Most popular works, as well as a number of technical papers, lump together all the alpine communities occurring in the Sierra as "alpine fell-fields," (*fell* being derived from a Gaelic word for rock) largely because the lack of basic ecological information has prevented finer distinctions. Some botanists dislike the term "fell-fields" because it suggests an analogy between Sierran alpine communities and comparable European formations — a relationship based primarily on superficial resemblances rather than specific similarities of ecology and flora. The widely used term "alpine tundra," which implies an analogous relationship between alpine communities and arctic tundra, is becoming less acceptable for the same reason.

Recently, botanists at the University of California at Davis have made detailed surveys of the alpine flora and habitats at Carson Pass and several locations in the central Sierra from Mt. Dana south to the headwaters of Convict Creek, just south of Mammoth Mountain. They divided the flora on each site into groups of species that tend to recur in certain habitats. Then, through computer analysis, they were able to sort out a number of distinctive vegetation associations composed of species from different groups whose ranges overlap on certain types of sites. Altogether, 31 site-specific plant associations were identified. These fall into two broad categories:

1. a mesic type dominated by sod-forming sedges and grasses, which shall here be called *alpine meadow;*

2. a xeric type dominated by widely spaced bunch-grasses and cushion plants, which shall here be called *alpine rock communities.*

Although the Davis researchers carried out their work in but a small section of the total Sierran alpine zone, it is likely that their broad division of alpine plant associations into wet and dry types is applicable to the zone as a whole.

Alpine Meadow

Alpine meadows and smaller patches of turf occur on soils ranging from moist to soggy during the summer. Typical sites include lake basins and level benches, streamsides, and areas downslope from lingering snowbanks and seeps. Snow cover is moderate to heavy on most sites, and soils tend to be cold, poorly aerated, and somewhat acidic. Frozen-ground phenomena are occasionally evident. Vegetation is dominated by sod-forming sedges and grasses, which reproduce largely by means of rhizomes. In addition, several species of broad-leaved herbs, though often few in number, are characteristic of most stands. These include alpine everlasting, *Antennaria alpina;* dwarf lewisia, *Lewisia pygmaea;* Drummond's cinquefoil, *Potentilla drummondii;* Sierra daisy, *Erigeron petiolaris;* alpine goldenrod, *Solidago multiradiata;* club-moss ivesia, *Ivesia lycopodioides;* and Lyall's lupine, *Lupinus lyalli.*

Few shrubs are found in alpine meadows, and those that are tend to be sprawling, rather inconspicuous types adapted to very wet soils. Locally, dwarf thickets composed of alpine willow, *Salix arctica,* Eastwood's willow, *S. eastwoodiae,* grayleaf Sierra willow, *S. orestera;* or on metamorphic soils in Mono County, the rare snow willow, *S. nivalis,* may occur in wet soils near lakes, streams, or in low-lying areas. Other shrubs include alpine laurel, *Kalmia polifolia* var. *microphylla;* dwarf huckleberry, *Vaccinium nivictum;* white mountain heather, *Cassiope mertensiana;* and red mountain heather, *Phyllodoce breweri.*

Sites beneath late-melting snowbanks or in marshy areas near lakes and streams are characterized by cold, soggy, highly acidic soils rich in peat. Many species common to drier meadows are scarce or absent in such areas, partly because the growing season may be too short, partly because of the soil conditions per se. A few species, however, are specially adapted to these adverse conditions and be-

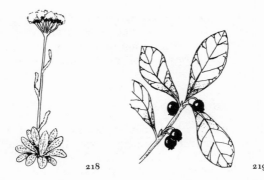

218   219

218. Alpine Everlasting, *Antennaria alpina*. Flower heads consisting of white, paperlike bracts with greenish black tips; leaves gray, linear, forming basal mat; stem 1 to 6 in (2.5 to 15 cm). Alpine everlasting is commonest near and above timberline, where it forms dense, spreading mats on more-or-less moist, rocky soils. Blooms July–August.

219. Dwarf Huckleberry (Sierra Bilberry), *Vaccinium nivictum*. Prostrate, spreading shrub only a few inches high; flowers tiny, pink, inconspicuous among leaves; deciduous leaves oval, barely 1 in (2.5 cm). This sprawling shrub is fairly common in moist soils, mostly in meadows or along lakeshores and streams, above 7000 ft (2150 m). Its edible fruit is sweet and much relished by small rodents. The leaves turn reddish in the fall.

come less common or do not grow at all where soils are warmer and less soggy. The most reliable indicator plant for these snowbank areas is sibbaldia, *Sibbaldia procumbens,* a creeping member of the rose family. Common plants in marshy areas include alpine shooting star, *Dodecatheon alpinum;* elephant's head, *Pedicularis groenlandica;* little elephant's head, *Pedicularis attolens;* primrose monkeyflower, *Mimulus primuloides;* mountain laurel; dwarf huckleberry; and several grasses and sedges.

Alpine Meadow Plants

Damp alpine sods are dominated by various sedges, notably alpine sedge, *Carex subnigricans,* and common sedge, *C. vernacula.* Brewer's shorthair grass, *Calamagrostis breweri,* is an abundant and characteristic associate. These plants will be found in the majority of stands. Numerous forbs and a few dwarf shrubs are also common in alpine meadows, but most are present only in small numbers and no single species will be found in all stands. For the purposes of this list the term *alpine meadow* also includes peat-bog areas, willow thickets, and snowbeds.

Alpine Meadow Wildflowers

The following species are among the most common and characteristic in damp alpine sods. Most also occur in moist meadows below the alpine zone.

Alpine Buttercup, *Ranunculus eschscholtzii,* Plate 6c (see description below).
Dwarf Knotweed, *Polygonum minimum.*
Alpine Shooting Star, *Dodecatheon alpinum.*
Subalpine Shooting Star, *Dodecatheon subalpinum,* Fig. 170.
Gentians, genus *Gentiana.*
Little Elephant's Head, *Pedicularis attolens.*
Greater Elephant's Head, *Pedicularis groenlandica,* Fig. 171.
Alpine Paintbrush, *Castilleja nana.*
Rosy Stonecrop, *Sedum rosea,* Plate 4c (see description on page 362).
Sierra Saxifrage, *Saxifraga aprica.*
Sibbaldia, *Sibbaldia procumbens.*
Drummond's Cinquefoil, *Potentilla drummondii,* Plate 7a (see description below).
Anderson's Alpine Aster, *Aster alpigenus,* var. *andersonii.*
Alpine Goldenrod, *Solidago multiradiata.*

Alpine Meadow Shrubs

The following shrubs are limited to meadows and damp sods in the subalpine and alpine zones.

Alpine Willow, *Salix arctica.*

Snow Willow, *Salix nivalis;* on metamorphic rocks only, un-
common.
White Mountain Heather, *Cassiope mertensiana,* Fig. 173.
Alpine Laurel, *Kalmia microphylla,* Plate 6B (see description
on page 374).
Sierra Bilberry, *Vaccinium nivictum.*
Western Blueberry, *Vaccinium occidentale.*

COLOR PLATES

Plate 4C. Rosy Stonecrop, *Sedum rosea.* Description, page
362.

Plate 6B. Alpine Laurel, *Kalmia microphylla.* Description,
page 374.

Plate 6C. Alpine Buttercup, *Ranunculus eschscholtzii.* Flowers bright yellow, waxy, 1 to 2 in (2.5 to 5 cm) across, with 5 petals; leaves rounded and deeply 3-lobed; stems to 6 in (15 cm). The
alpine buttercup occurs in damp turfs and rocky areas below lingering snowbanks, 8000 to 14,000 ft (2450 to 4250 m). It blooms
shortly after snowmelt, or somewhat later where moisture lingers.
Numerous species of buttercups occupy various habitats at all elevations in the Sierra.

Plate 7A. Drummond's Cinquefoil, *Potentilla drummondii.*
Flowers yellow, 5 petals alternating with 5 conspicuous sepals;
leaves nearly hairless, with 4 to 6 toothed leaflets; stem 12 to 20
inches (3 to 5 dm). The very similar Brewer's Cinquefoil, *P. breweri,* which grows in the same moist meadows and alpine turfs as
this species, can be told by the dense coating of fine, white hairs
on its leaves.

Alpine Rock Communities

The Sierran alpine flora is distinguished by a large
number of plants closely allied not to other alpine or arctic
floras, but to desert plants characteristic of Great Basin
communities. Specially adapted to thin, dry, rocky soils,
these plants tend to be members of a few genera—
Penstemon, Astragalus, Phlox, Draba, Eriogonum, Arabis,
and others—that were able to move upslope rapidly during
the interglacial periods, including the one in which we are
now living, which began about 10,000 years ago.

These desert plants were no doubt aided in their upslope
migration by adaptive features appropriate to both desert
and alpine conditions—succulence, hairiness, deep tap-

roots, light coloration, perenniality, prostrate or dwarf growth habits, and the like. Enroute, some species elaborated new forms even better able to withstand the colder climates at higher elevations; others may have managed the migration without changing much. Today, for example, a large number of these desert migrants can be found occupying dry, rocky sites over a wide elevational range, suggesting a high degree of tolerance for variations in air temperature. Pussypaws, *Calyptridium umbellatum,* is typical in this regard, occurring on xeric sites from 3000 to 12,000 feet (900 to 3650 meters). Alpine rock communities contain several cosmopolitan species such as pussypaws, as well as a large number that seldom or never occur below timberline.

GRAVEL FLATS   Alpine gravel flats are characteristic of both the subalpine and alpine zones, occurring on level or gently sloping ground where continued frost action on bedrock has fashioned a fractured, irregular surface littered with boulders, smaller rocks, gravel, and sand. The bedrock itself is often widely exposed and commonly shattered along joints. Boulders split by frost often show jigsaw-puzzle arrangements of carefully fitting pieces. The gaps and crevices between the rocks, as well as those on steeper slopes and among talus, are commonly occupied by plants, which here enjoy a more protected and possibly somewhat moister habitat than on open ground.

Blasted almost constantly by wind, subjected to extreme cold and intense illumination, sometimes swept free of snow during the winter, and forever contending with severe drought, gravel flats are among the harshest environments in the Sierra. In the cold air of the alpine zone, where temperatures commonly drop below freezing even in midsummer, frost action occurs nearly year-round on snowfree ground. Frost-shattered boulders are progressively reduced to increasingly smaller fragments, ranging down to fine gravels and sand, which form a thin veneer over the bedrock. In many places small rock fragments fitted closely together like the tiles of a mosaic form alpine "pavements" over a thin sublayer of sandy soil. Gravel-flat soils tend to be rudimentary in structure, with little humus and virtually no horizon development. Because of the large particles making up these soils, they often drain rapidly, leaving the upper levels extremely dry by midsummer.

Thanks to winds, snow depths range from moderate to nil, and except where boulders provide some shade, snow is often gone from such sites by the first of July.

Gravel-flat vegetation typically consists of widely spaced bunchgrasses and cushion plants, the latter possessing long taproots extending down to moister levels well below the surface. Mat plants and rosettes also occur on gravel flats, and these, along with the cushion plants, are variously adapted to the wind, cold, and soil aridity characteristic of such sites. Exposure to wind and cold during the winter, as well as moisture levels during the summer, are largely functions of snow depth, so it is not surprising that the kinds of plants growing on a site, as well as their relative abundance, are also largely determined by this factor.

Vegetation is sparsest and consists of fewest species on sites that are free of snow during the winter. Plants growing on such sites must endure subfreezing temperatures and high winds in winter followed by extreme aridity during the summer. Among the more common species able to tolerate such conditions are dense-leaved draba, *Draba densifolia,* alpine spring locoweed, *Astragalus kentrophyta,* and oval-leaved eriogonum, *Eriogonum ovalifolium,* all cushion plants; Coville's phlox, *Phlox covillei,* a sprawling mat plant; and alpine fescue, *Festuca brachyphylla,* a drought-tolerant bunchgrass.

Most of the above species also grow in areas covered by snow during the winter. Where snows are deep, plants are assured of ample soil moisture through the summer. Typical species on such sites include Sierra podistera, *Podistera nevadensis,* alpine paintbrush, *Castilleja nana,* club-moss ivesia, *Ivesia lycopodioides,* and alpine lupine, *Lupinus lyalli.*

Sites intermediate between these two, having some areas covered by snow and some exposed, present a heterogenous environment suitable to a relatively wide variety of species. Owing to moderate snow depths, these sites typically have abundant soil moisture early in the growing season, followed rapidly by pronounced aridity. Plants occupying such sites tend to develop rapidly and enter dormancy by mid-August. Characteristic species include silver raillardella, *Raillardella argentea;* frosty eriogonum, *Eriogonum incanum;* Nuttall's sandwort, *Arenaria nuttalli;*

220   221   222

220. Greenleaf Raillardella, *Raillardella scaposa.* Flower head of yellow to greenish yellow disk flowers; leaves linear, in basal tuft; stem leafless, 2 to 16 inches (5 to 40 cm). Greenleaf raillardella grows in dry, rocky or gravelly places in the subalpine and alpine zones, blooming July–August. It lacks the dense, fine white hairs of the silver raillardella, *R. argentea,* a somewhat lower plant found in similar places.

221. Sierra Primrose, *Primula suffrutescens.* Flowers red to rose, with yellow throat, tubular at base, with spreading starlike face composed of 5 notched petals; leaves spatula-shaped with toothed margins, in dense basal rosettes; leafless flower stem 1 to 4 in (2.5 to 10 cm). The Sierra primrose blooms July–August on moist rocky soils fed by late-melting snowbanks. It is largely restricted to sheltered, rocky places in the alpine zone.

222. Mountain Sorrel, *Oxyria digyna.* Flowers red or greenish, ¼ in (6 mm), in compact branching terminal clusters; leaves kidney-shaped, growing from base; stem 2 to 10 inches (5 to 25 cm). Mountain sorrel is common in rock crevices or damp scree above 8000 ft (2450 m). Its edible leaves have a pungent flavor.

squirreltail, *Sitanion hystrix,* a perennial bunchgrass; and pussypaws.

CREVICES AND BOULDER FIELDS Rock crannies and areas littered with large boulders offer more protected environments than do open gravel flats. Although the rock surfaces themselves are available only to lichens, the spaces between provide shelter from the wind and allow snow and soil to accumulate to greater depths than in open areas. Plants are therefore afforded not only protection from wind and cold during the winter, but a dependable moisture supply during the summer. Shrubs and taller herbs that would have a hard time surviving in open areas often are able to inhabit sheltered sites in crevices and among large boulders. Shrubs such as granite gilia, *Leptodactylon pungens,* whitestem goldenbush, *Haplopappus macronema,* and whitesquaw, *Ribes cereum,* are seldom found anywhere else in the alpine zone. Common crevice plants among the smaller shrubs and herbs include Sierra primrose, *Primula suffrutescens;* mountain sorrel, *Oxyria digyna;* showy polemonium, *Polemonium pulcherrimum;* Sierra cryptantha, *Cryptantha nubigena;* shaggy hawkweed, *Hieracium horridum;* dwarf daisy, *Erigeron pygmaeus;* alpine columbine, *Aquilegia pubescens;* and Davidson's penstemon, *Penstemon davidsonii.*

Plants of Alpine Rock Communities

Since alpine rock communities are as yet poorly defined, the following plants have been grouped instead under two broad habitats: (1) gravel flats and scree and (2) rock crannies. These two habitats are easily distinguished (see definition below), but each embraces variations in specific site conditions that may one day prove to be crucial to the definition of alpine plant communities. For the present, though, predictable plant associations have not been demonstrated for the Sierran alpine zone as a whole.

Trees are absent from the alpine zone, and shrubs are few in number and seldom common. The latter are rare or absent on gravel flats and are listed separately under Rock Crannies. With this single exception, the remainder of the plants listed below are herbaceous species, though a few may have more-or-less woody stems near the base.

Gravel Flats and Scree

The surface of such sites is mostly covered by fine-textured rock rubble, perhaps with a scattering of fist-sized stones but with very few or no boulders. *Scree* refers to such terrain when it occurs on slopes. Sites range from moist to very dry, but all are exposed to full sun and wind. Moist sites occur downslope from lingering snowbanks. Areas may or may not be covered by snow during the winter. Species preferring moist gravels are indicated in the list below. Plant coverage on gravel flats and scree is sparse. No species will be present in large numbers, and there are few that will be found on a majority of such sites. The following wildflowers, however, are among the more characteristic and widespread species on gravel flats and scree.

Rockcresses, genus *Arabis;* several species.
Drabas, genus *Draba,* Plate 7B (see description below); several species.
Sandworts, genus *Arenaria.*
Pussypaws, *Calyptridium umbellatum,* Fig. 214.
Dwarf Lewisia, *Lewisia pygmaea,* Fig. 215; moist sites.
Eriogonums, genus *Eriogonum,* Fig. 163 and Plate 7D (see description below); numerous species.
Mountain Sorrel, *Oxyria digyna,* Fig. 222; moist sites.
Kellogg's Knotweed, *Polygonum kelloggii;* moist sites.
Dwarf Knotweed, *Polygonum minimum;* moist sites.
Showy Polemonium, *Polemonium pulcherrimum.*
Spreading Phlox, *Phlox diffusa,* Fig. 167.
Coville's Phlox, *Phlox covillei.*
Little Elephant's Head, *Pedicularis attolens;* moist sites.
Alpine Saxifrage, *Saxifraga tolmei.*
Sibbaldia, *Sibbaldia procumbens;* moist sites.
Ivesias, genus *Ivesia,* Plate 7C (see description below); several species.
Alpine Lupine, *Lupinus lyalli;* moist sites.
Locoweeds, genus *Astragalus;* several species.
Gray's Cymopteris, *Cymopteris cinerarius.*
Sierra Podistera, *Podistera nevadensis.*
Dwarf Daisy, *Erigeron pygmaeus.*
Greenleaf Raillardella, *Raillardella scaposa,* Fig. 220.
Silver Raillardella, *Raillardella argentea.*
Alpine Everlasting, *Antennaria alpina,* Fig. 218.

Rock Crannies

Rock crannies include all sites where plants grow among large, bare rocks—boulder fields, talus, and rock crevices. Such sites usually provide some measure of shelter from the sun and wind. Soils are often better developed than on gravel flats, and moisture is often available through much of the growing season. Plant coverage ranges from sparse to fairly dense in small places where soil and moisture are ample. No species will be present in large numbers, and few will be found on a majority of such sites. The following wildflowers and shrubs are among the most characteristic and widespread species in rock crannies.

WILDFLOWERS

Alpine Columbine, *Aquilegia pubescens.*
Broad-Seeded Rockcress, *Arabis platysperma.*
Lemmon's Draba, *Draba lemmonii,* Plate 7B (see description below).
Sargent's Campion, *Silene sargentii.*
Pussypaws, *Calyptridium umbellatum,* Fig. 214.
Eriogonums, genus *Eriogonum,* Fig. 163 and Plate 7D (see description below).
Mountain Sorrel, *Oxyria digyna,* Fig. 222.
Sierra Primrose, *Primula suffrutescens,* Fig. 221.
Sky Pilot, *Polemonium eximium,* Fig. 216.
Showy Polemonium, *Polemonium pulcherrimum.*
Spreading Phlox, *Phlox diffusa,* Fig. 167.
Timberline Phacelia, *Phacelia frigida.*
Sierra Cryptantha, *Cryptantha nubigena.*
Davidson's Penstemon, *Penstemon davidsonii.*
Sierra Penstemon, *Penstemon heterodoxus.*
Stonecrops, genus *Sedum,* Plate 4C (see description on page 362).
Alpine Saxifrage, *Saxifraga tolmei.*
Drummond's Cinquefoil, *Potentilla drummondi,* Plate 7A (see description below).
Club-Moss Ivesia, *Ivesia lycopodioides,* Plate 7C (see description below).
Rock Fringe, *Epilobium obcordatum,* Plate 4B (see description on page 362).
Cutleaf Daisy, *Erigeron compositus,* Plate 6D (see description below).
Shaggy Hawkweed, *Hieracium horridum.*

Alpine Gold, *Hulsea algida.*
Alpine Everlasting, *Antennaria alpina,* Fig. 218.

SHRUBS

Alpine Prickly Currant, *Ribes montigenum.*
Whitesquaw, *Ribes cereum.*
Creambush, *Holodiscus microphyllus.*
Bush Cinquefoil, *Potentilla fruticosa.*
Red Mountain Heather, *Phyllodoce breweri,* Fig. 153.
Granite Gilia, *Leptodactylon pungens.*
Parish's Snowberry, *Symphoricarpos parishii.*
Goldenbushes, genus *Haplopappus.*

COLOR PLATES

Plate 4B. Rock Fringe, *Epilobium obcordatum.* Description, page 362.

Plate 4C. Rosy Stonecrop, *Sedum rosea.* Description, page 362.

Plate 6D. Cutleaf Daisy, *Erigeron compositus.* Like other members of the sunflower family (*Compositae*), cutleaf daisy has composite flower heads consisting of central disc flowers and radiating, petal-like ray flowers. Densely clustered disc flowers form a yellow button surrounded by white or pale purple ray flowers; leaves form a dense mat, leaf margins much divided; flower stalks 2 to 6 inches (5 to 15 cm). The cutleaf daisy most commonly occurs in rock crevices at or above timberline. Two related species, the dwarf daisy, *E. pygmaeus,* and sierra daisy, *E. petiolaris,* also frequent rock crevices, but lack the divided leaves that distinguish the cutleaf daisy. Blooms July–August.

Plate 7B. Lemmon's Draba, *Draba lemmonii.* Flowers yellow, at ends of leafless stalks 1 to 5 in (2 to 12 cm) long; leaves spatular, finely haired, less than ¾ in (2 cm) long, in dense basal cushion or tufts. Five species of Draba are rather common and widespread in the alpine zone, and several others occur there as well. Most are cushion plants, but Payson's Draba, *D. paysonii,* forms a spreading mat. Lemmon's Draba blooms July–August.

Plate 7C. Club-Moss Ivesia, *Ivesia lycopodioides.* Flowers yellow on leafless stems 2 to 8 in (5 to 20 cm) long; leaves hairless, in dense basal clusters, each with numerous leaflets that are themselves further divided. This strictly alpine species does not occur below 10,000 ft (3050 meters) in the Sierra, though several other ivesias do. Club-moss ivesia is named for the distinctive mossy appearance of its leaves. It blooms July–August.

Plate 7D. Oval-Leaved Eriogonum, *Eriogonum ovalifolium.*

Plants of Alpine Rock Communities

Flowers cream-colored, sometimes tinged with pink, densely clustered on tips of leafless stalks 4 to 8 in (1 to 2 dm) tall; leaves oval, about ½ in (15 mm) long, densely coated on both sides with fine white hairs; leaves sprout from short basal shoots to form a dense cushion. Dozens of species of eriogonum, or wild buckwheat, occur in California, and well over a dozen are common and widespread in the Sierra, notably the sulfur-flowered eriogonum (Fig. 163). Without the aid of botanical keys, most are rather difficult to identify with certainty. The oval-leaved eriogonum, also common, ranges downslope to 5000 ft (1500 m) on dry, rocky sites. It blooms May–July, depending on elevation.

Alpine Animals

Aside from insects and other invertebrates, very few animals reside in the alpine zone, where food and shelter are both in short supply. Even invertebrate life is far scarcer above timberline than below. Although plant species are numerous in the alpine zone, cover vegetation is for the most part sparse, and the zone has little to offer either plant or insect eaters. The very few animal species that occasionally breed in the zone are necessarily those able to nest or den among rocks, the only type of shelter available.

Of all the creatures occurring in the Sierra, only one, the gray-crowned rosy finch, is liable to be as common above timberline as below. It builds a nest of moss and fibers among rock crevices and feeds on seeds and on insects carried upslope by valley breezes. Loose flocks of rosy finches may sometimes be seen wheeling over alpine fields or feeding on stunned insects on snowpatches or glaciers.

The remnant bands of Sierra bighorn occurring in the central and southern parts of the range—mostly the latter—move upslope from their winter quarters in the sagebrush scrub at the base of the eastern slope to spend their summers near or above timberline. Their young, however, are born on the winter range. Sierra bighorns subsist largely on alpine herbs during the summer, since shrubs are few above timberline.

The most common mammals above timberline are the pika and yellow-bellied marmot, which occur where suitable rocky habitats are available. The alpine chipmunk may also occur locally in talus or on rocky benches where herbaceous vegetation is plentiful. All three creatures, however, are more common below timberline.

In addition to the above species, a number more common in the subalpine zone may casually wander above timberline during the summer. A variety of bird species are also seen flying over the range from time to time, particularly during fall migration. But the most common and widespread animal in the alpine zone is *Homo sapiens,* and sightings of any other species must be considered something of an occasion.

Animals of the Alpine Zone

The following species are common locally near or above timberline.

Gray-Crowned Rosy Finch, *Leucosticte tephrocotis.* Fig. 223. (See description below.)

Pika, *Ochotona princeps.* Fig. 194. (See Selected Forest Animals.)

Yellow-Bellied Marmot, *Marmota flaviventris.* Figs. 197 and 198. (See Selected Forest Animals.)

Heather Vole, *Phenacomys intermedius.*

The following species are scarce and local summer visitors to the alpine zone. Both are more likely to be seen below timberline.

Alpine Chipmunk, *Eutamias alpinus.* (See Selected Forest Animals.)

Sierra Bighorn, *Ovis canadensis.* Figs. 239 and 240. (See Selected Pinyon–Sagebrush Animals.)

The following species are occasional visitors from the subalpine zone.

Clark's Nutcracker, *Nucifraga columbiana.* Fig. 187. (See Selected Forest Animals.)

Mountain Blackbird, *Sialia currucoides.*

White-Tailed Jackrabbit, *Lepus townsendii.*

Red Fox, *Vulpes fulva;* rare.

Wolverine, *Gulo luscus;* rare. Fig. 181.

Short-Tailed Weasel, *Mustela erminea;* uncommon. (See Selected Forest Animals.)

223. Gray-Crowned Rosy Finch, *Leucosticte tephrocotis.*

Gray-Crowned Rosy Finch, *Leucosticte tephrocotis.*
Fig. 223. *Length:* 5¾ to 6¾ in (15 to 17 cm). *Color:* back, breast, and belly, rosy brown; head, dark brown with gray patch extending around back of head; rump, shoulder, and lower belly, pink. *Eggs:* 4 to 5. *Nest:* cup of mosses and dried grasses placed in rock crevices or even in *bergschrunds* of glacierets. *Food:* adults feed mostly on seeds, though some insects are also eaten; young are fed insects primarily. *Distribution:* locally common R, 9000 to 14,000+ft (2700 to 4200+m), mostly in alpine zone; ranges lower in winter, some spending much of the season in the pinyon woodland of the east slope. Above timberline flocks of a dozen or more gray-crowned rosy finches are often seen wheeling somewhat erratically over barren, rocky ridges and high basins, or feeding at the edges of snowbanks, glaciers, lakes, and meadows. Rarely found below 9500 ft (2900 m) during the summer, they may even spend the winter above tree limit, foraging for seeds on high ridgecrests and summits kept free of snow by high winds.

CHAPTER VIII

Edge of the Desert: Pinyon–Sagebrush Communities

THE EASTERN ESCARPMENT of the Sierra Nevada is the desert face of the range. It forms the steep, gaunt western wall of the Great Basin, which stretches eastward across Nevada to the Wasatch Mountains of Utah. Winter storms moving up the west slope of the Sierra are nearly wrung dry by the time they reach the crest, so that the east flank of the range and the lands beyond receive significantly less precipitation. At the north end of Owens Valley, for example, the town of Bishop, at an elevation of 4140 feet (1260 meters), averages just under six inches (15 centimeters) of precipitation a year, while on the west side of the crest sites at comparable elevation receive about 30 inches (76 centimeters) a year. In this same part of the Sierra, precipitation at 7000 feet (2150 meters) ranges from 15 to 20 inches (38 to 50 centimeters) on the east slope and 40 to 60 inches (100 to 150 centimeters) on the west.

Below 7000 feet on the east slope, vegetation is dominated by two communities characteristic of the arid Great Basin: pinyon–juniper woodland and sagebrush scrub. Together they define the pinyon–sagebrush zone, which extends downslope to about 4000 feet (1200 meters). This zone and the foothill zone of the lower western slope of the Sierra were once considered separate manifestations of Merriam's Upper Sonoran life zone (see page 147), but this view has been largely abandoned. Ecological differences between the two zones are far greater than their similarities. This is apparent in their largely different floras and plant communities. Foothill woodland and chaparral, for example, are absent from the east slope because at elevations high enough to supply them with adequate precipitation air temperatures are too cold and snow, rather than rain, is the rule.

East-slope forests and meadows are comparable to those on the west slope (and are discussed in Chapter V), but tend to be less extensive, represented by fewer tree species, and restricted either to streamsides or to relatively mesic sites above 7000 feet (2150 meters). The east-slope flora is distinguished at all elevations by a large desert element—xerophytic Great Basin genera that have profited from the greater aridity on this side of the range. Sagebrush and allied shrubs, along with a variety of desert herbs, range upslope nearly to timberline and in some cases

224. Sagebrush scrub and pinyon–juniper woodland.

above. Limber pine, an important Great Basin conifer, often replaces the more widespread whitebark pine in the east-slope subalpine forest.

This chapter focuses on the distinctively east-slope communities found in the pinyon–sagebrush zone, beginning with sagebrush scrub, which dominates the lowest slopes.

PINYON–SAGEBRUSH PLANT COMMUNITIES

Sagebrush Scrub

Sagebrush scrub, a treeless community of low, xerophytic shrubs, is the predominant vegetation on coarse, dry, well-drained soils below 5000 feet (1500 meters) elevation on the east slope of the Sierra and adjacent valley floors from Owens Lake north. At higher elevations sagebrush scrub forms an understory beneath pinyons, junipers, and such forest conifers as Jeffrey and lodgepole pines. On hot, dry slopes and ridges the community ranges nearly to timberline and recurs locally in comparable habitats in the

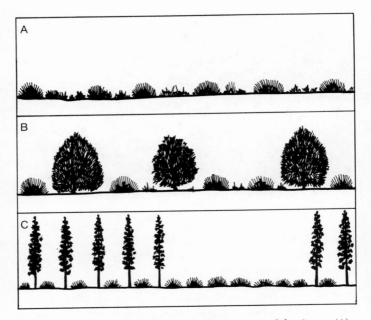

225. Sagebrush scrub dominates vast areas east of the Sierra (A), but also forms an understory in pinyon woodland (B) and conifer forests dominated by Jeffrey pine, ponderosa pine, or Washoe pine.

upper montane and subalpine zones on the west slope of the Sierra.

Shrubs tend to be widely spaced, with grasses and forbs forming a sparse, but characteristic understory between the larger plants. The community normally receives between 5 and 15 inches (13 and 38 centimeters) of precipitation a year, much of it arriving during the winter as snow. Temperatures in winter commonly drop below freezing. Summers tend to be hot and dry, though more rain falls on the east side of the Sierra at this time of year—largely from thunderstorms passing over the crest—than at comparable elevations on the west.

Sagebrush Species

Great Basin sagebrush, *Artemisia tridentata*, is the overwhelming dominant in most stands. It prefers deep, well-drained, sandy loams, but is able to tolerate a variety of soil types and moisture regimes. On the east side of the Sierra it is typically found on valley floors, outwash plains, alluvial fans, glacial moraines, and upland flats. A high-elevation form recognized as a distinct subspecies by some botanists ranges up to 11,500 feet (3500 meters). Sizeable stands of this alpine race are evident on dry flats near Donner Lake and south of Carson Pass.

Locally, Great Basin sagebrush may be replaced by low sagebrush, *A. arbuscula*, which prefers shallower, somewhat drier, rockier sites from 4000 to 9500 feet (1200 to 2900 meters) elevation, often pioneering on alkaline, or coarse, sterile, volcanic soils. Alpine sagebrush, *A. rothrockii*, a low, spreading plant, occurs on both slopes of the range from 6500 to 11,500 feet (2000 to 3500 meters), often forming fairly extensive stands on dry subalpine and alpine flats. Stands of this species can be seen near Soda Springs in Tuolumne Meadow, in the Gaylor Lakes Basin near Tioga Pass, near Fallen Leaf Lake, and along Little Cottonwood Creek a few miles south of Mt. Whitney, to name a few of the more accessible locations.

226. Several species of sagebrush are found along the east side of the Sierra, including (A) Great Basin Sagebrush, *Artemisia tridentata*, (B) Low Sagebrush, *A. arbuscula*, var. *nova*, (C) Low Sagebrush, *A. arbuscula*, (D) Alpine Sagebrush, *A. rothrockii*, and (E) Hoary Sagebrush, *A. cana*. See text for descriptions.

Some botanists consider low sagebrush and alpine sagebrush to be subspecies of Great Basin sagebrush. Others treat them as separate species, the procedure followed here. Great Basin sagebrush is the largest of the clan, typically ranging from three to six feet (one to two meters) tall. Low sagebrush is seldom more than 16 inches (four decimeters) tall, and alpine sagebrush rarely exceeds two feet (six decimeters). These two species, despite their comparable stature, are not likely to be confused because their ranges rarely, if ever, overlap in the Sierra.

Two other species of sagebrush also occur along the east side of the Sierra, neither of them members of the *A. tridentata* group. Spiny, or bud, sagebrush, *A. spinescens,* is an intricately branched shrub from four to twelve inches (one to three decimeters) tall. Flower heads grow on short spikes that become spines the following year. The foliage tends to be somewhat grayer than that of other sagebrushes. Bud sagebrush ranges along the east side of the Sierra on alkaline flats below 5000 feet (1500 meters) elevation.

Hoary sagebrush, *A. cana,* ranges in height from 16 inches to three feet (four to nine decimeters). Its leaves are rarely toothed and it possesses no spines. Ranging from 6500 to more than 10,000 feet (2000 to 3050 meters), hoary sagebrush commonly occurs along the shores of dry lakebeds, in grassy flats among rocks, and on gravelly sites.

Sagebrush was named for the pungent, sagelike fragrance of its leaves, but it is not a "true" sage of the genus *Salvia.* True sages are widespread and conspicuous members of coastal brush communities in Central and Southern California, but only three native species occur in the Sierra, two in the western foothills. Desert sage, *Salvia dorrii,* is the sole representative of the genus on the east side of the range, occurring mostly along the lower margin of the pinyon–juniper woodland at elevations up to 6800 feet (2100 meters).

Desert sage is also a shrub, usually less than three feet tall, and like sagebrush has aromatic leaves, though it can readily be distinguished from sagebrush by its leaves, stems, and flowers, which are quite different. Desert sage bears conspicuous terminal spikes of bluish or purplish flowers; sagebrush, numerous leafy clusters of small, rather inconspicuous, pale-yellow flowers. The leaves of desert sage are spoon-shaped; those of sagebrush are smaller, rather slender, and terminate in distinct lobes or teeth. Desert sage has roughly square stems; sagebrush, round ones. There are also other conspicuous differences, but these should serve to distinguish most specimens. True sages are members of the mint family; sagebrush is related to sunflowers and asters.

Shrub Associates

Despite the dominance of sagebrush species, several other shrubs occur as important associates in the sagebrush scrub: antelope bitterbrush, *Purshia tridentata;* desert bitterbrush, *P. glandulosa;* curl-leaf mountain mahogany, *Cercocarpus ledifolius;* rubber rabbitbrush, *Chrysothamnus nauseosus;* and desert peach, *Prunus andersonii.* Bitterbrush often forms nearly pure stands within the sagebrush scrub, especially on coarse, well-drained volcanic soils, such as those found along the west side of Owens Val-

227. Curl-Leaf Mountain Mahogany, *Cercocarpus ledifolius.* *Height:* usually 6 to 12 ft (2 to 3 m); sometimes small tree to 30 ft (9 m); bark smooth, gray on branchlets, dark and furrowed on older branches; leaves elliptical to lance-shaped, pointed at both ends, leathery, covered with white hairs below, margins smooth and rolled under; fruit, a small, dry, 1-seeded capsule with a twisted feathery plume attached. The curl-leaf, or desert, mountain mahogany grows on dry slopes in the pinyon–sagebrush zone along the east side of the Sierra. The birchleaf mountain mahogany, *C. betuloides,* of the foothill chaparral can be distinguished from the above by its serrated leaf margins.

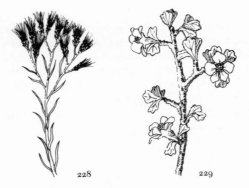

228   229

228. Rubber Rabbitbrush, *Chrysothamnus nauseosus. Height:* 1 to 7 ft (0.3 to 2.1 m); stems erect from base, much-branched, leafy, flexible, covered with woolly white hairs, foul smelling; leaves evergreen, linear, more or less woolly; flowers yellow, in terminal rounded tufts; no ray flowers. Rubber rabbit-brush, along with several other species and varieties, grows abundantly in the pinyon–sagebrush zone along the east side of the Sierra, where its yellow flowers are conspicuous from July through late fall or early winter.

229. Antelope Bitterbrush, *Purshia tridentata. Height:* 1½ to 6 ft (4.6 to 18 dm); bark brown or gray, young shoots woolly; leaves deciduous, woolly, in bundles, wedge-shaped with tips divided into 3 lobes, gray-green above, white below; flowers creamy yellow with spatula-shaped petals. Antelope bitterbrush is common or abundant in sagebrush scrub from Mono County north, where it dominates some stands. Southward, it is replaced by desert bitterbrush, *P. glandulosa,* the leaves of which are less wedge-shaped and often divided into 3 to 5 narrow lobes, or sometimes only toothed.

ley north of Independence. Antelope bitterbrush ranges higher and farther north than desert bitterbrush; however, the two commonly occur together along the east side of the Sierra in Inyo and Mono counties, from 3500 to 9000 feet (1050 to 2750 meters).

Other locally common shrubs in the sagebrush scrub include western chokecherry, *Prunus demissa;* horsebrushes, genus *Tetradymia;* Parry's rabbitbrush, *Chrysothamnus parryi;* common rabbitbrush, *C. viscidiflorus;* Mormon tea, *Ephedra viridis;* winter fat, *Ceratoides lanata;* and spiny hopsage, *Grayia spinosa;* as well as species of gooseberry, snowberry, goldenbush, and other shrubs commonly associated with forest communities bordering the sagebrush scrub.

Understory Herbs

The sagebrush scrub, unlike chaparral, has a well-developed and characteristic herbaceous understory that is dominated by grasses but also includes a large number of forbs. Common and widespread grasses in the community include Idaho fescue, *Festuca idahoensis;* desert needlegrass, *Stipa speciosa;* needle-and-thread, *S. comata;* western needlegrass, *S. occidentalis;* bluegrass, *Poa secunda;* bluebunch wheatgrass, *Agropyron spicatum;* and basin wild rye, *Elymus cinereus.* All of these species are native perennial bunchgrasses, which in many places have been replaced by alien annual grasses such as cheatgrass, *Bromus tectorum.*

As in the western foothills, overgrazing by livestock has been credited with the decline of native perennial bunchgrasses in the sagebrush scrub. Providing excellent forage, the bunchgrasses were favored by livestock over many of the alien annuals, as well as over such natives as squirreltail, *Sitanion hystrix,* which therefore flourished. Although the great majority of lands covered by sagebrush scrub lie

230. Prickly Poppy, *Argemone munita.* Flowers white with yellow stamens, 2 to 4 inches (5 to 10 cm) across; leaves coarse, lobed, with ruffled margins and spines; stem 2 to 4 ft (6 to 12 dm), prickly. The prickly poppy is abundant and conspicuous along roadsides on the east side of the Sierra, where its large, showy white flowers with yellow centers bloom April–July. It also occurs in the foothill zone of the west slope.

in the public domain, western ranchers have resisted attempts to limit grazing as a way of restoring the range to something approaching pristine condition.

Most forbs found in the sagebrush-scrub understory are annuals, which usually flower in spring or early summer, disseminating their seeds shortly thereafter. Germination may occur either in the fall or the following spring, depending on weather conditions. Obviously, these annuals rely on extremely rapid growth to make the most of those brief periods when optimal temperature and moisture conditions coincide. Abundant wildflowers grace the sagebrush scrub during May and June, the most conspicuous being the tall prickly poppy, *Argemone munita*, whose large white flowers with yellow centers bloom abundantly along roadsides. Other common wildflowers include Mariposa tulips, lupines, penstemons, locoweeds, paintbrushes, mule's ears, wild buckwheats, gilias, phloxes, and monkey-flowers.

Adaptations to Heat and Aridity

The shrubs of the sagebrush scrub exhibit a variety of adaptations to heat, drought, and intense sunlight. A number of these xerophytic adaptations were discussed in connection with chaparral shrubs, which must endure summer conditions that are comparable in many respects.

HAIRINESS The characteristic gray-green color of the sagebrush scrub is that of its dominant species, the Great Basin sagebrush, and is produced by the fine white hairs covering the leaves of this plant. Rabbitbrush, horsebrush, and winter fat are also hairy. To review, the hairs serve several functions: (1) they insulate the plants from summer heat and winter cold; (2) they protect the plants from dessicating winds; and (3) the light color of the hairs, which is responsible for the pastel shades of most desert shrubs, reflects sunlight, thus lowering the temperature of plant surfaces and reducing the deterioration of chlorophyll.

LEAVES AND THORNS Most of the desert shrubs are small and, like their counterparts in the chaparral, have tiny leaves, often tightly clustered about the stem. A large number, such as spiny sagebrush, desert peach, blackbush, horsebrush, and spiny hopsage, also have spines, or thorns.

These are produced by the abandonment of leaves and a subsequent hardening of stems. Fewer leaves reduce the volume of tissue that must be supplied with water, and spines may inhibit some animals from browsing, though several of these shrubs are important food sources for bighorns, mule deer, and livestock.

ROOTS Most of the shrubs in the sagebrush scrub have taproots for deep moisture sources and spreading surface roots to take advantage of occasional summer showers. This too is an adaptation to drought also found in chaparral shrubs.

Growing Season

Although the east slope receives more moisture than the west during the summer, the total annual precipitation is less. Summer rains allow plants of the sagebrush scrub to remain active during most of the season—indeed, many flower in the period from July through September—but maximum growth occurs during two or three weeks in May, when temperatures are warm and the ground still moist from winter storms. Sometimes, if rains arrive early and temperatures remain warm, a second growth period will occur in the fall. Dormancy is triggered by moisture stress. Most of the shrubs in the sagebrush scrub emerge from dormancy in late winter, when buds formed the previous year begin to open. From then on growth proceeds slowly until May, when as much as 60 percent of the year's new shoot length is added.

Range Fire

Great Basin sagebrush reproduces abundantly from seed following fire, while rabbitbrush, chokecherry, bitterbrush, and horsebrush are all sprouters, like so many of the chaparral shrubs. Some bitterbrush plants do not sprout, however, and where these are numerous a range fire can be disastrous. Sprouting shrubs may dominate postfire sites for two decades, though Great Basin sagebrush eventually reasserts its dominance on most sites. Herbaceous cover is also greater during the earlier postfire stages, thanks to reduced competition from shrubs. Along with overgrazing,

Sagebrush Scrub

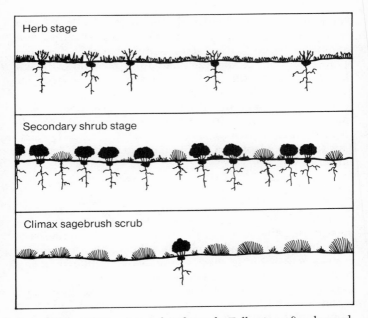

Herb stage

Secondary shrub stage

Climax sagebrush scrub

231. Fire succession in sagebrush scrub. Following a fire, burned areas once dominated by sagebrush are invaded by numerous herbaceous species, followed by sprouting shrubs present before the fire. Eventually, these shrubs (including rabbitbrush, bitterbrush, horsebrush, and chokecherry) crowd out the herbaceous cover and dominate recently burned sites for several years. Finally, they are crowded out in turn by sagebrush.

frequent fires—most of human origin—are believed to be one of the chief factors responsible for the widespread replacement of mature sagebrush stands by earlier successional stages.

Sagebrush Scrub Plants

The plants of the pinyon—sagebrush zone as a whole are listed in a single section beginning on page 475. The main floristic difference between the sagebrush scrub and the pinyon–juniper woodland is the presence in the latter community of the singleleaf pinyon. Most of the shrubs and herbs typical of sagebrush scrub are also found in the woodland.

Pinyon–Juniper Woodland

From 4000 to 5500 feet (1200 to 1700 meters) in the northern Sierra and from 5000 to 8000 feet (1500 to 2450 meters) in the south, sagebrush scrub forms an understory in a desert woodland dominated by singleleaf pinyon, *Pinus monophylla*. This pinyon–juniper woodland occurs sparsely southward to Alpine County and from there south forms a more or less continuous belt to Kern County. Since understory herbs and shrubs in this woodland are those of the sagebrush scrub, with which it is intimately associated, this section will concentrate on the dominant tree.

Singleleaf pinyon (or piñon) is the only pine in the western hemisphere having one needle per leaf bundle, and this characteristic, if nothing else, will serve to distinguish it from all other Sierra pines. It is a low, rounded, shrubby tree seldom exceeding 20 to 25 feet (6 to 7.5 meters) in height. Its scattered occurrence among the sagebrush indicates that annual precipitation has increased locally to at least 10 inches (25 centimeters), the bare minimum, and probably ranges between 12 and 20 inches (30 and 50 centimeters). Where conditions are especially favorable singleleaf pinyons may form rather dense groves, such as at

232. Singleleaf Pinyon, *Pinus monophylla. Height:* shrubby tree, 10 to 30 ft (3 to 9 m). *Leaves:* needles, gray-green, 1 to 2 in (2.5 to 5 cm) long, each growing singly, rather than in bundles; the only 1-needle pine native to the Sierra. *Fruit:* cones, 1 to 2½ in (2.5 to 6 cm) long, almost spherical; seeds, ½ in (12 mm), edible. *Range:* 6000 to 8000 ft (1800 to 2450 m), east slope, from Sierra County south; the dominant tree of the pinyon woodland; scattered, isolated stands occur on the west slope from Yosemite south.

the mouth of Rock Creek Canyon and at the summit of Sherwin Grade. Singleleaf pinyon ranges into Southern California and through Nevada and Arizona to southern Idaho and western Utah. It is the most common tree in Nevada and often the only kind found on the state's semi-arid mountain ranges.

Throughout most of the Great Basin, Utah juniper, *Juniperus osteosperma*, is a more or less constant associate of the singleleaf pinyon and in this region is the "juniper" in the pinyon–juniper woodland. For unexplained reasons, however, this shrubby tree is missing from the woodland on the east slope of the Sierra, though it may be found nearby on the Pine Nut and Sweetwater ranges, the Bodie Hills north of Mono Lake, Glass Mountain to the south of the lake and the White Mountain and Inyo ranges.

South of Walker Pass, in Kern County, at the extreme southern end of the Sierra, singleleaf pinyon occurs with California juniper, *Juniperus californica*, an association that extends southward into the mountains of Southern California. A few isolated pinyon stands occur on the west slope of the Sierra north to Rancheria Peak, which overlooks the Tuolumne River just east of Hetch Hetchy Reservoir. Along the upper limits of the pinyon woodland on the east slope of the Sierra, singleleaf pinyons commonly occur with Jeffrey pine and western juniper.

South of Lake Tahoe, between Monitor Pass and Sonora Pass, singleleaf pinyon occurs in a hybrid woodland–mixed coniferous forest association in which western juniper, Jeffrey pine, white fir, and lodgepole pine are common associates. The understory brush is also a hybrid mixture, comprising species common to sagebrush scrub—such as sagebrush, bitterbrush, and rabbitbrush—as well as others common to mixed coniferous forest—mountain snowberry, *Symphoricarpus vaccinoides;* tobacco brush, *Ceanothus velutinus;* western serviceberry, *Amelanchier pallida;* mountain spray, *Holodiscus microphyllus;* and plateau gooseberry, *Ribes velutinum.*

Humans and animals alike relish the delicious seeds of the singleleaf pinyon. Their flavor resembles that of the pine nuts of southern Europe, which are derived from a related species. Most Indian tribes on the east side of the Sierra relied heavily on pine nuts for food. The cones were harvested green and roasted whole in an open fire to vaporize the resinous pitch contained in them. The nuts were extracted and dried further to ensure their preservation. During the summer, Indians around Mono Lake traveled over the Sierra to the western foothills, where they traded pine nuts for acorns, the staple of most California tribes. Various parts of the singleleaf pinyon were also used by Sierra Indians for medicinal purposes.

Pinyon–Juniper Woodland Plants

Since the understory of the pinyon–juniper woodland consists of shrubs and herbs characteristic of adjacent sagebrush scrub, plants of both communities are listed together in a single section beginning on page 475.

Streamside Vegetation

Owing to the prevalence of shrubs on the lower east slope of the Sierra, streamside woodlands are much more conspicuous here than in the foothills and montane zones of the west slope, where they are usually obscured by adjacent woodlands and forest. On the east side of the Sierra, however, the vivid greens of black cottonwood, *Populus trichocarpa*, quaking aspen, *P. tremuloides*, water birch, *Betula occidentalis*, Jeffrey pine, *Pinus jeffreyi*, and white fir, *Abies concolor*, contrast dramatically with the pastel shades of desert rocks and scrub. Serpentines of trees following streams downslope into the sagebrush scrub are characteristic of the east-slope landscape and a familiar sight along roads leading into Sierra canyons. For example, travelers on State Highway 120 between Tioga Pass and the small town of Lee Vining, on the shore of Mono Lake, have a bird's-eye view of the well-developed woodland along Lee Vining Creek far below. The corridor of verdure marks the streamcourse as it meanders through the expanses of sagebrush and pinyon on either side.

Trees typical of the streamside woodland have also established themselves to some extent along manmade drainage

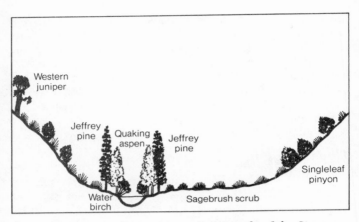

233. Cross section of a canyon on the east side of the Sierra, showing typical vegetation in such a situation.

and irrigation channels in the valleys east of the Sierra, but here the lovely, spirelike Lombardy poplar, *Populus nigra*, a native of southern Europe, is more common. Its rich, gold autumn foliage does much to enliven the small desert towns of the Owens Valley.

A number of trees that are common on the west slope of the Sierra occur at the east slope mainly along streams, and then only occasionally. These trees include Fremont cottonwood, *Populus fremontii;* arroyo willow, *Salix lasiolepis;* yellow willow, *S. lasiandra;* canyon oak, *Quercus chrysolepis;* and black oak, *Q. kelloggii.* South of the Tahoe region the latter two species are found sparingly only along streams entering Owens Valley. From Owens Lake south, Arizona ash, *Fraxinus velutina,* a small, deciduous tree typical of desert ranges in the Southwest, occurs along streams on the east slope of the Sierra.

Quaking Aspen

Streamside vegetation typically gives way within a few yards of the water to sagebrush scrub or pinyon woodland, though sometimes canyon flats may be moist enough to support more extensive thickets of aspen or cottonwood. Beavers, which are native to the Central Valley but not to

PINYON–SAGEBRUSH COMMUNITIES

the Sierra, were introduced some years ago to a few streams along the east slope. The animals found one of their favorite foods, aspen, in plentiful supply and forthwith cut down many of these trees to dam the streams. The water spread out behind the dams, not only forming ponds, but extending the influence of the stream far beyond what it had been before. Meadows expanded as the ponds filled with silt, and aspens found new territory to invade along the banks.

Although quaking aspens are found near meadows, streams, and moist flats on the west slope of the Sierra from 6000 to 10,000 feet (1800 to 3050 meters), they are most common and conspicuous along the east side of the range, particularly in the Sonora Pass region, where they form extensive stands. Anyone who has driven down the east slope of the Sierra from Sonora Pass to the junction of U.S. 395 during the fall will not soon forget the spectacular display of yellows, golds, oranges, and even shades of red provided by the abundant aspens along this route. Comparable stands of aspen occur northward along the east side of the Sierra to near Beckwourth Pass. South of Mono Lake, aspens are not uncommon, but they seldom form stands so extensive as those to the north.

234. Quaking Aspen, *Populus tremuloides. Height:* 10 to 60 ft (3 to 18 m). *Bark:* smooth, greenish white. *Leaves:* bright yellow-green, spade-shaped, 1 to 2½ in (2 to 6 cm) long; leaf stalks slender, flattened, causing leaves to tremble even in a slight breeze; deciduous, turning brilliant gold, orange, and even red in the fall. *Fruit:* catkins with tiny brown seeds; however, most aspens sprout from spreading roots, so that entire stands usually consist of genetically identical individuals united by a single root system and sharing a single parent. *Range:* common, moist slopes, talus, grassy flats, and meadow margins, 6000 to 10,000 ft (1800 to 3050 m), both slopes; the largest stands in the Sierra occur on the east slope from Tioga Pass north.

Aspens are commonly pioneers on talus slopes, which they help to stabilize by means of their elaborate network of interlocking roots. Aspens always occur in groves or thickets. Since all the trees in a stand sprout from and share the same network of roots, each is genetically identical to its neighbors, and in a real sense the organism we know as the quaking aspen consists not of one tree, but of the stand as a whole. Aspens are able to reproduce from seed but rarely do so because seed viability is rapidly lost and their ability to sprout from existing roots largely eliminates the need.

Water Birch

Along streams draining the Sierra escarpment west of Owens Valley, water birch, *Betula occidentalis,* is the most common tree, forming shrubby thickets from 10 to 25 feet (3 to 8 meters) tall. On the west slope of the range it is restricted to the headwaters of the Kings and Kern rivers, where it occurs sparsely. Like the foxtail pine, water birch has an odd, disjunctive range, which in California includes the Klamath Mountains and the southern Sierra Nevada, but not the 300 miles (480 kilometers) of comparable mountain terrain in between. Unlike the foxtail pine, water birch is not endemic to California, but extends eastward through the Rockies and out onto the Great Plains along streamcourses.

235. Water Birch, *Betula occidentalis. Height:* 10 to 25 ft (3 to 7.5 m). *Bark:* smooth, coppery or bronze; twigs warty. *Leaves:* dark green, 1 to 2 in (2.5 to 5 cm) long, heart-shaped, margins toothed; deciduous, turning yellow in autumn. *Fruit:* catkins 1½ to 2½ in (4 to 6 cm) long. *Range:* east slope streams draining into Owens Valley, 5000 to 8000 ft (1500 to 2450 m); rare and local in Kings Canyon National Park, west slope.

Plants of the
Pinyon–Sagebrush Zone

Available moisture is the most obvious factor governing the distribution of plants in the pinyon–sagebrush zone. They fall into two broad groups: plants that are more or less restricted to streamsides and other moist areas and plants that range over the open dry slopes and flats characteristic of this zone. The following plant lists are grouped accordingly.

Trees

The following lists include all native species found in the zone.

DRY SLOPES OR FLATS

Singleleaf Pinyon, *Pinus microphyllus*, Fig. 232.
Western Juniper, *Juniperus occidentalis*, Fig. 158.

STREAMSIDES OR OTHER MOIST PLACES

Jeffrey Pine, *Pinus jeffreyi*, Fig. 142.
Lodgepole Pine, *Pinus contorta*, var. *murrayana*, Fig. 152.
White Fir, *Abies concolor*, Fig. 136.
Arroyo Willow, *Salix lasiolepis;* often shrubby.
Yellow Willow, *Salix lasiandra;* often shrubby.
Quaking Aspen, *Populus tremuloides*, Fig. 234.
Fremont Cottonwood, *Populus fremontii*, Fig. 99; uncommon.
Black Cottonwood, *Populus trichocarpa.*
Canyon Live Oak, *Quercus chrysolepis;* local.
Black Oak, *Quercus kelloggii*, Fig. 90; local.
Water Birch, *Betula occidentalis*, Fig. 235. Owens Valley and adjacent Sierra canyons; often shrubby.
Arizona Ash, *Fraxinus velutina;* rare and local south of Owens Lake.

Shrubs

DRY SLOPES OR FLATS

The following species are the most common and widespread in the sagebrush scrub community.

Curl-leaf Mountain Mahogany, *Cercocarpus ledifolius*, Fig. 227.
Antelope Bitterbrush, *Purshia tridentata*, Fig. 229.
Desert Bitterbrush, *Purshia glandulosa*.
Hoary Sagebrush, *Artemisia cana*, Fig. 226.
Great Basin Sagebrush, *Artemisia tridentata*, Fig. 226.
Low Sagebrush, *Artemisia arbuscula*, Fig. 226.
Common Rabbitbrush, *Chrysothamnus viscidiflorus*.
Rubber Rabbit-brush, *Chrysothamnus nauseosus*, Fig. 228.

The following species are less common than the above in the sagebrush scrub, but some are abundant locally.

Mormon Tea, *Ephedra viridis*.
Winter Fat, *Ceratoides lanata*.
Hopsage, *Grayia spinosa*.
Plateau Gooseberry, *Ribes velutinum*.
Fern Bush, *Chamaebatiaria millefolium;* uncommon.
Blackbush, *Coleogyne ramosissima;* uncommon.
Desert Peach, *Prunus andersonii*.
Mohave Ceanothus, *Ceanothus vestitus*.
Beavertail Cactus, *Opuntia basilaris*.
Bud Sagebrush, *Artemisia spinescens*.
Alpine Sagebrush, *Artemisia rothrockii*, Fig. 226.
Littleleaf Brickellbush, *Brickellia microphylla*.
Cottonthorn, *Tetradymia axillaris*.
Spineless Horsebrush, *Tetradymia canescens*.
Littleleaf Horsebrush, *Tetradymia glabrata*.

One species occurs mostly along east-slope streams.

Arroyo Willow, *S. lasiolepis*.

STREAMSIDES OR OTHER MOIST PLACES

Arroyo Willow, *Salix lasiolepis*.
Yellow Willow, *Salix lasiandra*.
Narrowleaf Willow, *Salix exigua*.
Golden Currant, *Ribes aureum*.
California Wild Rose, *Rosa californica*.
Buffalo Berry, *Shepherdia argentea*.
Water Birch, *Betula occidentalis*, Fig. 235.

PINYON—SAGEBRUSH ANIMALS

Wildflowers

The following are a representative sample of some of the more common species and genera.

DRY SLOPES OR FLATS

Sagebrush Buttercup, *Ranunculus glaberrimus*.
Blazing Star, *Mentzelia laevicaulis*.
Kidneyleaf Violet, *Viola nephrophylla*.
Prickly Poppy, *Argemone munita*, Fig. 230.
Dagger Pod, *Phoenicaulis cheiranthoides*.
Rock Cresses, genus *Arabis*; numerous species.
Sierra Tansy Mustard, *Descurainia pinnata*.
Sandworts, genus *Arenaria*; several species.
Mountain Campion, *Silene montana*.
Pussypaws, *Calyptridium umbellatum*, Fig. 214.
Bitterroot, *Lewisia rediviva*, Plate 4D (see description on page 362).
Eriogonums, genus *Eriogonum*, Fig. 163.
Douglas' Knotweed, *Polygonum douglasii*.
Showy Milkweed, *Asclepias speciosa*.
Stansbury's Phlox, *Phlox stansburyi*, Plate 8A (see description below).
Nuttall's Linanthus, *Linanthus nuttallii*.
Bridges' Gilia, *Gilia leptalea*.
Ballhead, *Ipomopsis congesta*.
Scarlet Trumpet Flower, *Ipomopsis aggregata*.
Two-Leaved Phacelia, *Phacelia bicolor*.
Lowly Penstemon, *Penstemon humilis*.
Bridges' Penstemon, *Penstemon bridgesii*, Plate 8B (see description below).
Desert Paintbrush, *Castilleja chromosa*, Plate 8C (see description below).
Prairie Smoke, *Geum ciliatum*.
Common Silverweed, *Potentilla anserian*.
Dusky Horkelia, *Horkelia fusca*.
Nevada Pea, *Lathyrus lanzwertii*.
Tahoe Lupine, *Lupinus meionanthus*.
Locoweeds, genus *Astragalus*; several species.
Low Evening Primrose, *Oenothera caespitosa*.
Mountain Mule's Ears, *Wyethia mollis*, Plate 8D (see description below).
Nevada Daisy, *Erigeron nevadincola*.
Eaton's Daisy, *Erigeron eatonii*.
Sego Lily, *Calochortus nuttallii*.

Glaucous Larkspur, *Delphinium glaucum*.
Western Plantain Buttercup, *Ranunculus alismaefolius*.
Western Shooting Star, *Dodecatheon pulchellum*.
Brewer's Navarretia, *Navarretia breweri*.
Suksdorf's Monkeyflower, *Mimulus suksdorfii*.
Inyo Meadow Lupine, *Lupinus pratensis*.
Hooker's Evening Primrose, *Oenothera hookeri*.

COLOR PLATES

Plate 4D. Bitterroot, *Lewisia rediviva*. Description, page 362.

Plate 8A. Stansbury's Phlox, *Phlox stansburyi*. Flowers tubular, rose to nearly white, petals with small notch at tips; leaves linear, opposite; stem 4 to 8 in (1 to 2 dm). Stansbury's phlox grows in dry open places among sagebrush and pinyons. Several other species of phlox occur in the Sierra, the most common and widespread being spreading phlox, *Phlox diffusa* (Fig. 177). Stansbury's phlox is found only on the east slope. Blooms April–June.

Plate 8B. Bridges' Penstemon, *Penstemon bridgesii*. Flowers scarlet, tubular, with petals forming 2 lips—the upper protruding, the lower curled back; leaves linear, opposite, gray-green; stem 1 to 3 ft (3 to 9 dm). Bridges' penstemon occurs on both slopes of the Sierra, but is commoner on the east side in association with pinyons and sagebrush. It ranges eastward into the Great Basin. The lowly penstemon, *P. humilis*, which also occurs in the sagebrush scrub, is a smaller plant with bright blue flowers. Numerous species of penstemon occur in the Sierra, including mountain pride, *P. newberryi* (Fig. 166), and meadow penstemon, *P. rydbergii* (Plate 5C).

Plate 8C. Desert Paintbrush, *Castilleja chromosa*. Flowers red-margined, inconspicuous, sheathed in showy scarlet sepals and leaf bracts; leaves tinged with red, lower leaves deeply lobed; stem 4 to 16 in (1 to 4 dm). Desert paintbrush is common in sagebrush scrub and adjacent desert communities, blooming April–August. Numerous other species of paintbrush, including Indian paintbrush, *C. applegatei* (Plate 3D), and Lemmon's paintbrush, *C. lemmonii* (Plate 5B), occur in the Sierra.

Plate 8D. Mountain Mule's Ears, *Wyethia mollis*. Like other members of the sunflower family *(Compositae)*, mountain mule's ears has composite flower heads consisting of central disc flowers and radiating, petal-like ray flowers. Disc and ray flowers both bright yellow; leaves oblong, covered with fine white hairs, clumped at base, up to 24 in (6 dm) long and 7 in (2 dm) wide;

stems leafless, 1 to 3 ft (3 to 9 dm). Mountain mule's ears is common and widespread on both slopes of the Sierra, but especially on the east side. It prefers dry, often bare soils in open areas and will rapidly invade disturbed sites. Its abundance on the east slope is attributed to overgrazing by sheep at the turn of the century.

PINYON–SAGEBRUSH ANIMALS

Animal Life in the Pinyon–Sagebrush Zone

Among the several types of desert plant communities occurring in North America, the sagebrush scrub is one of the more congenial to animal life. The shrubs provide both food and shelter for numerous small birds and mammals, and the understory grasses and forbs supply abundant green vegetation or seeds, depending on the time of year. Along the upper margins of the community, stands of pinyon–juniper woodland constitute yet another important source of food and shelter and support a few species of animals less common in open sagebrush.

Throughout most of the vast intermontane region dominated by sagebrush scrub, water is normally scarce. But as in other arid and semiarid regions—the Sierra foothills, for example—animal residents are well adapted to this apparent limitation. These adaptations are discussed at some length in Chapter IV and include (1) light coloration to reduce heat absorption and resulting moisture loss, (2) the ability to obtain sufficient moisture from foods, (3) the reduction of the moisture content of urine and feces, and (4) nocturnality.

Along the east slope of the Sierra, which is drained by numerous streams, water is somewhat less of a problem than elsewhere in the sagebrush scrub. Woodlands and marshes found along these streams provide habitats for several kinds of animals that otherwise would not occur in the region, including a few that are more typical of forest communities upslope. Streamsides also provide an abundance of green grasses and forbs throughout the summer, when such foods are less common in drier areas, and thereby supplement the diets of sagebrush animals living near them.

Seasonal Conditions

Although winters are fairly cold in the pinyon–sagebrush zone, and precipitation during this season is usually in the form of snow, the region also experiences numerous sunny days when temperatures are well above freezing. As a result, even though occasional storms may drop up to several feet of snow, it seldom persists for long in open areas. Available plant foods during this season include the leaves, stems, bark and, in some cases, berries of shrubs. In warmer winters green plant shoots may also be available. Pinyon nuts are an important food source where they occur, as are the needles and bark of conifers.

Plant foods are abundant in the spring, when the shrubs begin to add new growth and the sagebrush scrub is carpeted with a profusion of grasses and forbs. Most of these plants are annuals that produce seed and die by midsummer, but some continue to supply green vegetation throughout the season. This is made possible in part because occasional rains are supplied by thundershowers generated by the passage of air over the mountains. Although the pinyon–sagebrush zone receives less precipitation than the Sierra foothills in the course of a year, what it does receive is more evenly distributed.

Migratory birds such as the gray flycatcher, Bell's vireo, and Brewer's sparrow, all common summer residents in the sagebrush scrub, arrive from April through early June, when food supplies are most abundant. Nesting is usually completed by midsummer, and the birds begin to move south in late August.

As winter settles over the high country to the west, a few subalpine birds begin to move downslope into the pinyon–sagebrush zone. Most notable among these are Clark's nutcracker, which stays close to stands of singleleaf pinyon and streamside conifers; the mountain bluebird, loose flocks of which roam the open lowlands; the gray-crowned rosy finch, which prefers pinyon–juniper woodland during this season; and the white-crowned sparrow, which occurs abundantly in the sagebrush scrub from autumn till late spring.

Mule deer also move downslope into the sagebrush scrub during the fall and remain there until snows begin to clear from the higher slopes. A few herds, however, remain in the pinyon–sagebrush zone throughout the year. The wintering deer arrive in the zone at the commencement of the rutting season, just as they do in the western foothills, and it is among the pinyons and sagebrush that mating occurs.

The few small bands of bighorn sheep remaining in the southern Sierra spend their winters at the base of the range in Owens Valley. Like the mule deer bucks, the bighorn rams begin to engage in mating contests in the fall and early winter. Lambs are born in June and shortly thereafter follow their mothers upslope to their summer range at and above timberline.

Browsers and Grazers

Mule deer, bighorn sheep, and pronghorn antelope were the primary browsers and grazers in the pristine sagebrush scrub along the east side of the Sierra, but today only the deer is common. Pronghorns are gone from the region, and bighorns are restricted to a few small bands. Cattle and sheep are now the most important consumers, and the community has changed—some would say suffered—as a result. Herbs and shrubs preferred by livestock have become scarce or absent in many stands, and Great Basin sagebrush, which is seldom browsed because it contains volatile oils that inhibit the action of stomach bacteria essential to digestion, has increased in both coverage and range throughout most of the region.

Wintering deer and bighorns feed primarily on shrubs such as bitterbrush, winter fat, spiny hopsage, horsebrush, and Mormon tea. They also like needlegrasses, wild buckwheats, and a variety of other herbs.

Desert Animals

A number of animals occurring in the pinyon–sagebrush zone are desert species that are scarce or absent elsewhere in the Sierra. Some range south into the Mohave Desert; others are distributed widely throughout the Southwest and Great Basin. Most have close ecological counterparts at higher elevations in the Sierra or in the western foothills of the range. Examples include the Great Basin spadefoot toad, desert horned lizard, speckled rattlesnake, sage grouse, black-billed magpie, pinyon jay, gray flycatcher, Brewer's sparrow, Nuttall's cottontail, sagebrush chipmunk, pinyon mouse, and sagebrush vole.

In addition, the pinyon–sagebrush and foothill zones share several animal species that are rarely found in the forest belt. These include the foothill yellow-legged frog, burrowing owl, mourning dove, house finch, and black-tailed jackrabbit.

The gray flycatcher, Brewer's sparrow, and the sage sparrow are common or abundant summer visitors to the sagebrush scrub. The flycatcher is one of several closely related species belonging to the genus *Empidonax*, of which five occur in various habitats on both slopes of the Sierra from the lowlands to timberline. These small flycatchers are difficult or impossible for most observers to distinguish in the field, even though the gray flycatcher—as its name suggests—is gray rather than greenish, as its cousins are.

Most sagebrush residents are grayer or lighter colored than their counterparts elsewhere. This is true, for example, of the sage sparrow, a somewhat darker race of which occurs in foothill chaparral. Brewer's sparrow, which belongs to the same genus as the chipping sparrow of the forest belt, is paler and has a finely streaked crown easily distinguished from its cousin's reddish-brown one. Desert species as a group tend to be paler than other animals, partly—as mentioned above—as a way of reducing body heat, partly as protective coloration matching that of desert sands and vegetation.

Pinyon–Juniper Woodland Animals

The animals found in this community are those of nearby sagebrush scrub. Pinyon stands may provide some measure of cover from predators, but they are most important as sources of pinyon nuts, which are relished by the pinyon jay, sagebrush chipmunk, and most humans who have ever tried them. The Indian tribes that once lived along the eastern base of the Sierra relied heavily on pinyon nuts and traded them to west-slope tribes for acorns and other commodities.

The pinyon jay is the only animal especially characteristic of the pinyon–juniper woodland on the east slope of the Sierra. Although this pale blue jay, like others of its kind, eats a wide variety of plant and animal matter, pinyon nuts form an important part of its diet. In addition, the pinyon jay seldom builds its nest anywhere but in the dense foliage of either pinyons or junipers. After the nesting season is over, foraging flocks range widely throughout the pinyon–sagebrush zone, and some even show up on the west slope of the Sierra from time to time.

The pinyon mouse, which is closely related to the more widespread deer mouse, commonly occurs in pinyon stands but is not restricted to them. It occurs in brushy or rocky areas not only on the east slope of the Sierra, but also in the western foothills.

Streamside Animals

Streamside vegetation and marshy areas support a number of animals found nowhere else along the eastern base of the Sierra. These include the foothill yellow-legged frog, belted kingfisher, yellow-headed blackbird (marshes only), red-winged blackbird, long-billed marsh wren (marshes only), Bell's vireo, yellow warbler, and yellowthroat. The western toad, Pacific treefrog, great horned owl (streamside woodlands), swallows, and song sparrow occur more widely, but prefer these habitats. The beaver, which is not native to the Sierra—though it is to the Central Valley—has been introduced along some east-slope streams, where supplies of aspen have provided suitable building materials for its dams.

Prey and Predators

Although sagebrush scrub provides better cover from predators than does open grassland, most small rodents living in the community occupy burrows. Examples include the antelope ground squirrel, northern pocket gopher, Great Basin pocket mouse, kangaroo rats, grasshopper mice, and the sagebrush vole. Three other important prey animals—the black-tailed jackrabbit, white-tailed jackrabbit, and Nuttall's cottontail—rely instead on the cover of the brush itself, as well as on their fleetness, to escape predators.

Except for a few species of snakes, all of the major predators in the pinyon—sagebrush zone are also present in other parts of the Sierra. The speckled rattlesnake, which replaces the Pacific rattlesnake south of Mono County, is comparable in foraging habits to its counterpart to the north. The coachwhip and striped whipsnake replace, in effect, the racer and striped racer of the western foothills. Major predators among birds and mammals include the great horned owl, golden eagle, red-tailed and Swainson's hawks (summers only), rough-legged hawk (winters only), coyote, and badger.

Perhaps the most unusual predators of the pinyon-sagebrush zone are grasshopper mice, which are the only small rodents in the Sierra that subsist almost entirely on animal matter. Though most of their diet consists of insects, grasshopper mice also prey on other small rodents, such as deer and pinyon mice and sagebrush voles.

Pinyon–Sagebrush Residents

The following species live in the pinyon–sagebrush zone the year around. Asterisks after some entries refer to further discussion in Selected Pinyon–Sagebrush Animals. Species described in detail in other chapters are so noted.

AMPHIBIANS

Great Basin Spadefoot, *Scaphiopus intermontanus*.
Western Toad, *Bufo boreas;* damp areas.
Pacific Treefrog, *Hyla regilla*.
Foothill Yellow-Legged Frog, *Rana boylei;* streams and ponds.

REPTILES

Common Leopard Lizard, *Crotaphytus wislizenii*
Western Fence Lizard, *Sceloporus occidentalis.* See Selected
  Forest Animals.
Desert Spiny Lizard, *Sceloporus magister.*
Desert Horned Lizard, *Phrynosoma platyrhinos.*
Southern Alligator Lizard, *Gerrhonotus multicarinatus.* See
  Selected Foothill Animals.
Coachwhip, *Masticophus flagellum.*
Striped Whipsnake, *Masticophus taeniatus.*
Gopher Snake, *Pituophis melanoleucus.*
Long-Nosed Snake, *Rhinocheilus lecontei.* *
Western Terrestrial Garter Snake, *Thamnophis elegans.*
Western Rattlesnake, *Crotalus viridis.*
Speckled Rattlesnake, *Crotalus mitchelli.* *

BIRDS

Golden Eagle, *Aquila chrysaetos.*
Sage Grouse, *Centrocercus urophasianus.* *
Burrowing Owl, *Speotyto cunicularia.*
Great Horned Owl, *Bubo virginianus.* See Selected Forest
  Animals.
Belted Kingfisher, *Megaceryle alcyon;* streamsides.
Horned Lark, *Eremophila alpestris.*
Black-Billed Magpie, *Pica pica;* agricultural areas.
Common Raven, *Corvus corax;* uncommon.
Pinyon Jay, *Gymnorhinus cyanocephalus.* *
Rock Wren, *Salpinctes obsoletus;* rocky areas.
Western Meadowlark, *Sturnella neglecta,* Fig. 114; grassy
  places. See Selected Foothill Animals.
Yellow-Headed Blackbird, *Xanthocephalus xanthocephalus,*
  Fig. 237. *
Red-Winged Blackbird, *Agelaius phoeniceus.*
Brewer's Blackbird, *Euphagus cyanocephalus.*
Brown-Headed Cowbird, *Molothrus ater.*
House Finch, *Carpodacus mexicanus.* See Selected Foothill
  Animals.

MAMMALS

Merriam's Shrew, *Sorex merriami.* *
Broad-Handed Mole, *Scapanus latimanus.*
Bats, order *Chiroptera.*

Animal Life in the Pinyon–Sagebrush Zone

Black-Tailed Jackrabbit, *Lepus californicus*. See Selected Foothill Animals.

White-Tailed Jackrabbit, *Lepus townsendii*.

Nuttall's Cottontail, *Sylvilagus nuttallii*.*

California Ground Squirrel, *Otospermophilus beecheyi*. See Selected Foothill Animals.

Antelope Ground Squirrel, *Ammospermophilus leucurus*.*

Sagebrush Chipmunk, *Eutamias minimus*.*

Northern Pocket Gopher, *Thomomys talpoides*.

Great Basin Pocket Mouse, *Perognathus parvus*.

Kangaroo Rats, genus *Dipodomys*.*

Pinyon Mouse, *Peromyscus truei*.

Deer Mouse, *Peromyscus maniculatus*, Fig. 179.

Grasshopper Mice, genus *Onychomys*.*

Sagebrush Vole, *Lagurus curtatus*.

Coyote, *Canis latrans*, Figs. 204 and 205. See Selected Forest Animals.

Badger, *Taxidea taxus*, Fig. 178.

Spotted Skunk, *Spilogale putorius*.

Striped Skunk, *Mephitis mephitis*, Fig. 110.

Mule Deer, *Odocoileus hemionus*, Figs. 210 and 211. See Selected Forest Animals.

Pinyon–Sagebrush Visitors: Migratory Birds

The following species are summer visitors to the pinyon–sagebrush zone, where they nest and rear their young.

Eared Grebe, *Podiceps nigricollis;* Mono Lake.

Red-Tailed Hawk, *Buteo jamicensis*. See Selected Foothill Animals.

Swainson's Hawk, *Buteo swainsoni;* uncommon.

Wilson's Phalarope, *Steganopus tricolor;* lakes and ponds.

California Gull, *Larus californicus;* lakes.

Mourning Dove, *Zenaida macroura*. See Selected Foothill Animals.

Poor-Will, *Phalaenoptilis nuttallii*.

Common Nighthawk, *Chordeiles minor*, Fig. 236.*

Say's Phoebe, *Sayornis saya*.

Gray Flycatcher, *Empidonax wrightii*.*

Violet-green Swallow, *Tachycinetta thalassina*.

Tree Swallow, *Iridoprocne bicolor;* uncommon.

Barn Swallow, *Hirundo rustica;* near buildings.

Cliff Swallow, *Petrochelidon pyrrhonota*.

White-breasted Nuthatch, *Sitta carolinensis;* uncommon.
Long-billed Marsh Wren, *Telmatodytes palustris;* marshes.
Bell's Vireo, *Vireo belli.*
Orange-Crowned Warbler, *Vermivora celata;* uncommon.
Yellow Warbler, *Dendroica petechia.*
Common Yellowthroat, *Geothlypis trichas.*
Lazuli Bunting, *Passerina amoena.*
Green-Tailed Towhee, *Chlorura chlorura.* *
Savanna Sparrow, *Passerculus sandwichensis.*
Vesper Sparrow, *Pooecetes gramineus.*
Lark Sparrow, *Chondestes grammacus.*
Sage Sparrow, *Amphispiza belli.*
Brewer's Sparrow, *Spizella breweri.* *
Song Sparrow, *Melospiza melodia.*

The following species are winter visitors to the pinyon–sagebrush zone.

Rough-Legged Hawk, *Buteo lagopus.*
Clark's Nutcracker, *Nucifraga columbiana,* Fig. 187. See Selected Forest Animals.
Mountain Bluebird, *Siala currucoides.* See Selected Forest Animals.
Gray-Crowned Rosy Finch, *Leucosticte tephrocotis,* Fig. 223. See Alpine Animals.
White-Crowned Sparrow, *Zonotrichia leucophrys.* See Selected Forest Animals.

Pinyon–Sagebrush Visitors: Mammals

The following two species move downslope from higher elevations in the fall and winter in the pinyon–sagebrush zone.

Mule Deer, *Odocoileus hemionus,* Figs. 210 and 211. See Selected Forest Animals.
Sierra Bighorn, *Ovis canadensis,* Figs. 239 and 240.* *

Selected Pinyon–Sagebrush Animals

Reptiles

Long-Nosed Snake, *Rhinocheilus lecontei. Length:* 20 to 42 in (5 to 11 dm). *Color:* black and red bands above; creamy white below; resembles California mountain king snake, except nose is cream-colored instead of black and rings do not completely surround the body but stop before reaching the belly; the habitats of the two snakes are also entirely different. *Food:* lizards, kangaroo rats, mice, insects. *Habitat:* desert scrub. *Distribution:* valleys east of Sierra south to Mojave Desert.

Speckled Rattlesnake, *Crotalus mitchelli. Length:* 2 to 4 ft (6 to 12 dm). *Color:* variable—tan, cream, yellow, brown, pink, speckled with darker shades; markings, usually vague bands, but other shapes possible; dark bands around tail. *Food:* kangaroo rats, mice, ground squirrels, lizards, birds. *Habitat:* rocky canyons, pinyon woodland, sagebrush scrub. *Distribution:* replaces the western rattlesnake south of Mono County. (For general information on rattlesnakes, see the discussion under Western Rattlesnake in Selected Foothill Animals.)

Birds

Abbreviations used in the following descriptions: R = year-around resident; SV = summer visitor breeding in the pinyon–sagebrush zone.

Sage Grouse, *Centrocercus urophasianus. Length:* male, 26 to 30 in (6.5 to 7.5 dm); female, 22 to 23 in (5.6 to 5.8 dm). *Color:* back, brown mottled with white; breast, white; belly, black; beak, cheeks, and chin, black; small yellowish spot over eye; black and white necklace stripes on throat; legs covered with buffy feathers. *Eggs:* 7 to 13. *Nest:* beneath sagebrush. *Food:* sagebrush leaves exclusively in fall and winter; seeds, green vegetation when available. *Habitat:* sagebrush scrub, often near meadows and permanent water sources. *Distribution:* R, formerly common along east side of Sierra south to Inyo County; now confined

236. Common Nighthawk, *Chordeiles minor.*

to scattered locales; large flock north of Lake Crowley in southern Mono County. Sage grouse have elaborate courtship and mating rituals. Male grouse, or cocks, congregate in an open arena among sagebrush each spring to strut, display their showy plumage, and engage in mock fights. During these displays, they spread their tail feathers, allow their wings to droop, and utter loud popping noises by means of air sacs located in the throat. Over a period of weeks the cocks establish a hierarchy among themselves consisting of a leader, or master cock, which mates repeatedly with the females of the flock; a runner-up, or subcock, which mates fewer times; and several guard cocks, which mate a few times on the sly and keep the unsuccessful males away from the mating area.

Common Nighthawk, *Chordeiles minor.* Fig. 236. *Length:* 8½ to 10 in (21 to 25 cm). *Color:* mottled gray or gray-brown; conspicuous white stripes across undersides of long, pointed wings. *Eggs:* 2. *Nest:* bare ground. *Food:* flying insects. *Distribution:* SV to pinyon–sagebrush zone; also found in higher forests on both slopes. Occasionally seen perched on rocks or fenceposts, more often flying overhead, especially near dusk; resembles large swallow or swift in manner of flight and swept-back wings; white wing bars distinctive; commonly utters a high metallic *peent* while flying.

Yellow-Headed Blackbird, *Xanthocephalus xanthocephalus.* Fig. 237. *Length:* 8 to 11 in (20 to 28 cm). *Color: male*—black with yellow head and throat; *female*—brown above, buffy on cheeks and throat, yellowish breast with white stripes. *Eggs:* 3 to 5. *Nest:* woven cup fastened to tules, cattails, or other tall marsh plants; nests in loose colonies. *Food:* forages in fields and open areas for insects,

237. Yellow-Headed Blackbird,
Xanthocephalus xanthocephalus.

spiders, and other invertebrates; some seeds and vegetable matter. *Distribution:* scattered colonies in marshes along east slope; less common in foothills of west slope.

Green-Tailed Towhee, *Chlorura chlorura. Length:* 6¼ to 7 in (16 to 18 cm). *Color:* brownish to olive green back, wings, and tail; breast and sides gray, belly white; reddish brown cap on head; white spot above beak and on chin and throat. *Eggs:* 4. *Nest:* substantial bowls of twigs and grass lined with hairs, soft vegetation, and the like; placed on ground beneath shrubs or just a few feet above ground. *Food:* seeds, berries, some insects; scratches for food in leaf litter beneath shrubs. *Distribution:* SV in pinyon and juniper woodlands and sagebrush scrub along east slope; also in brush and montane chaparral at higher elevations on both slopes. The green-tailed towhee has a distinctive call consisting of a catlike *meeoww*, which is unlike that of any other Sierra bird.

Gray Flycatcher, *Epidonax wrightii. Length:* 5½ in (14 cm). *Color:* gray above, white below; wings and tail dark brown; 2 white wingbars on each side. *Eggs:* 3 to 4. *Nest:* small woven-grass cup in sagebrush or small trees. *Food:* mostly flying insects; commonly perches on shrub and darts out to capture prey, then returns to same perch; may repeat this performance several times. *Distribution:* SV in sagebrush scrub, entire east slope. The gray flycatcher is difficult to distinguish during migration from the western, willow, dusky, and Hammond's flycatchers of the Sierra forest, but during the summer may be safely identified by its sagebrush habitat.

Pinyon Jay, *Gymnorhinus cyanocephalus. Length:* 9 to 11¾ in (23 to 30 cm). *Color:* blue-gray above, somewhat paler below. *Eggs:* 3 to 4. *Nest:* deep cup of twigs placed in singleleaf pinyon, western juniper, or other conifers. *Food:* primarily pinyon nuts, supplemented by other seeds and insects. *Distribution:* entire east slope in pinyon–juniper woodlands; ranges into adjacent forest and sagebrush areas; common R. Feeds in large, loose, noisy flocks; can be told from all other Sierra jays by its more-or-less uniform coloring; casual fall and winter visitor to west slope.

Brewer's Sparrow, *Spizella breweri. Length:* 5 to 6 in (13 to 15 cm). *Color:* pale brown above, white below; crown and back finely streaked; two faint white wingbars on each side. *Eggs:* 4. *Nest:* cup of twigs and rootlets in sagebrush. *Food:* seeds and some insects; forages on ground beneath shrubs. *Distribution:* abundant SV in sagebrush scrub.

Mammals

Merriam's Shrew, *Sorex merriami. Head and body:* 2¼ to 2½ in (6 to 6.5 cm). *Tail:* 1¼ to 1¾ in (3 to 4.5 cm). *Color:* grayish brown above, white below. *Food:* insects, other invertebrates. *Enemies:* few (most predators avoid shrews); owls and hawks perhaps. *Habitat:* bunchgrass in sagebrush scrub. *Distribution:* east slope of Sierra and adjacent valleys. (For general information on shrews see Selected Forest Animals.)

Nuttall's Cottontail, *Sylvilagus nuttallii. Head and body:* 12¼ to 13½ (31 to 34 cm). *Tail:* 1¾ to 2 in (4.5 to 5 cm). *Color:* grayish brown above, white below; tail, white. *Ears:* 2 to 2½ in (5 to 6 cm), slightly shorter than those of the Audubon cottontail of the western foothills. *Litter:* 6 to 8, early summer. *Nest:* depression in ground beneath dense shrubbery or in rockpiles. *Food:* grasses, tender shoots of herbs and shrubs. *Enemies:* coyote, hawks, owls, and other carnivores. *Habitat:* sagebrush scrub. *Sign:* small, flattened droppings. *Distribution:* sagebrush flats east of Sierra. Habits are similar to those of the Audubon cottontail (see Selected Foothill Mammals).

Antelope Ground Squirrel, *Ammospermophilus leu-*

curus. Head and body: 6 to 6¼ in (15 to 16 cm). *Tail:* 2½ to 2¾ in (6.5 to 7 cm). *Color:* grayish brown with one white stripe on each side; tail, white beneath. *Litter:* 6 to 10, possibly two litters a year. *Nest:* burrow. *Food:* seeds, green shoots; requires no drinking water, which it gets from its food. *Enemies:* coyotes, snakes, hawks, owls, and other carnivores. *Habitat:* sagebrush scrub. *Distribution:* sagebrush flats east of Sierra; often seen running across highways.

Sagebrush Chipmunk, *Eutamias minimus. Head and body:* 4 to 4½ in (6 to 7 cm). *Tail:* 2¾ to 3½ in (7 to 9 cm). *Color:* pale buffy gray with black and white stripes on back and head; tail, pale yellow beneath. *Litter:* 2 to 6, possibly two a year. *Nest:* burrow beneath stumps, fallen logs, rocks. *Food:* a variety of vegetation, seeds, nuts, fruits, some insects. *Enemies:* coyotes, hawks, snakes, and other carnivores. *Habitat:* sagebrush scrub, pinyon and juniper woodlands, open coniferous forest. *Distribution:* east slope, 6400 to 10,500 ft (1950 to 3200 m), south to Inyo County. (For general information on chipmunks see Selected Forest Animals.)

Kangaroo Rats, genus *Dipodomys.*

Two species of kangaroo rats appear along the east slope of the Sierra:

1. **Merriam Kangaroo Rat,** *Dipodomys merriami. Head and body:* 3¾ to 4 in (9.5 to 10 cm). *Tail:* 4¾ to 6¼ in (12 to 16 cm). *Habitat:* sagebrush scrub, mostly below pinyon belt. *Distribution:* east slope of Sierra north to Owens Valley.

2. **Great Basin Kangaroo Rat,** *Dipodomys microps. Head and body:* 4 to 4½ in (10 to 11 cm). *Tail:* 5½ to 6¾ in (14 to 17 cm). *Habitat:* sagebrush scrub, pinyon and juniper woodlands. *Distribution:* east slope of Sierra south to Owens Valley.

Litters: 1 to 4, spring, early summer; Merriam kangaroo rat has second litter in autumn. *Nest:* burrow near base of shrubs; plugged during the day with soft earth. *Food:* mostly seeds, some green vegetation. *Enemies:* coyotes, owls, snakes, and other carnivores.

Like kangaroos, kangaroo rats have large hindlegs and feet designed for leaping and standing more or less erect. The Merriam kangaroo rat has only four hind toes; the Great Basin kangaroo rat, five. The short forelegs are freed for gathering seeds and other food. Their tails, which are longer than their bodies, serve as counterbalances while they are at rest and as rudders when they jump. If alarmed, kangaroo rats will bound away in leaps of two to three feet, though normally they move about in short hops. More than a dozen species of kangaroo rats are found in arid or semiarid regions in the western United States. They obtain water from seeds through the oxidation of starches and reduce moisture loss by producing urine with low water content and limiting their activities to the nighttime hours. The Merriam kangaroo rat has two periods of peak activity: one at 9 P.M., a second at 4 A.M. During the day kangaroo rats remain in their burrows, the entrances of which are usually closed with earth to keep out heat and conserve humidity. Home ranges may exceed one-half acre, and females are known to defend territories.

Grasshopper Mice, genus *Onychomys.*

Two species of grasshopper mice inhabit the east slope of the Sierra:

1. **Northern Grasshopper Mouse,** *Onychomys leucogaster. Habitat and Distribution:* sagebrush scrub south to Mono County.

2. **Southern Grasshopper Mouse,** *Onychomys torridus. Habitat and Distribution:* sagebrush and desert scrub formations Mono County south.

Head and body: 3½ to 5 in (9 to 13 cm). *Tail:* 1½ to 2½ in (4 to 6.5 cm). *Color:* sandy brown or gray above (northern grasshopper mouse); cinnamon brown above (southern grasshopper mouse); both species white below. *Litter:* 3 to 6, three times a year. *Nest:* burrows of other small rodents. *Food:* grasshopper mice are the only rodents in the Sierra that are primarily carnivorous, animal matter making up 90 percent of their diets; mostly insects, spiders, and scorpions, but also small lizards, pocket mice, white-footed mice, and sagebrush voles; seeds eaten only when animal food not available. *Enemies:* coyotes, badgers, owls, and other carnivores. Grasshopper mice stalk and pounce on their prey, killing them by biting. Largely nocturnal, they are seldom seen, but their loud high-pitched calls can be heard at some distance. Their stomachs are adapted to accommodate the hard, chitinous exoskeletons of their insect prey.

Sierra Bighorn, *Ovis canadensis.* Figs. 238 and 239. *Head and body:* about 4 ft (12 dm); 3 to 3½ ft (9 to 10 dm) tall at shoulders. *Color:* gray or buffy brown with white rump patch and nose. The large spiraling horns of the male are distinctive; females have goatlike spikes curving backward; horns of the male may be 15 to 16 in (38 to 40 cm) in circumference at the base, with a tip-to-tip spread of 2 ft (6 dm). *Litter:* 1, sometimes 2 in spring. *Enemies:* none to speak of in the Sierra; severe winters cause heavy losses, especially among lambs. *Habitat: summer*—rocky areas near and above timberline; *winter*—sagebrush scrub. *Sign:* pointed, deerlike tracks; half-inch (1-cm) cylindrical droppings pointed at one end; flat, scraped resting areas among rocks. *Distribution:* in a few bands from Mt. Langley north to Mammoth Pass; near main crest in summer; in sagebrush along eastern base of range during winter; rarely west of main crest; some males may range widely during the summer and individuals have recently been observed as far north as Yosemite.

Before the coming of the white man to the Sierra, bighorn sheep were more or less common along some 260 mi (420 km) of the main crest. By 1950, however, the population had been reduced to about 390 sheep divided among five herds scattered between Convict Creek and Mt. Langley in the south-central Sierra. In 1970 the population was estimated at only 230 sheep. The smallest herd had been decimated in the intervening years, and another had been so reduced that its survival seems unlikely. Authorities generally agree that the decline of the Sierra bighorn was initially caused by: (1) competition for forage, first with domestic sheep, which were pastured in the high country in the latter half of the nineteenth century, and later with cattle and sheep allowed to range in the bighorn's wintering grounds along the eastern base of the Sierra; (2) scabies disease, which was transmitted to the bighorn by domestic sheep; and (3) illegal hunting. There is less agreement, however, about what has caused the continuing decline of the Sierra bighorn in recent years. Some authorities believe that increasing invasion of the high country by humans is at fault; others dispute this, pointing out that bighorns elsewhere have fared better than those in the Sierra even when human contacts were comparable.

238. Bighorn tracks.   239. Sierra Bighorn, *Ovis canadensis.*

Among the more elusive of the large Sierra mammals, the bighorn is seldom seen, even where it is fairly common. Despite its large size, the bighorn's gray or sandy coat blends in perfectly with the rocky terrain it frequents during the summer. Bighorns are wary and usually remain well away from humans, often scaling nearly inaccessible crags and cliffs. During its frequent daytime rest periods the bighorn remains almost perfectly still and may not be spotted even by someone looking directly at it.

In late autumn bighorns begin to migrate down the east slope of the Sierra to winter quarters in the sagebrush scrub along the base of the range, where they feed on bitterbrush, Mormon tea, wild buckwheats, California needlegrass, and other herbs and shrubs. Shortly after arriving on the wintering grounds, usually in November, the rams begin to fight for small bands of ewes. The contests consist of kicking and head butting, the victors being the only rams to mate that season. In this way only the strongest rams contribute to the herd's gene pool. In the butting contests two rams stand a few yards apart, rear up slightly on their hind legs, then rush each other, crashing head to head, horn to horn, with such force that the reports from the collisions can be heard some distance away. The battle continues until one of the rams departs from the field.

The lambs are born in early June, usually on a grassy ledge with a good view. They remain with their mothers in small bands of females and young throughout the summer. The rams wander off by themselves in loose bands, often

Selected Pinyon–Sagebrush Animals

roaming far afield. After the lambs are born, the bighorns begin to move upslope to their summer range near timberline, where they feed on subalpine and alpine herbs—grasses, sedges, buttercups, paintbrushes, wild buckwheats, mountain sorrel, penstemons, sky pilot, and their favorite, alpine gold, a bright yellow daisy that they dig up with their hooves and consume roots and all. Feeding begins shortly before dawn and continues through the day, interrupted by frequent rest periods, when the bighorns chew their cuds. At such times they rest on flat, oval-shaped day beds made by scraping the ground with their hooves.

APPENDIX A

USEFUL ADDRESSES

The Sierra Nevada embraces eight national forests, three national parks, and one national monument. These agencies can provide maps, wilderness permits, and information on campgrounds, weather, road conditions, and other matters pertinent to visiting the Sierra. Their addresses are listed below.

National Forests

> Eldorado National Forest
> 100 Forni Rd.
> Placerville, CA 95667
> (916) 622-5061

> Inyo National Forest
> 873 North Main St.
> Bishop, CA 93514
> (714) 873-5841

> Plumas National Forest
> PO Box 1500
> Quincy, CA 95971
> (916) 283-2050

> Sierra National Forest
> Federal Building
> 1130 O Street
> Fresno, CA 93721
> (209) 487-5155

> Sequoia National Forest
> 900 W. Grand Ave.
> Porterville, CA 93257
> (209) 784-1500

> Stanislaus National Forest
> 175 S. Fairview Lane
> Sonora, CA 95370
> (209) 532-3671

> Tahoe National Forest
> Highway 49
> Nevada City, CA 95959
> (916) 265-4531

Toiyabe National Forest
Federal Office Bldg.
324 25th St.
Ogden, UT 84401
(801) 399-6201

Information may also be obtained from:

U. S. Forest Service
California Region
630 Sansome St.
San Francisco, CA 94111
(415) 556-0122

National Parks and Monuments

Devils Postpole National Monument
c/o Superintendent
Sequoia and Kings Canyon National Parks
Three Rivers, CA 93262

Sequoia and Kings Canyon National Parks
Three Rivers, CA 93262

Yosemite National Park
Box 577
Yosemite National Park, CA 95389

Information may also be obtained from:

Western Regional Office
National Park Service
450 Golden Gate Ave.
San Francisco, CA 94102
(415) 556-4122

Los Angeles Field Office
National Park Service
300 N. Los Angeles St.
Los Angeles, CA 90012
(213) 688-2852

APPENDIX B

MAPS

The following maps are recommended for the Sierra Nevada:

1. United States Geological Survey (USGS) topographic maps. These are essential for backcountry hikers because they show with great accuracy topographic contours, elevations, and the location and configuration of landforms. These maps also show most major trails, but some may be out-of-date with regard to precise routes. The Sierra is covered by a series of 15-minute topo maps drawn to a scale of 1:62,500, or about one mile to the inch. In addition, Yosemite National Park and Sequoia–Kings Canyon National Parks are each covered in their entirety by a single large-scale (1:125,000) map sheet. Each is available with or without shaded relief. USGS "topo" maps can be obtained for a nominal charge from the USGS Map Store, 555 Battery St., San Francisco, CA 94111. The 15-minute series is also available at most backpacking, mountaineering, and ski shops throughout California.

2. The United States Forest Service publishes a map for each of the national forests in the Sierra Nevada. These maps do not indicate topographic contours but are the best sources of up-to-date information on campgrounds, access roads, and trail routes. A map of each national forest can be obtained from the appropriate office listed in Appendix A, or the entire set of maps covering all national forests in the Sierra (except Toiyabe) can be obtained from the California Region office in San Francisco.

SELECTED REFERENCES

General

Bakker, Elna S. *An Island Called California.* Berkeley: University of California Press, 1972.

Bowen, Ezra, and the Editors of Time-Life Books. *The High Sierra.* New York: Time-Life Books, 1972.

Brower, David, ed. *Gentle Wilderness.* San Francisco: Sierra Club Books, 1967.

Brown, Vinson, and George Lawrence. *The California Wildlife Region.* 2d rev. ed. Healdsburg, Calif.: Naturegraph, 1965.

Brown, Vinson, and Robert Livezey. *The Sierra Nevada Wildlife Region.* Rev. ed. Healdsburg, Calif.: Naturegraph, 1962.

Carrighar, Sally. *One Day on Beetle Rock.* New York: Alfred Knopf, 1956.

Farquhar, Francis. *History of the Sierra Nevada.* Berkeley: University of California Press, 1965.

Johnston, Verna R. *Sierra Nevada.* Boston: Houghton Mifflin Co., 1970.

Milne, Lorus J. and Margery, and the Editors of *Life. The Mountains.* New York: Time Inc., 1962.

Muir, John. *The Mountains of California.* New York: Doubleday and Co., Anchor Books, 1961.

Peattie, Roderick, ed. *Sierra Nevada, Range of Light.* New York: Vanguard Press, 1947.

Roth, Hal. *Pathway in the Sky.* Berkeley: Howell–North Books, 1965.

Schumacher, Genny. *Deepest Valley.* Berkeley: Wilderness Press, 1969.

————. *Mammoth Lakes Sierra.* 3d ed. Berkeley: Wilderness Press, 1969.

Storer, Tracy I. and Robert L. Usinger. *Sierra Nevada Natural History.* Berkeley: University of California Press, 1964.

Webster, Paul, and the Editors of *American West. The Mighty Sierra.* Palo Alto, Calif.: American West Publishing Co., 1972.

Geology

Alt, David D., and Donald W. Hyndman. *Roadside Geology of Northern California.* Missoula, Mont.: Mountain Press Publishing Co., 1975.

Bailey, Edgar H., ed. *Geology of Northern California.* San Francisco: California Division of Mines and Geology, 1966.

Curry, Robert. *Glacial and Pleistocene History of the Mammoth*

Lakes Sierra, California, a Geologic Guidebook. Missoula,
    Mont.: University of Montana Department of Geology, 1971.
Fryxell, Fritiof, ed. *Francois Matthes and the Marks of Time,
    Yosemite and the High Sierra.* San Francisco: Sierra Club,
    1962.
Hill, Mary. *Geology of the Sierra Nevada.* Berkeley: University of
    California Press, 1975.
Hinds, Norman E. A. *Evolution of the California Landscape.* San
    Francisco: California Division of Mines and Geology, 1952.
Jenkins, Olaf P. *Geologic Guidebook Along Highway 49—Sierran
    Gold Belt, The Mother Lode Country.* San Francisco: Califor-
    nia Division of Mines and Geology, 1948.
Matthes, Francois. *The Incomparable Valley.* Berkeley: Univer-
    sity of California Press, 1950.
————. *Sequoia National Park.* Berkeley: University of California
    Press, 1950.
Norris, Robert M., and Robert W. Webb. *Geology of California.*
    New York: John Wiley & Sons, 1976.
Oakeshott, Gordon B. *California's Changing Landscape.* New
    York: McGraw-Hill Book Co., 1971.

Weather and Climate

Anderson, Bette Roda. *Weather in the West.* Palo Alto, Calif.:
    American West Publishing Co., 1975.
Edinger, James G. *Watching for the Wind.* New York: Doubleday
    & Co., Anchor Books, 1967.
Gilliam, Harold, *Weather of the San Francisco Bay Region.*
    Berkeley: University of California Press, 1970.
LaChapelle, Edward R. *Field Guide to Snow Crystals.* Seattle:
    University of Washington Press, 1969.
Miller, Albert. *Meteorology.* 3d ed. Columbus, Ohio: Charles E.
    Merrill Publishing Co., 1967.
United States Forest Service. *Snow Avalanches.* Agricultural
    Handbook no. 194. Washington D.C., 1961.

Plants

Arno, Stephen F. *Discovering Sierra Trees.* Yosemite National
    Park, Calif.: Yosemite Natural History Association, Sequoia
    Natural History Association, 1973.
Balls, Edward K. *Early Uses of California Plants.* Berkeley: Uni-
    versity of California Press, 1970.
Barbour, Michael G., and Jack Major. *Terrestrial Vegetation of
    California.* New York: John Wiley & Sons, 1977.

Brockman, C. Frank. *Trees of North America*. New York: Golden Press, 1968.

Brown, Vinson. *Reading the Woods*. Harrisburg, Pa.: Stackpole Books, 1969.

Crampton, Beecher. *Grasses in California*. Berkeley: University of California Press, 1974.

Engbeck, Joseph H., Jr. *The Enduring Giants*. Berkeley: University Extension, University of California, 1973.

Griffin, James R. and William Critchfield. *The Distribution of Forest Trees in California*. Washington, D.C.: U.S. Department of Agriculture, Forest Service, Research Paper PSW–82, 1972.

Grillos, Steve J. *Ferns and Fern Allies of California*. Berkeley: University of California Press, 1971.

Hood, Mary and Bill. *Yosemite Wildflowers and Their Stories*. Yosemite, Calif.: Flying Spur Press, 1969.

Horn, Elizabeth L. *Wildflowers 3: the Sierra Nevada*. Beaverton, Oreg.: Touchstone Press, 1976.

McMinn, Howard E. *An Illustrated Manual of California Shrubs*. Berkeley: University of California Press, 1959.

McMinn, Howard E. and Evelyn Maino. *Pacific Coast Trees*. Berkeley: University of California Press, 1967.

Morgenson, Dana C. *Yosemite Wildflower Trails*. Yosemite National Park, Calif.: Yosemite Natural History Association, 1975.

Munz, Philip A., and David D. Keck. *A California Flora and Supplement*. Berkeley: University of California Press, 1973.

Munz, Philip A. *California Mountain Wildflowers*. Berkeley: University of California Press, 1969.

Niehaus, Theodore F., and Charles L. Ripper. *A Field Guide to Pacific States Wildflowers*. Boston: Houghton Mifflin Co., 1976.

Niehaus, Theodore F. *Sierra Wildflowers*. Berkeley: University of California Press, 1974.

Ornduff, Robert. *Introduction to California Plant Life*. Berkeley: University of California Press, 1974.

Peattie, Donald Culross. *A Natural History of Western Trees*. Boston: Houghton Mifflin Co., 1953.

Peterson, P. Victor, and P. Victor Peterson, Jr. *Native Trees of the Sierra Nevada*. Berkeley: University of California Press, 1975.

Smith, Alexander H. *A Field Guide to Western Mushrooms*. Ann Arbor, Mich.: University of Michigan Press, 1975.

Sudworth, George B. *Forest Trees of the Pacific Slope*. New York: Dover, 1967.

Thomas, John Hunter, and Dennis R. Parnell. *Native Shrubs of the Sierra Nevada*. Berkeley: University of California Press, 1974.

SELECTED REFERENCES

Weeden, Norman F. *A Survival Handbook to Sierra Flora*. 1975.
Zwinger, Ann H., and Beatrice E. Willard. *Land Above the Trees*. New York: Harper and Row, 1972.

Animals

Basey, Harold E. *Sierra Nevada Amphibians*. Sequoia National Park, Calif.: Sequoia Natural History Association, 1969.

Brown, Vinson. *Reptiles and Amphibians of the West*. Healdsburg, Calif.: Naturegraph, Publishers, 1974.

Burt, William H., and Richard P. Grossenheider. *A Field Guide to the Mammals*. Boston: Houghton Mifflin Co., 1964.

Grinnell, Joseph, and Tracy I. Storer. *Animal Life in the Yosemite*. Berkeley: University of California Press, 1924.

Grinnell, Joseph *et al. Fur-Bearing Mammals of California*. 2 vols. Berkeley: University of California Press, 1936.

———. *Vertebrate Natural History of a Section of Northern California Through the Lassen Peak Region*. Berkeley: University of California Press, 1930.

Hoffmann, Ralph. *Birds of the Pacific States*. Boston: Houghton Mifflin Co., 1927.

Ingles, Lloyd G. *Mammals of the Pacific States*. Stanford, Calif.: Stanford University Press, 1965.

Miller, Alden H. *An Analysis of the Distribution of the Birds of California*. Berkeley: University of California Press, 1951.

Moyle, Peter B. *Inland Fishes of California*. Berkeley: University of California Press, 1976.

Murie, Olaus J. *A Field Guide to Animal Tracks*. Boston: Houghton Mifflin Co., 1954.

Orr, Robert T. *Mammals of Lake Tahoe*. San Francisco: California Academy of Sciences, 1949.

Peterson, Roger Tory. *A Field Guide to Western Birds*. Boston: Houghton Mifflin Co., 1961.

Pickwell, Gayle. *Amphibians and Reptiles of the Pacific States*. Stanford, Calif.: Stanford University Press, 1947.

Pough, Richard H. *Audubon Western Bird Guide*. Garden City, N.Y.: Doubleday & Co., 1957.

Robbins, C. S. *et al. Birds of North America*. New York: Golden Press, 1966.

Small, Arnold. *The Birds of California*. New York: Winchester Press, 1974.

Stebbins, Cyral A. and Robert C. *Birds of Yosemite National Park*. Rev. ed. Yosemite National Park, Calif.: Yosemite Natural History Association, 1963.

Stebbins, Robert C. *Amphibians and Reptiles of California*.

Berkeley: University of California Press, 1972.

———. *Amphibians and Reptiles of Western North America.* New York: McGraw Hill, 1954.

———. *Field Guide to Western Reptiles and Amphibians.* Boston: Houghton Mifflin Co., 1966.

Sumner, Lowell, and Joseph S. Dixon. *Birds and Mammals of the Sierra Nevada.* Berkeley: University of California Press, 1953.

Trail Guides

Lowe, Don and Roberta. 100 *Northern California Hiking Trails.* Beaverton, Oreg.: Touchstone Press, 1971.

———. 100 *Southern California Hiking Trails.* Beaverton, Oreg.: Touchstone Press, 1972.

Roper, Steve. *The Climber's Guide to the High Sierra.* San Francisco: Sierra Club Books, 1976.

Schaffer, Jeffrey P. *The Tahoe Sierra.* Berkeley: Wilderness Press, 1975.

Schwenke, Karl, and Thomas Winnett. *Sierra North.* Rev. ed. Berkeley: Wilderness Press, 1976.

Starr, Walter A., Jr. *Starr's Guide to the John Muir Trail and the High Sierra Region.* 12th rev. ed. San Francisco: Sierra Club Books, 1976.

Winnett, Thomas, and Karl Schwenke. *Sierra South.* Rev. ed. Berkeley: Wilderness Press, 1975.

SELECTED REFERENCES

INDEX

Numbers in boldface refer to pages on which plants and animals are described, numbers in italic to pages with illustrations, including maps.

Cliff brake, 361; desert, 357

Climate, 97–130; factors in habitat, 133–34

Climax communities, 146

Clintonia uniflora, 314

Clones, 142

Clouds, 106–7, 127

Clover, carpet, 372; mustang, 295

Cnemidophorus hyperythrus, 251, 267, 271

Coachwhip, 484, 485

Coast Range, 65, 75, 315

Coffeeberry: California, 219, 226, 237, 246; Sierra, 351, 353

Colaptes auratus, 252, 260, 384, 393

Coleogyne ramosissima, 476

Coleotechnites milleri, 339

Collinsia spp.: *heterophylla*, **227-28**, pl. 2B; *torreyi*, 371

Collomia, 359

Collomia genus, 359

Coloma, 35, 57

Coluber constrictor, 251, 383

Columba fasciata, 262, 385

Columbine: alpine, 361, 450, 452; crimson, 357, **361–62**, pl. 3B

Commensalism, 181

Coneflower, California, 359

Conifers. *See* Forest, coniferous, *and individual species by name*

Constructive metamorphosis, 122

Contia tenuis, 264

Continental drift, 42

Convict Lake, 49, 94

Corallorhiza spp.: *maculata*, 332, 355; *striata*, 333, 355

Coralroot: spotted, 332, 333, 355; striped, 333 ,355

Cordillera, 40

Cornices, 123–24, *124*

Corn lily (false hellebore), 373, **374**, pl. 6A

Cornus spp.: *nuttallii*, 306, *314*, 324 *stolonifera*, 354

Corvus corax, 485

Corylus californica, 306, 308, 353

Cottontail: Audubon's, 253, 254, 281–82; Nuttall's, 484, 486, **491**

Cottonthorn, 476

Cottonwood, 365; black, 232, 306,

325, 471, 475; Fremont, *231*, 232, 306, 325, 472, 475

Cowbird, brown-headed, 253, 485

Coyote, 248, 253, 258, 261, 382, 384, 394, *418*, **418–19**; 484, 486; mountain, 201

Coyote brush, 226, 228, 240, 246

Coyote mint, *324*

Craters of the Moon National Monument, 293

Creambush, 348, 354, 453

Creeper, brown, 198, 384, 387, 393

Cress, American winter, 214, 234

Cretaceous period, 65

Crevice plants, 449–50

Critchfield, William, 303

Crossbill, red, 198, 379

Crotalus spp.: *mitchelli*, 485, 488; *viridis*, 252, 260, 267, **272–73**, 384, 485

Crotaphytus wislizenii, 485

Crown sprouts, 236–37

Crust, earth's, 43

Cryptantha, Sierra, 360, 450, 452

Cryptantha nubigena, 360, 450, 452

Cryptogramma acrostichoides, 361

Cupressus spp.: *macnabiana*, 225; *nevadensis*, 225

Currants, 185–86, 308, 313, 351, 352, 354; alpine prickly, 338, 348, 354, 453; chaparral, 226, 246; golden, 476; sticky, 332

Cyanocitta stelleri, 384, 393, **400**, *401*

Cyclones, 112, *112*, 113, 114

Cymopteris, Gray's, 451

Cymopteris cinerarius, 451

Cypress: MacNab, 225; piute, 225

Cystopteris fragilis, 359, 361

D

Dagger pod, 477

Daisy: cutleaf, 361, 435, **452**, pl. 6D; dwarf, 450, 451, 454; Eaton's, 477; loose, 361; Nevada, 477; Sierra, 443, 454; wandering, *368*, 372

Dardanelles Cone, 69

DDT, 340

Deer, mule, 191, 192 (range), 194 (range), 197, 258, 379, 385, **424–**

Lakes: cross section of, *365*; glacial, 93–95; moraine, 94; thermal circulation of, 125, *125*

Lake Tahoe, 30–31, 32, 94; formation of, 80–81, *81. See also* Tahoe Basin

Lampropeltis spp.: *getulus*, 252, 260, 267, **272**; *zonata*, 384, **398**

Lapse rate, 101, *103*

Lark, horned, 252, 485

Larkspurs, 214, 226, 234, 356, 357; glaucous, 478

Larus californicus, 486

Lasthenia chrysostoma, **215**, pl. 1C

Lateritic clay, 245

Lathyrus spp.: *langwertii*, 477; *nevadensis*, 355

Latitude, 108–9

Laurel: alpine, 368–69, 373, **374**, 443, 444, 446, pl. 6B; California, 223, 225, 232, 325

Layering of plants, 350, 441

Layia fremontii, *213*, 215

Leccinum scabrum, 183

Ledum glandulosum, 338, 354

Legumes, 183–84

Leptodactylon pungens, 323, 354, 450, 453

Lepus spp.: *californicus*, 253, 268, **281**, 486; *townsendii*, 394, 455, 486

Letharia spp., 296; *columbiana*, 327; *vulpina*, 297, 327

Leucosticte tephrocotis, 394, **456**, *456*, 487

Lewisia, dwarf, 436, *437*, 443, 451

Lewisia spp.: *pygmaea*, 436, *437*, 443, 451; *rediviva*, 359, **362–63**, 477, pl. 4D

Lichen, 181, 296–97, 297, 327

Life zones, 147–48, *149*

Lightning, 127–28, 327, *331*

Lignin, 303

Lilium spp.: *humboldtii*, 355; *pardalinum*, 358, 359; *washingtonianum*, 355

Lily: Humboldt, 355; leopard, *358*, 359; Sego, 477; Washington, 355; white globe, *217*

Limnanthes alba, 212, *213*, 214

Linanthus, Nuttall's, 477

Linanthus spp.: *dichotomus*, 214;

montanus, 295; *nuttallii*, 477

Linnet, *see* Finch, house

Lithocarpus densiflora, 225, 315, 325

Lithosols, 347, 433

Litter, forest, 302

Lizard: coast horned, 215, **270**; common leopard, 485; desert horned, 485; desert spiny, 485; northern alligator, 380, 383, 393; sagebrush, 393; southern alligator, 251, 267, **271–72**, 485; western fence, 260, 380, 383, 393, **397–98**, 485

Locoweed, 360, 451, 477; alpine spring, 448

Lodes, 56

Lomatium torreyi, 293

Lonicera spp., 233; *conjugalis*, 332, 354; *interrupta*, 236; *involucrata*, 354

Lophortyx californicus, 260, 267, 274–75

Lotus, 214, 360; narrowleaf, 359; Sierra Nevada, 295

Lotus spp., 214, 360; *nevadensis*, 295; *oblongifolius*, 359; *scoparius*, 240, 246

Lousewort, pine woods, 355

Lupine, 214, 227; alpine, 448, 451; Anderson's, 357; Brewer's, 357, 360; broadleaf, 358, **362**, pl. 3C; Coville's, 372; Inyo meadow, 478; Lyall's, 443, 448; Sierra, 372; silver, 226, 240; Tahoe, 477

Lupinus spp., 214, 227; *albifrons*, 226, 240; *andersonii*, 357; *breweri*, 357, 360; *confertus*, 372; *covillei*, 372; *latifolius*, 358, 362, pl. 3C; *meionanthus*, 477; *pratensis*, 478

Lynx rufus, 253, 261, **285–86**, 385

M

Madia, common, 214

Madia elegans, 214

Madrone, 315, 316, 325

Magma, 44–47 *passim*

Magmatic differentiation, 53, 54 (chart)

Magpie: black-billed, 485; yellow-billed, 252, 254, 260

397, 397

Ranges, 6–7, 192–94

Ranunculus spp., 214, 234, 371; *alismaefolius*, 357, 478; *eschscholtzii*, 445, **446**, pl. 6C; *glaberrimus*, 477; *hystriculus*, 357

Rat, domestic, 3. *See also* Kangaroo rat; Wood rat

Rattlesnake, 252; Pacific, 484; speckled, 484, 485, **488**; western, 249, 252, 258, 260, 267, 272, 382, 384, 485

Rattlesnake orchid, 315, 355

Raven, common, 485

Redberry, 236, 237, 246

Red bud, 223, 225, 236

Red mountain heather, 338, *338*, 354, 369, 443, 453

Regulus spp.: *calendula*, 262, 395; *satrapa*, 262, 395

Reithrodontomys megalotus, 252

Reproduction, alpine: vegetative, 440–41; from seed, 441–42

Reptiles, 251–52, 260, 264, 267, **270–73**, **383–84**, 393, **397–98**, 485, **488**

Rhamnus spp., 219; *californica*, 226, 237, 246; *crocea*, 236, 246; *purshiana*, 325; *rubra*, 351, 353

Rhinocheilus lecontei, 485, **488**

Rhizobium bacteria, 183–84

Rhizocarpon geographicum, 296, 297

Rhizomes, 142, *143*

Rhododendron occidentale, 308, *353*, 354

Rhus trilobata, 226, 246

Rhyolite, 55, 67–68, 72

Ribes spp., 308, 351, 352, 354; *amarum*, 225, 246; *aureum*, 476; *cereum*, 308, 348, 354, 450, 453; *lasianthum*, 354; *malvaceum*, 226, 246; *menziesii*, 246; *montigenum*, 338, 348, 354, 453; *quercetorum*, 225; *velutinum*, 470, 476; *viscossimum*, 332

Rime, 117, 123

Ringtail, 257–65 *passim*, **284–85**, *285*, 385

Riparian woodland, 208, 228–34

Ritter Range, 25–26, 50, 61

Rivers, 31–34

Robin, 197; American, 251, 252, 256, 262, 385, 390, 395

Rock: brake, 361; crannies, plants of, 452–53; flour, 87; outcrop, *295*

Rockcress, 359, 451, 477; broadseeded, 452

Rock fringe, 360, **362**, 452, pl. 4B

Rocks, 40–74, *51* (map); granitic, 52–56; igneous, 55 (table); volcanic, 66–74

Roof pendants, 49–50

Rorippa spp., 234, 358

Rosa spp., 308, 354; *californica*, 476, *spithamia*, 313

Rose, ground, 313; California wild, 476; wild, 308, 354

Rubber boa, 382, 383, **398**

Rubus spp.: *parviflorus*, 308, 354; *ursinus*, 226, 233

Rudbeckia californica, 359

Rushes, 364

Rye: basin wild, 465; gray wild, 371

S

Sacramento River, 31

Sage, desert, 462–63

Sagebrush, 27, 143 (range), 323, 348, *459*; alpine, 461, *461*, 476; bud (spiny), 462, 476; Great Basin, 323, 339, 461, *461*, 466, 467, 476; hoary, *461*, 462, 476; low, 461, *461*, 476; scrub, 459–69, *460*, 468

Salamander: arboreal, 259, 260, **269–70**; California slender, 256, 260, **269**; long-tailed, 393, Mt. Lyell, 193, 393; tiger, 260, 264

Salix spp., 228, *231*, 353, 373; *arctica*, 443, 445; *eastwoodiae*, 443; *exigua*, 476; *gooddingii*, 231, 232; *hindsiana*, 231, 232, 233; *laevigata*, 231, 232, 325; *lasiandra*, 231, 232, 325, 472, 475, 476; *lasiolepis*, 231, 232, 325, 472, 475, 476; *nivalis*, 443, 446; *orestera*, 443; *scouleriana*, 313, 325

Salpinctes obsoletus, 485

Salvia dorrii, 462–63

Sambucus spp.: *caerulea*, 226, 233; *melanocarpa*, 338; *microbotrys*, 354

San Andreas Fault, 44, 59

FIELD NOTES

FIELD NOTES

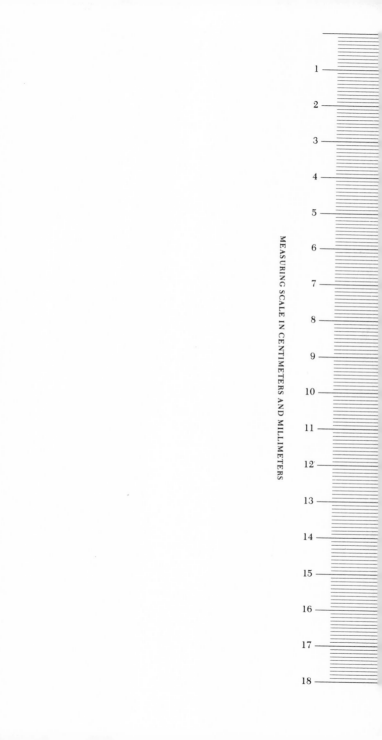

MEASURING SCALE IN CENTIMETERS AND MILLIMETERS

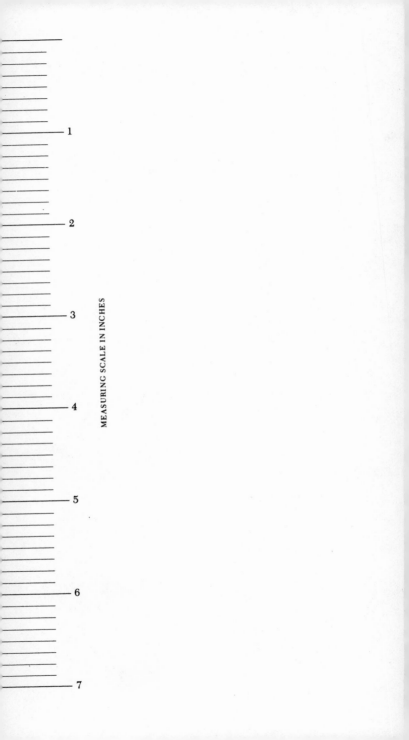

MEASURING SCALE IN INCHES